ENGINEERING GRAPHICS ESSENTIALS

with AutoCAD 2010 Instruction

by

Kirstie Plantenberg

University of Detroit Mercy

ISBN:
978-1-58503-517-5 (Text only)
978-1-58503-523-6 (Text bundled with 13-month license AutoCAD 2010)

PUBLICATIONS

Schroff Development Corporation

www.schroff.com

Schroff Development Corporation
P.O. Box 1334
Mission KS 66222
(913) 262-2664
WWW.**SCHROFF**.COM

Publisher: Stephen Schroff

Examination Copies:
Books received as examination copies are for review purposes only and may not be made available for student use. Resale of examination copies is prohibited.

Electronic Files:
Any electronic files associated with this book are licensed to the original user only. These files may not be transferred to any other party.

Trademarks
AutoCAD is a registered trademark of Autodesk, Inc.
IBM is a registered trademark of International Business Machines.
Windows XP is a registered trademark of Microsoft Corporation.

PREFACE

Engineering Graphics Essentials with AutoCAD 2010 Instruction is specifically designed to be used in a 1 or 2 credit introduction to engineering graphics course. It covers the main topics of engineering graphics, including tolerancing and fasteners, and gives engineering students a basic understanding of how to create and read engineering drawings. A two credit class should be able to cover all the topics presented in this book. A one credit class should be able to cover the basic topics. The advanced topics are marked by an asterisk in the table of contents.

This text is designed to encourage students to interact with the instructor during lecture. It has many 'instructor led' and 'in class student' exercises that require student participation.

Supplements

Power Point lecture materials accompany the *Engineering Graphics Essentials with AutoCAD 2010 Instruction* text. The presentations cover the entire book; however, they are segmented into basic and advanced topics. This allows instructors the flexibility to choose the material to be covered, based on the number of credits allocated to their course.

Some of the AutoCAD tutorials presented in this book require that you start with a pre-existing drawing. These AutoCAD tutorial files are on the disk accompanying the book or may be downloaded from www.engineeringessentials.com.

Questions? E-mail: ege2010@engineeringessentials.com

This book is dedicated to my family for their support and help.

Nassif, Summer and Lias Rayess
and
Phyllis Plantenberg

NOTES:

TABLE OF CONTENTS

Chapter 1: Drawing In AutoCAD

* = Advanced topics

* = Advanced topics

* = Advanced topics

Chapter 14: Pictorial Drawings

Chapter 15: Creating Isometric Pictorials in AutoCAD

Appendix A: Limits and Fits

Appendix B: Threads and Fastener Tables

Appendix C: References

* = Advanced topics

LIST OF EXERCISES

Chapter 14: Pictorial Drawings

DRAWING IN AUTOCAD

In Chapter 1 you will learn how to navigate through and create drawings within AutoCAD's 2-D drawing workspace. Entities within the AutoCAD environment are created within a coordinate framework. Objects such as Lines, Circles, Polygons, etc… are created using a set of defining coordinates points. Although this may sound complex, AutoCAD makes creating professional looking engineering drawings very simple. By the end of this chapter you will be able to create and edit complex geometries.

1.1) INTRODUCTION

AutoCAD allows you to visualize, document and share a design idea in either a 2-D or 3-D environment. Chapter 1 will focus on AutoCAD's 2-D drawing capabilities. AutoCAD gives you the tools to create accurate and professional looking detailed and assembly drawings. Figure 1-1 shows a detailed drawing created in AutoCAD's 2-D drawing workspace.

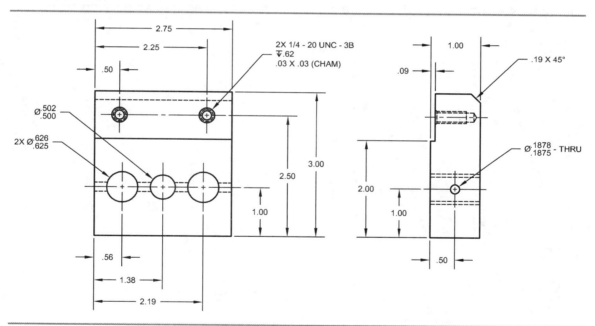

Figure 1-1: AutoCAD drawing example

1.1.1) Navigating through the AutoCAD Tutorials

The AutoCAD tutorials presented in this book have specific objectives which are stated at the beginning. Each tutorial is designed to introduce the user to a particular feature of AutoCAD or to a set of commands. As you will see, there are several ways to access AutoCAD's commands. For each command sequence, the tutorial will usually state one or two ways to access a command. This doesn't mean that you would not be able to access it in another way.

The format of each tutorial is consistent. For each step, a general statement of what is to be accomplished is given, followed by a command sequence that takes you step by step through the process. Within the tutorials the font, capitalization, and boldness of the text are used to convey information. The text format scheme used in each tutorial is as follows:

- <u>Underlined text</u>: Gives a location of where the command or options should be entered or selected.
- <u>*Italic* text</u>: Gives the name of a window or a field.
- <u>**Bold** text</u>: Text that should be typed in the *Command* window or into a field.
- <u>***Bold italic*** text</u>: Represents the name of a command, toggle, button or icon that should be selected.
- <u>`Bold Courier` font</u>: Indicates a key on the keyboard that needs to be pressed.
- <u>Normal text</u>: Gives instructions.
- <u>`Courier` font</u>: Represents AutoCAD prompts within the *Command* window.
- <u>**BOLD CAPITALIZED** text</u>: Indicates the command(s) that will be used to complete a task.

An example of a command sequence from one of the tutorials is given below. The command sequence illustrates the use of text format to convey information. The command sequence is used to create a line that is arrayed around an existing circle.

Example of an AutoCAD tutorial command sequence

1) Create a total of 16 sun rays using a polar **ARRAY**. Each sun ray **LINE** is 0.5 inches long.

   a) <u>Command:</u> **l** or **line** or   *Draw* toolbar:

   b) `Specify first point:` **quad** or   *Object Snap* toolbar:
      `of` Select the right side quadrant of the sun body circle.
   c) `Specify next point or [Undo]:` **@.5<0**
   d) `Specify next point or [Undo]:` **Enter**

   e) <u>Command:</u> **array** or   *Modify* toolbar:
   f) *Array* Window:
      i) Activate the **Polar Array** toggle
      ii) Click on the **Select Objects** icon and select the sun ray.
      iii) Select the center point of the array by clicking on the **Pick Center Point** icon and
      using the **CENTER** snap to select the center of the sun body. The cursor needs to hover over the circumference of the circle before it can locate the center.
      iv) The *Total number of items* is **16**
      v) The *Angle to fill* is **360**
      vi) **OK**.

1.2) AUTOCAD'S WORKSPACES AND USER INTERFACE

AutoCAD 2009 has three predefined workspaces; *AutoCAD Classic*, *2D Drafting & Annotation*, and *3D Modeling*. Each workspace allows for easy access to operations that are relevant to the current workspace.

AutoCAD's user interface is workspace dependent. The *AutoCAD Classic* and *2D Drafting & Annotation* workspace user interfaces are shown in Figure 1-2a and 1-2b respectively. The important areas of the interfaces are identified and will be discussed in the sections indicated.

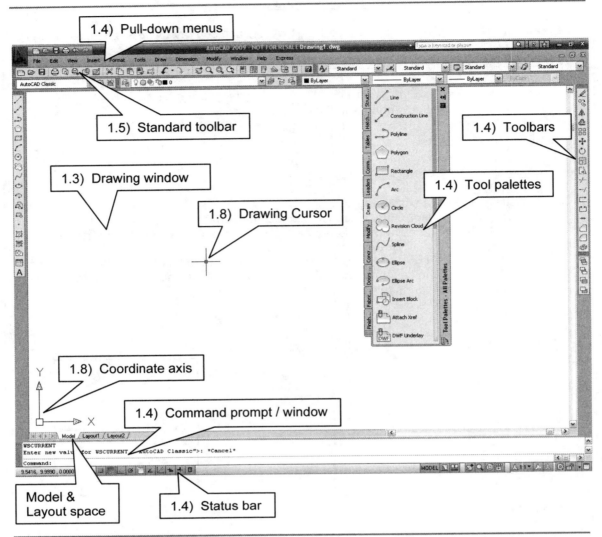

Figure 1-2a: *AutoCAD Classic* workspace user interface

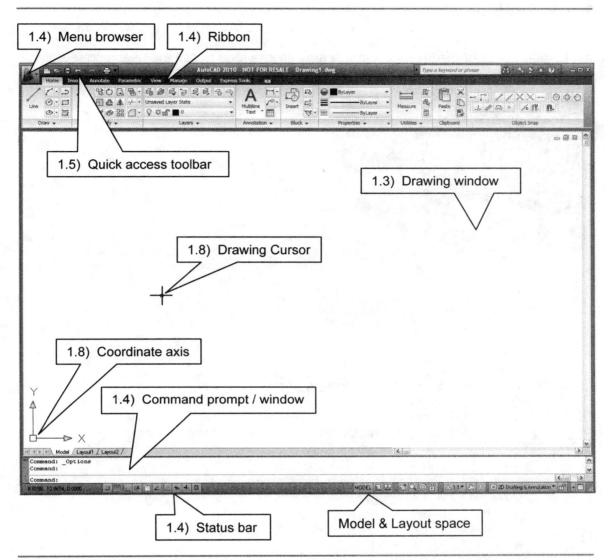

1.4) Menu browser

1.4) Ribbon

1.5) Quick access toolbar

1.3) Drawing window

1.8) Drawing Cursor

1.8) Coordinate axis

1.4) Command prompt / window

1.4) Status bar

Model & Layout space

Figure 1-2b: *2D Drafting & Annotation* workspace user interface

1.3) __THE DRAWING AREA__

The drawing area/window is the place where you create and view your drawing. The background color of the drawing window may be changed to suit the user's preference.

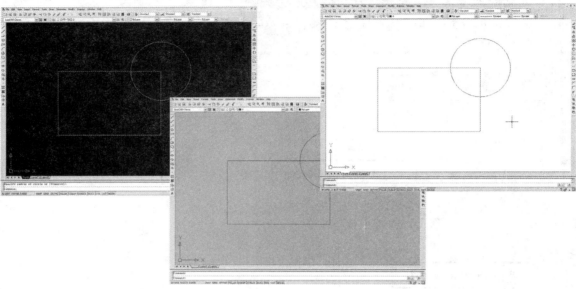

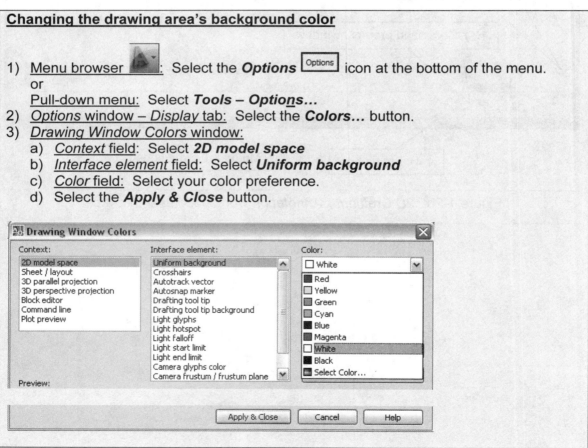

__Changing the drawing area's background color__

1) __Menu browser__ ▲▾ : Select the __Options__ [Options] icon at the bottom of the menu.
   or
   __Pull-down menu:__ Select __Tools – Options...__
2) __Options__ window – __Display__ tab: Select the __Colors...__ button.
3) __Drawing Window Colors__ window:
   a) __Context__ field: Select __2D model space__
   b) __Interface element__ field: Select __Uniform background__
   c) __Color__ field: Select your color preference.
   d) Select the __Apply & Close__ button.

The drawing area is as large as you need it to be. The usable drawing area does not just consist of the area that you can see. You can pan around the drawing area using the **PAN** command to reveal areas of your drawing that are out of view. You can also **ZOOM** in and out to reveal more or less of the drawing area. Both the PAN and ZOOM commands are located in the *Utilities* ribbon panel in the *Home* tab or the *Standard* toolbar. Because the drawing area is so large, it is a good idea to indicate the region that you wish to use. This is your drawing size or limits. This is usually the area that will be printed. You can change your drawing size using the **LIMITS** command.

Setting your drawing size

1) <u>Command:</u> **limits**
2) Specify lower left corner or [ON/OFF] <0.0000,0.0000>: **Enter** (The lower left corner of your limits should always remain 0,0.)
3) Specify upper right corner <420.0000,297.0000>: **280,216** (This changes a Metric drawing area to the equivalent of an 11 x 8.5 sheet of paper.)

The units (i.e. inches, millimeters, feet) used to draw objects in the drawing area can be selected using the **UNITS** command.

Setting your drawing units, precision and angle directions

1) <u>Command:</u> **units**
2) *Drawing Units* window: Use this window to set your units and precision.

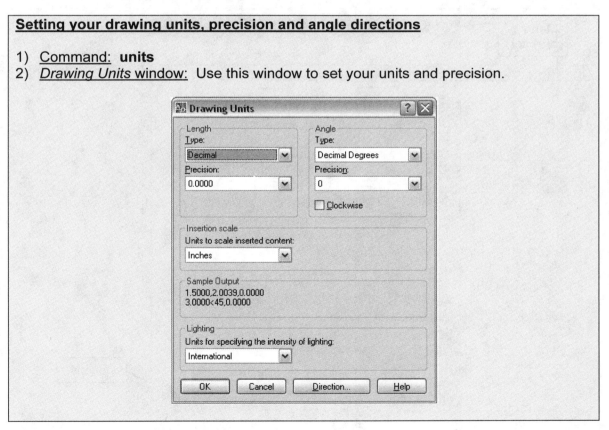

1.4) **ACCESSING AUTOCAD COMMANDS**

AutoCAD allows its users to access commands in many different ways. One of which will no doubt become your favorite. The most common ways of accessing AutoCAD's commands within the *2D Drafting & Annotation* workspace are through the menu browser, ribbon, command window, shortcut menus and status bar. The most common ways of accessing AutoCAD's commands within the *AutoCAD Classic* workspace are through the pull-down menus, toolbars, tool palettes, command window, shortcut menus and the status bar.

1.4.1) **Menu Browser**

Menus are available through the *Menu browser* in the upper left corner of the drawing window. These menus contain the commands used to create, save, print and manage your drawing. Figure 1-3 shows the *Menu browser* with the *New* item selected. The *Search menu* (near the top) allows you to perform a keyword command search. The search even works for commands that are not directly accessible through the *Menu browser*. Note the location of the **Options** button at the bottom. This button will be referenced several times in the upcoming tutorials.

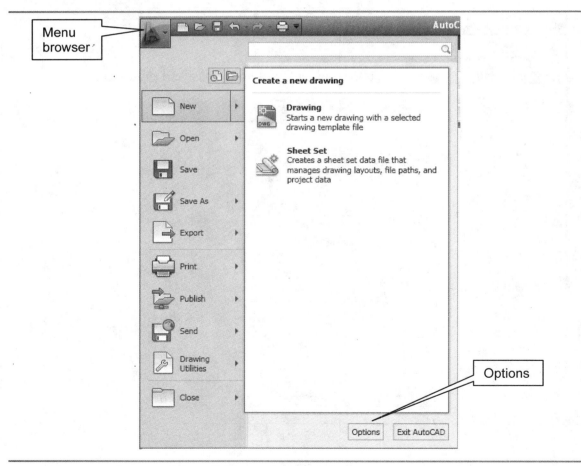

Figure 1-3: Menu browser

1.4.2) **Pull-down Menus** (AutoCAD Classic workspace)

Pull-down menus are available from the menu bar at the top of the drawing window. These menus contain the commands used to create, edit, and save your drawing. Figure 1-4 shows the pull-down menu with the *Draw* menu selected.

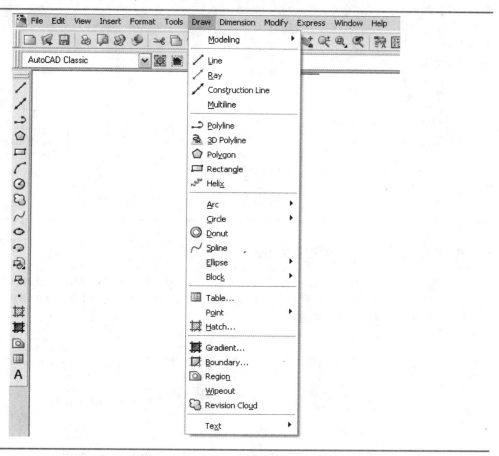

Figure 1-4: Pull-down menu

1.4.3) **The Ribbon**

The *Ribbon* provides, in a single location, commands that are relevant to the current workspace. It is organized into a series of tabs. Several ribbon panels are located in each tab area. Each panel contains related commands. Figure 1-5 shows the *2D Drafting & Annotation* workspace *Ribbon*. Individual ribbon panels may be expanded by clicking on the black arrow located in the bottom right corner of each panel. Once the mouse moves off of an expanded panel, the panel will collapse unless it is pinned. The ribbon may be docked horizontally or vertically. When it is docked vertically, the text tabs are replaced with icons. The ribbon as a whole or individual panels may float freely anywhere in the drawing window. Panels may also be added to or removed from a specific ribbon tab. This requires accessing the CUI (Customize User Interface) manager.

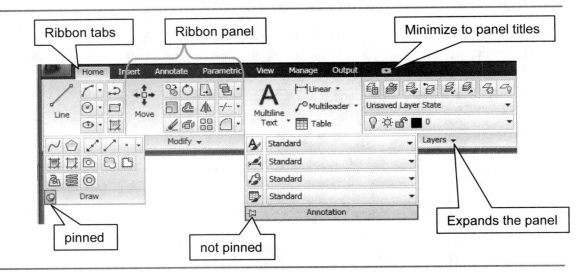

Figure 1-5: The Ribbon

Floating and docking ribbon panels

1) <u>Floating:</u> Click on a ribbon panel title and drag it to the drawing window.
2) <u>Docking:</u> Once the panel is floating, it may be moved, sent back to the ribbon, or the orientation may be changed.

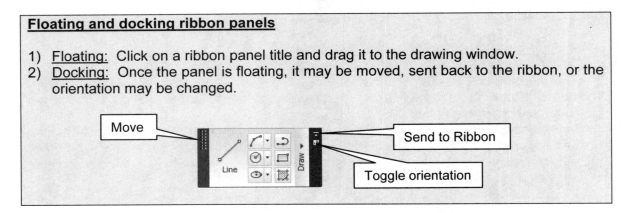

Tooltips appear when your mouse hovers over an icon. For the first few seconds an abbreviated tooltip appears. If the mouse remains over the icon, an expanded tooltip will appear as shown in Figure 1-6. The tooltips help you navigate through the command steps if you are uncertain how to proceed. Tooltip appearance may be modified by accessing in the **Display** tab of the **Options** window (*Menu browser – Options*).

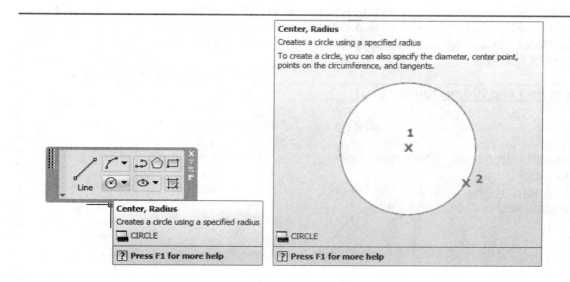

Figure 1-6: Tooltips

1.4.4) <u>Toolbars</u> (AutoCAD Classic workspace)

The toolbars are located along the edges of the drawing area. The icons located within these toolbars may be used to start commands. The name of the command will appear if you place the cursor over an icon without clicking.

Icons with a small black triangle in the lower-right corner are flyout toolbars that contain commands related to the icon shown. With the cursor over the icon, hold down the left mouse button until the flyout toolbar is displayed. Figure 1-7 shows an example of a revealed icon name and a flyout toolbar.

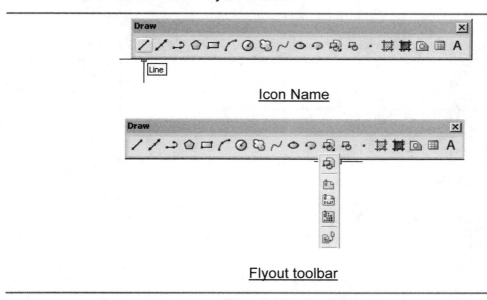

Figure 1-7: Toolbars

AutoCAD initially displays toolbars such as the *Standard* toolbar, the *Styles* toolbar and the *Layers* toolbar. Other toolbars may be displayed by right clicking on any existing toolbar and accessing its shortcut menu. Once a toolbar is active, it can be moved, docked or resized.

Displaying and hiding toolbars

1) Place your cursor over any existing toolbar and click your right mouse button. A shortcut menu will appear that lists the available toolbars. The active toolbars have a check mark next to them.
2) Shortcut menu: Select the toolbar you wish to display if unchecked or hide if checked.

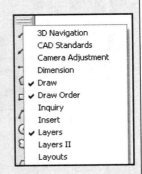

Moving and docking toolbars

1) Place your cursor over the double bar on a docked toolbar or the shaded bar on a floating toolbar, click and hold your left mouse button and then move the toolbar.
2) To dock a toolbar, move it near one of the edges of the drawing area. When the toolbar is in docking position, the toolbar outline will change from thick to thin.

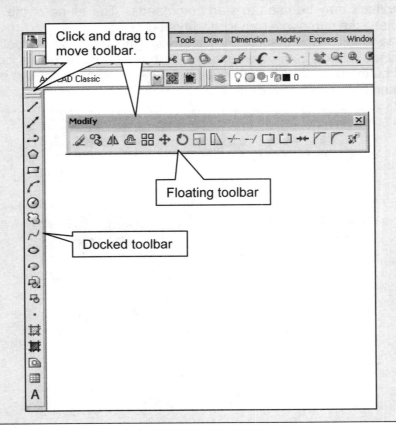

Click and drag to move toolbar.

Floating toolbar

Docked toolbar

1.4.5) Tool Palettes

Tool palettes are tabbed areas within the *Tool Palettes* window that provide an efficient method for organizing, sharing, and repeatedly using blocks, hatches, and your most frequently used commands. The Tool Palettes may be activated within the **Palettes** panel in the **View** tab.

The options and settings for the *Tool Palettes* are accessible from shortcut menus that are displayed when you right-click in different areas of the *Tool Palettes* window. The bottom portion of the shortcut menu, starting with *Dynamic Blocks,* are subsets of all the palettes. Other settings include:

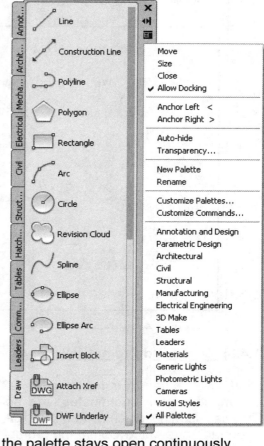

- Allow Docking: Toggles the ability to dock or anchor palette windows. If this option is selected, a window can be docked when you drag it over a docking area at the side of a drawing. Selecting this option also makes *Anchor Right* and *Anchor Left* available. Press the `Ctrl` key if you want to prevent docking as you move the *Tool Palettes* window.
- Auto-hide: Controls the display of the palette when it is floating. When this option is selected, only the tool palette title bar is displayed when the cursor moves outside the tool palette. When this option is cleared, the palette stays open continuously.
- Transparency: Sets the transparency of the Tool Palettes window so it does not obscure objects behind it.

The items within a tool palette are called tools. You can create your own tools by dragging objects such as dimensions, multiline text, polylines, blocks, hatches, etc... from your drawing area onto a tool palette. You can then use the new tool to create objects with the same properties as the object you dragged to the tool palette. Once you add a command to a tool palette, you can click on the tool to execute the command.

Adding a tool to a tool palette

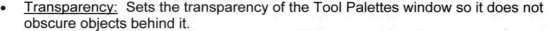

1) Place your cursor over the *Tool Palettes* window and click your right mouse button. A shortcut menu will appear.
2) Shortcut menu: Select **New Palette**.
3) Name the new palette **My Palette**.
4) Drawing area: Select the object you wish to add to your palette.
5) Place your cursor over your object, right click your mouse button and drag the object to the *My Palette*

---

area.
6) To create another object like the one used to create the tool, just click on the icon in the *My Palette* area.

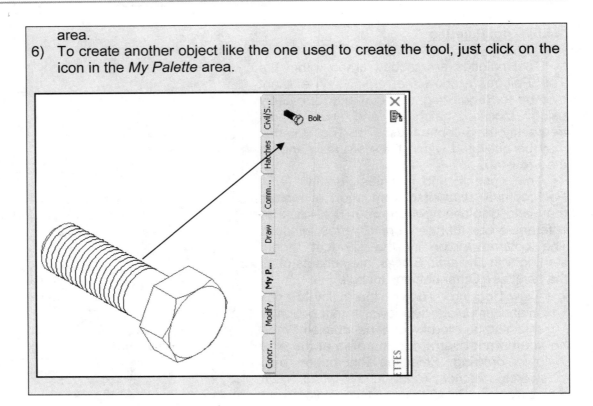

1.4.6) <u>Command Prompt / Window</u>

The *Command* window (Figure 1-8) is the place where you can type in AutoCAD commands, enter coordinates, and select what type of information you wish to enter. This is also the place where AutoCAD prompts you and asks you questions. It is important to read the *Command* prompt when working with an unfamiliar command. The *Command* window, by default, is located at the bottom of the drawing area. However, it can be moved and resized to suit the user's need.

To enter a command using the keyboard, type the command name on the *Command* line and press **Enter** or the **Spacebar**. Commands entered at the *Command* line are not case sensitive and you do not have to move the mouse over the *Command* window before you type. When the *Dynamic Input* is switched on and is set to display dynamic prompts, the entered commands will appear near the cursor.

Most commands may be abbreviated, for example: Line = L, Circle = C, Move = M and Copy = CO. Abbreviated command names are called command aliases and are defined in the acad.pgp file.

When you enter a command, you will see either a set of options or a dialog window. When AutoCAD prompts you to select an option, you only need to enter the capitalized letter(s) of the option. The *Command* window shown in Figure 1-5 shows the process used to draw a circle. First, **C** is entered to activate the CIRCLE command. Second, AutoCAD prompts us to enter a center point or choose another option. A center point was chosen with the mouse. Third, AutoCAD prompts you for a radius or the option of a diameter. **D** was entered to indicate that a diameter is to be entered. Lastly, AutoCAD prompts you for the circle's diameter. The diameter is then entered.

```
×  Command: c
►◄ CIRCLE Specify center point for circle or [3P/2P/Ttr (tan tan radius)]:
▤  Specify radius of circle or [Diameter]: d
   Specify diameter of circle: 1
⌣  Command: l
▭  LINE Specify first point:
```

Figure 1-8: The *Command* window

A command may be repeated by pressing **Enter** or the **Spacebar**. To find a command, you can type a letter on the command line and press **Tab** to cycle through all the commands that begin with that letter. To restart a recently used command, right click on the command line.

1.4.7) Shortcut Menus

Shortcut menus allow quick access to commands that are relevant to your current activity. You can display different shortcut menus when you right-click different areas of the screen and during a command. The shortcut menus shown in Figure 1-9 appear when you right click in the drawing window and during the LINE command.

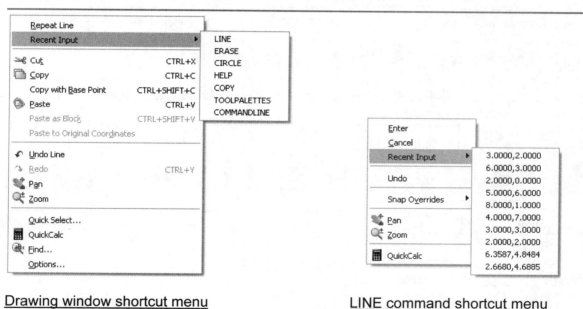

Drawing window shortcut menu   LINE command shortcut menu

Figure 1-9: Shortcut menu examples

1.4.8) Application Status Bar

The *Application Status Bar* displays the coordinate values of your cursor, drawing tools, navigation tools, and tools for quick view and annotation scaling. It is located at the bottom of the drawing area. Figure 1-10 shows the left side and right side parts of the *Status Bar* along with its shortcut menu. The buttons in the status bar are active or on when they are highlighted or light blue (they look gray when they are off). The left side of the status bar contains the coordinate readout. This reads the location of your cursor on in the drawing window. Next to the coordinate reading are the drawing tools. These command are frequently turned on and off throughout the drawing process.

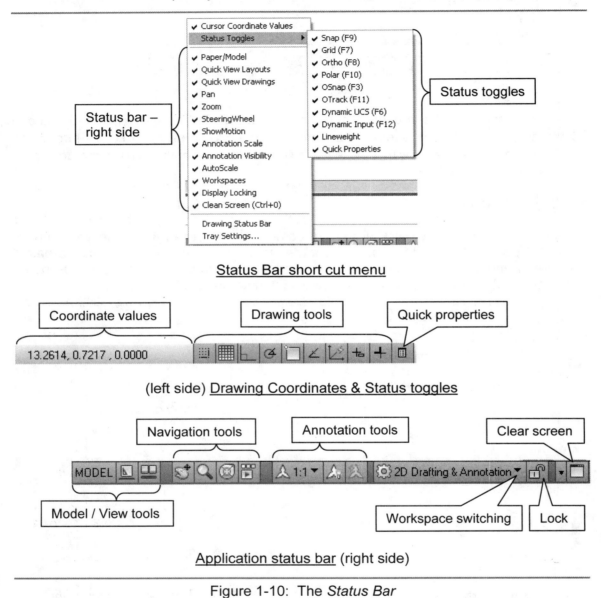

Status Bar short cut menu

(left side) Drawing Coordinates & Status toggles

Application status bar (right side)

Figure 1-10: The *Status Bar*

1.5) **STANDARD AND QUICK ACCESS TOOLBARS**

The *Standard* toolbar at the top of the drawing area is displayed by default in the *AutoCAD Classic* workspace. This toolbar is similar to those found in Microsoft Office programs. It contains frequently used AutoCAD commands such as PROPERTIES, PAN, and ZOOM, as well as commands such as NEW, OPEN, and SAVE. The *Standard* toolbar is shown in Figure 1-11a.

Figure 1-11a: The *Standard* toolbar

The *Standard* toolbar contains the following commands (reading left to right):

- <u>QNew:</u> Opens a new drawing.
- <u>Open...:</u> Opens an existing drawing. (Ctrl+O)
- <u>Save:</u> Saves the current drawing. (Ctrl+S)
- <u>Plot...:</u> Plots or prints the current drawing. (Ctrl+P)
- <u>Plot Preview:</u> Shows you a preview of what will be printed.
- <u>Publish...:</u> Prints the current drawing to either a DWF file or a plotting device.
- <u>3DDWF:</u> Exports the current drawing to a 3D DWF.
- <u>Impressions:</u> Exports to AutoDesk Impressions. Impression converts AutoCAD drawings to design illustrations.
- <u>Cut:</u> Copies the selected objects to the clip board and then deletes them from the drawing area. (Ctrl+X)
- <u>Copy:</u> Copies the selected objects to the clip board. (Ctrl+C)
- <u>Paste:</u> Inserts the objects from the clip board into the current drawing. (Ctrl+V)
- <u>Match Properties:</u> Applies the properties of one object to another.
- <u>Block Editor:</u> Allows you to create or edit a block.
- <u>Undo:</u> Used to undo previous command or actions.
- <u>Redo:</u> Used to redo commands that have been undone.
- <u>Pan Realtime:</u> Allows you to pan the drawing area so that you can see portions of your drawing that are outside the drawing window's boundaries.
- <u>Zoom Realtime:</u> Allows you to zoom in or out using the mouse.
- <u>Zoom Window:</u> Zooms to a selected window.
- <u>Zoom Previous:</u> Zooms to the previous view.
- <u>Properties:</u> Activates a *Properties* window that allows you to selectively change the properties of an object. (Ctrl+1)
- <u>Design Center:</u> Activates the *Design Center* window. With the Design Center, you can organize access to drawings, blocks, hatches, and other drawing content. (Ctrl+2)
- <u>Tool Palettes Window:</u> Activates the *Tool Palettes* which contain commands used to create and edit your drawing. (Ctrl+3)
- <u>Sheet Set Manager:</u> Activates the *Sheet Set Manager* window. The Sheet Set Manager helps you organize multiple drawing files into a single sheet set. (Ctrl+4)
- <u>Markup Set Manager:</u> Activates the *Markup Set Manager* window. The Markup Set Manager allows you to publish your drawing to DWF (Design Web Format) or review and mark up an existing DWF file. (Ctrl+7)
- <u>Quick Calc:</u> Activates a *Quick Calc* window that allows you to perform calculations on a scientific calculator. (Ctrl+8)
- <u>Help:</u> Opens an AutoCAD Help window.

The *Quick Access* toolbar, displayed in the *2D Drafting & Annotation* workspace is an abbreviated version of the *Standard* toolbar. This toolbar is located at the very top of the drawing window next to the *Menu browser*. The *Quick Access* toolbar may be customized by adding or removing commands. This is done by right clicking on the toolbar and selecting **Customize Quick Access toolbar...**, or selecting the arrow at the end of the toolbar. The *Quick Access* toolbar is shown in Figure 1-11b.

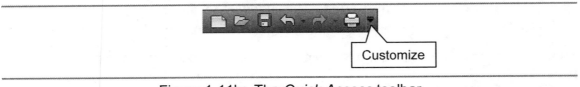

Customize

Figure 1-11b: The *Quick Access* toolbar

1.5.1) Starting a new drawing

When starting a new drawing (QNEW) you have a choice of either starting from the *Create New Drawing* window or the *Select Template* window. The *Create New Drawing* window allows you to set up a drawing to your preferences. You may set parameters such as the units (Imperial or Metric), the size of the drawing, and the degree of precision. The *Select Template* window allows you to choose from predefined templates. Figure 1-12 shows both startup windows. The **STARTUP** variable is used to choose which window will appear when you start a new drawing. If STARTUP = 0, then the *Select Template* window will appear. If STARTUP = 1, then the *Create New Drawing* window will appear.

Template drawings store all the settings for a drawing and may also include predefined layers, dimension styles, and views. Template drawings are distinguished from other drawing files by the .dwt file extension. Several template drawings are included in AutoCAD. You can make additional template drawings by changing the extensions of drawing file names to .dwt.

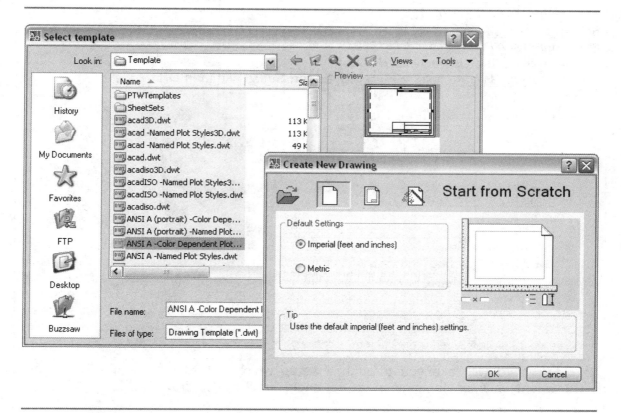

Figure 1-12: Startup window

Starting a new drawing using the *Create New Drawing* window

1) <u>Command:</u> **startup**
2) Enter new value for STARTUP <0>: **1**

3) *Quick Access* <u>toolbar:</u> [ ] or *Menu Browser.* **File – New...** (**Ctrl+N**).
   The *Create New Drawing* window will appear.
4) *Create New Drawing* <u>window:</u> Activate the **Start from Scratch** button, activate either **Imperial** or **Metric** toggle, and then select **OK**.

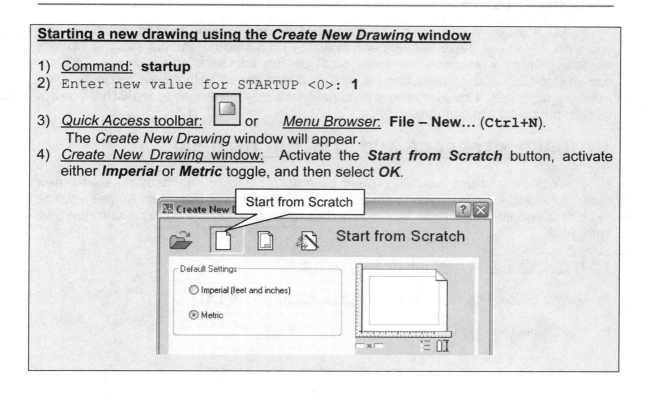

5) *Quick Access* toolbar:

6) *Create New Drawing* window:
   a) Activate the **Use a Wizard** button.
   b) *Select a Wizard* field: Select **Advanced Setup** and then **OK**.

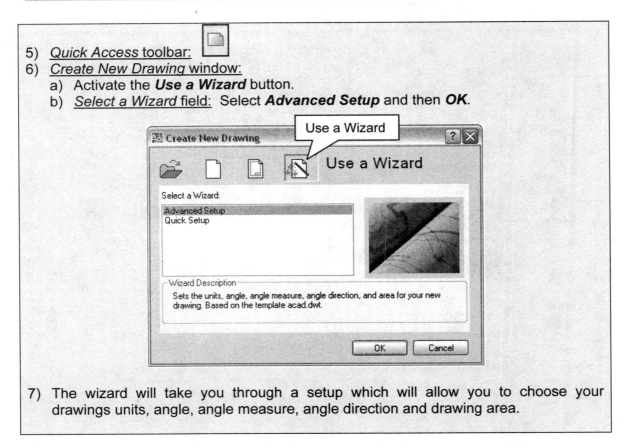

7) The wizard will take you through a setup which will allow you to choose your drawings units, angle, angle measure, angle direction and drawing area.

1.6) CUSTOMIZE USER INTERFACE (CUI)

The CUI allows you to adjust the user interface and drawing area to match the way you work. Many of these settings are available from shortcut menus and the *Options* window. Some workspace elements, such as the presence and location of ribbon panels, toolbars and palettes can be specified and saved using the *Customize User Interface* manager. However, you should not make major changes to the CUI if you are using a public access computer.

1.7) USER INTERFACE AND STARTUP TUTORIAL

The objective of this tutorial is to set up AutoCAD's user interface and start a new drawing. AutoCAD allows you to set up an interface that suits the user. As you become more familiar with using AutoCAD, you will develop an interface configuration that best suits you.

1.7.1) Setting up the user interface

1) View the *User Interface* video and read sections 1.1) to 1.6).

2) Start AutoCAD 2010.

3) An *Initial Setup* window may appear, if this is the first time that AutoCAD has been launched. This allows you to select settings for your workspace that suit your branch of engineering and other preferences. For the purposes of this book, it really doesn't matter, what settings you choose, because we will be working in the *2D Drafting & Annotation* workspace. These are the settings that I selected.
   a) <u>Page 1 of 3:</u> Select the **Mechanical, Electrical and Plumbing** radio button and then select **Next**.
   b) <u>Page 2 of 3:</u> Select nothing and then select **Next**.
   c) <u>Page 3 of 3:</u> Select the **Use AutoCAD 2010's default drawing template file** radio button and then select **Finish**.

Note: This initial setup window may be accessed at any time (*Options* window – *User Preferences* tab – *Initial setup…* button).

---

4) If a *New Features Workshop* window may appear. If so, select the **No, don't show me this again** radio button and then **OK**.

5) Select the **2D Drafting & Annotation** workspace.

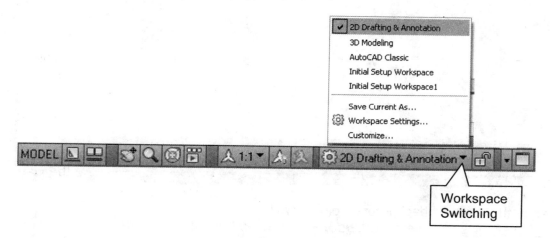

6) Your AutoCAD user interface should look something like the figure shown below. If it is slightly different, don't worry.

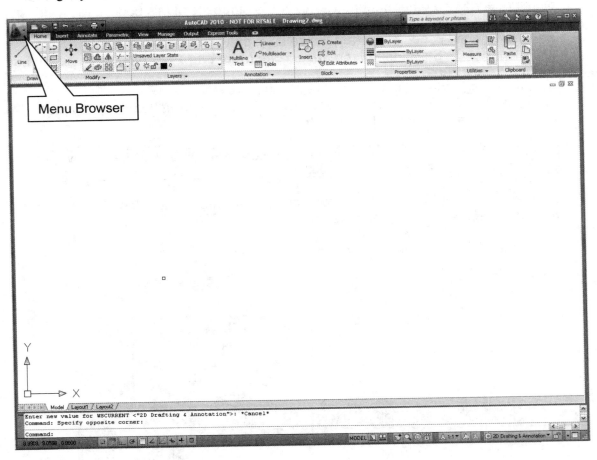

7) Change the screen's background color to white.
   a) *Menu Browser:* Select the **Options** icon at the bottom of the menu.
   b) *Options* window – *Display* tab: Select the **Colors...** button.
   c) *Drawing Window Colors* window:
      i. Context: **2D model space**
      ii. Interface element: **Uniform background**
      iii. Color: Select **White**.
   d) *Drawing Window Colors* window: Select the **Apply & Close** button.
   e) *Options* window: Select **OK**.

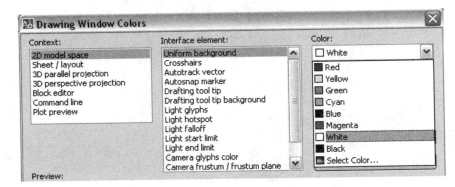

1.7.2) Starting a new drawing

1) Enable the *Create New Drawing* window.
   a) Command: **startup**
   b) Enter new value for STARTUP <0>: **1**

2) Set the units for your drawing.
   a) *Quick Access toolbar:*
      A *Create New Drawing* window will appear.
   b) *Create New Drawing window:* Activate the **Start from Scratch** button, select the **Metric** toggle and then select **OK**.

   Note: If you don't exit and re-enter the *Create New Drawing* window it will continue to use Imperial units.

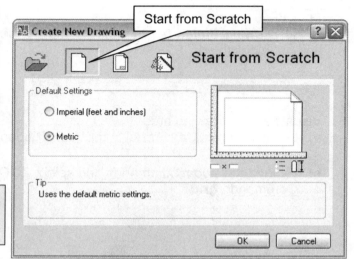

3) Enter the *Advanced Setup* wizard.

   a) *Quick Access* toolbar:
   b) *Create New Drawing* window:
      i. Activate the **Use a Wizard** button.
      ii. *Select a Wizard* field: Select **Advanced Setup**.
      iii. **OK**.

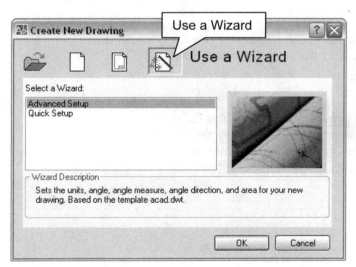

4) Step through the *Advanced Setup* wizard and set the following parameters.
   a) Set your *Units* to **Decimal** with a precision of **0**.
   b) Set your *Angle* to **Decimal Degrees** with a precision of **0**.
   c) Set your *Angle Measurement* to **East**.
   d) Set your *Angle Direction* to **Counter-Clockwise**.
   e) Set your *Area* to a width of **280** mm and a height of **216** mm.
   f) When you are done setting your parameters, select **Finish**.

5) In the *Drawing Status bar*, deactivate the **dynamic input** ⊞. It should look gray and not highlighted.

6) Visualize your drawing area.
   a) Locate the *Navigate* Panel in the *View* Ribbon tab.

   b) Expand the *Zoom* commands and select **ZOOM ALL**.
   c) Command: **grid**
   d) `Specify grid spacing(X) or ON/OFF/Snap/Major/aDaptive/ Limits/Follow/ Aspect]`
      `<10>:` **5**

   e) Notice that your *Grid* icon ⊞ in the *Drawing Status Bar* has become active. Click on the **GRID** icon to turn the grid off and then turn it back on again.

   f) *View* Ribbon tab – *Navigate* panel: [Realtime] (ZOOM REALTIME)
   g) Move your mouse to the center of the drawing area. Click and hold your left mouse button and move the mouse down until you can see the edges of your grid and then release your left mouse button.
   h) *View* Ribbon tab – *Navigate* panel: [Pan] (PAN REALTIME)
   i) Move your mouse to the center of the drawing area. Click and hold your left mouse button and move the mouse around the drawing area. When you are done, release your left mouse button.
   j) **Esc**
   k) [All] (ZOOM ALL)

6) Turn off your **GRID** ⊞.

1.7.3) Saving your drawing as a template

1) *Menu Browser.* 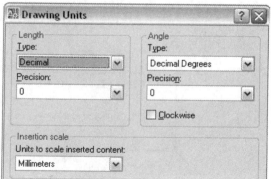 (**Ctrl+Shift+S**)
   a) *Save Drawing As* window: Select a file type of **AutoCAD Drawing Template (*.dwt)**, select a file location on your disk, flash drive or hard drive, name your file **set-mm.dwt**, and select **Save**. A *Template Description* window will appear.
   b) *Template Description* window: Describe your template file in the *Description* field, select your *Measurement* units and then select **OK**.

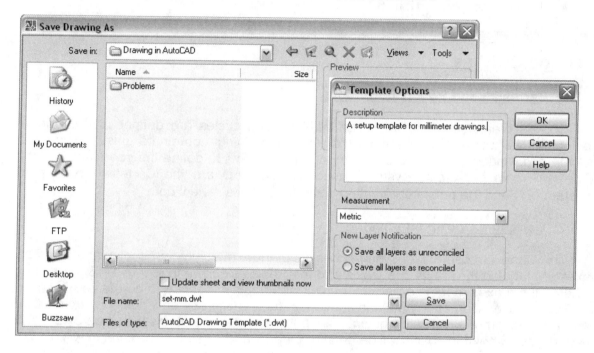

1.7.4) Checking your drawing parameters

1) Check your drawing units.
   a) <u>Command:</u> **un** or **units**
   b) *Drawing Units* window: Make sure that your units and precision are correct and then select **OK**.

2) Check the size of your drawing.
   a) <u>Command:</u> **limits**
   b) Specify lower left corner or [ON/OFF] <0.00,0.00>: **Enter**
   c) Specify upper right corner <280.00,216.00>: **Enter** (If needed, you can change your drawing size by entering larger or smaller numbers in this area.)

3) *Quick Access* toolbar: **Save**

In Class Student Exercise 1-1: User interface and startup

Create and save a **set-inch.dwt** drawing template with the following drawing parameters.
- Set your units to **Inches** with a precision of **0.00**. If the selected units are not Inches, then you need to select **Inches**, select **OK** and then re-enter the Create New Drawing window.
- Set your drawing size to **11** by **8.5**.
- Use the command **UNITS** to check your settings.

1.8) COORDINATES

1.8.1) Cartesian and Polar Coordinates

Objects created in AutoCAD such as lines and circles are defined by coordinate points. The user may specifically state the defining coordinate points using the Command window or use the geometry of other objects to define the coordinate points. The two main coordinate systems used by AutoCAD are the Cartesian coordinate system (x, y) and the polar coordinate system (r, θ). Let's review both.

1.8.2) Cartesian Coordinate System

The Cartesian coordinate system consists of three mutually perpendicular axes. The axes are labeled the x-axis, the y-axis and the z-axis as shown in Figure 1-13. The point where all the axes meet is called the origin. The origin is defined to be the zero location $(0,0,0)$. The location of any point in space can be identified by an x position, a y position and a z position relative to the origin. Since this chapter only deals with AutoCAD's 2-D capabilities, a point in space will be defined by an x and y value. The z value will always remain zero.

3-D Cartesian coordinate system   2-D Cartesian coordinate system

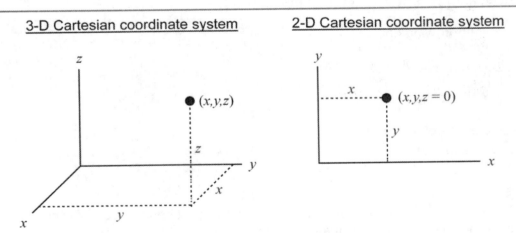

Figure 1-13: The Cartesian coordinate system

To illustrate the use of Cartesian coordinates in AutoCAD, let's look at the sequence of commands used to draw the line shown in Figure 1-14. As shown, the line lies in the x-y plane. It starts at the point $x = 2$ and $y = 1$. It ends at the point $x = 6$ and $y = 3$. The command sequence used to create this line in AutoCAD is:

- <u>Command:</u> **l** or **line**
- LINE Specify first point: **2,1**
- Specify next point or [Undo]: **6,3**
- Specify next point or [Undo]: Press **Enter** to end the LINE command.

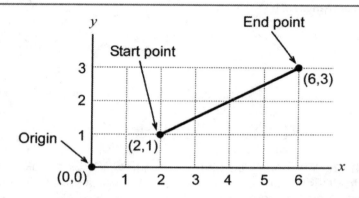

Figure 1-14: A line defined by Cartesian coordinate points

1.8.3) Polar Coordinates

The 2-D polar coordinate system consists of two mutually perpendicular axes. The axes are labeled the x-axis and the y-axis as shown in Figure 1-15. The point where the axes meet is called the origin. The origin is defined to be the zero location (0,0). The location of any point in space can be identified by the radial coordinate r and the angular coordinate θ. The radial coordinate is the shortest measured distance between the origin and the point under consideration, and the angular coordinate θ is the angle between the radial coordinate line and the x-axis.

The angular coordinate θ is measured positive counterclockwise starting at the positive x-axis. Therefore, if a point lies on the positive x-axis, its angular coordinate is zero. If a point lies on the y-axis, its angular coordinate is 90 degrees. The angular coordinate directions are illustrated in Figure 1-15.

2-D Polar Coordinate System

Polar Coordinate Directions

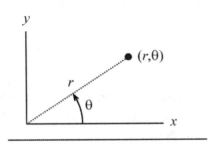
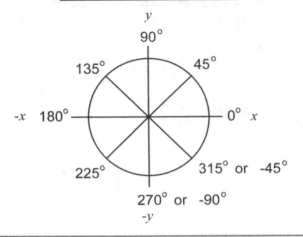

Figure 1-15: The polar coordinate system.

To illustrate the use of polar coordinates in AutoCAD, let's look at the sequence of commands used to draw the line shown in Figure 1-16. As shown, the line lies in the x-y plane. It starts at the point $r = 2.5$ and $\theta = 60$ degrees. It ends at the point $r = 7$ and $\theta = 10$ degrees. The command sequence used to create this line in AutoCAD is:

- Command: **l** or **line**
- LINE Specify first point: **2.5<60**
- Specify next point or [Undo]: **7<10**
- Specify next point or [Undo]: Press **Enter** to end the LINE command.

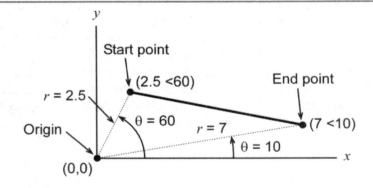

Figure 1-16: A line defined by polar coordinate points

1.8.4) Relative Coordinates

Many times the start point of a line is unknown or the length and angle of the line is known but not the coordinate for the end point. Therefore, AutoCAD allows you to enter coordinate points that are relative to the last point entered and not relative to the origin.

It is like making the last point entered a temporary origin. The symbol @ is placed before the coordinate point if it is to be relative to the last point entered.

To illustrate the use of relative coordinates, let's look at the sequence of commands used to draw the two lines shown in Figure 1-17. The command sequence used to create these lines in AutoCAD are:

Line 1

- <u>Command:</u> **l** or **line**
- LINE Specify first point: Using the mouse, select a point anywhere in the drawing area.
- Specify next point or [Undo]: **@4,2**
- Specify next point or [Undo]: Press **Enter** to end the LINE command.

Line 2

- <u>Command:</u> **l** or **line**
- LINE Specify first point: **2,1**
- Specify next point or [Undo]: **@5<25**
- Specify next point or [Undo]: Press **Enter** to end the LINE command.

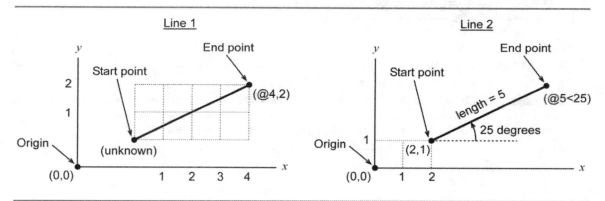

Figure 1-17: Lines defined by relative coordinates

1.8.5) <u>World Coordinate System (WCS) and User Coordinate System (UCS)</u>

AutoCAD has two different coordinate systems; the *world coordinate system* (WCS), which is fixed and cannot be moved, and the *user coordinate system* (UCS), which is movable. The WCS origin is always located in the same place. When opening a new drawing, it is located in the bottom left corner of the drawing window. The UCS origin may be translated and its axes rotated using the commands found in the *UCS* panel. The UCS is very useful when drawing objects that are relative to a point on an existing object. Figure 1-18 shows the coordinate axes for the WCS and a translated and rotated UCS. Notice that the WCS coordinate axes have a box at the origin and the UCS does not. Visually this is how you can tell them apart. The properties of the coordinate axes may be changed to suit the user's preferences.

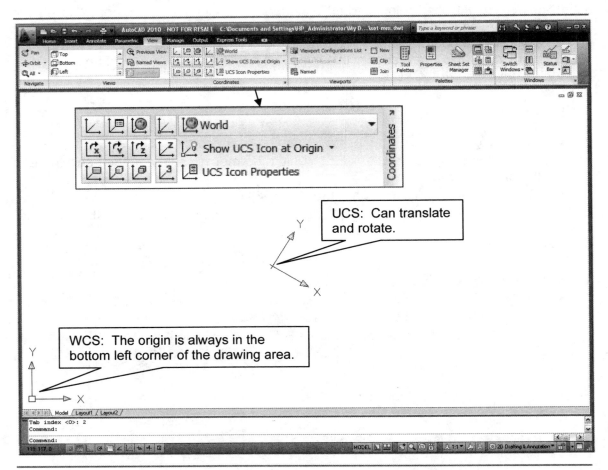

Figure 1-18: AutoCAD's coordinate axes

Changing properties of the UCS icon

1) *Coordinates* panel: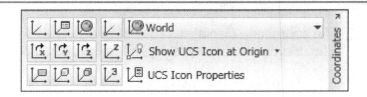
2) Within the *UCS Icon* window, you can change the UCS icon style, its size and its color.

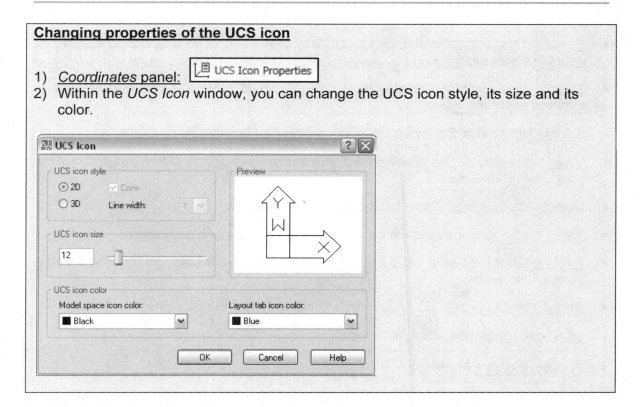

1.8.6) The Coordinates Panel

The *Coordinates* panel, shown in Figure 1-19, contains commands that allow you to switch back and forth between the WCS and the UCS. There are also several commands that manipulate the UCS.

Figure 1-19: The *Coordinates* panel

The *Coordinates* panel contains the following commands:

- UCS: Manages the user coordinate system.
- Named: Manages the defined user coordinate systems.
- World: Activates the WCS.
- Origin: Allows you to change the origin of your UCS.
- X: This command rotates the UCS coordinate system a specified number of degrees about the x axis.

- Y: This command rotates the UCS coordinate system a specified number of degrees about the y axis.

- Z: This command rotates the UCS coordinate system a specified number of degrees about the z axis.

- Z Axis Vector: Defines a UCS with a specified positive z-axis.

- View: Establishes a new coordinate system with the xy plane perpendicular to your viewing direction.

- Object: Defines a new UCS based on a 3D object.

- Face: Aligns the xy plane of the UCS with the face of a solid model.

- 3 Point: Defines a UCS using 3 points: an origin, a point on the x-axis and a point on the y-axis.

- Show/Hide UCS icon: Allows you to hide or show the coordinate axis.

- UCS Icon Properties: Allows you to change the look of the coordinate axis.

1.8.7) Coordinate Position

The coordinate position of your cursor is displayed at the bottom left of the drawing area. It dynamically states the x, y and z position of your cursor. To turn the coordinate display on and off, just click on the area where the coordinate numbers are displayed. The command **COORDS** controls whether the coordinate display is on or off and whether it displays absolute x,y,z coordinates or relative r,θ,z coordinates during a command. Figure 1-20 shows the coordinate display for the cursor position in both the x,y,z coordinates and the r,θ,z coordinates.

- Coords = 0: The coordinate display is off.
- Coords = 1: The coordinate display is on and reads absolute x,y,z coordinates at all times.
- Coords = 2: The coordinate display is on and reads absolute x,y,z coordinates before a command and relative r,θ,z coordinates during the command.

x,y,z coordinate display

5, 0, 0

r,θ,z coordinate display

2.19< 27 , 0.00

Figure: 1-20: Coordinate display

1.9) WCS/UCS COORDINATE SYSTEMS TUTORIAL

The objective of this tutorial is to familiarize the user with AutoCAD's coordinate systems. AutoCAD has two different coordinate systems; the world coordinate system (WCS), which is fixed and cannot be moved, and the user coordinate system (UCS), which may be translated and rotated.

1.9.1) Coordinates

1) View the *UCS* video and read section 1.8).

2) Open your **set-inch.dwt** drawing template (created in Exercise 1-1).

3) Save your template file as a drawing file named **WCS-UCS Coord Tut.dwg**.
    a) *Menu Browser: Save As...*
    b) *Save Drawing As* window:
        i. Select a file type of **AutoCAD 2010 Drawing (*.dwg)**.
        ii. Name your file **WCS-UCS Coord Tut.dwg.**
        iii. Select a location for your file.
        iv. Select **Save**.

4) (ZOOM ALL) or (**z Enter a Enter**)

5) Show your coordinate axis at the origin.

    a) *View* ribbon tab – *Coordinate* panel: Show UCS Icon at Origin

6) Pan your drawing a little to the right and a little up.

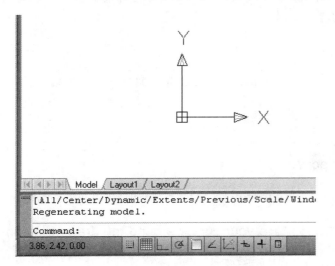

7) Move your cursor around the graphics screen and watch the coordinate display (located in the *Status Bar*) change as your cursor changes locations.

Coordinate display

8) Find the origin. It should be located at the intersection of the coordinate axes.

9) Turn your coordinate readings off by clicking on the coordinate display reading.

10) Turn your coordinate display back on.

1.9.2) Change to the *User Coordinate System* (UCS)

1) Change the location of your **UCS** origin to the middle of your drawing area.

   a) *View* ribbon tab - *Coordinate* panel: (UCS - ORIGIN)

   b) `Specify origin of UCS or Face/NAmed/OBject/Previous/View/ World/X/Y/Z/ ZAxis] <World>: _o`
      `Specify new origin point <0, 0, 0>:` Click the left mouse button somewhere in the middle of the drawing window. (Notice that the coordinate axis moves to the new origin point and the box at the origin disappears.)

2) Move your cursor around the graphics screen and watch the coordinate display change.

3) Find the origin.

4) Change back to the WCS.

   a) *View* ribbon tab - *Coordinate* panel:

1.9.3) Coordinate display and drawing

1) Change the value or your **COORDS** system variable so that the coordinate display will read absolute *x, y, z* coordinates.
   a) Command: **coords**
   b) `Enter new value for COORDS <2>:` **1**

2) Draw a **LINE**, but only enter the first point.
   a) Command: **l** or **line**
   b) `Specify first point:` Move your cursor to the center of your drawing area and click your left mouse button.
   c) `Specify next point or [Undo]:` Move your cursor around the drawing area and watch the coordinate display change. Notice that the coordinate position of your cursor is relative to the origin of the WCS. Press **Esc** when done.

3) Change the value of your **COORDS** system variable to **2** so that the coordinate display will read relative polar coordinates (r, θ).

4) Draw a **LINE**, but only enter the first point.
   a) <u>Command:</u> **l** or **line**
   b) `Specify first point:` Move your cursor to the center of your drawing area and click your left mouse button.
   c) `Specify next point or [Undo]:` Move your cursor around the drawing area and watch the coordinate display change. Notice that the coordinate position of your cursor is relative to the first point of the line. Press `Esc` when done.

1.9.4) Drawing using the UCS coordinate system

1) Draw a **RECTANGLE**, near the center of the graphics screen, which is 4 inches long and 3 inches high.
   a) <u>Command:</u> **rec** or **rectangle**
   b) `Specify first corner point or [Chamfer/Elevation/Fillet/ Thickness/Width]:` Select a point near the center of your drawing area.
   c) `Specify other corner point or [Area/Dimensions/Rotation]:` **d**
   d) `Specify length for rectangles <10.00>:` **4**
   e) `Specify width for rectangles <10.00>:` **3**
   f) `Specify other corner point or [Area/Dimensions/Rotation]:` Move your mouse around the drawing screen. Notice that the rectangle flips from one position to the next. Click your left mouse button to select a position.

   > **Problem?**
   > - If your rectangle is too small, you are probably in a metric drawing.
   > - If your rectangle is off the screen, use **PAN** to bring it into view.

2) Turn your object snap on.
   a) Activate the **OBJECT SNAP** icon ▢ in the *Drawing Status Bar*. It should look highlighted.

3) Draw a **CIRCLE** of radius 1 whose center is located at the geometric center of the rectangle.
   a) Change the origin of your **UCS** to the bottom left corner of the rectangle.
   c) *View ribbon tab - Coordinate panel:* ▱ (UCS – ORIGIN)
   d) `Specify origin of UCS or Face/NAmed/OBject/Previous/View/ World/X/Y/Z/ ZAxis] <World>: _o`
      `Specify new origin point <0, 0, 0>:` Move your cursor near the bottom left corner of the rectangle. As soon as a box appears locating the corner, click your left mouse button.

b) <u>Command:</u> **c** or **circle**

c) CIRCLE Specify center point for circle or [3P/2P/Ttr (tan tan radius)]: **2,1.5**

d) Specify radius of circle or [Diameter]: **1**

> **IMPORTANT!** The UCS is used to reference existing geometry. The UCS allows us to position an object relative to a particular feature on an existing object.

4) Save your drawing.

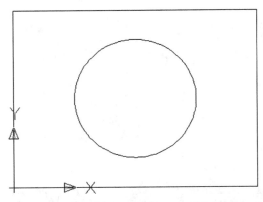

1.10) DRAWING USING COORDINATES TUTORIAL

The objective of this tutorial is to familiarize the user with using both absolute and relative coordinates. You can enter the location and/or size of an object in AutoCAD by using either Cartesian (x,y) or polar coordinates $(r < \theta)$. Both coordinate systems can be entered on an absolute basis (relative to the UCS or WCS origin) or a relative basis (relative to the last point entered). Relative coordinates are preceded by the symbol @.

> **IMPORTANT!:** If you make a mistake when drawing, type **u** or **undo**. This will undo the last point or command that you entered. The UNDO command may be used repeatedly to undo several mistakes.

1.10.1) Drawing a rectangle using Cartesian coordinates

We will be drawing the following rectangle using lines defined by absolute and relative Cartesian coordinates.

1) View the *Coordinates* video.

2) Open your **set-inch.dwt** drawing template.

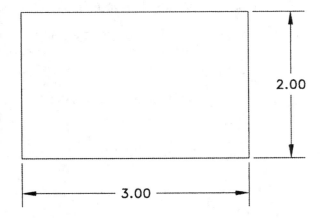

3) *Menu Browser:* **Coordinate Tut – a.dwg**

4) Turn your **OBJECT SNAP**, **POLAR TRACKING** and **DYNAMIC INPUT** off by clicking on them in your *Drawing Status Bar* at the bottom of the drawing area. They should not look gray.

5) Turn your **GRID** on and set the grid spacing to be 1 inch by 1 inch.

> How?
> **a)** <u>Command:</u> **grid**
> **b)** `Specify grid spacing(X) or [ON/OFF/Snap/Major/aDaptive/`
>   `Limits/Follow/ Aspect] <0.25>:` **1**

> Problem?
> • If your grid is too dense, you are probably in a metric drawing.

6) Draw a 3x2 rectangle using absolute coordinates.

> **Note:** An **absolute coordinate** is measured from the WCS origin. The figure shows the actual coordinate points used to create the rectangle.

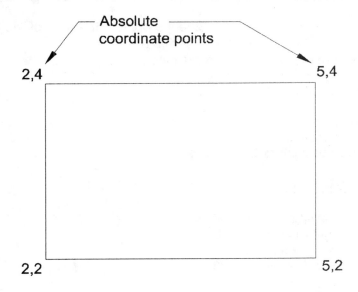

Absolute
coordinate points

2,4   5,4

2,2   5,2

a) <u>Command:</u> **l** or **line**
b) `LINE Specify first point:` **2,2**
c) `Specify next point or [Undo]:` **5,2**
d) Follow the figure and enter the remaining points. **Enter** when done.

> Problem?
> • If your rectangle is too small, you are probably in a metric drawing.

7) Use the grid to confirm that the rectangle is 3 inches wide and 2 inches high.

8) Draw the same rectangle using relative coordinates.

> **Note:** A **relative coordinate** is measured from the last point drawn. The advantage of using relative coordinates is that you do not have to know where the original coordinate point is. We use the symbol @ to tell AutoCAD that we are entering a relative coordinate.

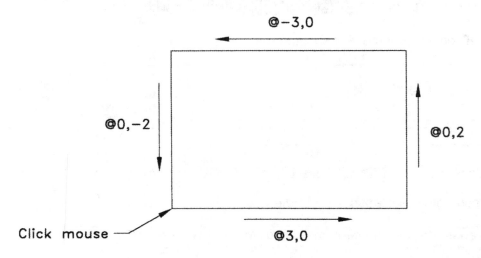

a) <u>Command:</u> **l** or **line**
b) LINE Specify first point: Select a point to the right of the first rectangle.
c) Specify next point or [Undo]: **@3,0**
d) Follow the figure and enter the remaining points. **Enter** when done.

9)

1.10.2) Drawing using relative polar coordinates

1) Review section 1.8.3).

2) **ERASE** all the previously drawn objects.
a) <u>Command:</u> **e** or **erase**
b) Select object: **all**
c) Select object: **Enter**

3) *Menu Browser:* [Save As] **Coordinate Tut – b.dwg**

4) Draw the object shown below using relative polar coordinates.
   a) <u>Command:</u> **l** or **line**
   b) Specify first point: **3,2** (at "A") or choose any point near the bottom left corner of your drawing area.
   c) Specify next point or [Undo]: **@6<0** (to "B")
   d) Specify next point or [Undo]: **@5<90** (to "C")
   e) Specify next point or [Close/Undo]: **@3<180** (to "D")
   f) Specify next point or [Close/Undo]: **@4<270** (to "E")
   g) Follow the figure and enter the remaining points. **Enter** when done.

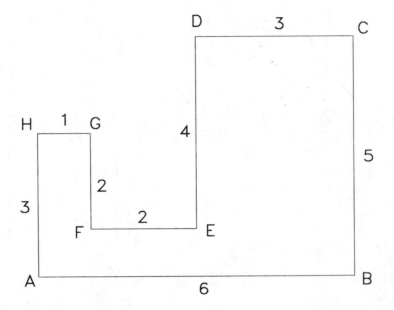

5)

1.10.3) <u>Drawing using both Cartesian and polar coordinates</u>

1) **ERASE** all previously drawn objects.

2) *Menu Browser:* **Coordinate Tut – c.dwg**

3) Draw the object shown below using a combination of polar and Cartesian coordinates.
   a) <u>Command:</u> **l** or **line**
   b) `Specify first point:` **2,2** (at "A") or choose any point near the bottom left corner of your drawing area.
   c) `Specify next point or [Undo]:` **@3<90** (to "B")
   d) `Specify next point or [Undo]:` **@2,2** (to "C")
   e) Follow the figure and enter the remaining points. **Enter** when done.

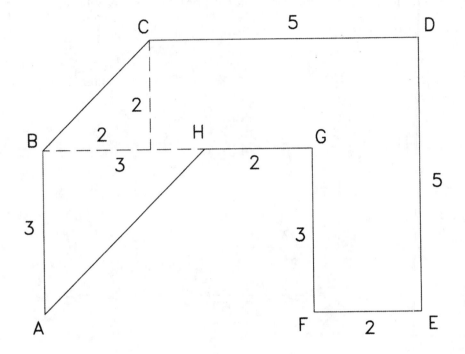

4)

1.11) PRINTING

When you print or plot a drawing, you need to specify what region you would like to print. From within *Paper* space you usually print the *Layout*. However, in *Model* space, there are four different ways of selecting a region to print. (Note: *Model* and *Paper* space will be discussed in Chapter 3.)

1. <u>Display:</u> Prints everything that you can see, at the moment, in the drawing area.
2. <u>Extents:</u> Prints the minimum area which will include everything that is drawn.
3. <u>Limits:</u> Prints the area that you have defined as your drawing size.
4. <u>Window:</u> Prints the area that you select using a window.

Figure 1-21a and b shows a drawing and the printing results using the first three region selection methods. The line around the drawing's title block indicates the limits/drawing size.

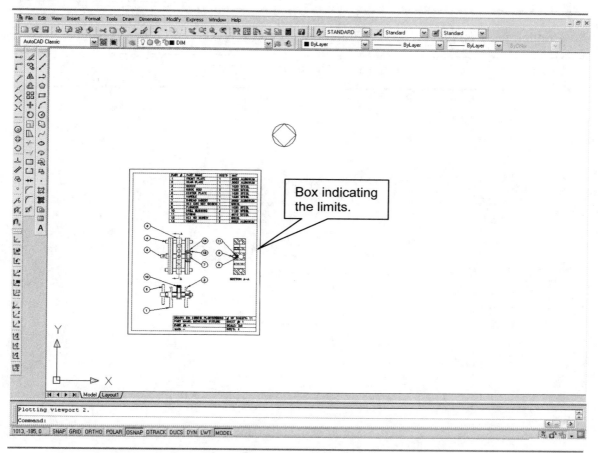

Figure 1-21a: Drawing as displayed in AutoCAD.

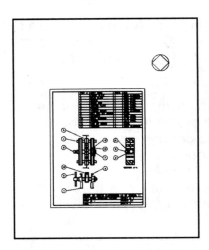

Printing the *Display*

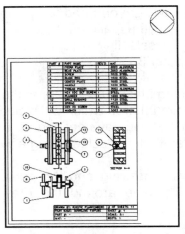

Printing the *Extent*

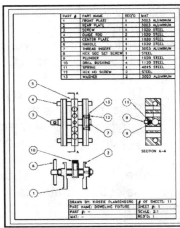

Printing the *Limits*

Figure 1-21b: Printing regions.

1.11.1) Page Setup

Printing preferences for a particular drawing may be set in the *Page Setup - Model* window. These settings are drawing specific which means that they are stored in the drawing or template file and not in the program. To access the *Page Setup - Model* window select **Menu Browser – Print – Page Setup...** and then click on the **Modify...** button. Figure 1-22 shows the *Page Setup - Model* window with the important features identified.

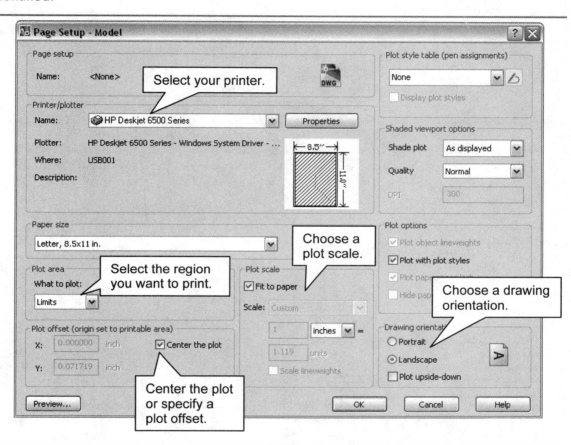

Figure 1-22: *Page Setup - Model* window

1.11.2) Plot

The *Plot – Model* window allows you to send your drawing to a printer or plotter. The default settings used to print your drawing are specified in the *Page Setup – Model* window. The *Plot – Model* window allows you to change some of these default settings without having to access the *Page Setup – Model* window again. To access the *Plot - Model* window select **Menu Browser - Print - Plot...**. Figure 1-23 shows the *Plot – Model* window with the important features labeled.

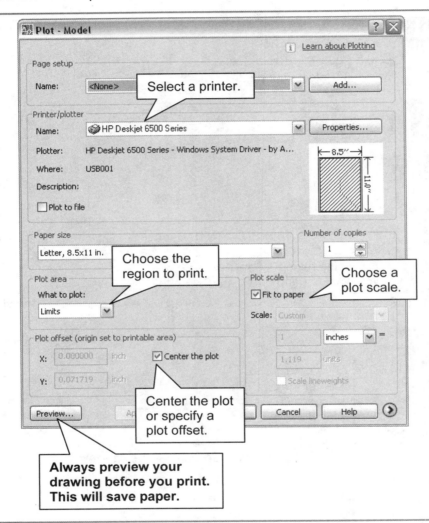

Figure 1-23: Plot – Model window

1.11.3) Printing to Scale

Print scale expresses the ratio between the printed size of an object to its actual size. If a drawing is printed full-scale, it implies that a feature dimensioned as 1 inch measures 1 inch with a ruler on the printed drawing. This is referred to as a 1 to 1 scale. Printing full scale, in most cases, is difficult to achieve unless you have access to a large plotter. In a classroom setting, most engineering drawings are printed on a standard 8.5" x 11" sheet of paper regardless of the object's size. The scale at which the part is printed should allow all details of the part to be seen clearly and accurately. **Even though a drawing may not be able to be printed full scale, they should always be drawn full scale in the CAD environment.**

Since it is impractical to print all drawings full scale, we employ printing to half scale, quarter-scale and so on. For example, if a drawing is printed half-scale, a feature that is dimensioned 1 inch will measure 0.5 inch on the printed drawing. The scale at which the drawing is printed should be indicated on the drawing next to the text "SCALE" in the title block. On a drawing, half-scale may be denoted in the following ways.

1/2   or   1:2   or   0.5

Although it is nice to print to scale, the ASME standard states that no dimension should be measured directly from the printed drawing. For drawings that are not prepared to any scale, the word "NONE" should be entered after "SCALE" in the title block.

1.12) PRINTING TUTORIAL

The objective of this tutorial is to familiarization the user with different printing methods. We will set up a drawing that will be printed in three different ways; *limits*, *extents*, and *display*. These three methods may all give similar results or vastly different results depending on the drawing. We will also go through the steps used to print an object to scale.

1.12.1) Creating the drawing

1) Read section 1.11).

2) Open up your *set-mm.dwt* drawing template.

3) Check your paper size.

> How?
> a) <u>Command:</u> **limits**
> b) Specify lower left corner or [ON/OFF] <0,0>: **Enter**
> c) Specify upper right corner <280,216>: **Enter** (Your paper size should be **280** by **216**. If it is not, set it to this size now.)

4)  **Printing Tut.dwg**

5) Turn your **OBJECT SNAP** and your **DYNAMIC INPUT** off (*Drawing Status bar*).

6) Enter your World coordinate system .

> Where? *View* ribbon tab – *Coordinate* panel:

7) Draw a **RECTANGLE** whose lower left corner is located at (0, 0) and is 280 mm long by 216 mm high. (This rectangle indicates the edge of paper or limits.)

> How?
> a) <u>Command:</u> **rec** or **rectangle**
> b) Specify first corner point or [Chamfer/Elevation/Fillet/ Thickness/Width]: **0,0**
> c) Specify other corner point or [Area/Dimensions/Rotation]: **d**
> d) Specify length for rectangles <10>: **280**
> e) Specify width for rectangles <10>: **216**
> f) Specify other corner point or [Area/Dimensions/Rotation]: Select a point in the middle of your drawing area.

8) . (ZOOM ALL)

9) Draw a **CIRCLE** of radius **50**, and center located at **350,100**. (Don't worry, this circle is off of your paper.)

> How?
> a) <u>Command:</u> **c** or **circle**
> b) Specify center point for circle or [3P/2P/Ttr (tan tan radius)]: **350,100**
> c) Specify radius of circle or [Diameter]: **50**

10) . (ZOOM ALL)

1.12.2) Printing

1) *Menu Browser:* **Print – Plot...**

2) <u>*Plot – Model* window</u>:
   a) Choose a printer.
   b) Activate the **Fit to Paper** toggle.
   c) Select **Extents** as your plot area.
   d) Activate the **Center the plot** toggle.
   e) Select the **Preview...** button. Take note of what is being printed and then hit Esc to exit the plot preview.
   f) Select **Display** as your plot area.
   g) Select the **Preview...** button. Take note of what is being printed and then hit Esc to exit the plot preview.
   h) Select **Limits** as your plot area.
   i) Select the **Preview...** button. Take note of what is being printed and then hit Esc to exit the plot preview.
   j) Select the **Cancel** button.

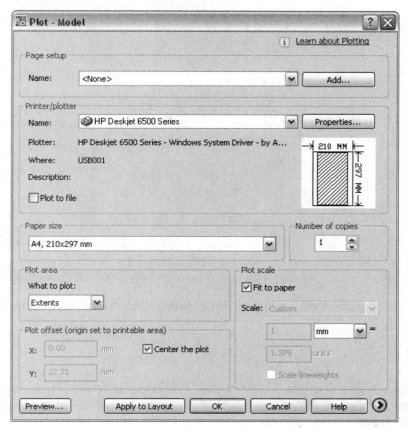

3)   Pan  the drawing so that the rectangle is in the center of the drawing area.

Where? *View* ribbon tab – *Navigate* panel:

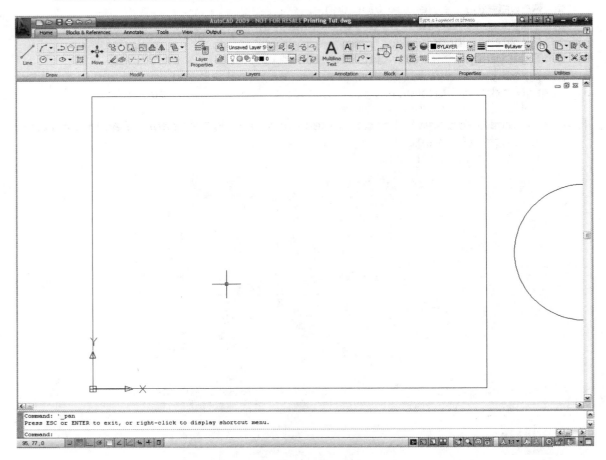

4)   Repeat step 2). and notice that this time all three printing methods give different results.

1.12.3) **Printing to scale**

You may find a situation where you need to print your drawings to scale. This means that the drawings must be printed at exactly the size that it was drawn, or at a specific ratio or scale to the exact size.

1) **MOVE** the circle anywhere inside the rectangle.
   a) Command: **m** or **move**
   b) Select objects: Place your cursor over the circumference of the circle and click your left mouse button.
   c) Select objects: **Enter**
   d) Specify base point or [Displacement] <Displacement>: Select a point inside the circle.
   e) Specify second point or <use first point as displacement>: Move the circle inside the rectangle and click your left mouse button.

2) Type your name inside the circle.
   a) <u>Command:</u> **text**
   b) `Specify start point of text or [Justify/Style]:` **Select a point inside the circle.**
   c) `Specify height <3>:` **3**
   d) `Specify rotation angle of text <0>:` **Enter**
   e) Type your name and hit **Enter** twice when you are done.

3) Print your drawing using *Limits* as your region and the *Fit to paper* option.

4) Print your drawing using *Limits* as your region and a *1:1 scale*. Note that not all of the rectangle will be printed.

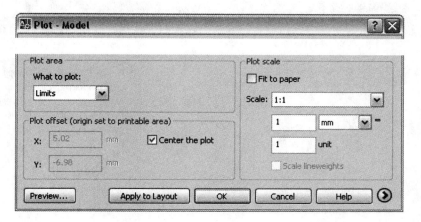

5) Measure both printed circles and indicate their measured diameters.

6)

1.12.3) Printing to PDF

You may find a situation where you need to print your drawings to PDF or another format. AutoCAD allows you to do this using its export feature.

1) *Menu Browser:* **Export – PDF...**
   a) Select the file location.
   b) File name: Name the file
   c) Export: **Window** (Select what you want to print)
   d) Page Setup: If you have already setup your page you can select **Current**. If you have not setup your page us *Override* and setup your page.
   e) If you want to view you print, select the **Open in viewer when done toggle**.

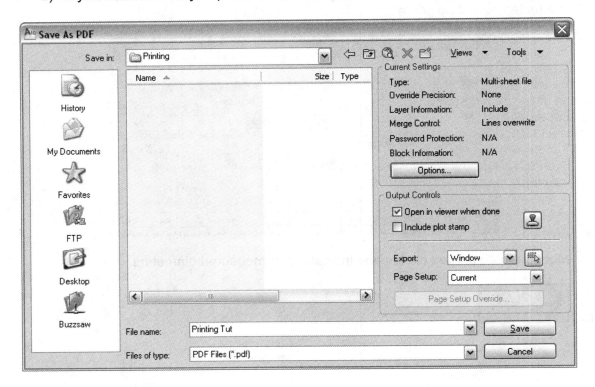

1.13) DRAW COMMANDS

The *Draw* panel (Figure 1-24) contains commands that allow you to draw standard geometries. The *Draw* commands can be used to create new objects such as lines and circles. Most AutoCAD drawings are composed purely and simply from these basic components. A good understanding of the *Draw* commands is fundamental to the efficient use of AutoCAD. To determine the name of the command associated with each icon in the *Draw* panel, place the cursor over each icon in turn and the associated command name will pop up and then in a few second an extended tooltip will appear.

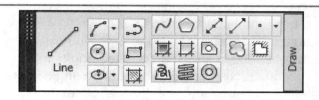

Figure 1-24: *Draw* panel

As is usual with AutoCAD, the *Draw* commands can be accessed in one of several ways: typing the command in the *Command* window, from the *Draw* panel, from the *Draw* tool palette, and from the *Draw* toolbar (AutoCAD Classic workspace).

1.13.1) The LINE Command

Lines are probably the most simple of AutoCAD's objects. Using the **LINE** command, a line can be drawn between any two points picked within the drawing area. A line drawn between two points is often called a vector. This terminology is used to describe the type of drawings that AutoCAD creates. AutoCAD drawings are generically referred to as "vector drawings". Vector drawings are extremely useful where precision is the most important criterion because they retain their accuracy irrespective of scale.

With the LINE command you can draw a simple line from one point to another or you can continue picking points and AutoCAD will draw a straight line between each picked point and the previous point. Each line segment drawn is a separate object and can be moved or erased as required. While the LINE command is active, you can un-enter the last point by using the **UNDO** option available in the *Command* window. You can also close a sequence of lines (connect the start and end point) using the **CLOSE** option.

The LINE command may be accessed in the following way.

- *Draw* panel: [Line]
- *Command* window: **l** or **line**

1.13.2) Construction Line

The construction line (**XLINE**) command creates a line of infinite length which passes through two picked points. Construction lines are very useful for creating construction frameworks or grids. Construction lines are not normally used as objects in finished drawings. Therefore, it is usual to draw all your construction lines on a separate layer which will be turned off or frozen prior to printing. Because of their nature, the ZOOM EXTENTS command ignores construction lines.

The construction line command may be accessed in the following way.

- *Draw* panel: [icon]
- *Command* window: **xl** or **xline**

Construction line options (`Specify a point or [Hor/Ver/Ang/Bisect/ Offset]:`).
- **Hor:** Creates a horizontal construction line.
- **Ver:** Creates a vertical construction line.
- **Ang:** Creates a construction line at a specified angle.
- **Bisect:** Create a construction line that bisects an angle defined by 3 points.
- **Offset:** Creates a construction line that is offset from an existing line by a specified distance.

1.13.3) Polyline

Polylines (**PLINES**) differ from lines in that they are more complex objects. A single polyline can be composed of a number of straight-line or arc segments. Polylines can also be assigned line widths to make them appear solid. Figure 1-25 shows a number of polylines to give you an idea of the flexibility of this type of line. Because of their complexity, polylines use up more memory than the equivalent line. As it is desirable to keep file sizes as small as possible, it is a good idea to use LINEs rather than polylines unless you have a particular requirement.

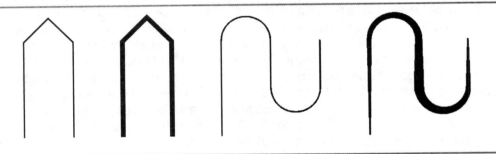

Figure 1-25: Polylines

The PLINE (polyline) command may be accessed in the following way.

- *Draw* panel:
- *Command* window: **pl** or **pline**

Polyline LINE options (`Specify next point or [Arc/Halfwidth/Length/ Undo/Width]:`).
- **Halfwidth:** Enables you to set the halfwidth of the start and end of the line.
- **Length:** Enables you to specify the length of the line.
- **Undo:** Removes the most recent segment added to the polyline.
- **Width:** Enables you to set the start and end widths of the line.

Polyline ARC options (`Specify endpoint of arc or [Angle/CEnter/CLose/ Direction/Halfwidth/Line/Radius/Second pt/Undo/Width]:`).

- Angle: Enables you to specify the included angle of the arc segment.
- CEnter: Enables you to specify the center point of the arc.
- Direction: Enables you to specify the starting direction of the arc.
- Halfwidth: Enables you to set the halfwidth of the start and end of the arc.
- Radius: Enables you to specify the radius of the arc.
- Second pt: Enables you to specify the second point of a three point arc.
- Undo: Removes the most recent segment added to the polyline.
- Width: Enables you to set the start and end widths of the arc.

The **UNDO** option is particularly useful. This allows you to unpick polyline vertices, one at a time so that you can easily correct mistakes. Also, polylines may be edited after they are created using the command **PEDIT**.

1.13.4) Polygon

The **POLYGON** command can be used to draw any regular polygon from 3 sides up to 1024 sides. This command requires four inputs from the user, the number of sides, a pick point for the center of the polygon, whether you want the polygon inscribed or circumscribed and then a pick point which determines both the radius of this imaginary circle and the orientation of the polygon. This command also allows you to define the polygon by entering the length of a side using the EDGE option.

The POLYGON command may be accessed in the following way.

- *Draw* panel:
- *Command* window: **pol** or **polygon**

1.13.5) Rectangle

The **RECTANGLE** command is used to draw a rectangle whose sides are, by default, vertical and horizontal. However, you may draw a rectangle at a specified angle.

The RECTANGLE command may be accessed in the following way.

- *Draw* panel:
- *Command* window: **rec** or **rectangle**

RECTANGLE options (`Specify first corner point or [Chamfer/ Elevation/Fillet/Thickness/Width]:`).

- Chamfer: Creates a rectangle with chamfered corners.
- Elevation: Enables you to specify the elevation of the rectangle.
- Fillet: Creates a rectangle with filleted corners.
- Thickness: Enables you to specify the thickness of the rectangle.
- Width: Enables you to specify the line width of the rectangle.

RECTANGLE options after picking the first corner point (`Specify other corner point or [Area/Dimensions/Rotation]:`).

- <u>Area:</u> Enables you to specify the area and length of the rectangle.
- <u>Dimension:</u> Enables you to specify the length and width of the rectangle.
- <u>Rotation:</u> Enables you to specify the angle of the line that connects the first and second corner of the rectangle.

1.13.6) <u>Arc</u>

The **ARC** command allows you to draw an arc of a circle. There are numerous ways to define an arc; the default method uses three pick points, a start point, a second point and an end point. Using this method, the drawn arc will start at the first pick point, pass through the second point and end at the third point. Others ways of defining an arc can be accessed through the fly-out menu under the ARC icon.

The ARC command may be accessed in the following way.

- <u>*Draw* panel:</u>
- <u>Command window:</u> **a** or **arc**

1.13.7) <u>Circle</u>

The **CIRCLE** command is used to draw circles. There are a number of ways that you can define a circle. The default method is to pick the center point and then to either pick a second point on the circumference of the circle or to enter the circle's radius in the *Command* window. Others ways of defining a circle can be accessed through the fly-out menu under the CIRCLE icon.

The CIRCLE command may be accessed in the following way.

- <u>*Draw* panel:</u>
- <u>Command window:</u> **c** or **circle**

1.13.8) <u>Spline</u>

A **SPLINE** is a smooth curve that is fitted along a number of control points. The FIT TOLERANCE option can be used to control how closely the spline conforms to the control points. A low tolerance value causes the spline to form close to the control points. A tolerance of 0 (zero) forces the spline to pass through the control points.

Splines can be edited after they have been created using the **SPLINEDIT** command. Using this command, you can change the tolerance, add more control points, move control points and close a spline. However, if you just want to move spline control points, it is best to use the grips boxes.

The SPLINE command may be accessed in the following way.

- *Draw* panel: [icon]
- *Command* window: **spl** or **spline**

1.13.9) Ellipse

The **ELLIPSE** command gives you a number of different creation options. The default option is to pick the two end points of an axis and then a third point to define the eccentricity of the ellipse. Others ways of defining an ellipse can be accessed through the fly-out menu under the ELLIPSE icon.

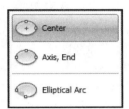

The ELLIPSE command may be accessed in the following way.

- *Draw* panel: [icon]
- Command window: **el** or **ellipse**

1.13.10) Point

The **POINT** command will insert a point marker in your drawing at a position which you pick or at any coordinate location which you enter in the *Command* window. Others ways of defining a point can be accessed through the fly-out menu under the POINT icon. The default point style is a simple dot, which is often difficult to see but you can change the point style to something more easily visible or elaborate using the point style dialogue box.

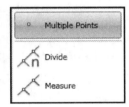

The POINT command may be accessed in the following way.

- *Draw* panel: [icon]
- *Command* window: **po** or **point**

You can access the *Point Style* window with the command **DDPTYPE** or you can access it from the pull-down menu at ***Format - Point Style...*** To change the point style, just pick the picture of the style you want and then click the *OK* button (see Figure 1-26). You will need to use the **REGEN** (regenerate) command to update your existing points. Any new points created after the style has been set will automatically display in the new style.

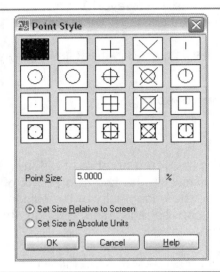

Figure 1-26: *Point Style* window

1.14) <u>TEXT</u>

Text may be added to any location of your drawing and is present in your drawing dimensions. AutoCAD's text is very flexible. It offers all of the standard Windows® fonts plus a few extra fonts. Various text commands and settings may be found in the *Annotation* panel in the *Home* tab shown in Figure 1-27.

Figure 1-27: Annotation panel

1.14.1) <u>Style</u>

The default text font and size may be set in the *Text Style* window. Many text styles may be created and saved under a style name. Properties such as the text direction and the text angle may also be set. The *Text Style* window shown in Figure 1-28 may be accessed by typing the command **STYLE** or **ST**, or from the pull-down menu at *Format – Text Style...*. Figure 1-30 also shows some examples of different text effects performed on an Arial font.

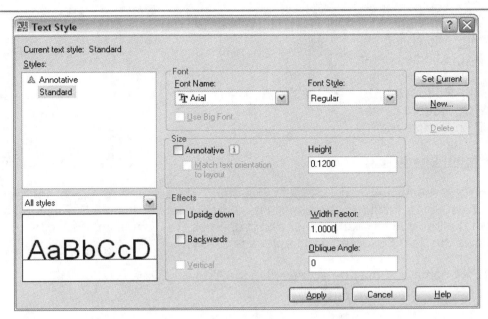

Figure: 1-28: *Text Style* window and text effects examples

1.14.2) Single-Line Text

The **TEXT** command creates a single-line of text. When creating text, you can click anywhere in a drawing to create a new text block. The advantage of using single line text is its wide variety of justification options. If TEXT was the last command entered, pressing **Enter** at the Specify Start Point of Text: prompt skips the prompts for height and rotation angle and enters the text directly underneath the previously entered text. The command **DDEDIT** may be used to edit existing text.

The TEXT command may be accessed in the following way.

- *Annotation* panel: [A↓]
- *Command* window: **text** or **dt** or **dtext**

JUSTIFY options (Enter an option [Align/Fit/Center/Middle/Right/TL/ TC/TR/ ML/MC/MR/BL/BC/BR]:).
- Align: Allows you to specify the left and right boundary of your text. The text will automatically adjust its height to fit the boundary.
- Fit: Allows you to specify the left and right boundary of your text. The text will automatically adjust its width to fit the boundary.
- Center: Allows you to specify the center of the text.
- Middle: Allows you to specify the middle of the text.
- Right: Justify right.
- TL: Top left.

- <u>TC:</u> Top center.
- <u>TR:</u> Top right.
- <u>ML:</u> Middle left.
- <u>MC:</u> Middle center.
- <u>MR:</u> Middle right.
- <u>BL:</u> Bottom left.
- <u>BC:</u> Bottom center.
- <u>BR:</u> Bottom right.

1.14.3) <u>Multi-Lined Text</u>

Using the multi-lined text (**MTEXT**) command activates an in-place text editor and adds a *Text Editor* tab to the ribbon. The *Text Editor* tab includes a several different panels that allow you to change your text properties (i.e. font, size, justification). Figure 1-29 shows the *Text Editor* tab and in-place text editor.

The MTEXT command may be accessed in the following way.

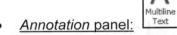

- *Annotation* panel:
- *Command* window: **mt** or **mtext**

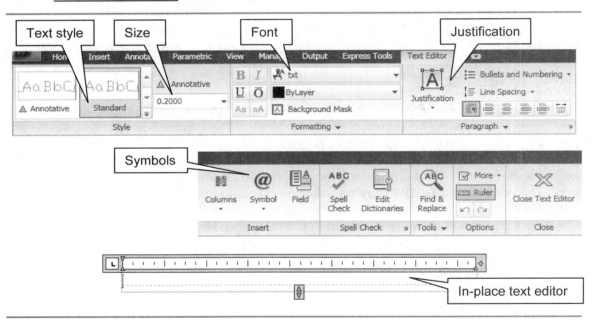

Figure 1-29: In place text editor.

1.15) <u>MODIFY COMMANDS</u>

AutoCAD drawings are rarely completed simply by drawing lines, circles and other geometries available within the *Draw* commands. It is more than likely that you will need to modify these basic objects, in some way, to create the shape you need. The *Modify* panel (Figure 1-30) contains commands that allow you to change standard geometries.

AutoCAD provides a wide range of *Modify* commands such as MOVE, COPY, ROTATE and MIRROR. As you can see, the command names are easily understandable. However, the way these commands work is not always obvious. It is very important to read the prompt displayed in the *Command* window while applying a *Modify* command.

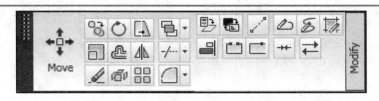

Figure 1-30: Modify panel

As is usual with AutoCAD, the *Modify* commands may be accessed in one of several ways: typing the command in the *Command* window, from the *Menu browser*, and from the *Modify* panel.

1.15.1) Selecting Objects

All *Modify* commands require you to select the object or objects you wish to modify. The simplest way to select an object is to place your cursor over the object and click your left mouse button. The selected object will become dashed or dotted. You may select several objects if necessary. If you accidentally select an object that should not be included in the *Modify* command, type **R** or **REMOVE** in the *Command* window and select the object again. It will be removed from the selection set. If you then need to add an object to the selection set after applying the REMOVE option, you need to type **A** or **ADD** and then select the object.

1.15.2) Erase

The **ERASE** command is one of the simplest AutoCAD commands and is one of the most used. The command erases or deletes any selected object(s) from the drawing.

The ERASE command may be accessed in the following way.

- *Modify* panel: 🖋
- *Command* window: **e** or **erase**

1.15.3) Copy

The **COPY** command can be used to create one or more duplicates of any object(s) which have been previously created.

The COPY command may be accessed in the following way.

- *Modify* panel: 🖿
- *Command* window: **cp** or **copy**

Copying an object(s)

1) <u>Command:</u> **c** or **copy** or   *Modify* panel: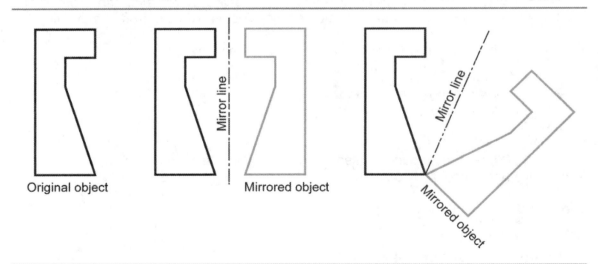

2) Select objects: **Select an object that you want to copy.**

3) Select objects: **Select an object that you want to copy or hit Enter to stop selecting objects.**

4) Specify base point or [Displacement/mOde] <Displacement>: **o**

5) Enter a copy mode option [Single/Multiple] <Multiple>: **m**

6) Specify base point or [Displacement/mOde] <Displacement>: **Select a base point (see selecting base points).**

7) Specify second point or <use first point as displacement>: **Select a second base point.**

8) Specify second point or [Exit/Undo] <Exit>: **To make another copy, select another second base point or hit Enter to exit.**

Selecting base points

- <u>Copying an object(s) a specified distance:</u> The two base points are simply used to indicate the distance and direction of the copied object from the original object. The first *base point* does not have to be picked on or near the object, just select a point anywhere on the drawing area. The *second base point* is specified as a relative (@) coordinate. This relative coordinate gives the specified distance and direction.

- <u>Copying an object(s) to a specific location:</u> In this situation, the base points need to have a geometric relationship with the object and its subsequent final location. The first *base point* should be a geometric location on the object and the *second base point* should be either a coordinate point or a geometric location on an existing object.

1.15.4) Mirror

The **MIRROR** command allows you to mirror selected objects in your drawing by picking them and then defining the position of an imaginary mirror line using two points. To create a perfectly horizontal or vertical mirror lines turn the ORTHO command on. Figure 1-31 shows examples of mirroring.

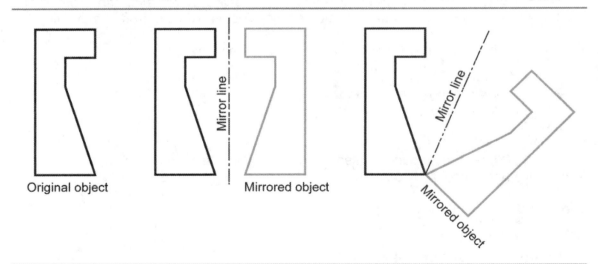

Original object   Mirror line   Mirrored object   Mirror line   Mirrored object

Figure 1-31: Mirroring an object

The MIRROR command may be accessed in the following way.

- *Modify* panel: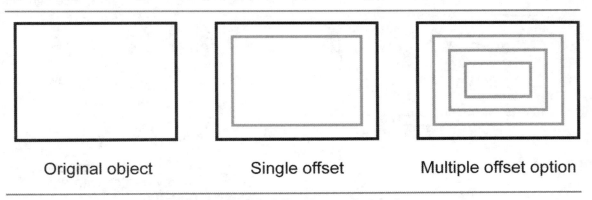
- *Command* window: **mi** or **mirror**

Mirroring an object(s)

1) <u>Command:</u> **mi** or **mirror** or   *Modify* panel:
2) `Select objects:` Select an object that you want to mirror.
3) `Select objects:` Select an object that you want to mirror or hit **Enter** to stop selecting objects.
4) `Specify first point of mirror line:` Select a point
5) `Specify second point of mirror line:` Select a point
6) `Erase source objects? [Yes/No] <N>:` (Entering **Y** will erase your originally selected objects)

1.15.5) Offset

The **OFFSET** command creates a new object parallel to or concentric with a selected object. The new object is drawn at a user defined distance (the offset) from the original and in a direction chosen. The OFFSET command may only be used on one object or entity at a time. Figure 1-32 shows a rectangle being offset. This effect could not be obtained by offsetting a rectangle that was created using four lines.

Original object   Single offset   Multiple offset option

Figure 1-32: Offsetting a rectangle

The OFFSET command may be accessed in the following way.

- *Modify* panel:
- *Command* window: **offset**

Offsetting an object

1) Command: **offset**   or   *Modify* panel:
2) `Specify offset distance or [Through/Erase/Layer] <1.0000>:` Specify the distance to offset.
3) `Select object to offset or [Exit/Undo] <Exit>:` Select an object.
4) `Specify point on side to offset or [Exit/Multiple/Undo] <Exit>:` Select a point on either side of the object to specify the direction of offset. Select the option MULTIPLE if you want to perform multiple offsets. The offset will be relative to the last offset object.
5) `Select object to offset or [Exit/Undo] <Exit>:` Select another object to be offset by the distance specified above or hit **Enter** to exit the command.

1.15.6) Array

The **ARRAY** command makes multiple copies of selected objects in a rectangular pattern (columns and rows) or a polar (circular) pattern. Figure 1-33 shows an example of a rectangle and a polar array.

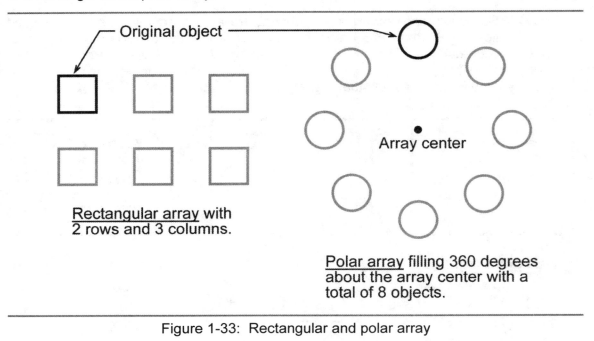

Rectangular array with 2 rows and 3 columns.

Polar array filling 360 degrees about the array center with a total of 8 objects.

Figure 1-33: Rectangular and polar array

The ARRAY command may be accessed in the following way.

- *Modify* panel:
- *Command* window: **ar** or **array**

Creating a rectangular array

1) Command: **ar** or **array**   or   *Modify* panel:
2) *Array* window:
   a) Select the ***Rectangular Array*** toggle.
   b) Click on the ***Select objects*** icon and select the object(s) that you want to array.
   c) Hit `Enter` or `Space` when you are finished selecting objects.
   d) Enter the number of ***Rows*** and ***Columns***.
   e) Enter the distance between the rows or the ***Row offset*** and the distance between the columns or the ***Column offset***. These distances may also be entered by referencing geometry that exists in the drawing area using the *pick offset* icons.
   f) Enter the angle that your array is rotated using the ***Angle of array*** field.
   g) Select the ***Preview*** button.
   h) Select ***OK***.

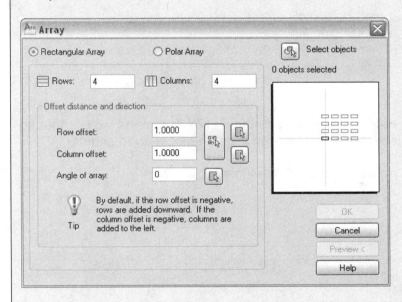

Creating a polar array

1) Command: **ar** or **array**   or   *Modify* panel:
2) *Array* window:
   i) Select the ***Polar Array*** toggle.
   j) Click on the ***Select objects*** icon and select the object(s) that you want to array.
   k) Hit `Enter` or `Space` when you are finished selecting objects.
   l) Enter the X and Y value of the array ***Center point*** or select it using the Pick *Center Point* icon.
   m) Select the array ***Method***.
   n) Enter the ***Total number of items***.
   o) Enter the ***Angle to fill*** or select the angle using the *Pick Angle to Fill* icon.
   p) Usually the items in a polar array are rotated as they are copies. However, you can deactivate this option if required.
   q) Select the ***Preview*** button.
   r) Select ***OK***.

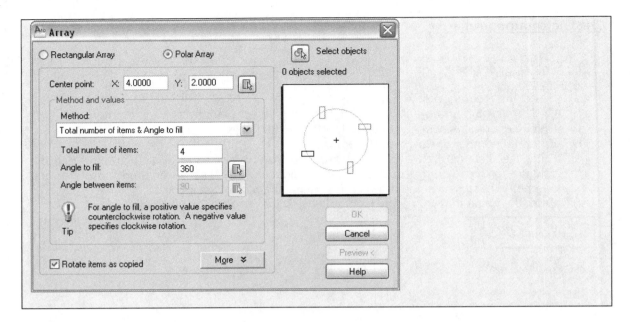

1.15.7) Move

The **MOVE** command works in a similar way to the COPY command except that no copy is made, the selected object(s) is simply moved from one location to another.

The MOVE command may be accessed in the following way.

- *Modify* panel:
- *Command* window: **m** or **move**

Moving an object(s)

1) Command: **m** or **move** or   *Modify* panel:
2) Select objects: Select an object that you want to move.
3) Select objects: Select an object that you want to move or hit **Enter** to stop selecting objects.
4) Specify base point or [Displacement] <Displacement>: Select a base point (see selecting base points).
5) Specify second point or <use first point as displacement>: Select a second base point.

Selecting base points
- Moving an object(s) a specified distance: The two base points are simply used to indicate the distance and direction of the final location from the original location. The first *base point* does not have to be picked on or near the object, just select a point anywhere on the drawing area. The *second base point* is specified as a relative (@) coordinate. This relative coordinate gives the specified distance and direction.
- Moving an object(s) to a specific location: In this situation, the base points needs to have a geometric relationship with the object and its subsequent final location. The first *base point* should be a geometric location on the object and the *second base point* should be either a coordinate point or a geometric location on an existing object.

1.15.8) Rotate

The **ROTATE** command allows an object or objects to be rotated about a point selected by the user. AutoCAD prompts for a second rotation point or an angle which can be typed in the *Command* window. Figure 1-34 shows examples of rotating.

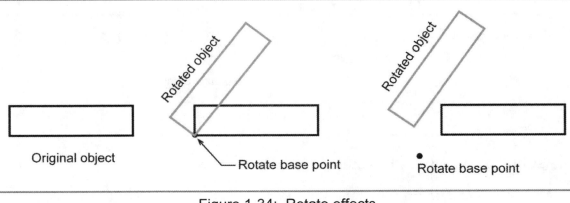

Figure 1-34: Rotate effects

The ROTATE command may be accessed in the following way.

- *Modify* panel:
- *Command* window: **ro** or **rotate**

Rotating an object(s)

3) Command: **ro** or **rotate**   or   *Modify* panel:
4) Select objects: Select an object that you want to rotate.
5) Select objects: Select an object that you want to rotate or hit **Enter** to stop selecting objects.
6) Specify base point: Select the point to rotate about.
7) Specify rotation angle or [Copy/Reference] <0>: Enter the angle of rotation or select the COPY option is you want to keep the original object.

1.15.9) Scale

The **SCALE** command can be used to change the size of an object or group of objects. You are prompted for a base point about which the selection set will be scaled. Scaling can then be completed by picking a second point or by entering a scale factor. Figure 1-35 shows examples of scaling.

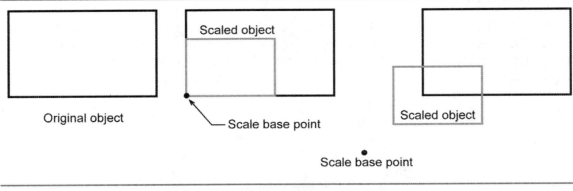

Original object

Scaled object

Scale base point

Scaled object

Scale base point

Figure 1-35: Scale effects

The SCALE command may be accessed in the following way.

- *Modify* panel:
- *Command* window: **sc** or **scale**

Scaling an object(s)

1) Command: **sc** or **scale**   or   *Modify* panel:
2) Select objects: Select an object that you want to scale.
3) Select objects: Select an object that you want to scale or hit **Enter** to stop selecting objects.
4) Specify base point: Select a scale reference point.
5) Specify scale factor or [Copy/Reference] <1.000>: Enter the scale factor or select the COPY option is you want to keep the original object.

1.15.10) Stretch

The **STRETCH** command can be used to move one or more vertices of an object while leaving the rest of the object unchanged. In Figure 1-36, a rectangle has been stretched by moving one vertex to create an irregular shape.

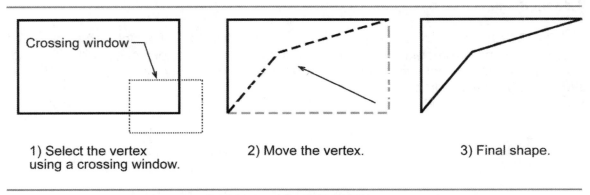

1) Select the vertex using a crossing window.

2) Move the vertex.

3) Final shape.

Figure 1-36: Using the STRETCH command

The STRETCH command may be accessed in the following way.

- *Modify* panel: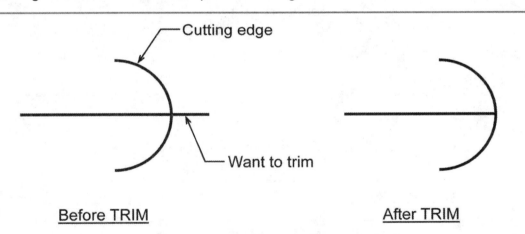
- *Command* window: **stretch**

Stretching a vertex

1) Command: **stretch** or   *Modify* panel:
2) Select objects to stretch by crossing-window or crossing-polygon...
   Select objects: **c** (for crossing window)
3) Specify first corner: Select the first corner of the window.
4) Specify opposite corner: Select the opposite corner of the window.
5) Select objects: Press **Enter** or **Space** to discontinue selecting objects.
6) Specify base point or [Displacement] <Displacement>: Select the vertex to stretch.
7) Specify second point or <use first point as displacement>: Select the final position of the vertex or enter relative coordinates to specify the distance to move relative to its original position.

1.15.11) Trim

The **TRIM** command can be used to trim off part of an object. In order to trim an object you must draw a second object which forms the cutting edge. Cutting edges can be lines, xlines, rays, polylines, circles, arcs or ellipses. Blocks and text cannot be trimmed or used as cutting edges. At each trimming step you are given the option to UNDO the previous trim. This can be very useful if you inadvertently pick the wrong object. Figure 1-37 shows an example of trimming.

Cutting edge

Want to trim

<u>Before TRIM</u>   <u>After TRIM</u>

Figure 1-37: An example of trimming

The TRIM command may be accessed in the following way.

- *Modify* panel:
- *Command* window: **tr** or **trim**

Trimming an object

1) <u>Command:</u> **tr** or **trim** or   <u>*Modify* panel:</u>

2) `Select cutting edges ...`
   `Select objects or <select all>:` **Select an object that will be used as a cutting edge** (this object usually is not trimmed.)

3) `Select objects:` **Select another cutting edge or hit Enter or Space to discontinue selecting cutting edges.**

4) `Select object to trim or shift-select to extend or [Fence/Crossing/Project/ Edge/eRase/Undo]:` **Select the portion of the object that you wish to trim.**

5) `Select object to trim or shift-select to extend or [Fence/Crossing/Project/ Edge/eRase/Undo]:` **Select another object to trim or select the Undo option to undo your last trim.**

1.15.12) Extend

The **EXTEND** command extends a line, polyline or arc to meet an existing object (known as the boundary edge). You can tell AutoCAD which direction to extend the object by picking a point to one side or the other of the midpoint. If the object does not extend, it means that you are either picking the wrong end of the object or the object you are trying to extend will not meet the boundary edge. The solution is to either pick nearer the end you want to extend, move the boundary edge so that the extended object will intersect it, or use the EDGE option. The EDGE/EXTEND option will create an imaginary boundary for the object to intersect. Figure 1-38 shows an example extending an object.

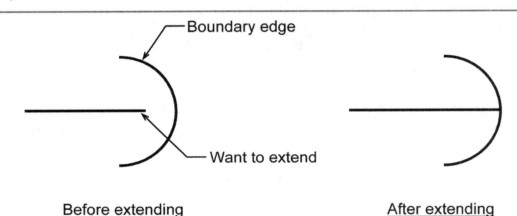

Before extending   After extending

Figure 1-38: Extending an object

The EXTEND command may be accessed in the following way.

- <u>*Modify* panel:</u>
- <u>*Command* window:</u> **ex** or **extend**

Extending an object

1) Command: **ex** or **extend** or   *Modify* panel: ![icon]
2) `Select boundary edges ...`
   `Select objects or <select all>:` **Select the object to be used as the boundary edge.**
   `Select objects:` **Select another boundary edge object or hit Enter or Space to end the selection.**
3) `Select object to extend or shift-select to trim or [Fence/Crossing/Project/Edge/Undo]:` **Select the object to extend or select the EDGE option if your extended object and boundary object will not intersect.**
4) `Select object to extend or shift-select to trim or [Fence/Crossing/Project/Edge/Undo]:` **Select the object to extend or hit Enter or Space to end the command.**

1.15.13) Break

The **BREAK** command enables you to break (remove part of) an object by defining two break points. In Figure 1-39, a corner of a rectangle has been removed using the BREAK command. The remaining lines are still part of one entity. By default, AutoCAD assumes that the point used to select the object is the first break point. However, you can use the FIRST POINT option to override this. If you need to break an object into two without removing any part of it, use the **BREAK AT POINT** command ![icon].

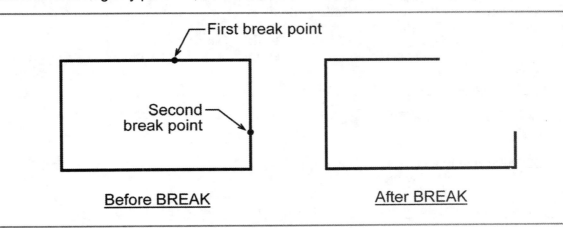

Before BREAK   After BREAK

Figure 1-39: Breaking an object

The BREAK command may be accessed in the following way.

- *Modify* panel: ![icon]
- *Command* window: **br** or **break**

1.15.14) Join

The **JOIN** command joins to separate objects into one object. The command prompt will change depending on the source object. The restrictions of the JOIN command for the following source objects are:

- Line: The lines must be collinear (lying on the same infinite line), but can have gaps between them.

- Polyline: The joined objects can be lines, polylines, or arcs. The objects cannot have gaps between them and must lie on the same plane parallel to the UCS xy plane.
- Arc: The arcs must lie on the same imaginary circle, but can have gaps between them. The CLOSE option converts the source arc into a circle. The arcs are joined counterclockwise beginning from the source object.
- Elliptical Arc: The elliptical arcs must lie on the same ellipse, but can have gaps between them. The CLOSE option closes the source elliptical arc into a complete ellipse. The elliptical arcs are joined counterclockwise beginning from the source object.
- Spline: The spline or helix objects must be contiguous (lying end-to-end). The resulting object is a single spline.
- Helix: The helix must be contiguous (lying end-to-end). The resulting object is a single spline.

The JOIN command may be accessed in the following way.

- *Modify* panel:
- *Command* window: **j** or **join**

Joining a line to a line

1) Command: **j** or **join** or   *Modify* panel:
2) Select source object: Select the first line.
3) Select lines to join to source: Select a line to join to the first line.
4) Select lines to join to source: Select a line to join or hit **Enter** or **Space** to end selection.
5) If the join was successful the prompt will read: 1 line joined to source.

Joining an arc to create a complete circle

1) Command: **j** or **join** or   *Modify* panel:
2) Select arc: Select the arc.
3) Select arc to join to source or [cLose]: close
4) If the join was successful the prompt will read: Arc converted to a circle.

1.15.15) Chamfer

The **CHAMFER** command enables you to create a chamfer (an angled corner) between any two non-parallel lines or any two adjacent polyline segments. A chamfer is usually applied to intersecting lines. The lines do not have to intersect, but their separation cannot be more than the chamfer distance. The CHAMFER icon may be under the FILLET icon .

The CHAMFER command may be accessed in the following way.

- *Modify* panel:
- *Command* window: **cha** or **chamfer**

CHAMFER options (Select first line or [Undo/Polyline/Distance/ Angle/Trim/mEthod/Multiple]:).

- <u>Undo:</u> Enables you to undo the last chamfer while in the multiple mode.
- <u>Polyline:</u> Enables you to chamfer polylines.
- <u>Distance:</u> Enables you to specify two distances that defines the chamfer size.
- <u>Angle:</u> Enables you to specify an angle and a distance that defines the chamfer size.
- <u>Trim:</u> Enables you to specify whether you want the original line trimmed or not trimmed.
- <u>mEthod:</u> Controls whether a chamfer is created using two distances or a distance and an angle.
- <u>Multiple:</u> Allows you to create several chamfers within the same command.

1.15.16) <u>Fillet</u>

The **FILLET** command is a very useful tool which allows you to draw a tangent arc between two objects. The objects are usually intersecting. The objects do not have to intersect, but their separation cannot be more than the fillet radius. It's worth experimenting with this command. It can save you a lot of time and enables you to construct shapes which otherwise would be quite difficult. The FILLET icon may be under the CHAMFER icon .

The FILLET command may be accessed in the following way.

- *Modify* panel:
- *Command* window: **f** or **fillet**

FILLET options (Select first object or [Undo/Polyline/Radius/ Trim/Multiple]:).

- <u>Undo:</u> Enables you to undo the last fillet while in the multiple mode.
- <u>Polyline:</u> Enables you to fillet polylines.
- <u>Radius:</u> Enables you to specify the radius of the fillet.
- <u>Trim:</u> Enables you to specify whether you want the original line trimmed or not trimmed.
- <u>Multiple:</u> Allows you to create several fillets within the same command.

1.15.17) <u>Explode</u>

The **EXPLODE** command is used to break apart single objects into their constituent parts. In other words, the command is used to return blocks, polylines, rectangles, etc... (which may be composed of a number of component objects) back to their individual component parts.

The EXPLODE command may be accessed in the following way.

- *Modify* panel:
- *Command* window: **explode**

1.16) OBJECT SNAP COMMANDS

The *Object Snap* commands (Osnaps for short) are drawing aids which are used in conjunction with other commands to help you draw accurately. Osnaps allow you to snap to specific geometric locations on an existing object. For example, you can accurately pick the end point of a line or the center of a circle. Osnaps are so important that you cannot draw quickly or accurately without them. For this reason, you must develop a good understanding of what the Osnaps are and how they work.

The *Object Snap* panel shown in Figure 1-40 contains commands that allow you to snap to the geometry of an existing object. The *Object Snap* panel is not usually displayed by default, but you can add it through the CUI.

Figure 1-40: The *Object Snap* panel

When using Osnaps, you only need to pick a point which is near the desired point because AutoCAD automatically snaps to the location implied by the particular Osnap you are using. While drawing, notice that when you move the cursor close enough to an Osnap location, it is highlighted with an Osnap marker. Each Osnap has a different marker. Figure 1-41 shows the different Osnap markers.

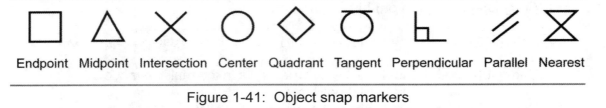

Endpoint Midpoint Intersection Center Quadrant Tangent Perpendicular Parallel Nearest

Figure 1-41: Object snap markers

Object snaps are so important that AutoCAD automatically detects an object's geometric locations while you are drawing. This automatic feature may be turned on and off in the *Status Bar* by clicking on the **Object Snap** icon. To override an automatically chosen Osnap, you can select your preferred Osnap in the *Object Snap* panel or type the command in the *Command* window.

1.16.1) Endpoint

The **ENDPOINT** Osnap snaps to the end points of lines and arcs and to polyline vertices.

The ENDPOINT command may be accessed in the following way.

- *Object Snap* panel:
- *Command* window: **end** or **endpoint**

1.16.2) Midpoint

The **MIDPOINT** Osnap snaps to the midpoint of a line, an arc and a polyline segment.

The MIDPOINT command may be accessed in the following way.
- *Object Snap* panel:
- *Command* window: **mid** or **midpoint**

1.16.3) Intersection

The **INTERSECTION** Osnap snaps to the physical intersection of any two drawn objects (i.e. where lines, arcs or circles cross each other) and to polyline vertices. However, this Osnap can also be used to snap to intersection points which do not physically exist. This feature is called the *Extended Intersection*. To use the extended intersection feature, you must pick two points to indicate which two objects should be used.

The INTERSECTION command may be accessed in the following way.
- *Object Snap* panel:
- *Command* window: **int** or **intersection**

1.16.4) Apparent Intersection

The Apparent Intersection (**APPINT**) Osnap snaps to the point where objects (on different planes) appear to intersect in the current view. For example, you may be looking at a drawing in plan view where two lines cross; however, since AutoCAD is a 3 dimensional drawing environment, the two lines may not physically intersect.

The Apparent Intersection (APPINT) command may be accessed in the following way.
- *Object Snap* panel:
- *Command* window: **appint**

1.16.5) Extension

The **EXTENSION** Osnap enables you to snap to some point along the imaginary extension of a line, arc or polyline segment. To use this Osnap, you must hover the cursor over the end of the object. When the end is found, a small cross appears at the endpoint and a dashed extension line is displayed from the endpoint to the cursor. The tool tip for the extension displays the relative polar coordinate of the current cursor position. This can be a useful guide for positioning your next point. In the case of the arc extension, the tool tip displays the distance along the arc. Once the extension is visible the distance from the endpoint may be entered. Figure 1-42 shows the extension snap in action.

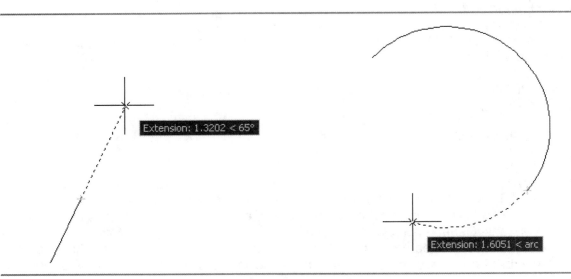

Figure 1-42: Extension snap

The EXTENSION command may be accessed in the following way.

- *Object Snap* panel: [icon]
- *Command* window: **ext** or **extension**

1.16.6) Center

The **CENTER** Osnap snaps to the center of a circle, arc or polyline arc segment. The cursor must pass over the circumference of the circle or the arc before the center can be found.

The CENTER command may be accessed in the following way.

- *Object Snap* panel: [icon]
- *Command* window: **cen** or **center**

1.16.7) Quadrant

The **QUADRANT** Osnap snaps to one of the four circle quadrant points located at north, south, east and west or 90, 270, 0 and 180 degrees respectively.

The QUADRANT command may be accessed in the following way.

- *Object Snap* panel: [icon]
- *Command* window: **quad** or **quadrant**

1.16.8) Tangent

The **TANGENT** Osnap snaps to a tangent point on a circle or arc. This Osnap works in two ways. For example, you can either draw a line from a point to the tangent point or you can draw a line between two tangent points. The second method does not give you a rubber band line to view when selecting the second point.

The TANGENT command may be accessed in the following way.

- *Object Snap* panel: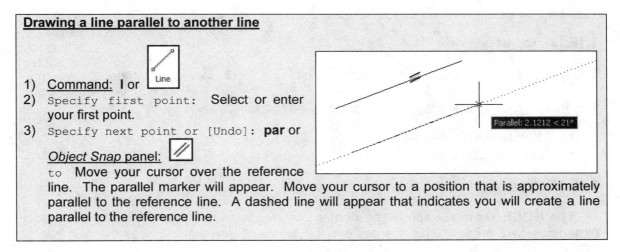
- *Command* window: **tan** or **tangent**

1.16.9) Perpendicular

The **PERPENDICULAR** Osnap snaps to a point which forms a 90 degree angle between the selected object and the object being drawn.

The PERPENDICULAR command may be accessed in the following way.

- *Object Snap* panel:
- *Command* window: **per** or **perpendicular**

1.16.10) Parallel

The **PARALLEL** Osnap is used to draw a line parallel to any other line in your drawing.

The PARALLEL command may be accessed in the following way.

- *Object Snap* panel:
- *Command* window: **par** or **parallel**

Drawing a line parallel to another line

1) Command: **l** or [Line]
2) Specify first point: Select or enter your first point.
3) Specify next point or [Undo]: **par** or

   Object Snap panel:

   to Move your cursor over the reference line. The parallel marker will appear. Move your cursor to a position that is approximately parallel to the reference line. A dashed line will appear that indicates you will create a line parallel to the reference line.

Parallel: 2.1212 < 21°

1.16.11) Nearest

The **NEAREST** Osnap snaps onto an existing object. This Osnap is useful if you want to make sure that the point lies on an object but you don't necessarily mind exactly where it is located.

The NEAREST command may be accessed in the following way.

- *Object Snap* panel:
- *Command* window: **nea** or **nearest**

1.16.12) Snap From

The SNAP **FROM** Osnap is a little more complicated than the other object snaps but it can be very useful. The SNAP FROM Osnap does not snap to an object, rather it snaps to a point at some distance or offset from an object snap location.

The SNAP FROM command may be accessed in the following way.

- *Object Snap* panel:
- *Command* window: **from**

Using the SNAP FROM Osnap

The following command sequence creates a line that starts 1 unit away from the midpoint of an existing line.

1) <u>Command:</u> **l** or

2) Specify first point: **from**   or   *Object Snap* panel:

3) Base point: **mid** or   *Object Snap* panel:
   of **Select the midpoint of the reference line.**

4) <Offset>: **1**

5) Specify next point or [Undo]: **Select the second point.**

1.16.13) Insert

The **INSERT** Osnap snaps to the insertion point of a block, text or an image.

The INSERT command may be accessed in the following way.

- *Object Snap* panel:
- *Command* window: **ins** or **insert**

1.16.14) Node

The **NODE** Osnap snaps to the center of a point, a dimension definition point or a dimension text origin. This Osnap can be useful if you have created a number of POINTS with the MEASURE OR DIVIDE commands.

The NODE command may be accessed in the following way.

- *Object Snap* panel:
- *Command* window: **node**

1.16.15) Object Snaps Settings

Individually picking or entering the *Object Snaps* commands can sometimes be a time consuming process. With *Object Snap* set to on, AutoCAD will automatically snap to a geometric location of an object. The specific snaps that AutoCAD will detect can be set in the *Object Snap* tab of the *Drafting Settings* window (Figure 1-43). This can be accessed by selecting the **Object Snap Settings** icon, by right clicking on OSNAP in the *Status* bar and selecting **Settings...** or by entering **OSNAP** in the *Command* window. The snaps that have a check mark next to them will be automatically detected. You can set the *AutoSnap Markers Size* and *Aperture Size* by selecting the *Options...* button (Figure 1-44). The aperture size controls the size of the area around the current cursor position used to search for object snaps.

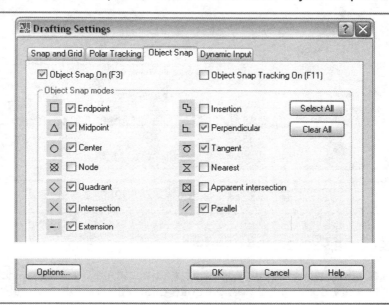

Figure 1-43: *Object Snap* settings

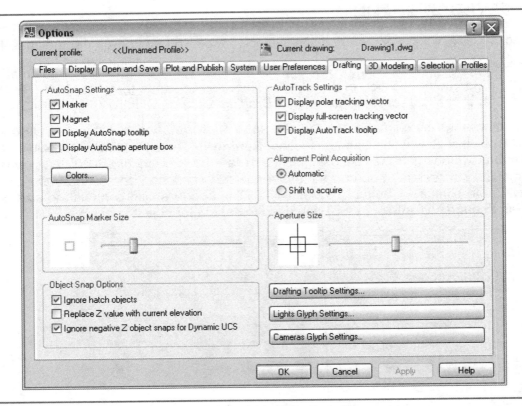

Figure 1-44: *Object Snap* options

1.16.16) Object Snap Cycling and Aperture

Using object snaps is a great way to construct accurate drawings. However, when a drawing becomes very complex, it can be quite difficult to pick the exact point you want. This is particularly problematic if there are a number of possible snap points in close proximity. There are several ways to circumvent this problem. You can identify the particular Osnap that you wish to use by selecting it in the *Object Snap* panel or entering it in the *Command* window, or you can decrease the size of your aperture box.

Another option is to use the object snap cycling feature. This allows you to cycle through all valid snap points within the aperture area until you find the one you want.

This feature only works when *Object Snap* is turned on. Once a snap marker appears, you can cycle through other local snap points by pressing the **Tab** key. Each time **Tab** is pressed, the next snap point is highlighted along with the object or objects to which it belongs. Using this feature, you can be absolutely sure that you are selecting the point you want, no matter how complex the arrangement of objects.

1.17) <u>WAGON TUTORIAL</u>

The objective of this tutorial is to draw several different entities such as LINES, CIRCLES, POLYGONS, etc..., and use several different modifying commands such as MOVE and COPY.

AutoCAD allows you to draw many predefined entities or shapes. Some entities can be defined in many different ways. For example, a circle can be defined by a center point coordinate and a radius, or by two tangent points and a radius. During each command, look at the command prompt and make note of the different options. Also, notice the commands enclosed in angled brackets   < >. They are the default values or options and are selected by pressing the **Enter** or **Space** key.

1.17.1) <u>Preparing to draw</u>

1) View the *Modify*, *Move & Copy* and *Text* videos and read sections 1.13) to 1.16).

2) Open your ***set-inch.dwt*** template.

3)  **Wagon Tut.dwg**.

4) Set your default text font and size.
   - Command: **style**
   - *Text Style* window: Set your text *Font Name* to **Arial** and your text *Height* to **0.24**, select **<u>A</u>pply** and then **<u>C</u>lose**.

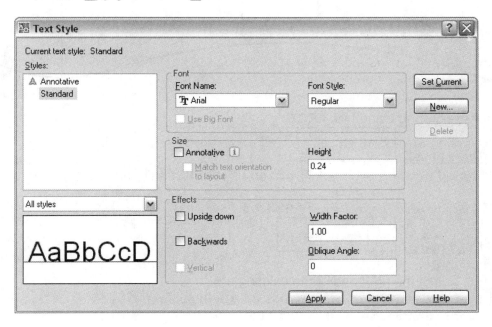

5) Activate a **GRID** that is **0.5** x 0.5.

6)  (ZOOM ALL).

7) Enter your WCS ⌖ (*View* tab - *Coordinates* panel).

8) Turn your **Dynamic input** off and your **Object Snap** off in the *Status* bar.

1.17.2) Drawing.

You will be drawing the following scene.

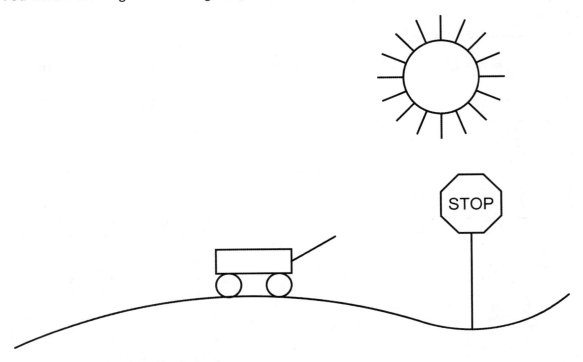

1) Draw the ground using two **ARCS**.

   a) *Draw* panel: [⌒ 3-Point]
   b) `Specify start point of arc or [Center]:` **0,1**
   c) `Specify second point of arc or [Center/End]:` **4,2**
   d) `Specify end point of arc:` **8,1.5**

   e) Draw panel: [⌒ Start, End, Radius]
   f) `Specify start point of arc or [Center]:` **end**
      `of` Select the right end of the existing arc.
   g) `Specify second point of arc or [Center/End]:` `_e`
      `Specify end point of arc:` **11,2**
   h) `Specify center point of arc or [Angle/Direction/Radius]:` `_r`
      `Specify radius of arc:` **3**

> **Note:** By selecting a specific type of arc from the pull-down menu, AutoCAD automatically inputs the correct options.

2) Create the wagon wheels.

a) Draw a **CIRCLE** | Center, Diameter | that has a <u>diameter</u> of **0.5** inches and whose center is located at **4.25,2.25**.

> How?
>   ii.   <u>Command:</u> **c** or **circle**
>   iii.   Specify center point for circle or [3P/2P/Ttr (tan tan radius)]: **4.25,2.25**
>   iv.   Specify radius of circle or [Diameter] <1.00>: **d**
>   v.   Specify diameter of circle <2.00>: **0.5**

b) **COPY** the circle 1 inch to the right.

   i.   <u>Command:</u> **co** or **copy**   or   *Modify* panel:
   ii.   Select object: Use the square cursor to select the circle with the mouse. Place the square on the border of the circle and click the left mouse button.
   iii. Select object: **Enter**
   iv.   Specify base point or [Displacement/mOde] <Displacement>:**o**
   v.   Enter copy mode option [Single/Multiple] <Multiple>: **s**
   vi.   Specify base point or [Displacement/mOde] <Displacement>: Pick a point anywhere within the drawing area.
   vii. Specify second point or <use first point as displacement>: **@1<0** (This moves the circle 1 inch to the right or at an angle of 0 degrees)

3) Create the body of the wagon by drawing a **1.5 x 0.5 RECTANGLE** whose lower left corner starts at (**4,2.5**).

> How?
>   a)   <u>Command:</u> **rec** or **rectangle** or
>   b)   Specify first corner point or [Chamfer/Elevation/Fillet/Thickness/Width]: **4,2.5**
>   c)   Specify other corner point or [Area/Dimensions/Rotation]: **d**
>   d)   Specify length for rectangles <10.00>: **1.5**
>   e)   Specify width for rectangles <10.00>: **0.5**
>   f)   Specify other corner point or [Area/Dimensions/Rotation]: Select a point above the two wheels.

4) Draw the handle of the wagon using a **LINE** that is **1** inches long at a **30** degree angle and starts at the midpoint of the right side of the wagon.

a) <u>Command:</u> **line** or **l** or
b) LINE Specify first point: **mid**
   of Select the midpoint of the right side of the wagon.
c) Specify next point or [Undo]: **@1<30**
d) Specify next point or [Undo]: **Enter**

5) Create the sun body using a **CIRCLE** of radius **0.75** and whose center is located at **8.5,6.5**.

6) Create the sun rays using a polar **ARRAY**. Each sun ray is 0.5 inches long.

   a) Command: **l** or **line** or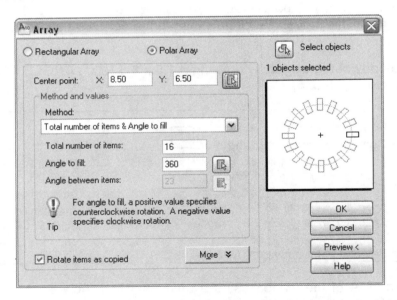

   b) Specify first point: **quad**
      of Select the right side quadrant of the sun body circle.

   c) Specify next point or [Undo]: **@.5<0**

   d) Specify next point or [Undo]: **Enter**

   e) Command: **array** or *Modify* panel:

   f) *Array* Window:
      i.   Activate the ***Polar Array*** toggle
      ii. Click on the ***Select Objects*** icon and select the sun ray and then hit **Enter**.
      iii. Select the center point of the array by clicking on the ***Pick Center Point*** icon and using the **CENTER** snap to select the center of the sun body. The cursor needs to hover over the circumference of the circle before it can locate the center.
      iv. The *Total number of items* is **16**
      v.   The *Angle to fill* is **360**
      vi. Select **OK**.

7) Create the stop sign post using a **LINE** that starts at the **QUADRANT** of the second ground arc and is **2** inches long and travels vertically upward.

8) Create the stop sign using an octagon (**POLYGON**) that is circumscribed in a circle of radius **0.75** at the top of the sign post.

   a) <u>Command:</u> **pol** or **polygon** or   *Draw* panel:
   b) `Enter number of sides <4>:` **8**
   c) `Specify center of polygon or [Edge]:` **ext** or **extension**
      `of` Place your cursor over the top end of the sign post. Once AutoCAD locates the end, move your cursor up to create an extension line. Enter **0.6** in the *Command* window without losing the extension line.
   d) `Enter an option [Inscribed in circle/Circumscribed about circle] <I>:` **c**
   e) `Specify radius of circle:` **0.6**

9) Enter the word STOP in the middle of the stop sign.

   a) <u>Command:</u> **text**   or   *Annotation* panel:
   b) `Specify start point of text or [Justify/Style]:` **j**
   c) `Enter an option [Align/Fit/Center/Middle/Right/TL/TC/TR/ML/MC/MR/BL/BC/BR]:` **m**
   d) `Specify middle point of text:` Use the **EXTENSION** snap to locate a point **0.6** inches above the stop sign post like we did before.
   e) `Specify rotation angle of text <0>:` **Enter**
   f) Type the word **STOP** and hit `Enter` twice.

10)

1.17.3) <u>Using *Modify* commands</u>

For the following commands, you will need to select objects that contain more than one entity. The easiest way to do this is to use a window. When the command asks you to *select object*, you will draw a window around the entire object using the following steps. Click you left mouse button and release, drag the mouse so that the box encloses the entire object, and click the left mouse button again. If an entity was not selected, use the mouse to select the entities individually. If an entity was selected and you do not want it to be selected, type an **R** for *remove* and select the entity.

> **IMPORTANT!** While performing the following commands, READ THE COMMAND PROMPT to see what AutoCAD is wanting.

1)  **Wagon Tut Modified.dwg**

2) On your own, **MOVE** the sun directly to the left by 6 inches and **SCALE** the sun by half using the center of the sun body as the base point.

3) On your own, **OFFSET** the wagon body to the inside by **0.125** to produce a double line.

4) On your own, **MIRROR** the entire wagon using a vertical mirror line. Delete the original wagon.

5) On your own, **ROTATE** the stop sign **45** degrees using the bottom of the sign post as the base point.

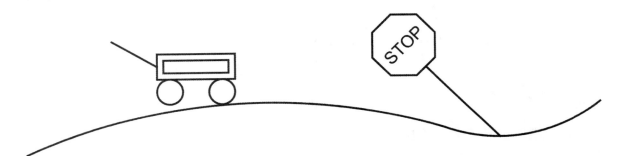

6) Print the completed drawings using **Limits** as your print area and the **Scale to Fit** option.

7)

In Class Student Exercise 1-2: Text Style

1) Open your **set-mm.dwt** template file. Set your text font to **Arial**, text height to **3** mm and make the text **Annotative**. Resave your file.
2) Open your **set-inch.dwt** template file. Set your text font to **Arial**, text height to **0.12** inch and make the text **Annotative**. Resave your file.

Shown below is the inch *Text Style* window.

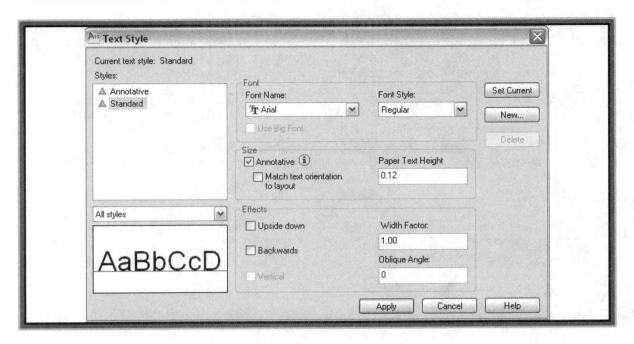

1.18) **SELECTING OBJECTS**

When you start a *Modify* command such as ERASE, two things happen. First, the cursor changes from the usual *crosshairs* to a *pickbox* and second, you will see the `Select objects:` prompt in the *Command* window. Both of these cues are there to let you know that AutoCAD is expecting you to select one or more objects. When an object has been picked it is highlighted in a dashed line to show that it is part of the current selection and the *Command* window reports `1 found`. The `Select objects:` prompt will continue to appear so that you can continue adding more objects to the current selection or you can press **Enter** or **Space** to complete the selection. The most commonly used selection options are explained below.

- Selecting objects by picking: To select an object, place the *pickbox* over part of the object and click your left mouse button.
- Window selection: The WINDOW option is invoked by typing **W** in response to the `Select objects:` prompt or by just clicking the mouse button. The WINDOW option allows you to define a rectangle using two points. Once the window is defined, all objects that lie entirely within the window will be selected.
- Crossing window selection: The CROSSING WINDOW option is invoked by typing **C** in response to the `Select objects:` prompt. Once the window is defined, all objects that lie inside or cross the window will be selected.

If you accidentally selected an object that you do not want to include in the modify command, type **R** or **REMOVE** in the *Command* window and select the object again. It will be removed from the selection group. If you then need to add another object to the selection group, you need to type **A** or **ADD** and then select it.

The **PICKADD** command controls whether subsequent selections replace the current selection group or add to it. If PICKADD = 0, then the object will replace the selected object. If PICKADD = 1, the object will be added to the selection group.

The size of the pickbox may be set in the *Options* window (Figure 1-45). If you click on the *Visual Effect Settings...* button, you can set the selection preview effect and the area selection effect. The selection preview indicates when you are in position to select an object, but have not selected it yet. The area selection effect controls how your selection window looks. To access the *Options* window select **Options icon** in the *Menu browser* and then the **Selection** tab.

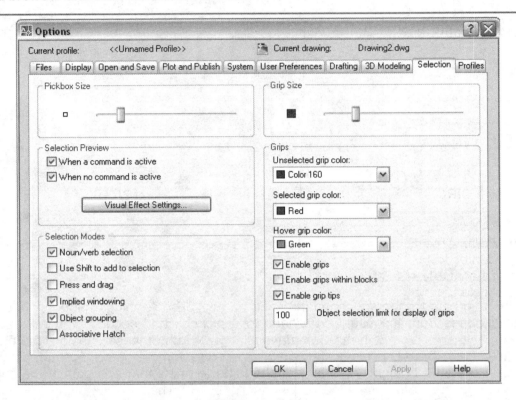

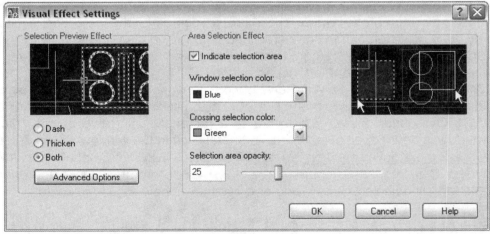

Figure 1-45: Selection settings

1.19) <u>OBJECT SELECTION TUTORIAL</u>

AutoCAD has a whole range of tools which are designed to help you select just the objects you need. This tutorial is designed to familiarize you with these selection options.

1.19.1) <u>Selecting objects using the pickbox.</u>

1) View the *Selection* video and read section 1.18).

2) Open your **set-mm.dwt** template file.

3)  **Selection Tut.dwg**.

4) Draw a **CIRCLE** of radius **20** mm whose center is located at **75,100**.

5) **ARRAY** the *Circle* using the following settings.
   a) *Polar Array*
   b) Center point = **150,150**
   c) Total number of items = **10**
   d) Angle to fill = **360**

6) **ZOOM ALL**

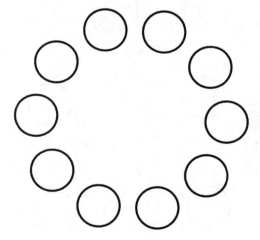

7)

8) Use the pickbox to **ERASE** objects.

   a) <u>Command:</u> **e** or **erase**   or   *Modify* panel:

   b) `Select objects:` **all**

   c) `Select objects:` **r** (Note: This command allows you to remove an object from your selection set.)

   d) `Select objects:` Select all but the left and right circles using the pickbox as shown in the figure on the left.

   e) `Select objects:` **a**

   f) `Select objects:` Select the bottom two circles using the pickbox as shown in the figure on the right.

   g) `Select objects:` **Enter**

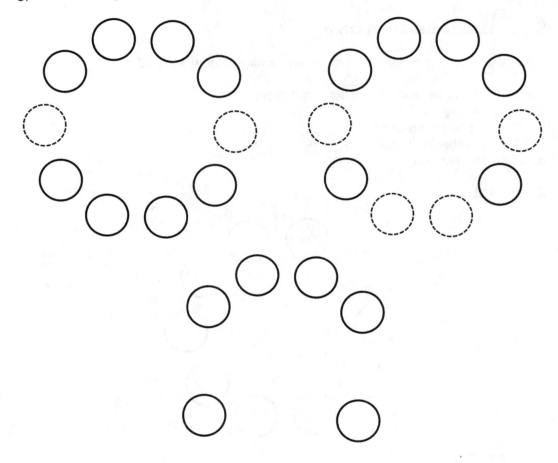

1.19.2) Selecting objects using a window

1) **ERASE** the bottom two circles using a window.
   a) <u>Command:</u> **e** or **erase** or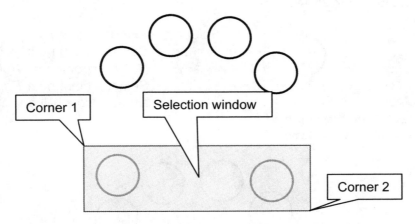
   b) Select objects: Move your pickbox to the approximate location of *Corner 1* and click your left mouse button once (do not click and hold).
   c) Specify opposite corner: Drag the mouse down and to the right and click your left mouse button again at the approximate location of *Corner 2*. (Only objects that are completely enclosed in the window will be selected.)
   d) Select objects: **Enter**

Corner 1   Selection window   Corner 2

2) **ERASE** the top four circles using the crossing window option.
   a) <u>Command:</u> **e** or **erase** or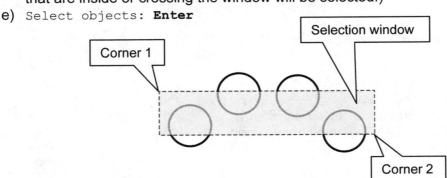
   b) Select Objects: **c**
   c) Specify first corner: Move your pickbox to the approximate location of *Corner 1* and click your left mouse button once (do not click and hold).
   d) Specify opposite corner: Drag the mouse down and to the right and click your left mouse button again at the approximate location of *Corner 2*. (All objects that are inside or crossing the window will be selected.)
   e) Select objects: **Enter**

Selection window   Corner 1   Corner 2

1.19.3) Selecting objects using advanced techniques

1) 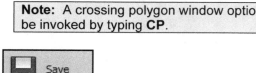 and <u>don't</u> save your drawing and reopen **Open** **Selection Tut.dwg**. This will give you your full array of circles back. If you forget to save or saved in between steps, you will need to draw the circle array again. (Draw the array of circles as described in Section 1.19.1) steps 4) and 5).)

2) **ERASE** selected circles using a **FENCE LINE**.

   a) <u>Command:</u> **e** or **erase** or ✏️
   b) `Select objects:` **f**
   c) `Specify first fence point:` Select a point near *Point 1*.
   d) `Specify next fence point or [Undo]:` Select a point near *Point 2*.
   e) `Specify next fence point or [Undo]:` Select a point near *Point 3*.
   f) `Specify next fence point or [Undo]:` Select a point near *Point 4*.
   g) `Specify next fence point or [Undo]:` **Enter** (Note: All objects that cross the fence line are selected.)
   h) `Select object:` **Enter**

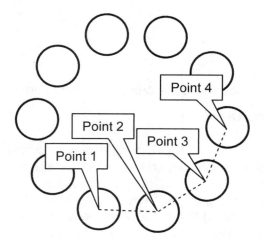

3) **ERASE** selected circles using a **WINDOW POLYGON**.

   a) <u>Command:</u> **e** or **erase** or ✏️
   b) `Select objects:` **wp**
   c) On your own, create the selection window shown. **IMPORTANT!** To end the polygon window hit **Enter**.

   > **Note:** A crossing polygon window option may be invoked by typing **CP**.

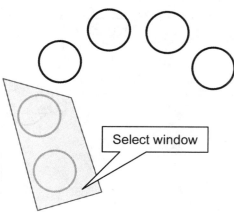

Select window

4) 💾 Save

1.20) **OBJECT SNAP TUTORIAL**

The objective of this tutorial is to familiarize the reader with the OSNAP and TRIM commands. Object snaps automatically select specified geometric locations on an existing object such as the endpoint or the center. Osnaps help you draw accurately and quickly. In this tutorial we will be using the Automatic Object Snaps. Therefore, you will not have to type the OSNAP command in the *Command* window. For the most part, AutoCAD will automatically detect them

1.20.1) **Drawing using Osnaps**

We will be drawing the following object.

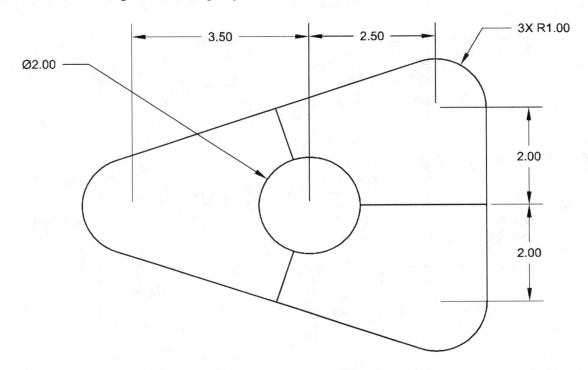

1) View the *Object Snaps* video and review section 1.16).

2) 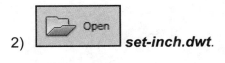 **set-inch.dwt**.

3) 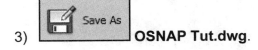 **OSNAP Tut.dwg**.

4) Add the *Object Snap* panel to the *Home* tab.

a) *Manage* tab – *Customization* panel: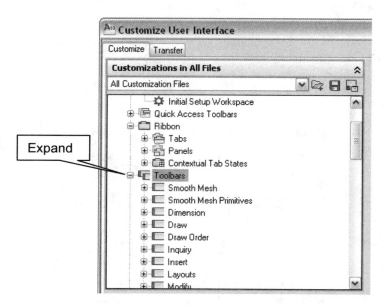

b) *Customize User Interface* window: Expand the *Toolbars* in the tree view on the left side of the window.

c) Scroll down until you see the *Object Snap* toolbar. Right click and select **Copy to Ribbon Panels**.

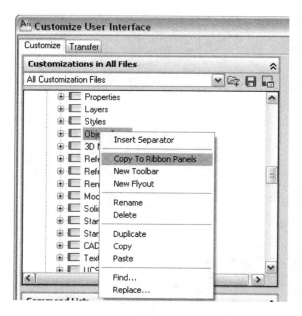

d) Select **Yes** in the *CUI Editor – Confirm Copy to Ribbon Panels Node* Window, if one appears.

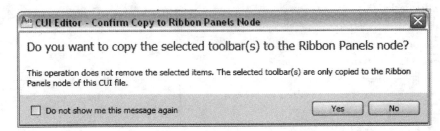

e) Scroll up and expand the *Ribbon* and *Panels* in the tree view on the left side of the window.

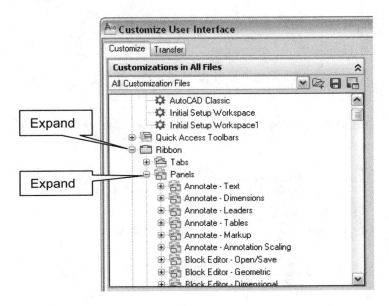

f) Scroll down until you see the *Object Snap* panel. Right click and select **Copy**.

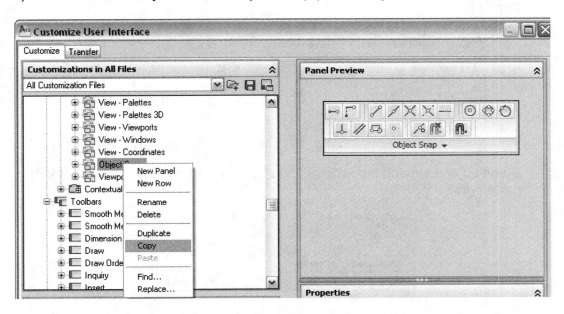

g) Scroll up and expand the *Ribbon* and *tabs* in the tree view on the left side of the window.

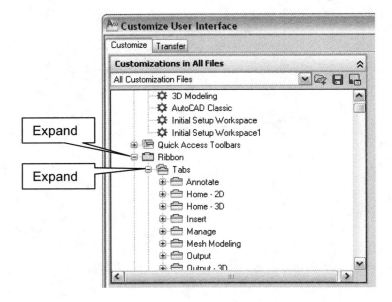

h) Right click on the *Home 2D* tab and select **Paste**.

i) Select **OK**.

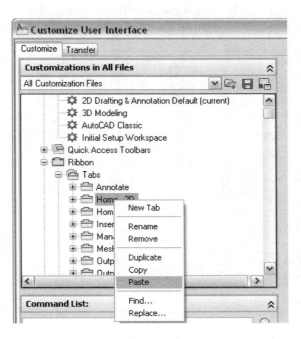

j) The Object Snap panel should automatically show up in the *Home* tab. You can hide or show panels by right clicking on an existing panel and selecting panel. The check mark means that the panel is showing.

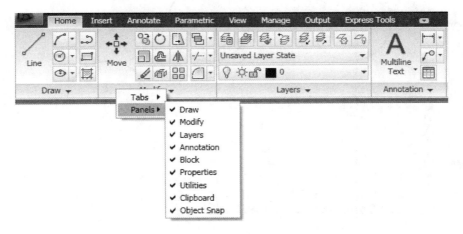

5) Draw a **CIRCLE** of <u>diameter</u> **2** whose center is located at **5,4**.

6) **COPY** the circle to create the three outer circles. Look at the initial drawing to get the distances. Try to do this without looking at the How? box.

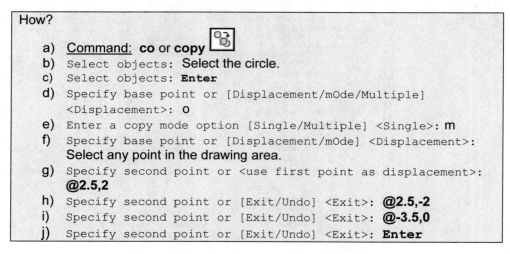

How?

a) <u>Command:</u> **co** or **copy**

b) Select objects: **Select the circle.**

c) Select objects: **Enter**

d) Specify base point or [Displacement/mOde/Multiple] <Displacement>: **o**

e) Enter a copy mode option [Single/Multiple] <Single>: **m**

f) Specify base point or [Displacement/mOde] <Displacement>: **Select any point in the drawing area.**

g) Specify second point or <use first point as displacement>: **@2.5,2**

h) Specify second point or [Exit/Undo] <Exit>: **@2.5,-2**

i) Specify second point or [Exit/Undo] <Exit>: **@-3.5,0**

j) Specify second point or [Exit/Undo] <Exit>: **Enter**

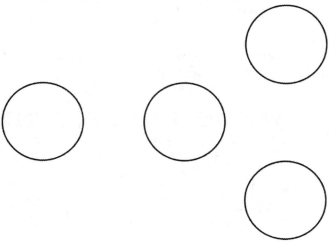

7) **ZOOM ALL**

8) Turn your **Object Snap** on in the *Status Bar*.

9) Set up your *Object Snap* options.

    a) <u>Command:</u> **OSNAP**   or   *Object Snap* panel: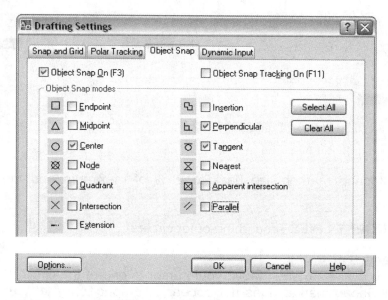

    b) *Drafting Settings* window – *Object Snap* tab: Activate the *Object Snap modes* shown and then click the **Options...** button. These are the only object snaps that the computer will automatically detect.

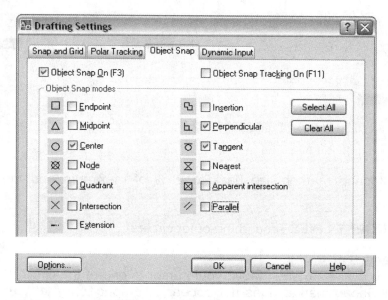

    c) *Options* window – *Drafting* tab: Set the *AutoSnap Marker Size* to maximum and then click the **Colors...** button.

    d) *Drawing Window Colors:* Set the autosnap marker color to **red** and then click on the **Apply & Close** button.

    e) Click **OK** in the *Options* windows.

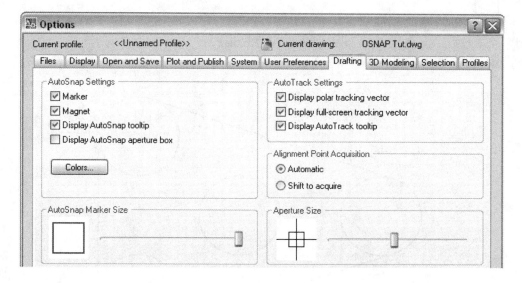

10) Visualize the autosnap markers.
   a) Start a **LINE** any where in the drawing area.
   b) Move your cursor around the circles and locate each one of the automatic snap markers (Center, Perpendicular, Tangent).
   c) Hit **Esc** to exit the LINE command.

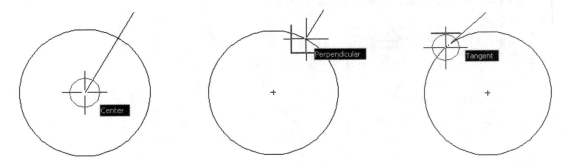

11) Set the autosnap marker size back to 25% of maximum and the color to your preference.

12) Draw 3 **TANGENT LINES** around the outer circles.

   a) <u>Command:</u> **l** or ◺
   b) `Specify first point:` Move your cursor to one of the circles. Notice that the tangent Osnap marker does not appear. To specifically tell AutoCAD that you want to detect the tangent, type **tan** or select ⊚.
       `to` Select the circle.
   c) `Specify next point or [Undo]:` Move your cursor to the circle at the other end of the line. Again, AutoCAD will not detect the tangent. Type **tan** or select ⊚.
       `to` Select the circle.
   d) `Specify next point or [Undo]:` **Enter**
   e) Complete the other two lines.

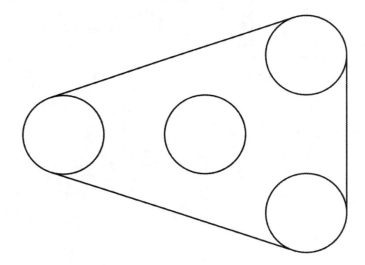

13) Draw the 3 **LINES** from the **CENTER** point of the middle circle to **PERPENDICULAR** to the outer tangent lines. Use the Osnap markers to guide you. (Note: To acquire the center of the circle you need to hover over its circumference.)

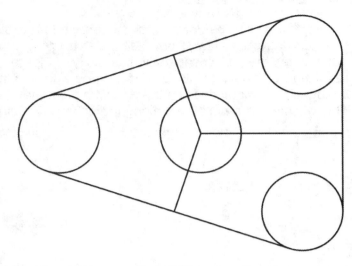

1.20.2) Trimming unwanted lines

1) **TRIM** the unwanted lines.
   a) <u>Command:</u> **trim**   or

   <u>*Modify* panel:</u> [icon]

   b) `Select cutting edges ...`
      `Select objects or <select all>:` Select the 3 tangent lines and the middle circle.

   Problems?
   - If AutoCAD will not let you multiple select change your PICKADD variable to 1.
   ---

   c) `Select objects:` **Enter**
   d) `Select object to trim or shift-select to extend or [Fence/` `Crossing/Project/Edge/eRase/Undo]:` Select the inner portion of the outer circles and the lines inside the middle circle.
   e) `Select object to trim or shift-select to extend or [Fence/` `Crossing/Project/Edge/eRase/Undo]:` **Enter**

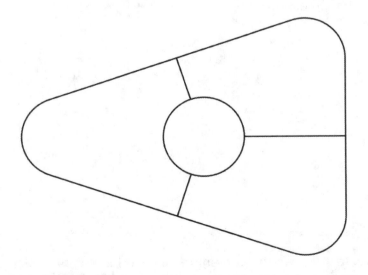

1.21) POLAR TRACKING

Polar tracking restricts cursor movement to specified angles. When you are creating or modifying objects, you can use polar tracking to display temporary alignment paths defined by the polar angles you specify. Figure 1-46 shows a polar tracking path restricting a line to be along a 15 degree angle. Once a polar tracking path has been snapped to, a distance from the previous point may be entered in the *Command* window. This will place the next point along the polar path at the specified distance.

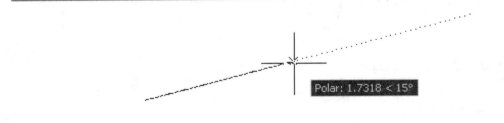

Figure 1-46: Polar tracking path

Polar angles are relative to the orientation of the WCS or the current user coordinate system (UCS). You can turn your polar tracking on and off by clicking on the *Polar Tracking* icon in the *Status Bar*. To change the increment of the tracking angle you can use the **POLARANG** command, or right click on the *Polar Tracking* icon in the *Status Bar* and select **Settings...**. Figure 1-47 shows the *Polar Tracking* settings window.

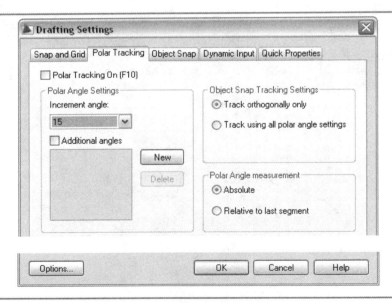

Figure 1-47: Polar tracking settings

Polar snap restricts cursor movement to specified increments along a polar tracking path. You can turn on the polar snap by setting your **SNAPTYPE** variable to 1 (a value of 0 is for standard snap). You can set the polar snap distance with the **POLARDIST** command.

1.22) OBJECT SNAP TRACKING

Object snap tracking enables you to track along alignment paths that are based on object snap points. After you acquire a point, horizontal, vertical, or polar alignment paths relative to the point are displayed as you move the cursor. You can acquire up to seven snap points at a time. Acquired snap points are displayed as a small plus sign (+). You can turn your object snap tracking on and off by clicking on the *Object Snap*

Tracking icon in the *Status Bar* or by hitting **F11**. Figure 1-48 shows a line being drawn with the help of object snap tracking. The end of the line will be drawn where the center of the circle aligns with the endpoint of the existing line.

A temporary track point is a point that is not associated with the geometry directly, but with the alignment paths that come off the geometry. You can select a temporary

track point by typing **TT** or selecting the *Temporary Track Point* icon in the *Object Snap* panel and then selecting the point.

Object snap tracking is set to create paths at 0, 90, 180, and 270 degrees. However, you can use polar tracking angles instead by setting the **POLARMODE** variable to 2.

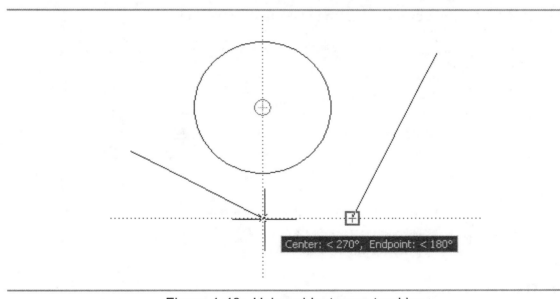

Center: < 270°, Endpoint: < 180°

Figure 1-48: Using object snap tracking

1.23) TRACKING TUTORIAL

The objective of this tutorial is to familiarize the user with AutoCAD's tracking ability. AutoCAD allows you to track along polar paths. Polar paths are created at angle increments that you specify. Distances along a polar path may be entered to identify the location of the next point. Object snap tracking is also available. This allows you to place a point at the intersection of multiple paths. These paths extend from acquired object snap points.

1.23.1) Polar tracking

1) View the *Tracking* video and read sections 1.21) and 1.22).

2) 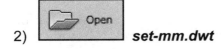 *set-mm.dwt*

3)  **Tracking Tut.dwg**

4) *Status Bar:* Turn your **Object Snap** and **Polar Tracking** on and your **Dynamic Input** off.

5) Set your polar tracking angle increment to 15 degrees.
   a) Command: **polarang**
   b) Enter new value for POLARANG <90>: **15**

6) Access the **Osnap settings** and activate the snaps shown.

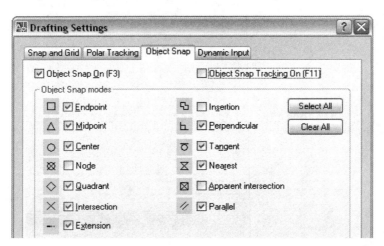

7) **ZOOM ALL**

8) Draw the following object using polar tracking. The object is symmetric.
   a) Start a **LINE** at **30,30**.
   b) Move your cursor around the drawing area until you snap to the 60 degree polar path.
   c) Type **40** and then hit **Enter**.
   d) Use polar tracking to complete the object.

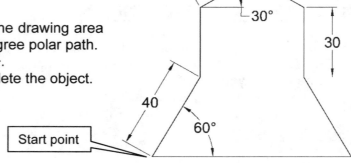

9) **MIRROR** your entire drawing. The first point of the mirror line should be **140,20**. Use the **90°** polar path to snap the second point of the mirror line. Do not erase the original drawing.

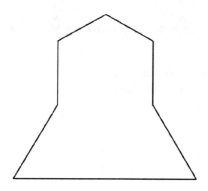 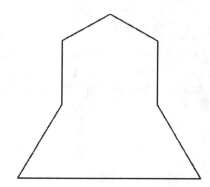

10) *Status Bar:* Turn your *Object Snap Tracking* on.

11) Set your **POLARMODE** variable to **2**. (This allows you to track using polar paths.)

12) Draw an octagon that is aligned on a 15 degree path from *Point 1* and a 90 degree path from *Point 2*.

a) <u>Command:</u> **polygon** or *Draw* panel:

b) `Enter number of sides <4>:` **8**

c) `Specify center of polygon or [Edge]:` Acquire Point 1 by moving your cursor over it. A small cross will appear when the point is acquired. Move the cursor out along the 15 degree polar path. Acquire point 2. Move the cursor along the 90 degree polar path until the 15 degree path appears. Select the point where the paths intersect.

d) `Enter an option [Inscribed in circle/Circumscribed about circle] <I>:` **i**

e) `Specify radius of circle:` **15**

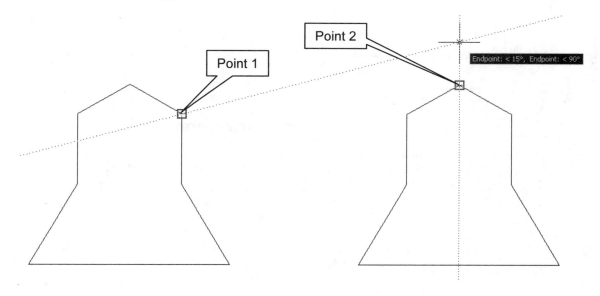

13) Draw a hexagon in the middle of the two main objects using a temporary tracking point.

    a) <u>Command:</u> **polygon**   or   *Draw* toolbar:

    b) `Enter number of sides <8>:` **6**

    c) `Specify center of polygon or [Edge]:` Select the ***Temporary Track Point*** icon in the *Object Snap* panel

    d) `Specify temporary OTRACK point:` Acquire the intersection of the two extensions shown and then select the point where the extensions cross.

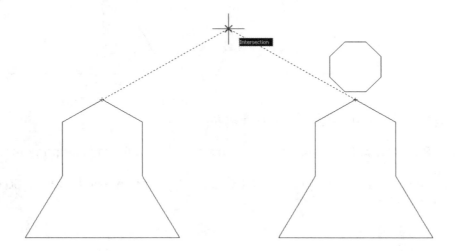

    e) `Specify center of polygon or [Edge]:` Use the 90 degree path off of the temporary track point and the 0 degree path off of *Point 1* to establish the center of the polygon.

    f) `Enter an option [Inscribed in circle/Circumscribed about circle] <I>:` **i**

    g) `Specify radius of circle:` **30**

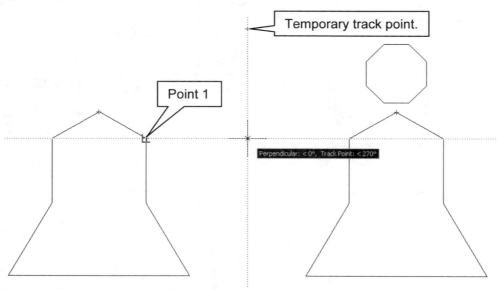

Temporary track point.

Point 1

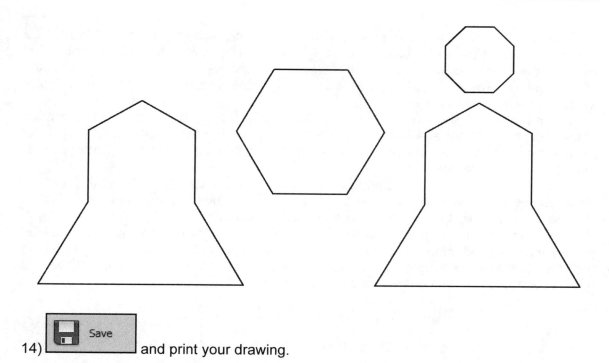

14) 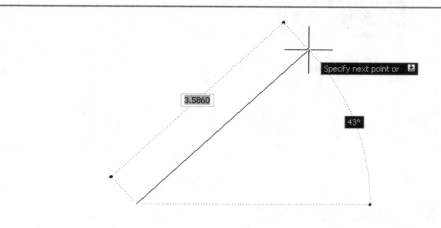 and print your drawing.

1.24) DYNAMIC INPUT

Dynamic input provides a command interface near the cursor to help you keep your focus in the drawing area. When the dynamic input is on, a tooltip displays information near the cursor that is dynamically updated as the cursor moves. You can enter a response in the tooltip area instead of in the *Command* window. If you press the **Down Arrow** key, you can view and select options. Pressing the **Up Arrow** key displays recent input. Figure 1-49 shows the use of dynamic inputs in the creation of a line.

Figure 1-49: An example of dynamic inputs

The dynamic input may be turned on and off by clicking on the *Dynamic Input* icon in the *Status Bar* or by using the F12 key. To set the dynamic input controls, right click on the *Dynamic Input* icon in the *Status Bar* and select *Settings...* or from the *Menu browser*, *Tools – Drafting Settings... - Dynamic Input* tab. Figure 1-50 shows the *Dynamic Input* settings window.

When the *pointer input* (see Figure 1-50) is on and a command is active, the location of the crosshairs is displayed as coordinates in a tooltip near the cursor. Use the *pointer input* settings to change the default format for coordinates and to control when *pointer input* tooltips are displayed.

When the *dimensional input* (see Figure 1-50) is on, the tooltip displays distance and angle values when prompted for a second point. The values in the dimensional tooltips change as you move the cursor. You can press Tab to move to the value you want to change. When you use grip boxes to edit an object, the dimensional input tooltips can display the following information: original length, a length that updates as you move the grip, the change in the length and angle, and the radius of an arc. Which one of these is displayed may be set in the *dimension input* settings.

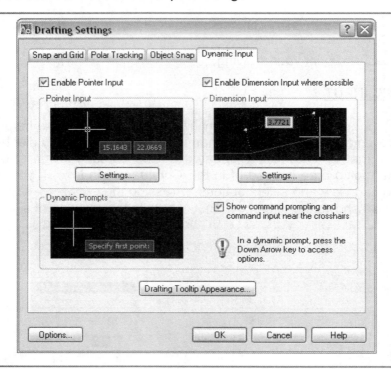

Figure 1-50: Dynamic input settings

1.25) DYNAMIC INPUT TUTORIAL

The objective of this tutorial is to familiarize the user with using dynamic inputs and the different settings that are available. The dynamic input allows you to enter commands and select options in an area near the cursor and the object being drawn.

1.25.1) Dynamic input settings

1) Read section 1.24).

2) [Open icon] *set-inch.dwt*.

3) [Save As icon] **Dynamic input Tut.dwg**

4) *Status Bar:* Turn your **Dynamic Input** [icon] on and your **Polar Tracking** [icon] and **Object Snap Tacking** [icon] off.

5) Activate a **1** x 1 **GRID**.

6) Change the dynamics input settings.
   a) *Status Bar:* Right click on the **Dynamic Input** icon and select **Settings...**
   b) *Drafting Settings* window – *Dynamic Input* tab: Select the **Settings...** button under *Pointer Input*.
   c) *Pointer Input Settings* window: Activate **Polar format**, **Absolute coordinates** and **When a command asks for a point** radio buttons.
   d) Select **OK** in both windows.

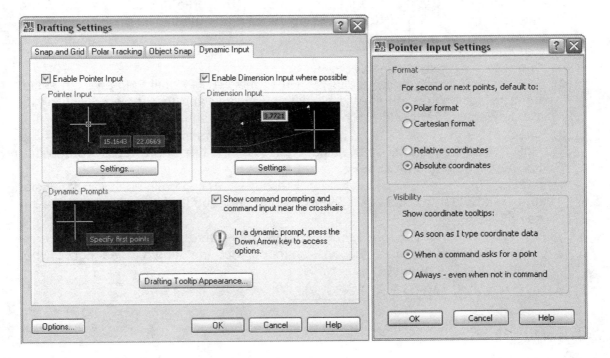

7) Draw a **LINE** from (2,2) to (3,3) with the dynamic input on.

    a) <u>Command:</u> **l** or

    b) Specify first point: Move your cursor around the drawing area. Notice the coordinates near the cursor. When finished, enter the first point without taking your cursor down to the *Command* window **2,2**.

    c) Specify next point or [Undo]: Move your cursor around the screen and see the length of the line and angle change. When finished enter the second point **3,3** without taking your cursor down to the *Command* window and then **Enter** to exit the command.

    d) Note the coordinate of the second point relative to the WCS.

8) *Pointer Input Settings* <u>window:</u> Change *Absolute coordinates* to **Relative coordinates**.

9) Draw a **LINE** from **4,4** to **5,5** as in step 7). (Notice that the second point is relative to the first point and not to the WCS.)

10) **ERASE** the two lines that you have drawn and **ZOOM ALL**.

11) *Pointer Input Settings* <u>window:</u> Change *Relative coordinates* to **Absolute coordinates**.

1.25.2) Locking a coordinate

1) Draw a **LINE** from **2,2** that is **3** inches long at a **45** degree angle. From the end of the previous line, draw a **LINE** that is **2** inches long at a **30** degree angle.

    a) <u>Command:</u> **l** or

    b) Specify first point: **2,2**

    c) Specify next point or [Undo]: Press the **Tab** key until the angle dimension turns red or just the number is highlighted in grey and then type **45** and hit the **Tab** key again. Notice the lock that appears on the angle dimension.

    d) Specify next point or [Undo]: Move your cursor around the drawing area. Notice that the length of the line changes, but the angle does not. When finished, type **3** and hit **Enter**.

    e) Specify next point or [Undo]: Press the **Tab** key until the linear dimension turns red or just the number is highlighted in grey and then type **2** and hit the **Tab** key again.

    f) Specify next point or [Undo]: Move your cursor around the drawing area. Notice that the angle of the line changes, but the length does not. When finished, type **30** and hit **Enter** twice.

2)

1.26) <u>GRIP BOXES</u>

Object grips or grip boxes are usually blue boxes that appear on a selected object if no command is active. Once the grip boxes appear, you can use them to MOVE, COPY, SCALE, ROTATE, MIRROR and STRETCH the object. To understand how grip boxes work, let's look at a simple line (Figure 1-51). If you click on the line, grip boxes will appear at the ends and the middle. If you click on the middle grip box, you can move the entire line. If you click on one of the end grips, you can stretch the line. For more advanced options, click on a grip and then right click to access a shortcut menu.

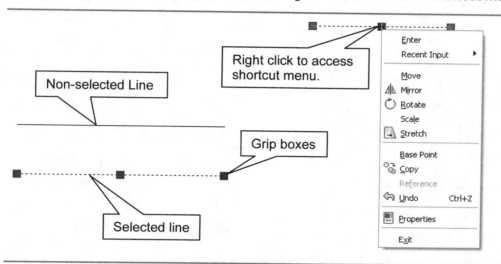

Figure 1-51: Grip boxes

The grip box mode may be turn off by setting the **GRIPS** variable to 0 and turned on by setting it to 1. The size of the grip boxes are controlled by the **GRIPSIZE** variable. Grip box settings are also available in the *Selections* tab of the *Options* window (Figure 1-52).

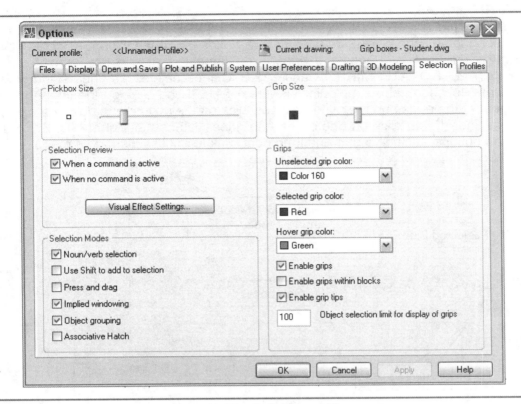

Figure 1-52: Grip box settings

1.27) GRIP BOX TUTORIAL

The objective of this tutorial is to use object grips or grip boxes and the *Properties* window to edit a drawing. Grip boxes allow you to quickly modify an object without having to enter a command.

1.27.1) Preparing to draw

1) Read section 1.26).

2) ▢ Open the preexisting file **grip_boxes_student_2010.dwg**.

3) ▢ Save As **Grip boxes Tut.dwg**

4) *Status Bar.* Turn your **Object Snap** ▢, **Object Snap Tracking** ▢ and **Polar Tracking** ▢ on and your **Dynamic Input** ▢ off.

5) Deactivate all but the following automatically detected object snaps: **Endpoint**, **Center**, and **Perpendicular**.

1.27.2) <u>**Fixing the drawing:**</u> We need to fix the areas indicated in the figure.

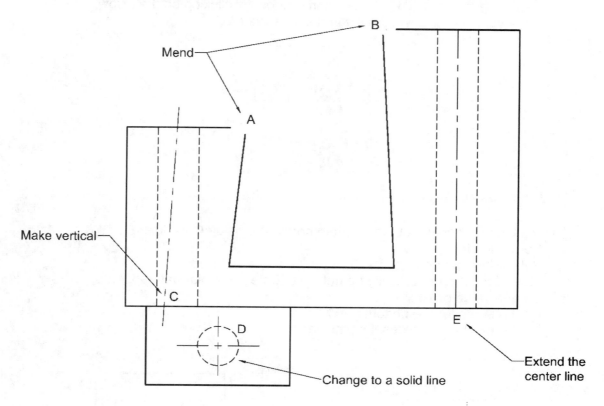

1) Repair corner A.
   a) Select the vertical line at corner A.
   b) Click on the top grip box.
   c) Move your cursor and see the end of the line move.
   d) Move your cursor over to right end of the horizontal line at corner A. Once the END snap marker appears, click your left mouse button.
   e) Hit the **Esc** to deselect the line.

2) Using the same procedure to repair corner B.

3) Make line C vertical.
   a) Select line C (the centerline).
   b) Click on the bottom grip box.
   c) Acquire the top end of the centerline by moving your cursor over it.
   d) Move your cursor vertically downward until the 0 degree tracking path appears and then click your left mouse button.
   f) Hit the **Esc** to deselect the line.

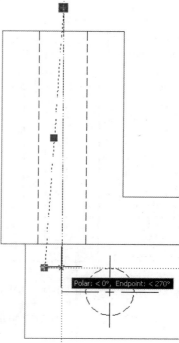

4) Change circle D to a solid line.
   a) Select circle D.
   b) Locate the *Layers* panel.
   c) Select the layers pull down selection window by clicking on the arrow.
   d) Move your cursor down the list and select **Visible**.

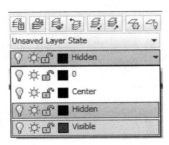

   g) Hit the **Esc** to deselect the circle.

5) Extend Line E past the top and bottom horizontal visible/solid lines.
   a) Select line E.
   b) Select the top grip box.
   c) Move your cursor vertically up until the 90 degree polar path appears.
   d) Enter a value of **10**.
   e) Do the same for the bottom grip box.
   f) Hit the **Esc** button to deselect the line.

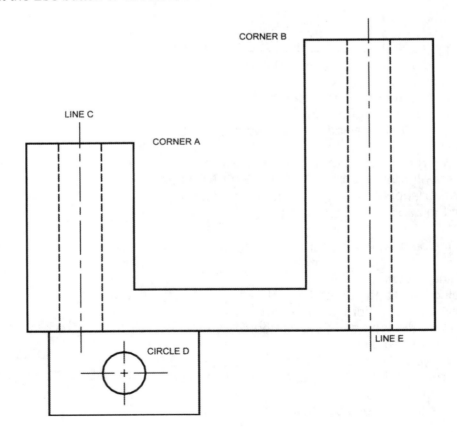

1.27.3) Modifying the drawings shape

The following figure lists the modifications that we will perform.

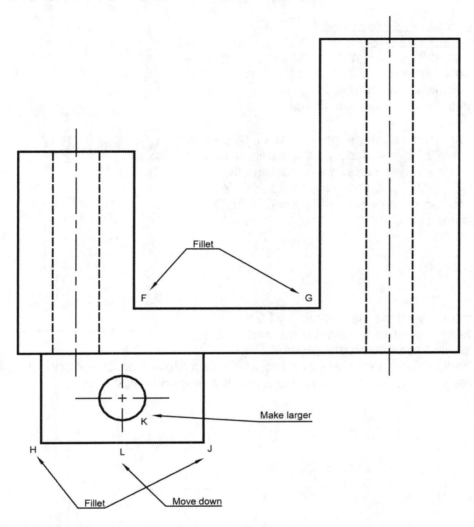

1) Apply an R5 (radius = 5) **FILLET** to corners F and G.

   a) <u>Command:</u> **fillet**   or   *Modify* panel:
   b) Select first object or [Undo/Polyline/Radius/Trim/Multiple]: **r**
   c) Specify fillet radius <10.0000>: **5**
   d) Select first object or [Undo/Polyline/Radius/Trim/ Multiple]: Select one of the two lines that make up corner F.
   e) Select second object or shift-select to apply corner: Select the other line that makes up corner F.
   f) <u>Command:</u> Hit the **Space** bar to repeat the last command and apply the same fillet to corner G.

2) Apply a **R10 FILLET** to corners H and J. This time use the **MULTIPLE** option.

3) Change the size of Circle K.
   a) Select Circle K.

   b) *View* tab – *Palettes* panel:
   c) *Properties window:* Change the circle's *Diameter* to **30** and click on the graphics screen to watch the changes occur. Close the window when you are done.
   d) Hit the **Esc** to deselect the circle.

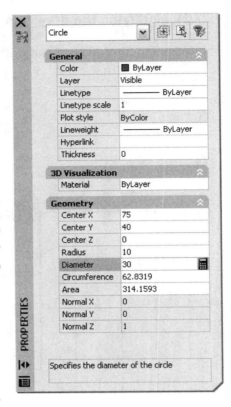

4) On your own, change the length of the vertical centerline of circle K so that it extends past the circle border but does not stop directly at any other line. Use polar tracking to do this. You may need to temporarily turn off your *Object Snap* to accomplish this.

5) Move line L and the fillets down by 20 mm.
   a) Using a window to select line L and both fillets.
   b) Left click on the middle grip box.
   c) Right click on the middle grip box and select ***Move*** from the shortcut menu.
   d) Use polar tracking to move line L and the fillets down **20** mm.

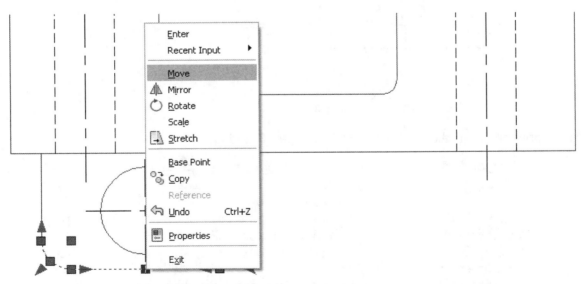

6) Use grip boxes to connect the ends of the vertical lines to the fillets.

7)  and print your drawing.

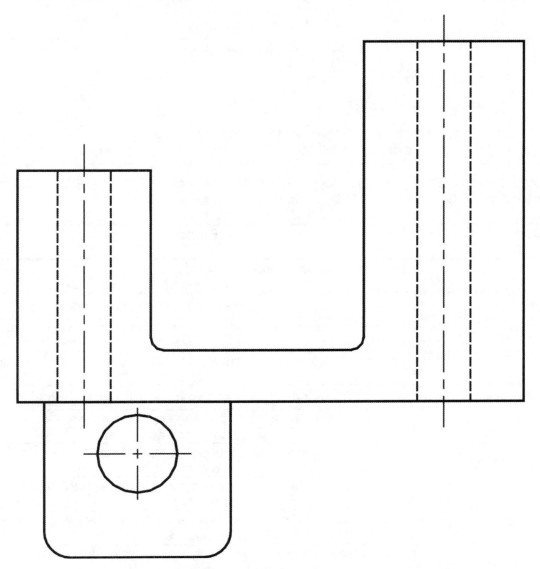

1.28) PARAMETRIC DRAWING

The commands located in the *Parametric* panel allow you to apply geometric and dimensional constraints to 2D drawings (shown in Figure 1-53). The power of parametric drawing becomes apparent during the design phase of a part. Parametric drawing allows you to apply key functional constraints and play with or adjust the rest of the part design without worrying about losing the constraints that you have already applied.

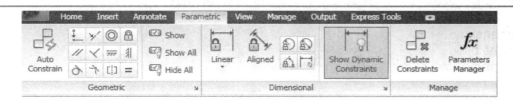

Figure 1-53: Parametric panel

1.28.1) Geometric Constraints

Geometric constraints control the orientation relationship between two elements or of a single element. For example, you are able to force an element to be horizontal, or you can make two lines be perpendicular to each other. Table 1-1 describes the available geometric constraints. This command may be access through the *Parametric* ribbon tab or by using the **GEOMCONTRAINT** command.

Constraint Type	Icon	Purpose
Coincident		Constrains two points to coincide, or a point to lie on an object or an extension of an object.
Colinear		Constrains two lines to lie on the same infinite line.
Concentric		Constrains two circles, arcs or ellipses to have the same center point.
Fix		Constrains a point or a curve to a fixed location and orientation with respect to the WCS.
Parallel		Constrains two lines to maintain the same angle.
Perpendicular		Constrains two lines or polyline segments to maintain a 90 degree angle to each other.
Horizontal		Constrains a line or a pair of points to lie parallel to the x-axis of the current UCS.
Vertical		Constrains a line or a pair of points to lie parallel to the y-axis of the current UCS.
Tangent		Constrains two curves to maintain a point of tangency to each other or their extensions.
Smooth		Constrains a spline to be contiguous and maintain G2 continuity with another spline, line, arc or polyline.
Symmetric		Constraints two curves or points on objects to maintain symmetry about a selected line.
Equal		Constrains two line or polyline segments to maintain equal lengths, or circles and arcs to maintain equal radii.

Table 1-1: Geometric Constraints

1.28.2) Dimensional Constraints

Dimensional constraints control size and angle. You can apply a dimensional constraint between two elements, two points on one element or to control the overall size or angle of an element. The size of the element will automatically change if the value of the dimension is changed. The dimension contains both a name and a value. This allows you the ability to relate one dimension to another through an equation (see Figure 1-54). Dimensional constraints may be accessed in the *Parametric* ribbon tab or by using the **DIMCONSTRAINT** command.

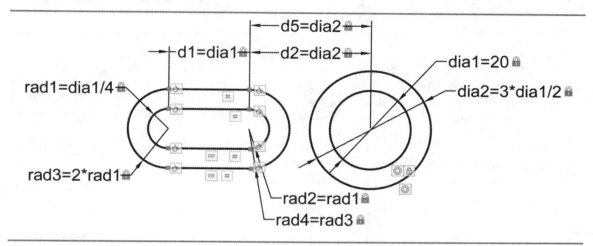

Figure 1-54: Example of parametric constraints.

1.29) APPLYING PARAMETRIC CONSTRAINTS TUTORIAL

The objective of this tutorial is to familiarize you with applying geometric and dimensional constraints to a pre-drawn part.

1.29.1) Applying geometric constraints

1) Read section 1.28).

2) [Open] the preexisting drawing *Parametric – Student – 2010.dwg*.

3) [Save As] **Apply Parametric Tut.dwg**

4) Our goal is to make the drawing on the left look like the drawing on the right without having to redraw it.

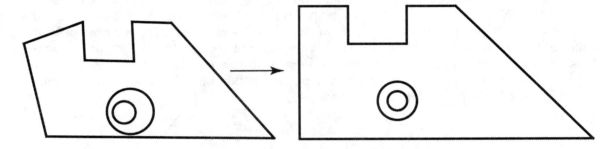

5) We start by applying the geometric constraints. The first thing you might think about doing is to make the bottom line horizontal, the left line vertical, followed by a few more orientation constraints. However, as you can see in the figure that doesn't work out too well. I have found the best constraint to start with is the coincident constraint ⬚. Find everything that needs to be fixed together and apply that first and then apply the orientation constraints.

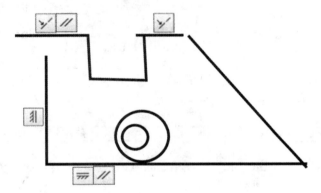

6) Apply a **COINCIDENT** constraint to every corner.

a) *Parametric* ribbon tab – *Geometric* panel: ⬚

b) `Enter constraint type [Horizontal/Vertical/Perpendicular/Parallel/Tangent/Smooth/Coincident/CONcentric/COLinerar/Symmetric/Equal/Fix]` *<last used constraint>*`: _Coincident`
`Select the first point or [Object/Autoconstrain] <Object>:` Hover over the bottom line near the bottom left corner of the part. Once you get this symbol ⊗ at the corner, select the line.
`Select the second point or [Object] <Object>:` Hover over the left line near the bottom left corner of the part. Once you get this symbol ⊗ at the corner, select the line. A blue square should appear at the corner.

c) Apply a coincident constraint to the remaining corners using a similar procedure.

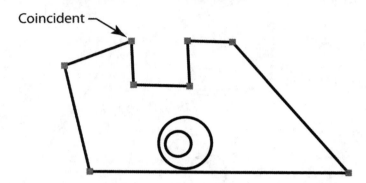

Coincident

7) Make the bottom line **HORIZONTAL** and the left line **VERTICAL**.

a) *Parametric* ribbon tab – *Geometric* panel:

d) `Enter constraint type [Horizontal/Vertical/Perpendicular/Parallel/Tangent/Smooth/Coincident/CONcentric/COLinerar/Symmetric/Equal/Fix] <last used constraint>: _Horizontal`
`Select an Object or [2Points] <2Points>:` Select the bottom line.

e) Apply a vertical constraint to the left line using a similar procedure.

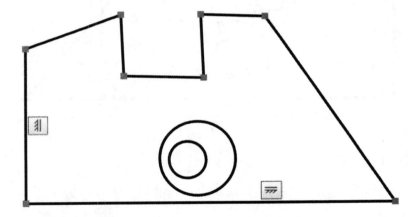

8) On your own apply the following constraints. See the figures below to guide you.

a) **FIX** the bottom horizontal line.

b) Apply a **COLINEAR** constraint to the top two lines.

c) Make the right side top line **PARALLEL** to the bottom line.

d) Make the two short nearly vertical lines **PARALLEL** to the left vertical line.

e) Make the short nearly horizontal line **PERPENDICULAR** to the right side short vertical line.

f) Make the two top lines **EQUAL** in length.

g) Make the two circle **CONCENTRIC** .

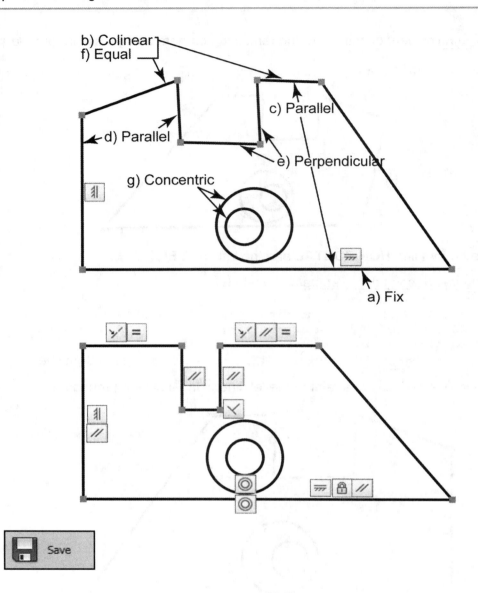

9) Save

1.29.2) Applying Dimensional Constraints

Now that our part is completely constrained geometrically, let's add some size constraints.

1) Add the **LINEAR** dimensions to the part.

a) *Parametric* ribbon tab – *Dimensional* panel:

b) `Current settings: Constraint form = Dynamic`
`Select associative dimension to convert or`
`[Linear/Horizontal/Vertical/Aligned/Angular/Radial/Diameter/Form]`
`<last used>: _Linear`
`Specify first constraint point or [Object] <Object>:` Hover over the left vertical line near the bottom left corner of the part. Once you get this symbol ⬡ at the corner, select the line.

c) `Specify second constraint point:` Hover over the left vertical line near the top left corner of the part. Once you get this symbol ⬡ at the corner, select the line.

d) `Specify dimension line location:` Pull the dimension away from the part and click the left mouse button.

e) `Dimension text = 67` Don't worry about the dimension value right now, just hit **Enter**.

f) Place the rest of the **LINEAR** dimensions shown in the figure below using a similar procedure. To place the linear dimensions between the lines and the center of the circle, select the line first and then the border of the circle.

2) On your own, add the **ANGULAR** 📐 dimension. Read the command prompt for guidance.

3) On your own, add the **DIAMETER** 🛇 dimensions.

Don't worry if your dimensions are named differently than the figure.

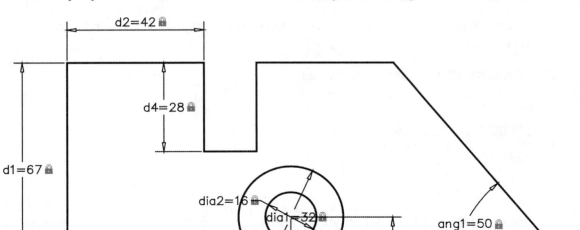

4) Double click on the angular dimension and type **ang1=45** Enter. Notice that to maintain the EQUAL constraint applied to the top two lines, the center cut got smaller.

5) Use the same procedure to set both the dimension NAME and VALUE of all the constraints to be the same as those shown in the figure below. You may need to create some temporary dummy names if you have a duplicate dimension name.

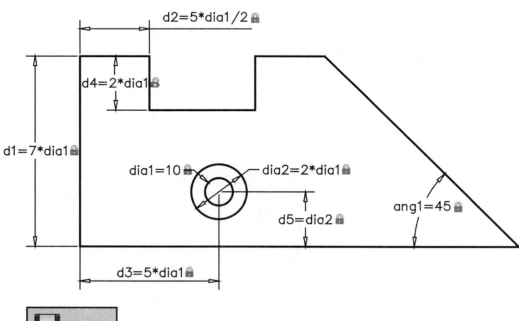

6)

7) As you can see, in the above figure, we have related every dimension to *dia1*. Therefore, if we change the value of *dia1*, the entire part should change size. Change *dia1* to **30**. As you can see, something went terribly wrong. This is a clear sign that we did not completely constrain our part. Can you figure out what dimension we missed? **UNDO** until the part is back to its correct shape and size.

8) Add the LINEAR dimension that controls the total length of the bottom line and set its length to **15*dia1**.

9) Change *dia1* to **30**. This time the result is completely different.

10) 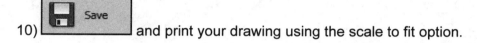 and print your drawing using the scale to fit option.

1.30) <u>AUTOMATIC PARAMETRIC CONSTRAINTS TUTORIAL</u>

The objective of this tutorial is to familiarize the reader with apply parametric constraints to an already correctly drawn part.

1)  *set-mm.dwt* and **Auto Parametric Tut.dwg**

2) Draw the following object using the proper OSNAPS. Do not include the dimensions, but draw it to the correct size.

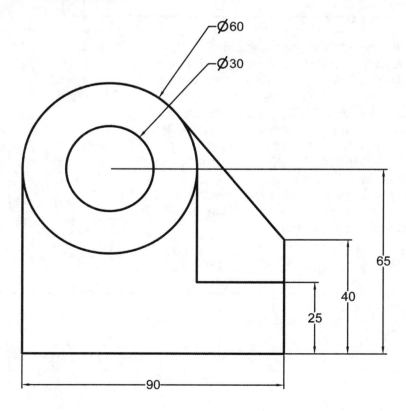

3) Automatically apply the geometric constraints based on your drawing.

a) <u>Command:</u> **autoconstrain**   or   *Parametric* tab – *Geometric* panel:

b) Select objects or [Settings]: **all**

c) Select objects or [Settings]: **Enter**

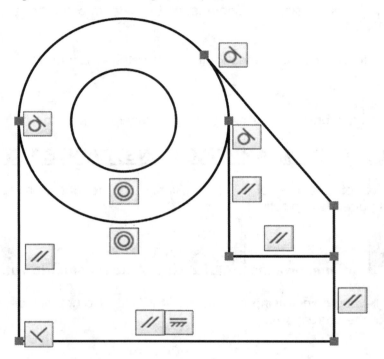

d) Notice the constraints that were made. Your constraints may be slightly different depending on how you drew the object. Most of the constraints are obvious. However the PARALLEL constraints are not so clear. Which elements are parallel to which elements? To find out, hover you mouse over the constraint and connecting constraints will highlight. You will also notice that an X will appear below the constraint. If you click on this X, the constraint will be deleted (don't do this right now).

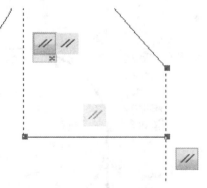

4) Apply the following dimensional constraints. If you name your dimensions the same as shown in the figure, it will make it easier later on. It is hard to see in the figure, but **dia1 = 30** and **dia2 = 60**.

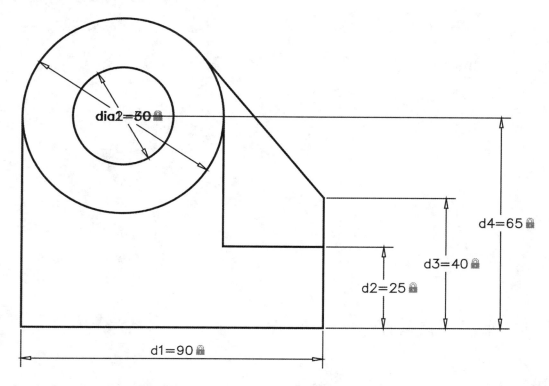

5) Apply functional relationships between the dimensional constraints.

a) <u>Command:</u> **parameters** or *Parametric* tab – *Geometric* panel:

b) *Parameters Manager* window: Input the following functional relationships between the dimensional constraints. The *Parameters Manager* allows you to change the name and value of every dimension. Refer to the above figure to relate the name to the original value.

c) Close the *Parameters Manager* window.

6) Change **d1** to **60** and make sure all the constraints are properly applied.

7) Save and print you drawing using the scale to fit option.

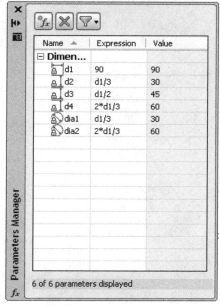

<u>NOTES:</u>

DRAWING IN AUTOCAD CROSSWORD PUZZLES

Name: _____ Date: _____

CP1-1) User interface, drawing area, accessing commands, standard and quick access
toolbars, CUI, user interface and startup tutorial.

Across

1. The workspace that mainly relies on toolbars to access commands.
4. The system variable that determines whether the *Select Template* window or the *Create New Drawing* window appears when starting a new drawing.
6. A place that gives you quick access to commands that are frequently turned on and off.
10. The window and tab that you need to access in order to change the drawing window's color.
12. Command used to select your unit of measure and precision.

Down

2. One way to access AutoCAD's commands.
3. To access a shortcut menu, you need to ....
5. The workspace that mainly relies on the ribbon to access commands.
7. Allows you to quickly repeat your last command.
8. Command used to set your paper size.
9. One way to access AutoCAD's commands.
11. Customize User Interface

Name: _____   Date: _____

CP1-2) Coordinates, UCS panel, WCS/UCS coordinate systems tutorial, Drawing using coordinates tutorial, printing, printing tutorial.

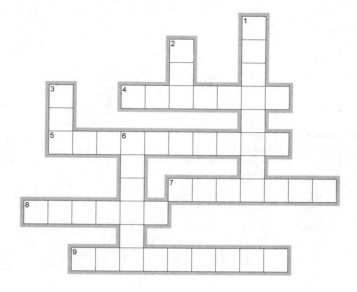

Across

4. The printing option that prints everything that you can currently see.
5. The printing option that will expand/reduce your drawing to fit the paper.
7. The printing option that prints everything that has been drawn.
8. An absolute coordinate is measured relative to the ....
9. Relative coordinates are measured relative to the .... entered.

Down

1. @
2. The coordinate system that is stationary.
3. The coordinate system that can be translated and rotated.
6. The printing option that prints everything within your defined paper size.

NOTES:

Name: _____   Date: _____

CP1-3) Draw commands, Text, Modify commands, Wagon tutorial.

Across
_____

4.   What is the rotation basepoint?

Rotated circle

Original circle

5.   The typed command used to access text settings.
6.   A polygon that is drawn on the outside of a circle.
7.   An arc may be defined by its START, END and ....

Down

1.   What is the scale basepoint?

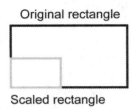

Original rectangle

Scaled rectangle

2.   When moving an object using relative coordinates, the first base point may be ....
3.   A circle may be defined by its CENTER and ....

Name: _____ Date: _____

CP1-4) Selecting objects, Object selection tutorial.

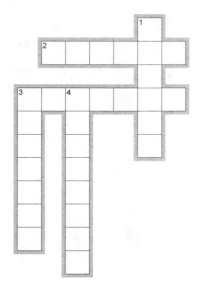

Across

2. You know when an object is selected because it turns ....
3. When AutoCAD is waiting for you to select an object, the crosshairs turn into a ....

Down

1. After selecting several objects to erase, what command would you type if you wanted to remove an object(s) from the selection set?
3. What system variable controls whether an object gets added to a selection set or replaces the object already in the selection set?
4. What type of selection window selects everything touching and inside the defined window?

NOTES:

Name: _____   Date: _____

CP1-5) Object snap commands, Object snap tutorial.

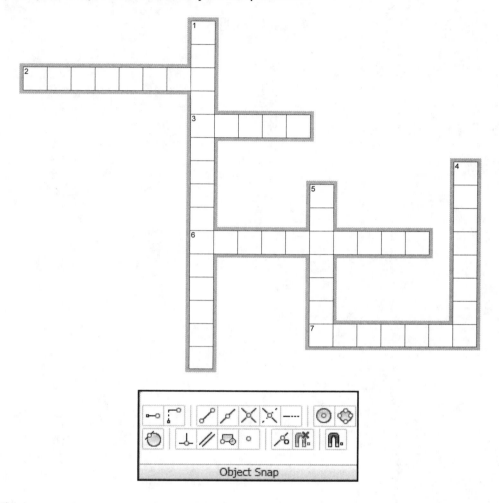

Across

2. *Object Snap* panel: Top row, ninth icon from the left?
3. You may access the object snap settings right clicking on the *Object Snap* icon in the status bar or by typing what command?
6. Object snaps not only speed up the drawing process, you cannot draw .... without them unless you enter coordinates.
7. The object snap that will not show where the first point of a line is located until the second point is selected.

Down

1. The window and tab where you can access the *Autosnap Marker* size.
4. *Object Snap* panel: Top row, third icon from the left?
5. *Object Snap* panel: Second row, sixth icon from the left?

<u>NOTES:</u>

Name: _____ Date: _____

CP1-6) Polar tracking, Object snap tracking, Tracking tutorial, Dynamic input, Dynamic input tutorial, Grip boxes, Grip box tutorial.

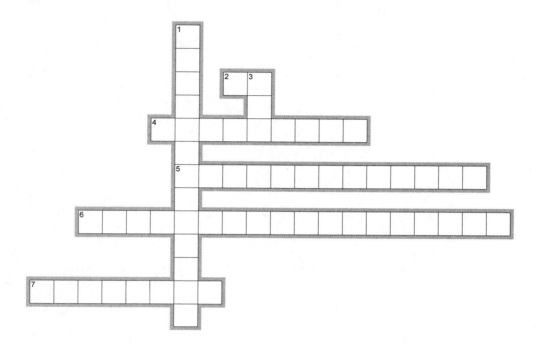

Across

2. What letters do you type to indicate that you want to create a temporary track point.
4. Clicking on an object, while not currently in a command, access the ....
5. The grip box options may be accessed by .... on one of the boxes.
6. This icon, located in the status bar, allows you to create tracking lines off of object snap points.
7. The typed command that allows you to change the polar tracking angle.

Down

1. This enables you to snap along angled track lines.
3. What key do you press to cycle through the dynamic input dimensions?

NOTES:

DRAWING IN AUTOCAD PROBLEMS

Name: _____ Date: _____

P1-1) (May be attempted after completing the *Drawing using Coordinates Tutorial* in section 1.10) Write down the relative Cartesian coordinates needed to create the following object in the direction indicated in the figure. Assume that the start point is created by clicking the mouse; therefore, we do not know its exact coordinate position.

Start point: Click mouse anywhere

Next point: _____

Next point: _____

Next point: _____

Next point: _____

Next point: _____

Next point: _____

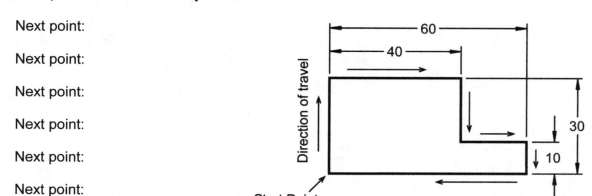

Write down the relative polar coordinates needed to create the following object.

Start point: Click mouse anywhere

Next point: _____

Next point: _____

Next point: _____

Next point: _____

Next point: _____

Next point: _____

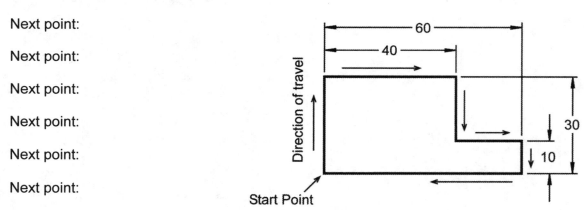

NOTES:

Name: _____   Date: _____

P1-2) (May be attempted after completing the *Printing Tutorial* in section 1.12) Using the ruler provided, determine the scale that should be indicated on the drawing for the following objects.

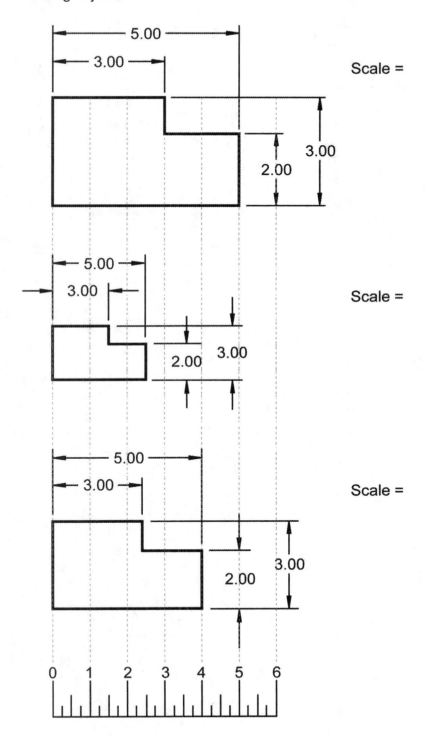

Scale =

Scale =

Scale =

NOTES:

Name: _____ Date: _____

P1-3) (May be attempted after completing the *Drawing using Coordinates Tutorial* and the *Printing Tutorial* in sections 1.10 and 1.12) Fill in the table below with the appropriate relative coordinates needed to draw this object in AutoCAD and then draw the object in AutoCAD. Print using a window and the scale to fit option. Dimensions are in inches.

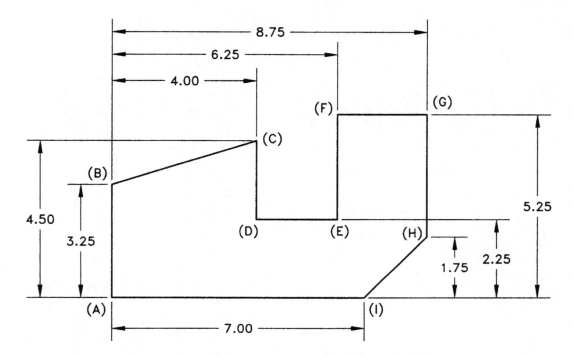

To Point	Relative Coordinate
A to B	@
B to C	@
C to D	@
D to E	@
E to F	@
F to G	@
G to H	@
H to I	@
I to A	@

NOTES:

Name: _____   Date: _____

P1-4) (May be attempted after completing the *Drawing using Coordinates Tutorial* and the *Printing Tutorial* in sections 1.10 and 1.12) Fill in the table below with the appropriate relative coordinates needed to draw this object in AutoCAD and then draw the object in AutoCAD. Print using a window and the scale to fit option. Dimensions are in millimeters.

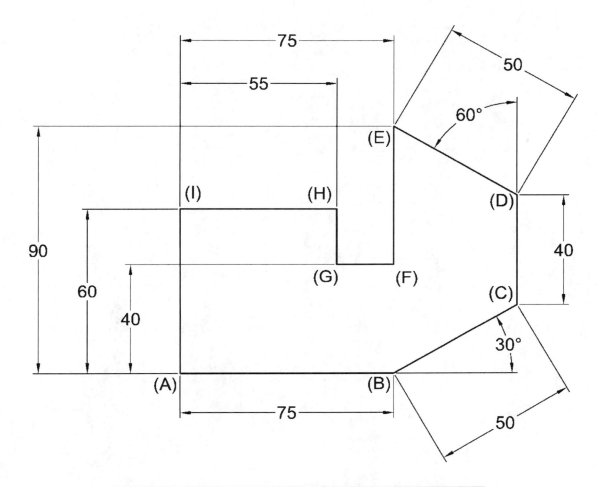

To Point	Relative Coordinate
A to B	@
B to C	@
C to D	@
D to E	@
E to F	@
F to G	@
G to H	@
H to I	@
I to A	@

NOTES:

Name: _____   Date: _____

P1-5) (May be attempted after completing the *Drawing using Coordinates Tutorial* and the *Printing Tutorial* in sections 1.10 and 1.12) Draw the following object using relative Cartesian and/or relative polar coordinates. Draw the object starting at the point indicated and in the direction indicated. To connect the start point and end point, type CLOSE while still in the LINE command. Write down the relative coordinates used to create the object in the table. Print using a window and the scale to fit option. Dimensions are in millimeters.

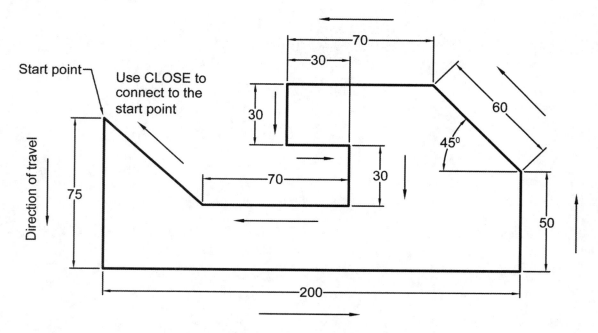

To Point	Relative Coordinate
Start point to next point	@
to Next point	@
to Next point	@
to Next point	@
to Next point	@
to Next point	@
to Next point	@
to Next point	@
to Next point	@
to Next point	CLOSE

NOTES:

P1-6) (May be attempted after completing the *WCS/UCS Coordinate Systems, Drawing using Coordinates* and the *Printing Tutorials* in sections 1.9, 1.10 and 1.12) Draw the following object in AutoCAD. HINT: To draw the circle and square, try changing your UCS to one of the corners of the main body. Print using a window and the scale to fit option. Dimensions are in inches.

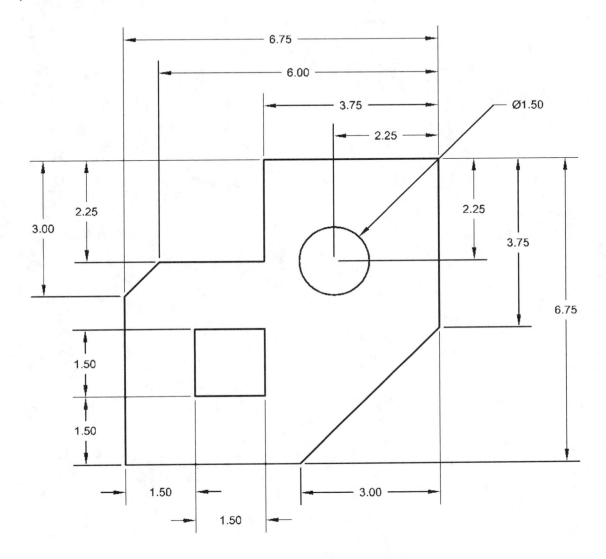

P1-7) (May be attempted after completing the *WCS/UCS Coordinate Systems, Drawing using Coordinates* and the *Printing Tutorials* in sections 1.9, 1.10 and 1.12) Draw the following object in AutoCAD. HINT: To draw the circles, try changing your UCS to the corners of the main body. Print using a window and the scale to fit option. Dimensions are in millimeters.

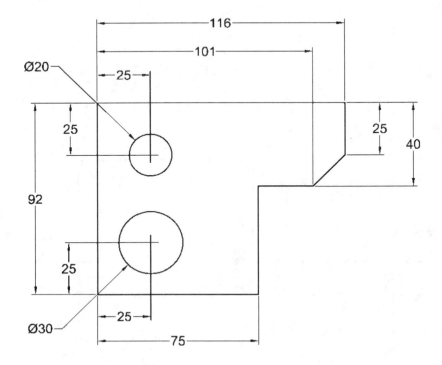

P1-8) (May be attempted after completing the *Object Snap Tutorial* in section 1.20) Draw the following object using object snap commands where necessary. Put your name on the drawing and then print it using a *Window* and the *Scale to Fit* option. Dimensions are in millimeters.

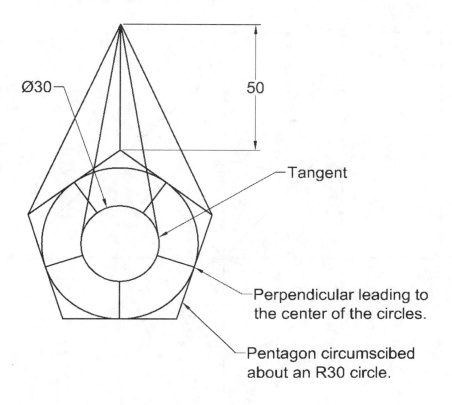

Ø30

50

Tangent

Perpendicular leading to the center of the circles.

Pentagon circumscibed about an R30 circle.

P1-9) (May be attempted after completing the *Object Snap Tutorial* in section 1.20) Draw the following object in AutoCAD using object snap commands where necessary. Put your name on the drawing and then print it using a *Window* and the *Scale to Fit* option. Dimensions are in inches.

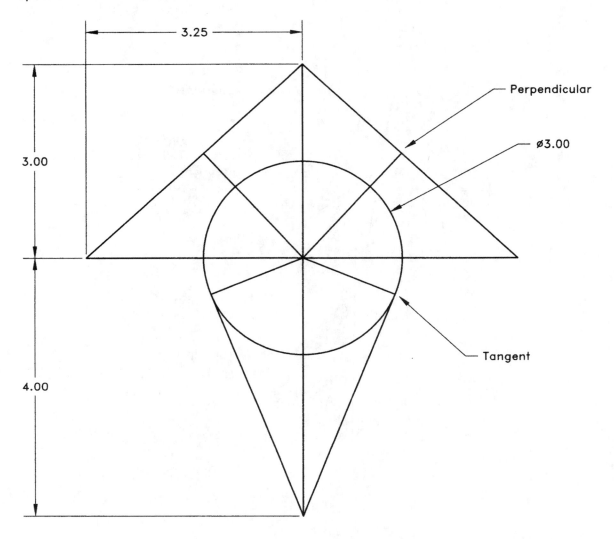

P1-10) (May be attempted after completing the *Object Snap Tutorial* in section 1.20) Draw the following object in AutoCAD using object snap commands where necessary. Put your name on the drawing and then print it using a *Window* and the *Scale to Fit* option. Dimensions are in inches. Hint: To create the arc, choose the start point, then the end point, and then the radius. Remember that arcs are drawn according to the right hand rule.

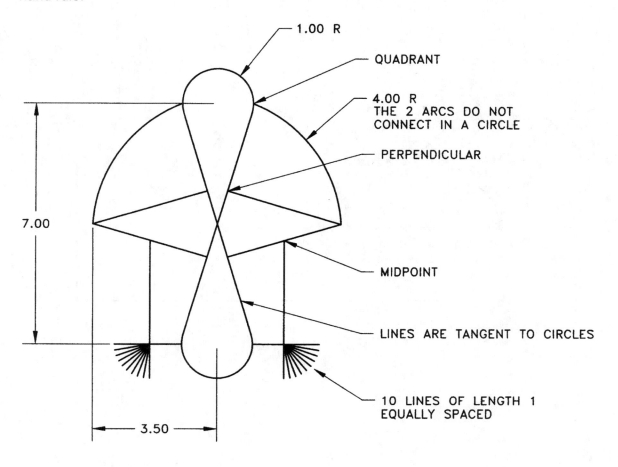

P1-11) (May be attempted after completing the *Tracking Tutorial* in section 1.23) Draw the following object with the help of track points. Put your name on the drawing and then print using a 1 to 1 scale. Dimensions are in millimeters.

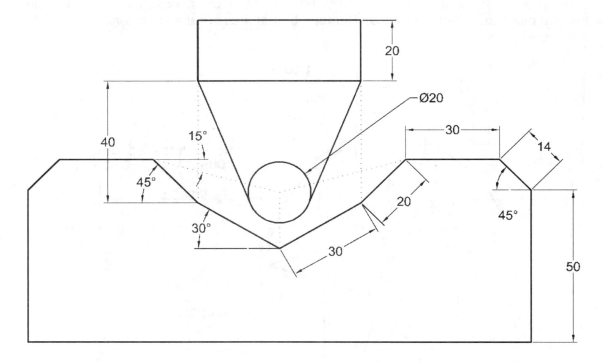

P1-11) (May be attempted after completing the *Object Snap Tutorial* in section 1.20) Draw the following object in AutoCAD. Put your name on the drawing and then print it using a *Window* and the *Scale to Fit* option. Dimensions are in millimeters.

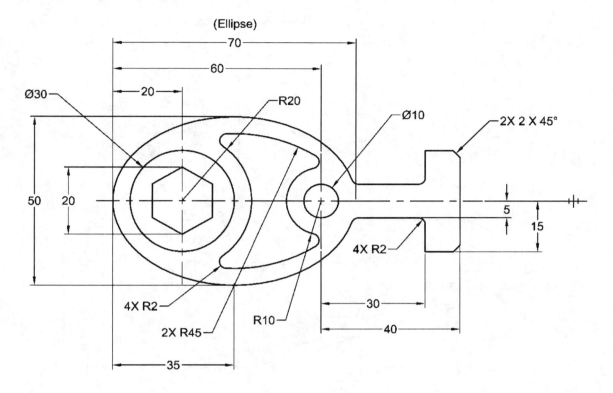

P1-12) (May be attempted after completing the *Object Snap Tutorial* in section 1.20) Draw the following object in AutoCAD. Put your name on the drawing and then print it using a *Window* and the *Scale to Fit* option. Dimensions are in millimeters.

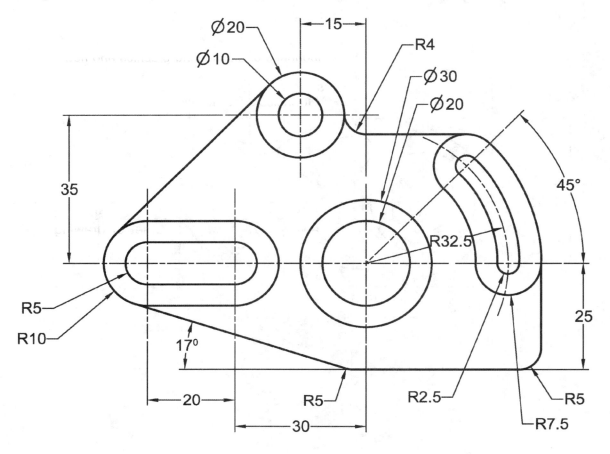

ORTHOGRAPHIC PROJECTION

In Chapter 2 you will learn the importance of engineering graphics and how to create an orthographic projection. An orthographic projection describes the shape of an object. It is a two dimensional representation of a three dimensional object. Different line types are used to indicate visible, hidden and symmetry lines. By the end of this chapter, you will be able to create a technically correct orthographic projection using proper projection techniques.

2.1) INTRODUCTION TO ENGINEERING GRAPHICS

Engineering graphics is a set of rules and guidelines that help you create an engineering drawing. An engineering drawing is a drawing or a set of drawings that communicates an idea, design, schematic, or model. Engineering drawings come in many forms. Each engineering field has its own type of engineering drawings. For example, electrical engineers draw circuit schematics and circuit board layouts. Civil engineers draw plans for bridges and road layouts. Mechanical engineers draw parts and assemblies that need to be manufactured. This book focuses on the latter. This is not to say that only students in a mechanical engineering curriculum will benefit from learning engineering graphics. It benefits everyone from the weekend carpenter who wants to draw plans for his/her new bookshelf to the electrical engineer who wants to analyze electrical component cooling using a CAE program. Engineering graphics teaches you how to visualize and see all sides of an object in your mind. Being able to visualize in your mind will help you in several aspects of critical thinking.

2.2) ORTHOGRAPHIC PROJECTION INTRODUCTION

An *orthographic projection* **enables us to represent a 3-D object in 2-D** (see Figure 2-1). An orthographic projection is a system of drawings that represent different sides of an object. These drawings are formed by projecting the edges of the object perpendicular to the desired planes of projection. Orthographic projections allow us to represent the shape of an object using 2 or more views. These views together with dimensions and notes are sufficient to manufacture the part.

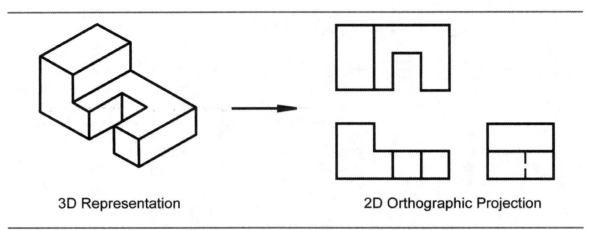

3D Representation   2D Orthographic Projection

Figure 2-1: Orthographic projection.

2.2.1) The Six Principle Views

The 6 principle views of an orthographic projection are shown in Figure 2-2. Each principle view is created by looking at the object in the directions indicated in Figure 2-2 and drawing what is seen as well as what is hidden from view.

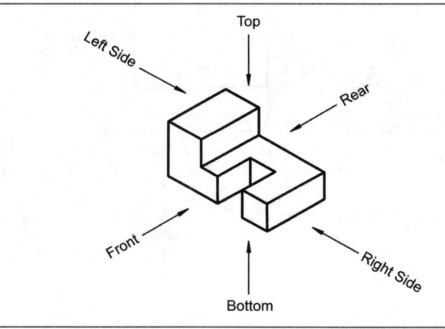

Figure 2-2: The six principle views.

2.3) **THE GLASS BOX METHOD**

To obtain an orthographic projection, an object is placed in an imaginary glass box as shown in Figure 2-3. The sides of the glass box represent the six principle planes. Images of the object are projected onto the sides of the box to create the six principle views. The box is then unfolded to lie flat, showing all views in a 2-D plane. Figure 2-4 shows the glass box being unfolded to create the orthographic projection of the object.

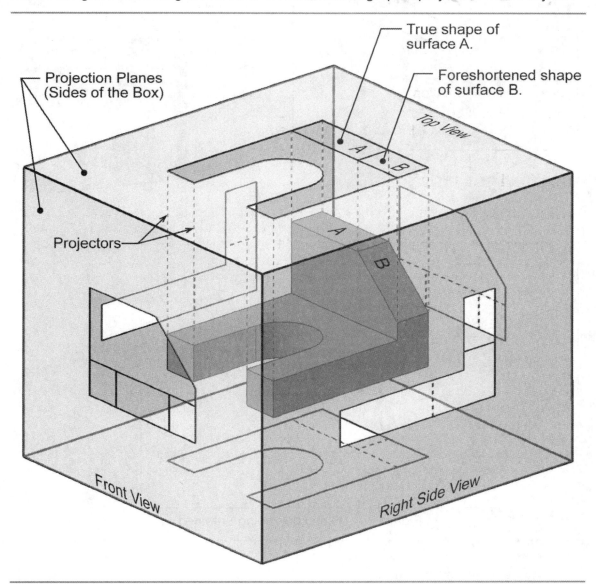

Figure 2-3: Object in a glass box.

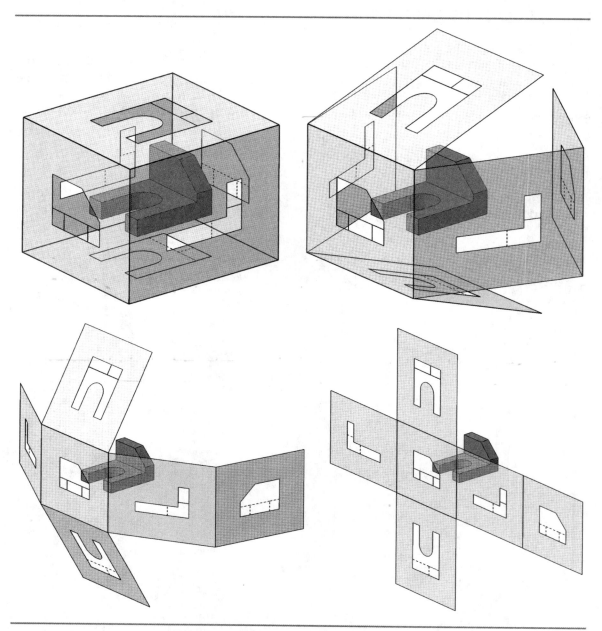

Figure 2-4: Glass box being unfolded.

Instructor Led Exercise 2-1: Principle views

Label the five remaining principle views with the appropriate view name.

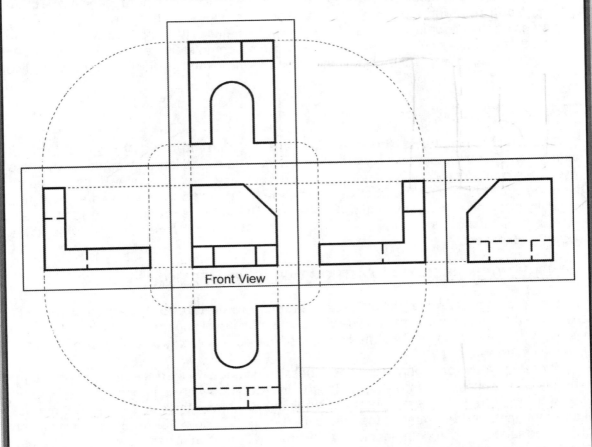

Front View

What are the differences between the *Right Side* and *Left Side* views?

What are the differences between the *Top* and *Bottom*, and *Front* and *Rear* views?

Which view(s) have the least number of hidden or dashed lines?

2.4) THE STANDARD VIEWS

When constructing an orthographic projection, we need to include enough views to completely describe the true shape of the part. The more complex a part, the more views are needed to describe it completely. Most objects require three views to completely describe them. **The standard views used in an orthographic projection are the *front, top,* and *right side* views.** The other views (bottom, rear, left side) are omitted since they usually do not add any new information. It is not always necessary to use the three standard views. Some objects can be completely described in one or two views. For example, a sphere only requires one view, and a block only requires two views.

2.4.1) The Front View

The *front view* **shows the most features or characteristics of the object.** It usually contains the least number of hidden lines. The exception to this rule is when the object has a predefined or generally accepted front view. All other views are based on the orientation chosen for the front view. The top, front, and bottom views are all aligned vertically and share the same width dimension. The left side, front, right side, and rear views are all aligned horizontally and share the same height dimension (see the figure shown in Exercise 2-1).

2.5) LINE TYPES USED IN AN ORTHOGRAPHIC PROJECTION

Line type and *line weight* **provide valuable information to the print reader.** For example, the type and weight of a line can answer the following questions: Is the feature visible or hidden from view? Is the line part of the object or part of a dimension? Is the line indicating symmetry?

There are four commonly used line types: continuous, hidden, center and phantom. The standard recommends using, no less than, two line widths. Important lines should be twice as thick as the less important thin lines. Common thicknesses are 0.6 mm for important lines and 0.3 mm for the less important lines. However, to further distinguish line importance, it is recommended to use four different thicknesses or weights: thin, medium, thick, and very thick. The actual line thickness should be chosen such that there is a visible difference between the line weights; however, they should not be too thick or thin making it difficult to read the print. The thickness of the lines should be adjusted according to the size and complexity of the part. The following is a list of common line types and widths used in an orthographic projection.

1. Visible lines: Visible lines represent visible edges and boundaries. The line type is **continuous** and the line weight is **thick** (0.5 - 0.6 mm).

2. Hidden lines: Hidden lines represent edges and boundaries that cannot be seen. The line type is **dashed** and the line weight is **medium thick** (0.35 - 0.45 mm).

3. Center lines: Center lines represent axes of symmetry and are important for interpreting cylindrical shapes. Crossed center lines should be drawn at the centers of circles. They are also used to indicate circle of centers and paths of motion. The line type is **long dash – short dash** and the line weight is **thin** (0.3 mm).

4. Phantom lines: Phantom lines are used to indicate imaginary features. For example, they are used to indicate the alternate positions of moving parts, and adjacent positions of related parts. The line type is **long dash – short dash – short dash** and the line weight is usually **thin** (0.3 mm).

5. Dimension and Extension lines: Dimension and extension lines are used to show the size of an object. In general, a dimension line is placed between two extension lines and is terminated by arrowheads, which indicates the direction and extent of the dimension. The line type is **continuous** and the line weight is **thin** (0.3 mm).

6. Cutting plane lines: Cutting plane lines are used to show where an imaginary cut has been made through the object in order to view interior features. The line type is **phantom** and the line weight is **very thick** (0.6 to 0.8 mm). Arrows are placed at both ends of the cutting plane line to indicate the direction of sight.

7. Section lines: Section lines are used to show areas that have been cut by the cutting plane. Section lines are grouped in parallel line patterns and usually drawn at a 45° angle. The line type is usually **continuous** and the line weight is **thin** (0.3 mm).

8. Break lines: Break lines are used to show imaginary breaks in objects. A break line is usually made up of a series of connecting arcs. The line type is **continuous** and the line weight is usually **thick** (0.5 – 0.6 mm).

Instructor Led Exercise 2-2: Line types

Using the line type definitions, match each line type name with the appropriate line type.

- Visible Line

- Hidden Line

- Center Line

- Phantom Line

- Dimension and Extension Lines

- Cutting Plane Line

- Section Lines

- Break Line

Instructor Led Exercise 2-3: Line use in an orthographic projection

Fill the following dotted orthographic projection with the appropriate line types.

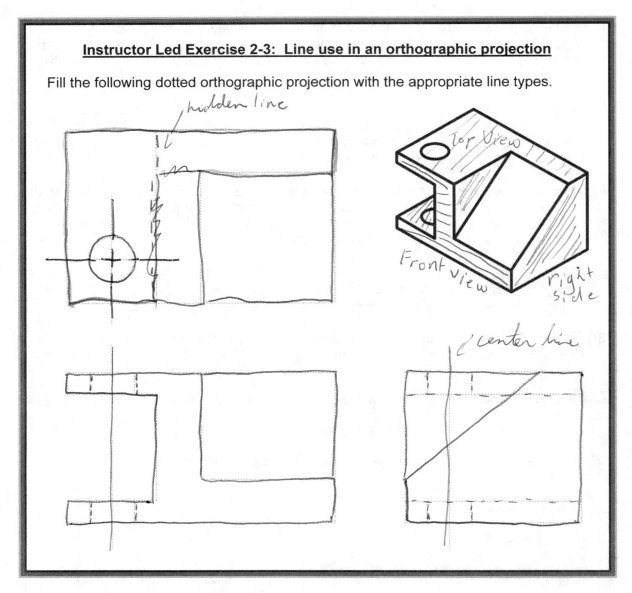

2.6) RULES FOR LINE CREATION AND USE

The rules and guide lines for line creation should be followed in order to create lines that are effective in communicating the drawing information. However, due to computer automation, some of the rules may be hard to follow.

2.6.1) Hidden Lines

Hidden lines represent edges and boundaries that cannot be seen.

Rule 1.   The length of the hidden line dashes may vary slightly as the size of the drawing changes. For example, a very small part may require smaller dashes in order for the hidden line to be recognized.

Rule 2.   Hidden lines should always begin and end with a dash, except when the hidden line begins or ends at a parallel visible line (see Figure 2-5).

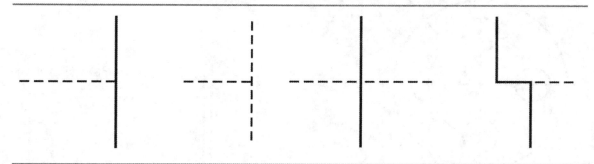

Figure 2-5: Drawing hidden lines.

Rule 3.   Dashes should join at corners (see Figure 2-6).

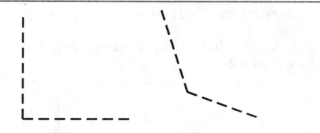

Figure 2-6: Hidden lines at corner.

2.6.2) Center Lines

Center lines represent axes of symmetry and are important for interpreting cylindrical shapes (Figure 2-7). They are also used to indicate circle of centers and paths of motion as shown in Figure 2-8.

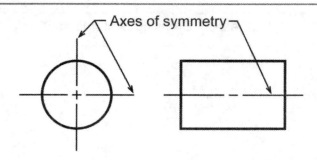

Figure 2-7: Axes of symmetry

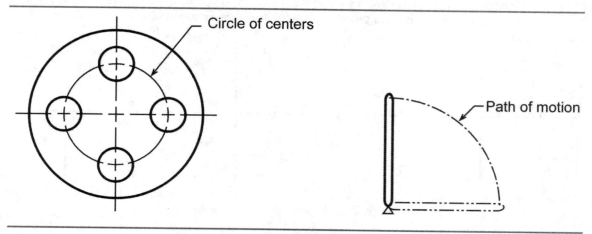

Figure 2-8: Center line uses

Rule 1.   Center lines should start and end with long dashes (see Figure 2-8).

Rule 2.   Center lines should intersect by crossing either the long dashes or the short dashes (see Figure 2-9).

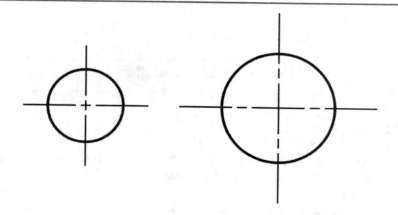

Figure 2-9: Crossing center lines.

Rule 3.   Center lines should extend a short distance beyond the object or feature.   They should not terminate at other lines of the drawing (see Figure 2-10).

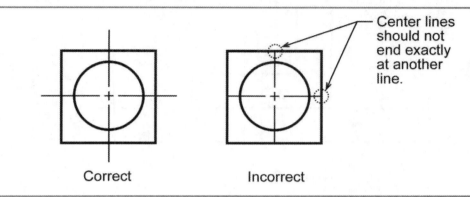

Center lines
should not
end exactly
at another
line.

Correct   Incorrect

Figure 2-10: Terminating center lines.

Rule 4.   Center lines may be connected within a single view to show that two or more features lie in the same plane as shown in Figure 2-11. However, they should not extend through the space between views.

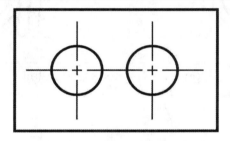

Figure 2-11: Connecting center lines.

2.6.3) Phantom Lines

Phantom lines are used to indicate alternate positions of moving parts (see Figure 2-8). They may also be used to indicate adjacent positions of related parts and repeated detail as shown in Figures 2-12 and 2-13. They are also used to show fillets and rounds in the view that does not show the radius. In this case, the phantom lines are used to show a change in surface direction (see Figure 2-14).

Rule 1. Phantom lines should start and end with a long dash.

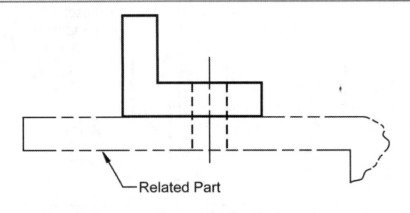

Figure 2-12: Related part.

Figure 2-13: Repeated detail.

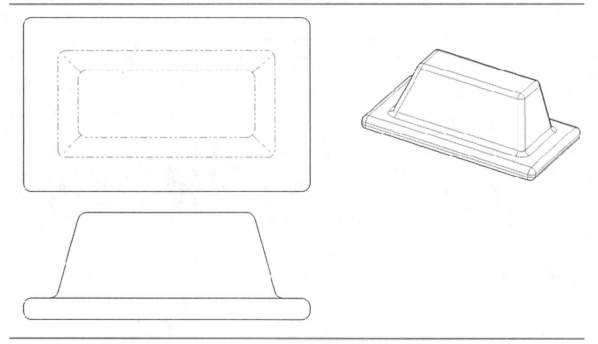

Figure 2-14: Phantom lines used to indicated a change in surface direction

2.6.4) Break Lines

Break lines are used to show imaginary breaks in an object. For example, when drawing a long rod, it may be broken and drawn at a shorter length as shown in Figure 2-15.

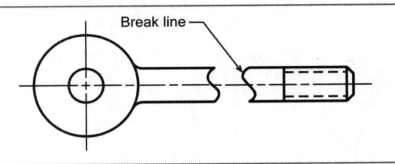

Figure 2-15: Using break lines.

There are two types of break lines. A break line may be a series of connecting arcs, as shown in Figure 2-15, or a straight line with a jog in the middle as shown in Figure 2-16. If the distance to traverse is short the series of connecting arcs is used. This series of arcs is the same width as the visible lines on the drawing. If the distance is long the thin straight line with a jog is used.

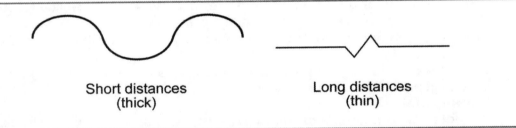

Short distances
(thick)

Long distances
(thin)

Figure 2-16: Types of break lines.

2.6.5) Line Type Precedence

Some lines are considered more important than other lines. **If two lines occur in the same place, the line that is considered to be the least important is omitted.** Lines in order of precedence/importance are as follows:

1. Cutting plane line
2. Visible line
3. Hidden line
4. Center line

2.7) CREATING AN ORTHOGRAPHIC PROJECTION

The steps presented in this section are meant to help you create a technically correct orthographic projection using the 3rd angle projection standard. To understand and visually see how views are created using the 3rd angle projection standard, put your right hand on a table palm up. You are looking at the front view of your hand. Now rotate your hand so that your thumb points up and your little finger is touching the table. This is the right side view of your hand. Put your hand back in the front view position. Now rotate your hand so that your finger tips are pointing up and your wrist is touching the table. This is the top view of your hand.

The following steps will take you through the creation of an orthographic projection. Once you become experienced and proficient at creating orthographic projections, you will develop short cuts and may not need to follow the steps exactly as written. These steps are visually illustrated in Figure 2-17.

1. **Choose a front view.** This is the view that shows the most about the object.
2. **Decide how many views are needed** to completely describe the object. If you are unable to determine which views will be needed, draw the standard views (front, top and right side).
3. **Draw the visible features of the front view.**
4. **Draw projectors off of the front view** horizontally and vertically in order to create the boundaries for the top and right side views.
5. **Draw the top view.** Use the vertical projectors to fill in the visible and hidden features.
6. **Project from the top view back to the front view.** Use the vertical projectors to fill in any missing visible or hidden features in the front view.
7. **Draw a 45° projector** off of the upper right corner of the box that encloses the front view.
8. **From the top view, draw projectors over to the 45° line and down** in order to create the boundaries of the right side view.
9. **Draw the right side view.**
10. **Project back to the top and front view** from the right side view as needed.
11. **Draw center lines where necessary.**

Following the aforementioned steps will insure that the orthographic projection is done correctly. That is, it will insure that:

√ The front and top views are vertically aligned.
√ The front and right side views are horizontally aligned.
√ Every point or feature in one view is aligned on a projector in any adjacent view (front and top, or front and right side).
√ The distance between any two points of the same feature in the related views (top and right side) are equal.

Figure 2-17 identifies the *adjacent* and *related* views. Adjacent views are two adjoining views aligned by projectors. Related views are views that are adjacent to the same view.

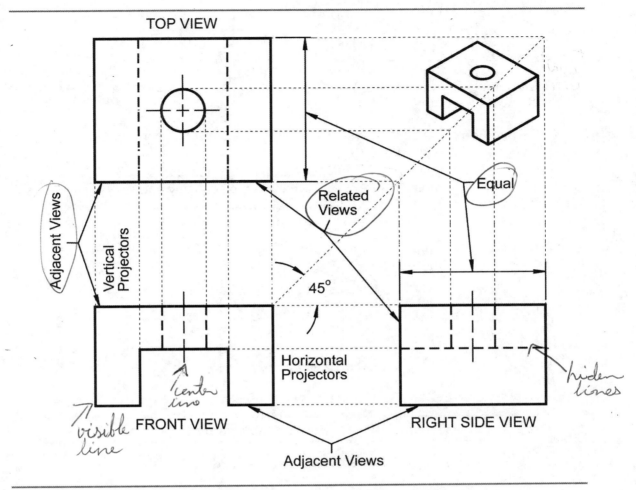

Figure 2-17: Creating an orthographic projection

2.7.1) Projection Symbol

In the United States, we use 3rd angle projection to create an orthographic projection. This is the method of creating orthographic projections that is described in this chapter. In some parts of Europe and elsewhere 1st angle projection is used. To inform the print reader what projection method was used, the projection symbol should be placed in the bottom right hand corner of the drawing. If the drawing uses metric units, the text "SI" is placed in front of the projection symbol. The projection symbols are shown in Figure 2-18. Figure 2-19 shows the projection symbol's proportions.

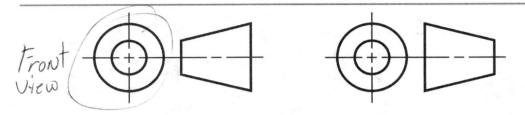

Front
View

Third Angle Projection Symbol
(Our national standard)

First Angle Projection Symbol

Figure 2-18: First and third angle projection symbols.

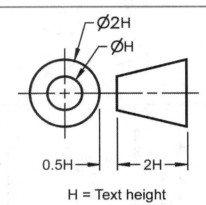

$\emptyset$2H

$\emptyset$H

0.5H ⟶| |⟵ 2H ⟶|

H = Text height

Figure 2-19: Projection symbol proportions.

In Class Student Exercise 2-4: Missing lines 1

Name: _____ Date: _____

Fill in the missing lines in the front, right side, and top views. **Hint:** The front view
has one missing visible line. The right side view has one missing visible line and
two missing hidden lines. The top view has five missing visible lines and two
missing hidden lines.

TOP

FRONT   RIGHT SIDE

NOTES:

In Class Student Exercise 2-5: Missing lines 2

Name: _____ Date: _____

Fill in the missing lines in the top, front, and right side views. **Hint:** The top view has one missing visible line. The front view has four missing visible lines and four missing center lines. The right side view has two missing hidden lines and one missing center line.

TOP

FRONT   RIGHT SIDE

NOTES:

<u>Video Exercise 2-6: Beginning Orthographic Projection</u>

This video exercise will take you through creating an orthographic projection for the object shown.

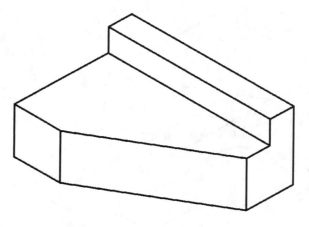

Video Exercise 2-7: Intermediate Orthographic Projection

This video exercise will take you through creating an orthographic projection for the object shown.

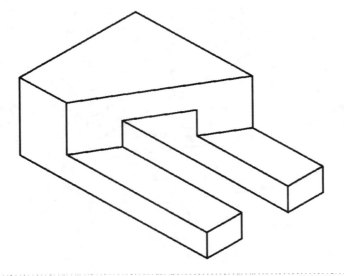

In Class Student Exercise 2-8: Drawing an orthographic projection 1

Name: _____ Date: _____

Shade in the surfaces that will appear in the front, top, and right side views. Estimating the distances, draw the front, top, and right side views. Identify the surfaces with the appropriate letter in the orthographic projection.

TOP ↓

FRONT   RIGHT SIDE

NOTES:

In Class Student Exercise 2-9: Drawing an orthographic projection 2

Name: _____ Date: _____

Identify the best choice for the front view. Estimating the distances, draw the front, top, and right side views.

NOTES:

Video Exercise 2-10: Advanced Orthographic Projection

This video exercise will take you through creating an orthographic projection for the object shown. Note: The object is not completely dimensioned; however, the missing dimensions will be made apparent in the video.

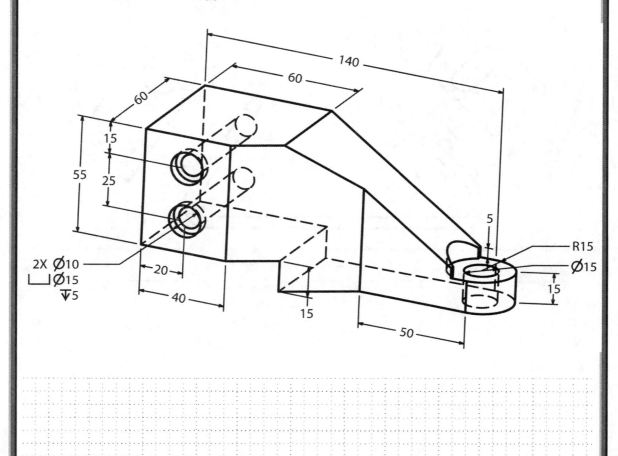

2.8) <u>AUXILIARY VIEWS</u>

Auxiliary views are used to show the true shape of features that are not parallel to any of the principle planes of projection. Auxiliary views are aligned with the angled features from which they are projected. Partial auxiliary views are often used to shown only a particular feature that is not described by true projection in the principle views. Figure 2-20 shows the use of auxiliary views.

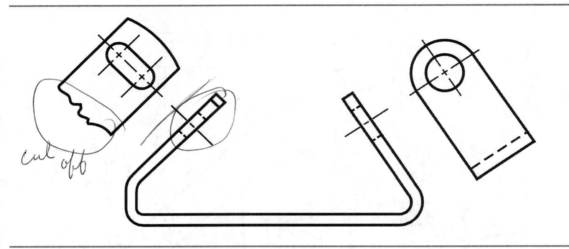

Figure 2-20: Auxiliary views.

Video Exercise 2-11: Auxiliary Views

This video exercise takes you through creating the auxiliary views for the following object.

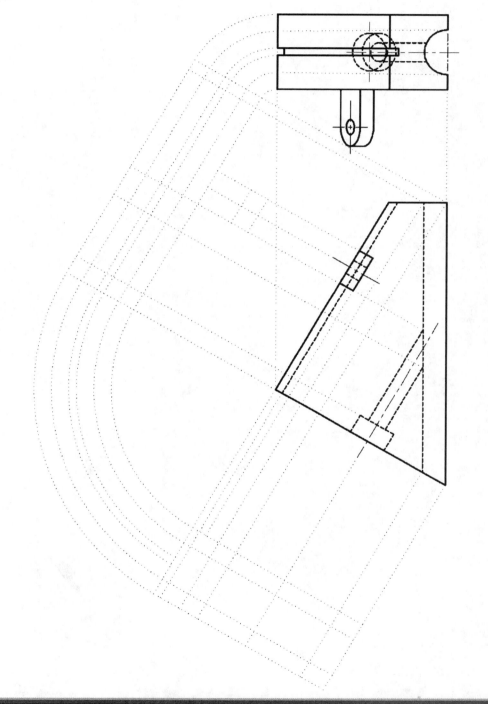

NOTES:

In Class Student Exercise 2-12: Auxiliary view

Name: _____ Date: _____

Draw the auxiliary view for this object.

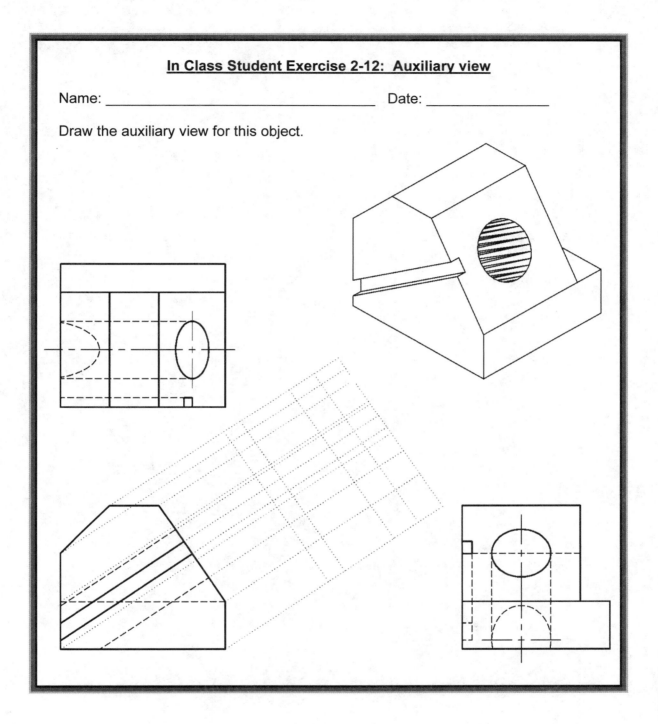

NOTES:

ORTHOGRAPHIC PROJECTION CROSSWORD PUZZLE

Name: _____ Date: _____

CP2-1)

Across

2. The thickest line type on a non-sectioned orthographic projection.
6. The standard views used in an orthographic projection in alphabetical order.
10. The front and right side views are aligned ....
11. Projection or construction lines are not shown on the final drawing. (true, false)
12. An orthographic projection is a .... representation of an object?
13. Phantom line use: Used to indicate ....

Down

1.   Phantom line use: Used to indicate ....
3.   Center line use: Used in indicate axes of ....
4.   The top and front views are aligned ....
5.   The view that generally contains the least number of hidden lines.
7.   If a hidden line and center line appear in exactly the same location on a drawing, which one do you delete?
8.   To indicate line importance we draw line using different line ....
9.   Should a center line end at the boundary of an object?
11. In the United States .... angle projection is used.

ORTHOGRAPHIC PROJECTION PROBLEMS

Name: _____   Date: _____

P2-1) 3-D pictorials of two objects are shown with labeled surfaces. Identify those surfaces on the corresponding 2-D orthographic projections. Dashed circles and leaders point to hidden surfaces and edges.

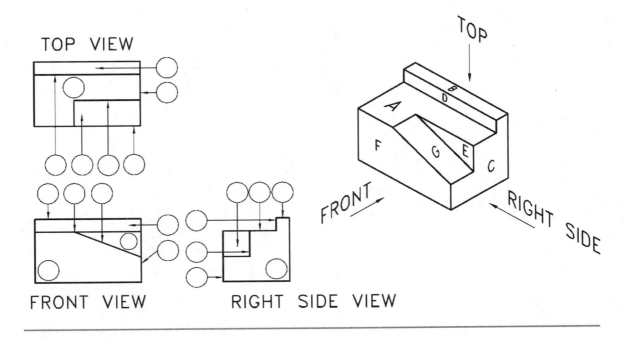

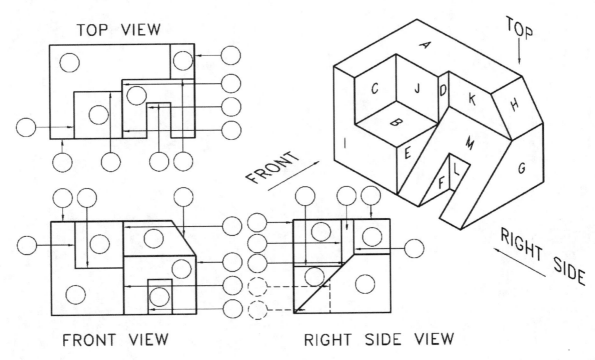

NOTES:

Name: _____ Date: _____

P2-2) Sketch the front, top and right side views of the following object. Use the grid provided.

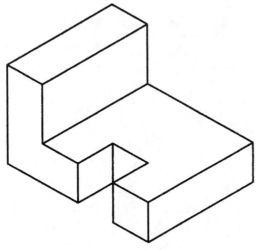

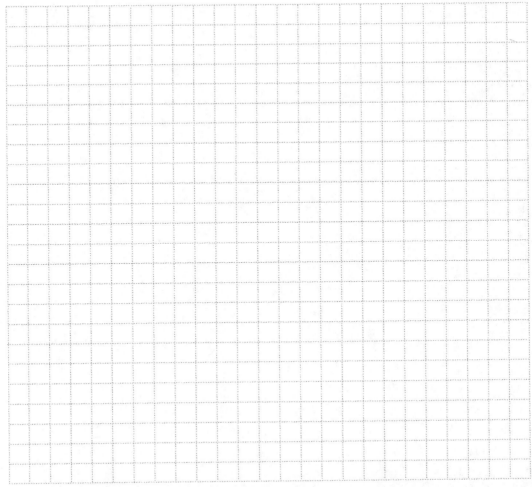

NOTES:

Name: _____ Date: _____

P2-3) Sketch the front, top and right side views of the following object. Use the grid provided.

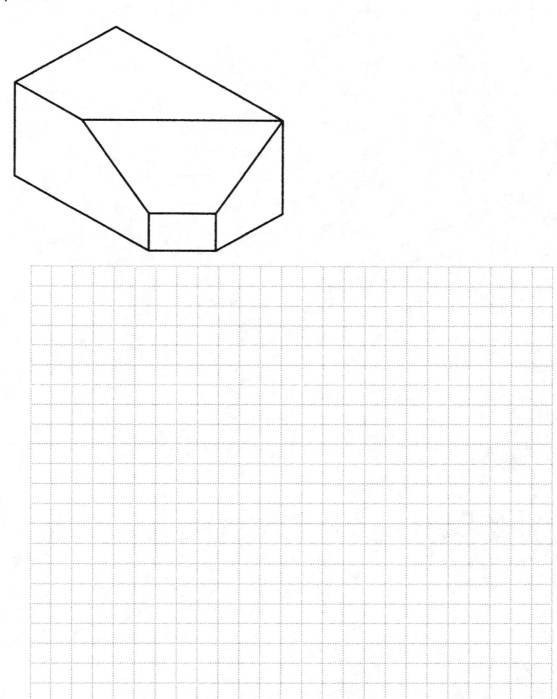

NOTES:

Name: _____ Date: _____

P2-4) Sketch the front, top and right side views of the following object. Use the grid provided.

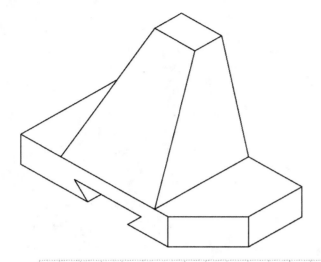

NOTES:

Name: _____ Date: _____

P2-6) Sketch the front, top and right side views of the following object. Use the grid provided.

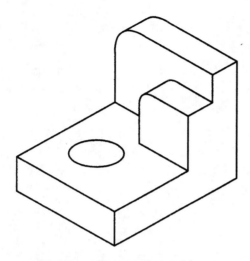

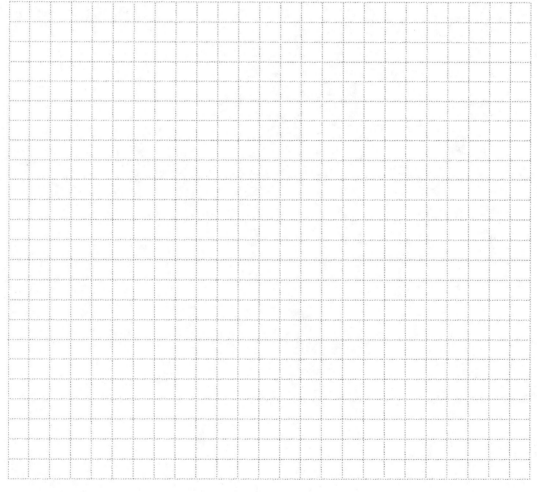

NOTES:

Name: _____ Date: _____

P2-7) Sketch the front, top and right side views of the following object. Use the grid provided.

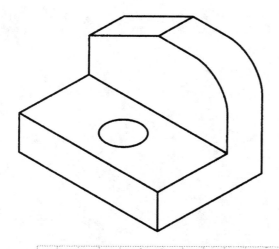

NOTES:

Name: _____ Date: _____

P2-9) Sketch the front, top and right side views of the following object. Use the grid provided.

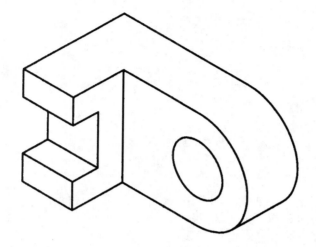

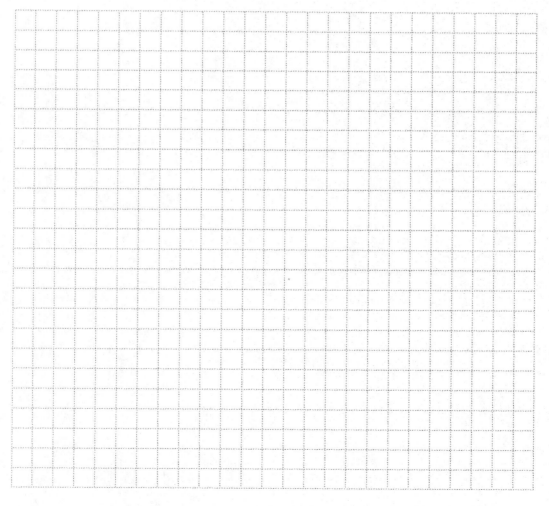

NOTES:

Name: _____ Date: _____

P2-10) Sketch the front, top and right side views of the following object. Use the grid provided.

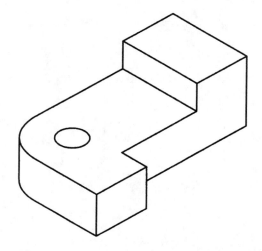

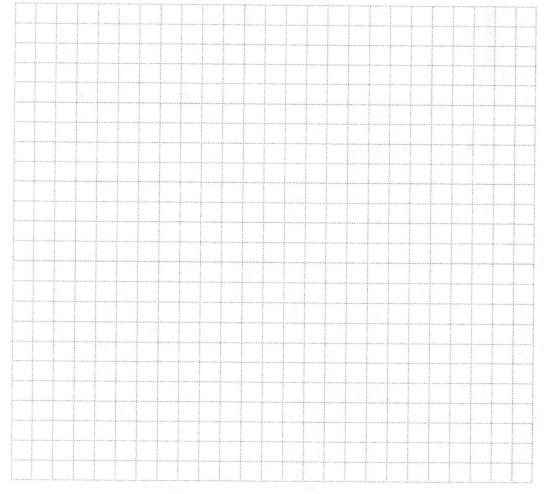

NOTES:

Name: _____ Date: _____

P2-11) Sketch the front, top and right side views of the following object. Use the grid provided.

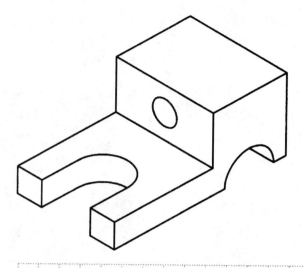

NOTES:

Name: _____   Date: _____

P2-12) Sketch the front, top and right side views of the following object. Use the grid provided.

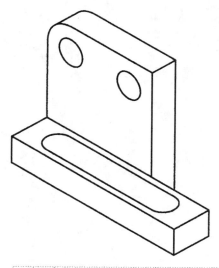

NOTES:

Name: _____ Date: _____

P2-13) Sketch the front, top and right side views of the following object. Use the grid provided.

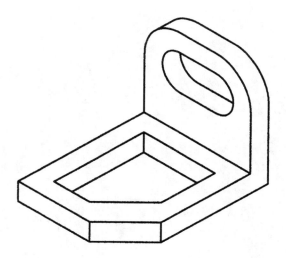

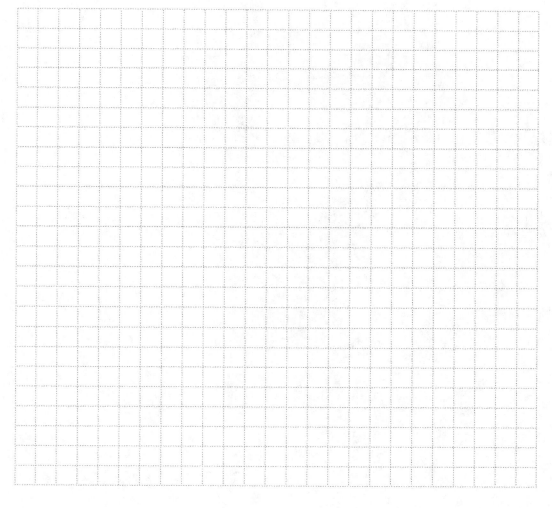

NOTES:

Name: _____ Date: _____

P2-14) Sketch the front, top and right side views of the following object. Use the grid provided.

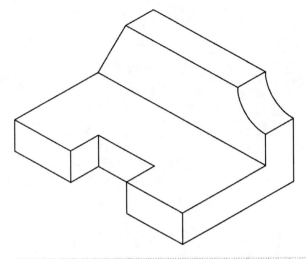

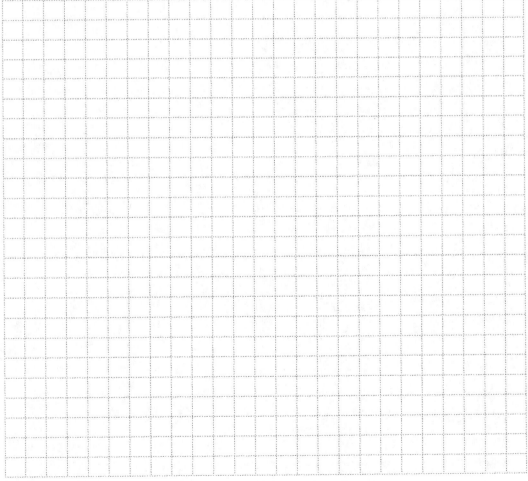

NOTES:

Name: _____ Date: _____

P2-15) Sketch the front, top and right side views of the following object. Use the grid provided.

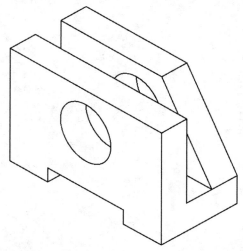

NOTES:

Name: _____ Date: _____

P2-16) Sketch the front, top and right side views of the following object. Use the grid provided.

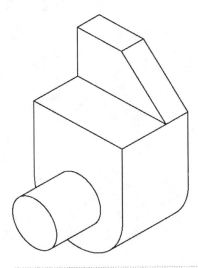

<u>NOTES:</u>

Name: _____ Date: _____

P2-17) Sketch the front, top and right side views of the following object. Use the grid provided.

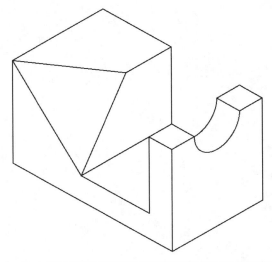

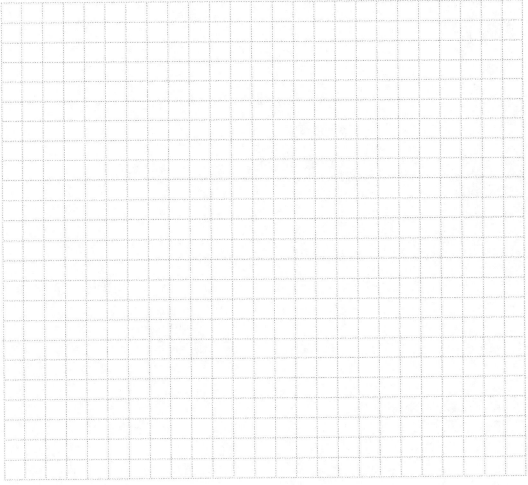

NOTES:

Name: _____ Date: _____

P2-18) Sketch the front, top and right side views of the following object. Use the grid provided.

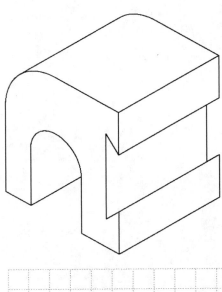

NOTES:

Name: _____ Date: _____

P2-19) Sketch the front, top and right side views of the following object. Use the grid provided.

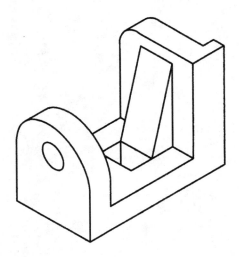

<u>NOTES:</u>

Name: _____   Date: _____

P2-20) Sketch the front, top and right side views of the following object. Use the grid provided.

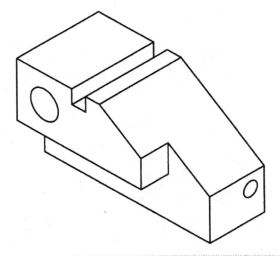

NOTES:

Name: _____ Date: _____

P2-21) Given two complete views, sketch in the missing view.

NOTES:

Name: _____ Date: _____

P2-22) Given two complete views, sketch in the missing view.

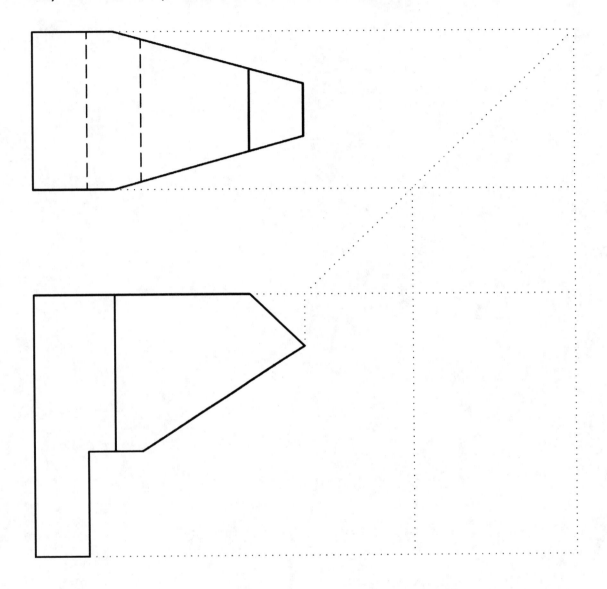

NOTES:

Name: _____ Date: _____

P2-23) Given two complete views, sketch in the missing view.

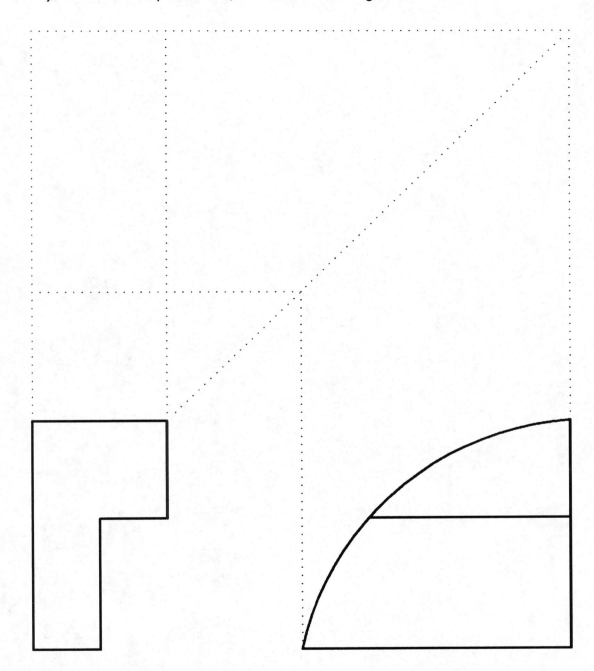

NOTES:

Name: _____ Date: _____

P2-24) Given two complete views, sketch in the missing view.

NOTES:

Name: _____ Date: _____

P2-25) Given two complete views, sketch in the missing view.

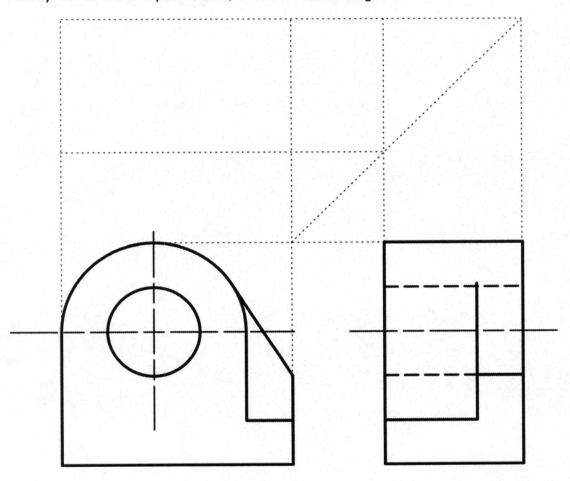

NOTES:

Name: _____ Date: _____

P2-26) Given two complete views, sketch in the missing view.

NOTES:

Name: _____ Date: _____

P2-27) Given two complete views, sketch in the missing view.

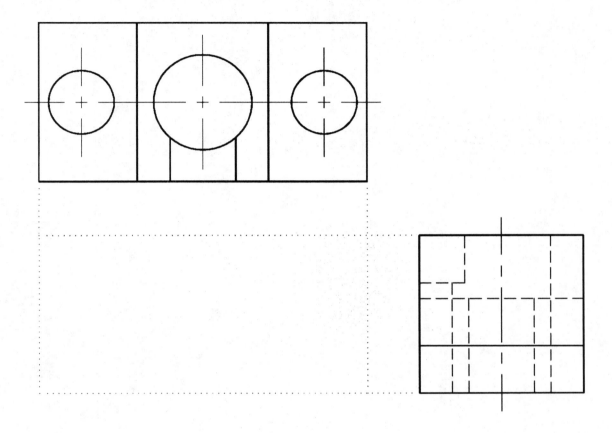

NOTES:

Name: _____ Date: _____

P2-28) Given two complete views, sketch in the missing view.

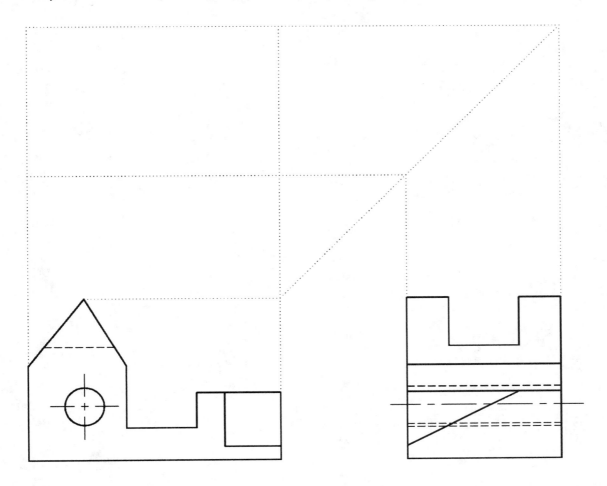

NOTES:

Name: _____ Date: _____

P2-29) Sketch in a complete auxiliary view in the space indicated.

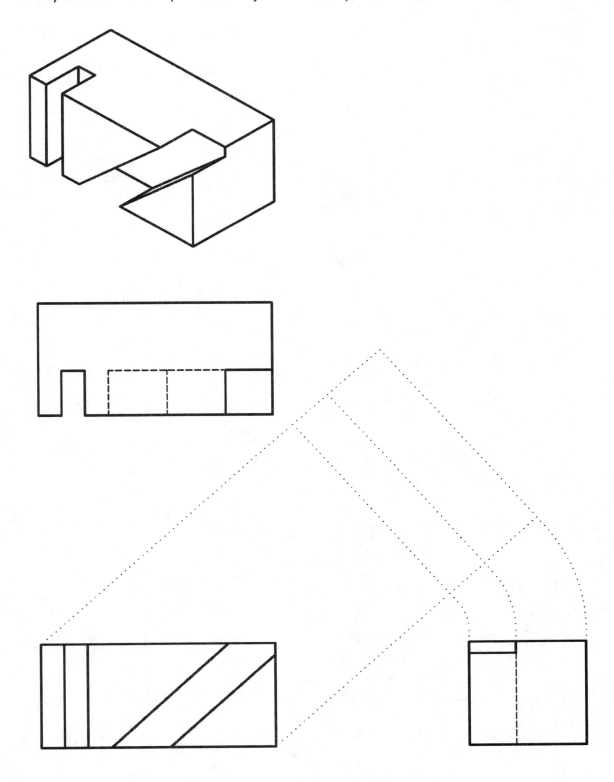

NOTES:

Name: _____ Date: _____

P2-30) Sketch in a complete auxiliary view in the space indicated.

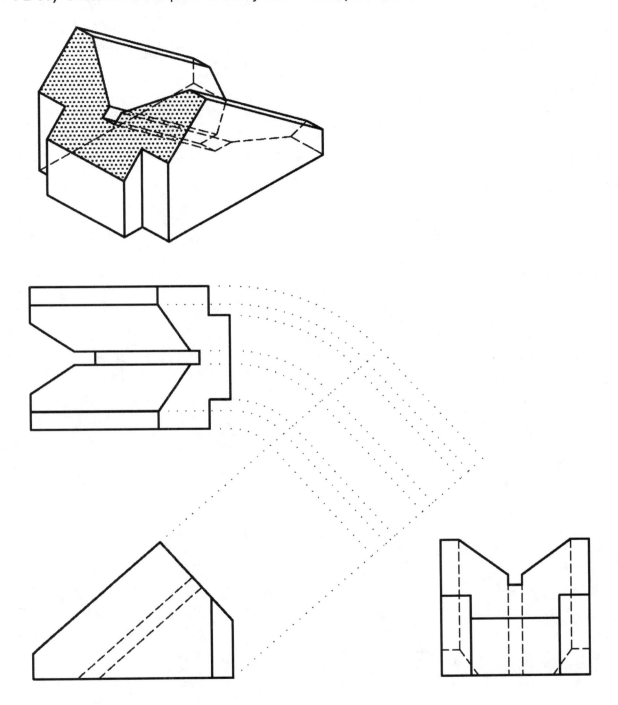

NOTES:

Name: _____ Date: _____

P2-31) Finish the two incomplete auxiliary views.

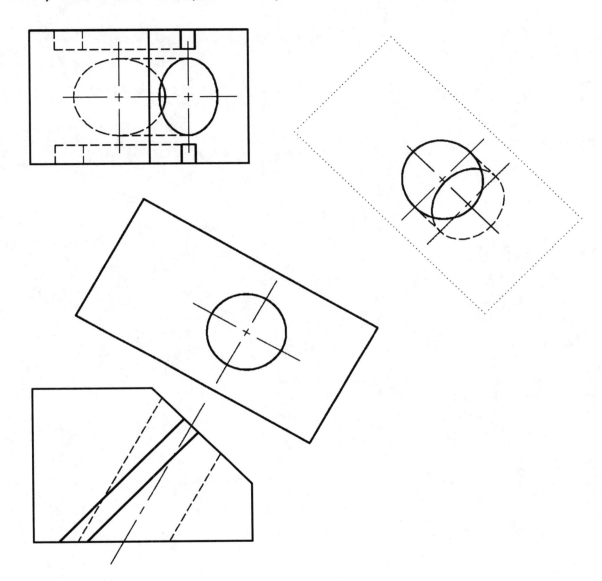

<u>NOTES:</u>

CREATING ORTHOGRAPHIC PROJECTIONS IN AUTOCAD

In Chapter 3 you will learn how to draw an orthographic projection in AutoCAD. Layers will be used which allow a drawing to contain different line types and to print using different line widths. You will draw and title block and border that can be repeatedly used. By the end of this chapter, you will be able to create a technically correct orthographic projection using proper line types and weights.

3.1) INTRODUCTION

An orthographic projection is a 2-D representation of a 3-D part. The line types and line weights used to create the orthographic projection give valuable information to the drawing or print reader. AutoCAD enables you to draw orthographic projections using different line types and to print drawings using different line weights. This is accomplished through the use of layers.

3.2) LAYERS

Layers are like transparencies, one placed over the top of another. Each transparency/layer contains a different line type or a different part of the drawing. One layer may be used to create visible lines, while another layer may be used to create hidden lines. One layer may draw objects in red while another layer may draw objects in blue and so on. Assigning a different line type and color to each layer helps you control and organize the drawing. Before beginning to draw, many layers will be created and their properties assigned. While drawing, the current or active layer (the layer you are drawing on) will be switched from one to another depending on what feature of the drawing you are working on.

Figure 3-1a shows an orthographic projection that uses different line types and line weights. The line type for each layer is set directly as a layer property. The line thickness is controlled by the color in which it is drawn. Figure 3-1b shows a possible layer organization scheme that could be used to create the orthographic projection shown in Figure 3-1a.

Layers not only facilitate the use of line types and weights, but they can also help you visualize, create and edit your work. For example, layers can be turned on or off. This is very useful when using a projection/construction line. Construction lines are helpful in the creation of an orthographic projection. However, they are not part of the final drawing. It would be tedious if you had to erase all the construction lines individually. A better way is to create a separate *Construction* layer and just turn it off (make it invisible) when they are no longer needed. Layers can also be locked. This means that you can see the layer but you cannot select any of the objects on the layer. This is very useful when your drawing is very complex and you need to isolate objects that are on a particular layer.

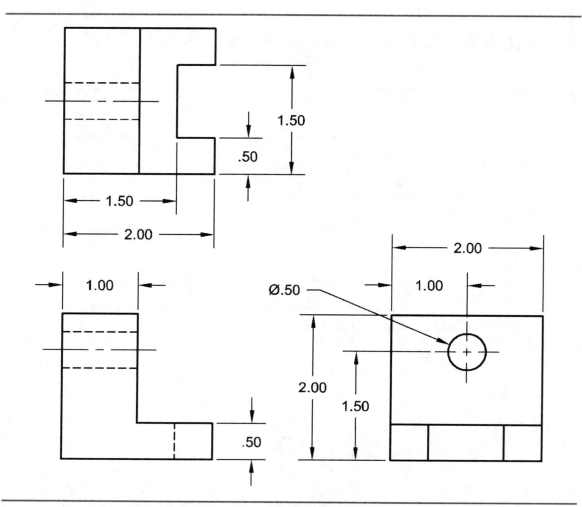

Figure 3-1a: A typical orthographic projection

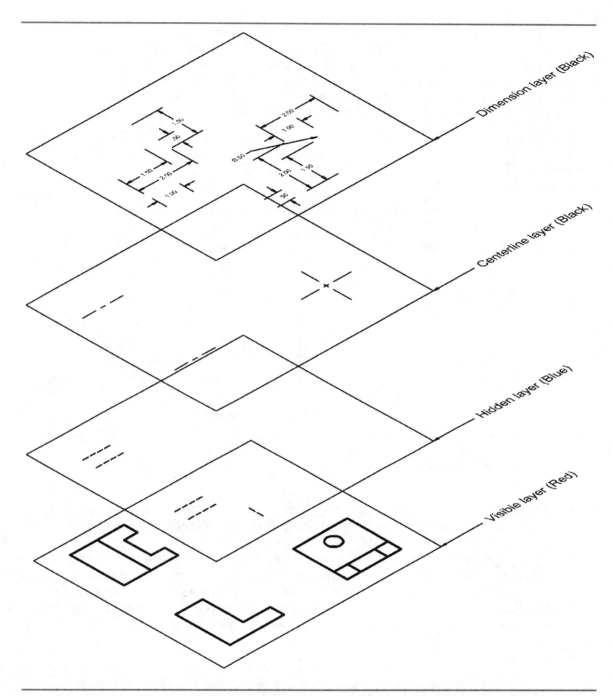

Figure 3-1b: Layer organization of an orthographic projection

3.2.1) The *Layers* panel

The *Layers* panel is shown in Figures 3-2. The most frequently used commands/areas in the *Layers* panel are the *Layers Properties Manager* icon and the *Layers pull-down selection* menu. The *Layers Properties Manager* is used to create, name, assign line types and manage layers. The *Layers* menu allows you to quickly switch from one layer to the next and turn layers on and off.

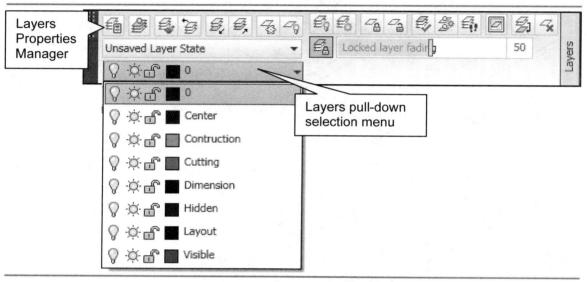

Figure 3-2: The *Layers* panel

The icons/features of the *Layers* panel are:

- *Layers Properties Manager* window: This icon brings up a *Layers Properties Manager* window. This window is the place where layers are created and the layer properties are assigned.
- Layer pull-down selection window: This pull-down window shows all of the available layers, allows you to switch between layers and enables you to change an object from one layer to another. To the left of each layer name is a set of quick access layer status settings that may be turned on or off. To turn these settings on and off, just click on them. Reading from left to right these settings are:
  - On/Off: The ON\OFF status of a layer is indicated by the light bulb. If it is yellow, the layer is ON and the objects on this layer can be seen. If it is gray, the layer is OFF and the objects on this layer can not be seen.
  - Freeze/Thaw: The FREEZE/THAW status of a layer is indicated by two suns. The big yellow sun freezes/thaws all viewports and the small sun freezes/thaws only the current viewport. If a layer is FROZEN, the sun will turn into a snowflake. Objects on a frozen layer are not displayed, regenerated, or plotted. Freezing layers shortens regenerating time.

- o Lock/Unlock: 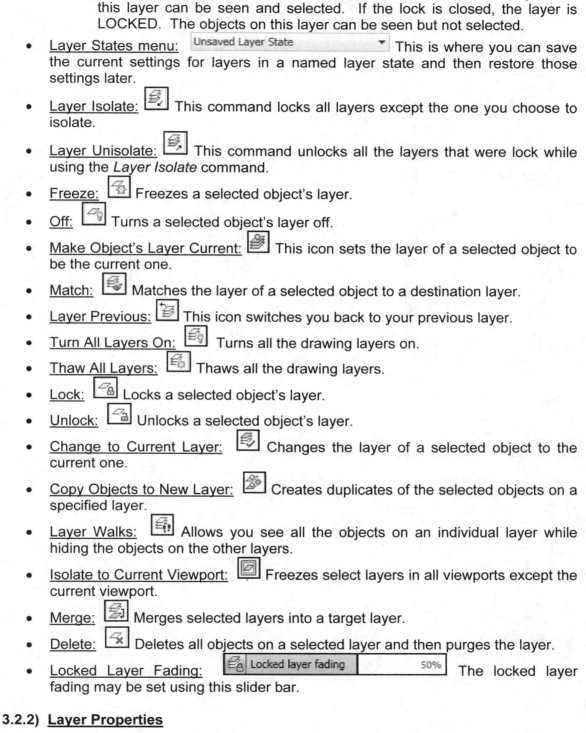 The LOCK/UNLOCK status of a layer is indicated by the pad lock. If the lock is open, the layer is UNLOCKED. The objects on this layer can be seen and selected. If the lock is closed, the layer is LOCKED. The objects on this layer can be seen but not selected.

- Layer States menu: Unsaved Layer State ▼ This is where you can save the current settings for layers in a named layer state and then restore those settings later.

- Layer Isolate: This command locks all layers except the one you choose to isolate.

- Layer Unisolate: This command unlocks all the layers that were lock while using the *Layer Isolate* command.

- Freeze: Freezes a selected object's layer.

- Off: Turns a selected object's layer off.

- Make Object's Layer Current: This icon sets the layer of a selected object to be the current one.

- Match: Matches the layer of a selected object to a destination layer.

- Layer Previous: This icon switches you back to your previous layer.

- Turn All Layers On: Turns all the drawing layers on.

- Thaw All Layers: Thaws all the drawing layers.

- Lock: Locks a selected object's layer.

- Unlock: Unlocks a selected object's layer.

- Change to Current Layer: Changes the layer of a selected object to the current one.

- Copy Objects to New Layer: Creates duplicates of the selected objects on a specified layer.

- Layer Walks: Allows you see all the objects on an individual layer while hiding the objects on the other layers.

- Isolate to Current Viewport: Freezes select layers in all viewports except the current viewport.

- Merge: Merges selected layers into a target layer.

- Delete: Deletes all objects on a selected layer and then purges the layer.

- Locked Layer Fading: Locked layer fading 50% The locked layer fading may be set using this slider bar.

3.2.2) Layer Properties

The *Layer Properties Manager* window is the place where you can create layers and set their properties. This window may be accessed using the command **LAYER** or by clicking on the *Layer Properties Manager* icon in the *Layers* panel. Figure 3-3 shows the *Layer Properties Manager* window with the important features identified. Most of the features are self explanatory except for the layer filter. The *New Property Filter* window is a place where you may create filters based on one or more layer properties.

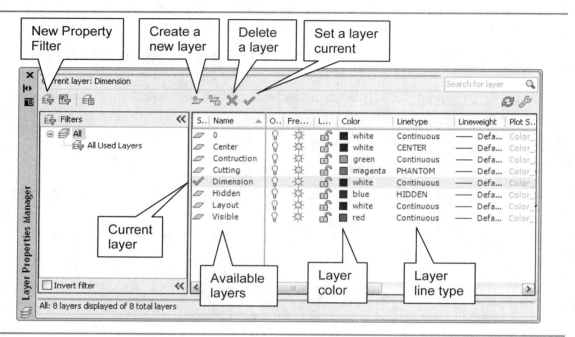

Figure 3-3: The *Layer Properties Manager* window

Creating a new layer and setting layer properties

1) Command: **layer**   or   *Layers* panel:
2) *Layer Properties Manager* window:

   a) Click on the *New Layer* icon
   b) Name your layer.
   c) Click on the square colored box under the heading *Color*. A *Select Color* window will appear.

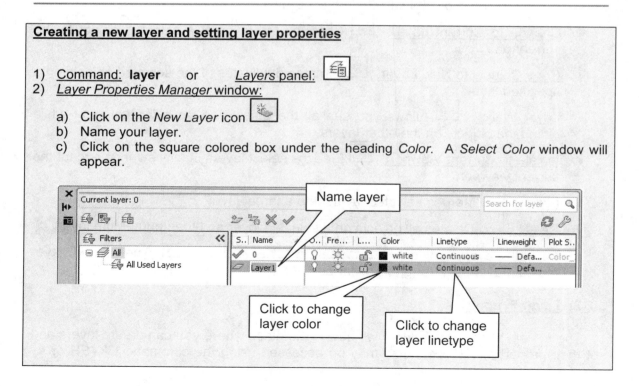

3) *Select Color* window – *Index Color* tab:
   a) Select a color for your layer. It is best to select a standard color. Note: The color *White* and *Black* are the same.
   b) **OK**

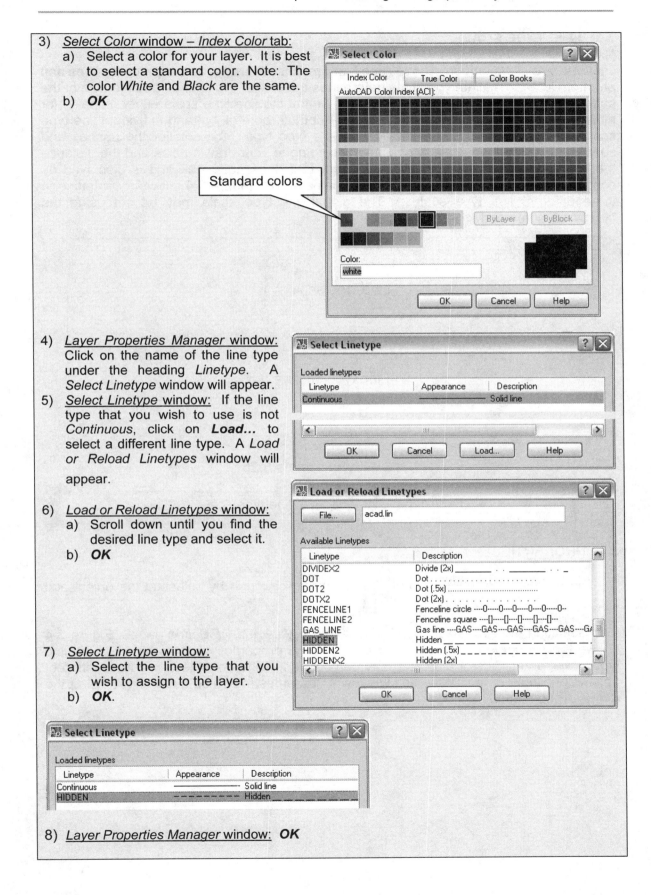

Standard colors

4) *Layer Properties Manager* window: Click on the name of the line type under the heading *Linetype*. A *Select Linetype* window will appear.
5) *Select Linetype* window: If the line type that you wish to use is not *Continuous*, click on **Load...** to select a different line type. A *Load or Reload Linetypes* window will appear.

6) *Load or Reload Linetypes* window:
   a) Scroll down until you find the desired line type and select it.
   b) **OK**

7) *Select Linetype* window:
   a) Select the line type that you wish to assign to the layer.
   b) **OK**.

8) *Layer Properties Manager* window: **OK**

3.3) LINE TYPE SCALE

Line type scale only applies to lines that break, such as, hidden lines, centerlines and phantom lines. The line type scale determines the size of the dashes and the size of the spaces between dashes or dots. You can control the line type scale either globally (for all lines) or individually for each object. By default, both global and individual line type scales are set to 1.00. The smaller the line type scale, the smaller the dashes and spaces. The line type scale is adjusted according to your drawing size and the distance that a line traverses. A short line segment that does not break and is displayed as continuous will need to have a smaller line type scale. Figure 3-4 shows a centerline at three different line type scales. The global line type scale may be set using the **LTSCALE** command.

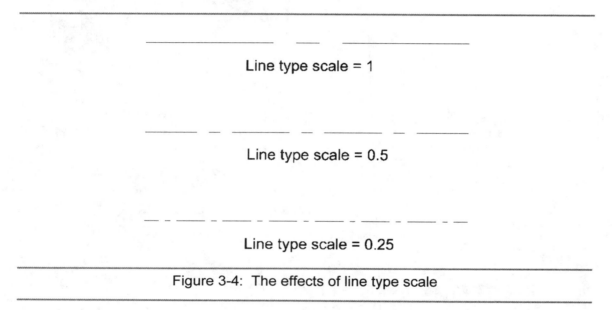

Line type scale = 1

Line type scale = 0.5

Line type scale = 0.25

Figure 3-4: The effects of line type scale

3.4) PROPERTIES

The properties of an individual object may be changed by selecting the object and then selecting the *Properties* icon in the *View* tab - *Palettes* panel. Figure 3-4 shows the *Properties* window of a circle. Several properties such as object layer, line type scale, and radius or diameter may be changed. Different objects will have different options available in the *Properties* window. Properties may also be changed using the **CHPROP** command.

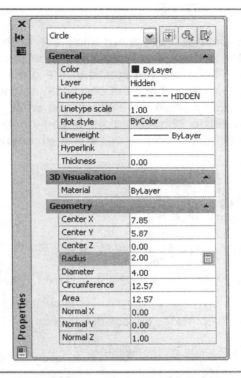

Figure 3-5: Properties window for a circle

3.4.1) The *Properties* panel

The *Properties* panel (Figure 3-6) is located in the *Home* tab. It allows you to change the color, line type and line weight of a selected object. It is my suggestion that these properties always remain on ByLayer (the default properties of the object's layer). If you need to change one of these properties, your first action should be to move the object to a layer that has those properties. This creates a much more organized drawing. Changing the ByLayer settings in the properties toolbar should be reserved for occasional use only. Two useful command found in the *Properties* panel are *Match Properties* and *List*. The **List** command lists the property data for a selected object.

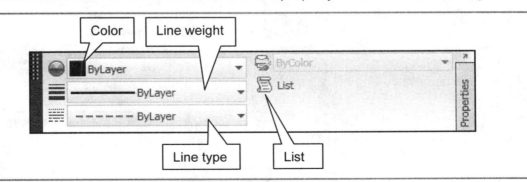

Figure 3-6: The *Properties* panel

3.5) <u>PRINTING USING PEN WIDTHS</u>

The color of an object dictates the printed thickness of that object. This is why we will specify a different color to each line type/layer. The pen widths are stored in files that are computer specific. They are not stored in the drawing file. If you are using a public computer, it is a good idea to check the pen width settings before printing.

You may print in color, grey scale or in black and white. If you are printing to an inkjet and in color, you need to choose colors based on how they look. If you are printing to a laser printer it is best to print in black and white and not in grey scale.

Setting pen widths

1) *Menu browser*: **Print – Page Setup...**
2) *Page Setup Manager* window: **Modify...**
3) *Page Setup – Model* window:
   a) In the *Plot style table (pen assignments)* area, select **momochrome.ctb** from the pull-down menu.
   b) *Question* window (Assign this plot style table to all layouts?): **Yes**

   c) Select the **Edit...** 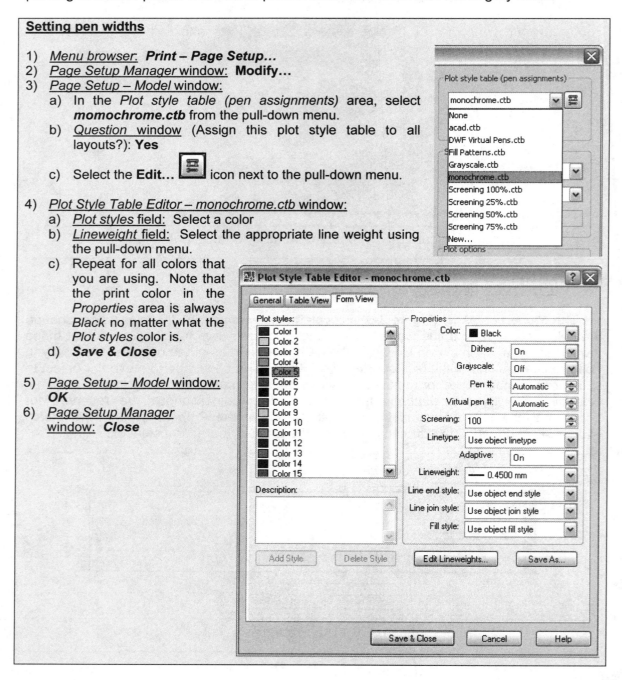 icon next to the pull-down menu.

4) *Plot Style Table Editor – monochrome.ctb* window:
   a) *Plot styles* field: Select a color
   b) *Lineweight* field: Select the appropriate line weight using the pull-down menu.
   c) Repeat for all colors that you are using. Note that the print color in the *Properties* area is always *Black* no matter what the *Plot styles* color is.
   d) **Save & Close**

5) *Page Setup – Model* window: **OK**
6) *Page Setup Manager* window: **Close**

3.6) CREATING LAYERS TUTORIAL

The objective of this tutorial is to create a set of standard layers that will be used to create orthographic projections. These layers will be saved to a template file so that they can be used repeatedly.

3.6.1) Setting drawing parameters

1) View the *Layers* video and read sections 3.1) through 3.5).

2) Open your **set-inch.dwt**. Your *set-inch* template file should have the following settings. If it does not, change them at this point.
- **UNITS**
   a. Units = inches
   b. Precision = 0.00
- **LIMITS** = 11,8.5
- **STYLE**
   a. Text font = Arial
   b. Text height = 0.12
   c. Make sure the **Annotative** toggle is checked.

3) Set the global line type scale to 0.5.
   a) Command: **ltscale**
   b) Enter new linetype scale factor <1.0000>: **0.5**

3.6.2) Creating layers

1) Command: **layer**   or   *Layers* panel:
2) *Layer Properties Manager* window:

   a) Click on the *New Layer* icon
   b) Name your layer **Hidden**.
   c) Click on the square colored box under the heading *Color* that is associated with the *Hidden* layer. A *Select Color* window will appear.

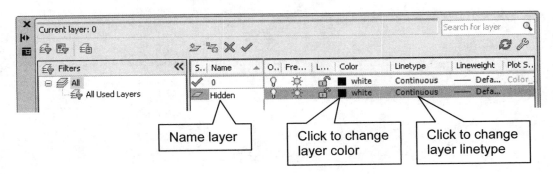

3) *Select Color* window – *Index Color* tab:
   a) Select the color **Blue** from the standard colors bar.
   b) **OK**

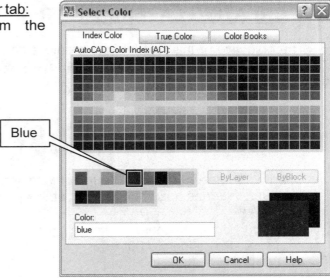

4) *Layer Properties Manager* window: Click on the name of the line type under the heading *Linetype* that is associated with the *Hidden* layer. A *Select Linetype* window will appear.

5) *Select Linetype* window: Click on **Load…**. A *Load or Reload Linetypes* window will appear.

6) *Load or Reload Linetypes* window:
   a) Scroll down until you find the **HIDDEN** line type and select it.
   b) **OK**

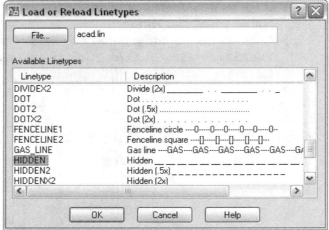

7) *Select Linetype* window:
   a) Select the **HIDDEN** line type.
   b) **OK**.

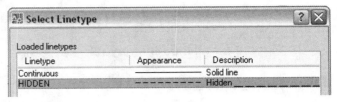

8) In a similar fashion, create the following layers.
   - **Visible**, color = *red*, linetype = **Continuous**
   - **Center**, color = *white*/black, linetype = **CENTER**
   - **Dimension**, color = *white*/black, linetype = **Continuous**
   - **Cutting**, color = *magenta*, linetype = **PHANTOM**
   - **Construction**, color = *green*, linetype = **Continuous**
   - **Layout**, color = *white*/black, linetype = **Continuous**

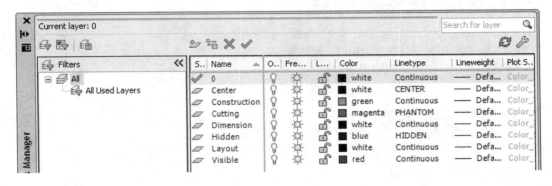

9) Save **set-inch.dwt**.

3.6.3) Drawing on different layers

1) Draw a line an each layer to see if the layer properties were set correctly.
   a) Set the **Visible** layer to be current.
      i. *Layers* panel: Expand the *Layer pull-down* menu and select **Visible**.

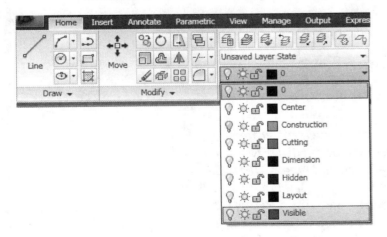

   b) Draw a **LINE**. It should be red.

c) Set the *Hidden* layer to be current and draw 2 **LINE**s. They should be blue and dashed.

d) Repeat for all the other layers.

3.6.4) Line type scale

1) Change the global line type scale (**LTSCALE**) to 0.25. Notice that the dashes and spaces between the dashes become smaller.

> How?
> a) <u>Command:</u> **ltscale**
> b) Enter new linetype scale factor <0.5000>: **0.25**

2) Change your **LTSCALE** back to **0.5**.

3) Change the line type scale of one of the hidden lines to twice that of the global line type scale.

a) Select one of the hidden lines.

b) *View tab - Palettes panel:* Properties

c) *Properties window:* Change the *Linetype scale* to **2**.

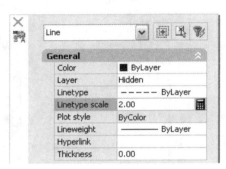

3) **Save As** **Layers Tut.dwg** and print your drawing.

In Class Student Exercise 3-1: Creating layers

Open your **set-mm.dwt**, make sure that it has the following settings and create the layers indicated. Then, resave your template file.

<u>Settings:</u>
- **UNITS** (Millimeters, Precision = 0)
- **LIMITS** = 280,216
- **STYLE** (Text font = Arial, Text height = 3, Annotative)
- **LTSCALE** = 0.5

<u>Layers:</u>
- **Visible**, color = *red*, linetype = *Continuous*
- **Hidden**, color = *blue*, linetype = *HIDDEN*
- **Center**, color = *white*/black, linetype = *CENTER*
- **Dimension**, color = *white*/black, linetype = *Continuous*
- **Cutting**, color = *magenta*, linetype = *PHANTOM*
- **Construction**, color = *green*, linetype = *Continuous*
- **Layout**, color = *white*/black, linetype = *Continuous*

3.7) TITLE BLOCKS

Every engineering drawing should have both a border and a title block. The border defines the drawing area and the title block gives pertinent information about the part or assembly being drawn. There are several different types of title blocks, but they all contain similar information. The information that is included depends on the drawing type, field of engineering, and viewing audience.

3.7.1) Title Block Contents

The information contained in a title block may include, but is not limited to, the following:

1. Name of drafter
2. Checked by
3. School or Company
4. Drawing title
5. Part name
6. Part number
7. Material of part
8. Number of required parts
9. Sheet number
10. Number of sheets
11. Scale of drawing
12. Date
13. Last revision

3.7.2) Date

The drawing date is given numerically in order of *year-month-day*. For example, the date, May 31, 2009, would be indicated as 2009-05-31 or 2009/05/31. The date is placed in the title block next to the word "DATE".

3.7.3) Sheet Layout

In a class room setting most drawings are printed out on an 8.5" x 11" sheet of paper. Figure 3-7 shows a typical drawing sheet layout. Figures 3-8a and 3-8b show two different simple title block forms.

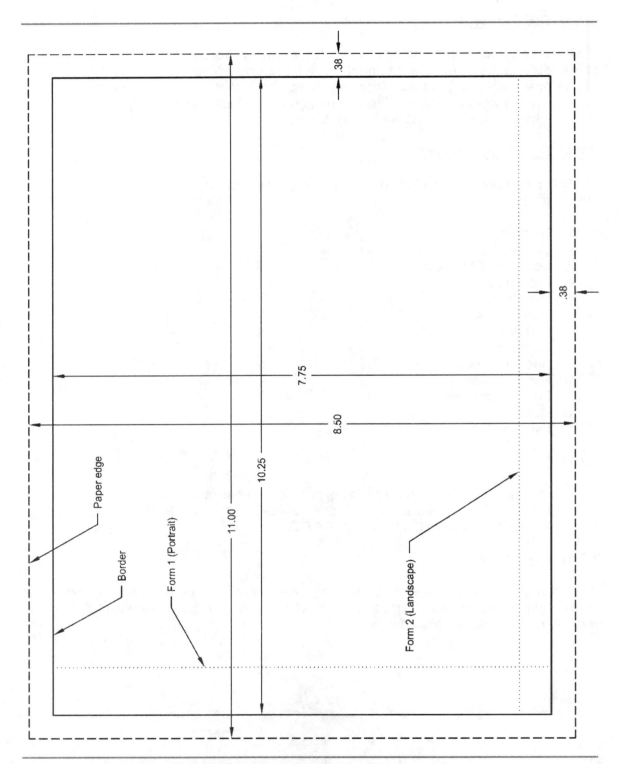

Figure 3-7: Sheet layout for an 11 x 8.5 sheet of paper.

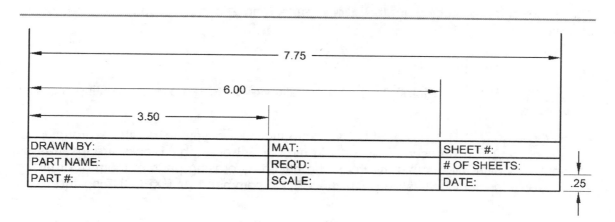

Figure 3-8a: Form 1 (portrait title block)

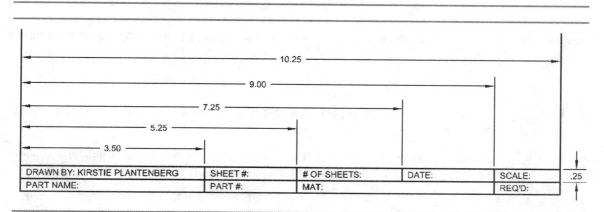

Figure 3-8b: Form 2 (landscape title block)

3.8) BLOCKING

Blocks are a grouping of objects that can be used repeatedly. The command **BLOCK** allows you to define a particular drawing as an entity. It groups all the lines, circles, and other geometric shapes into one entity. This means that you can insert this group into a drawing without having to redraw it. The commands that are relevant for creating and using blocks are grouped in the *Block* panel shown in Figure 3-9.

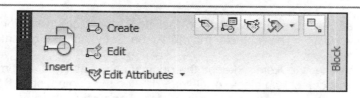

Figure 3-9: *Block* panel

The commands contained in the *Block* panel and the other commands related to blocking are:

- **INSERT:** The INSERT command allows you to retrieve an existing block or wblock.

- **BLOCK:** The BLOCK command allows you to create a grouping of objects that can be used repeatedly in the current drawing. Blocks are inserted as entities, which means that they can't be edited by erasing parts of them or breaking lines within them unless you use the BEDIT command or EXPLODEing the block first.

- **BEDIT:** The block edit command allows you to select and edit an existing block. The block edit command temporarily adds a *Block Editor* tab to the ribbon.

- **WBLOCK:** This command writes a block to a file. This allows you to use the block in all drawings not just the current one.

- **EXPLODE:** Allows you to separate a block into its individual parts. The EXPLODE command may be accessed in the *Modify* panel.

- **BASE** (Set Base point): Set the insertion base point for the current drawing. The base point is the reference point used when creating and inserting your block. This point should not be arbitrary. It should have some relationship with the block and with the object or space in which it will be inserted.

Creating blocks

1) <u>Command:</u> **block** or <u>*Block* panel:</u> Create
2) *Block Definition* window:
   a) Name the block.
   b) *Base point* area: Pick a base point/insertion point. This can be accomplished by directly entering a coordinate or by selecting the **Pick point** icon.
   c) *Objects* area:
      i. Select all objects that you wish to include in the block definition using the **Select objects** icon. (The objects may also be selected before entering the BLOCK command.)
      ii. Activate either the *Retain* (keeps the original object as is), *Convert to block* (converts the original object to a block) or *Delete* (deletes the original object) radio button.
   d) *Behavior* area: Activate **Allow exploding** and **Annotative** checkboxes.
   e) If necessary, set the *Block units*.
   f) **OK**

Note: A block is defined within the current drawing and cannot be used in other drawings unless a WBLOCK is created.

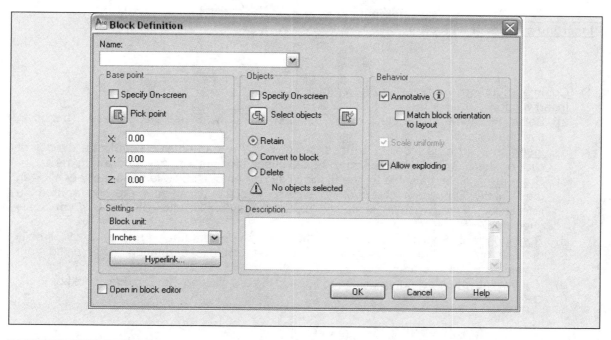

Creating a wblock

1) <u>Command:</u> **wblock**
2) *Write Block* window:
   a) Select the ***Block*** radio button.
   b) Select the block you wish to write to a file in the pull-down menu.
   c) Select a location for the file by clicking on the file path icon [...].
   d) Select the *Insert units*.
   e) ***OK***

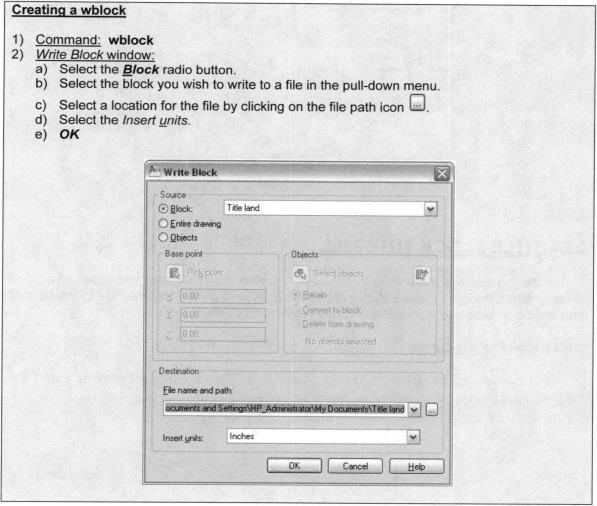

Inserting a block or wblock

1) Command: **insert**   or   *Block* panel: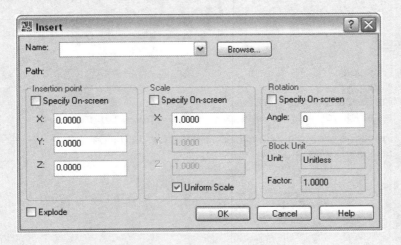
2) Insert window:
   a) Select the name of the block in the pull-down window, or use the ***Browse...*** button to select a wblock.
   b) *Insertion point* area: Select an insertion point. You can enter a coordinate directly or click on the *Specify On-screen* checkbox to choose a point with in your drawing area.
   c) *Scale* area: Select a scale for the block. You can enter a scale factor directly or click on the *Specify On-screen* checkbox to choose a scale using your drawing area as a reference. If you wish to scale the block non-uniformly, click off the *Uniform Scale* checkbox.
   d) *Rotation* area: Specify the rotation of the block. You can enter a rotation angle directly or click on the *Specify On-screen* checkbox to choose a rotation angle using your drawing area as a reference.
   e) If you want your block to be exploded upon insertion, click on the *Explode* checkbox.
   f) ***OK***

3.9) <u>TITLE BLOCK TUTORIAL</u>

At the end of this tutorial you will have created a border and title block similar to Form 2 illustrated in Figure 3.8b. We will BLOCK and WBLOCK the title block so that you will be able to use it on all landscape drawings that you create.

3.9.1) <u>Drawing the Border</u>

Your border will be drawn such that there is a 3/8 inch space between it and the edge of your paper.

1) View the *Blocking* video and read sections 3.7) and 3.8)

2) 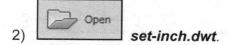 **set-inch.dwt**.

3)  **Title Block Land Tut.dwg**.

4) Get into your *World Coordinate System* ◉.

5) **ZOOM ALL**

6) Activate a **0.50** x 0.50 **GRID**.

7) In the **Visible** layer, draw a **RECTANGLE** that will become the border. The rectangles lower left corners is located at **0.375, 0.375** and is **10.25** long and **7.75** wide.

8) Explode the RECTANGLE. This will break the rectangle into individual lines.

    a) <u>Command:</u> **explode** or   *Modify* panel: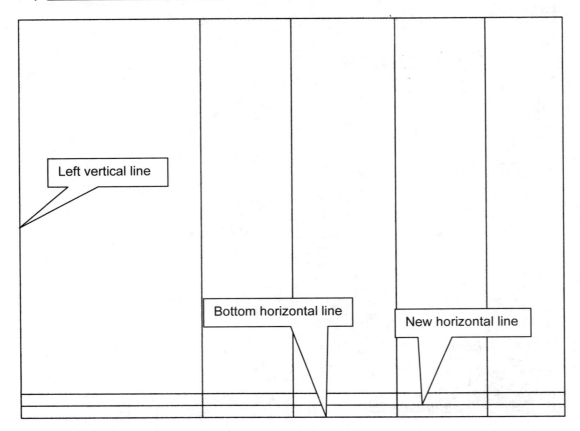

    b) `Select object:` Select the rectangle.

    c) `Select object:` **Enter**

3.9.2) **Framing in the title block**

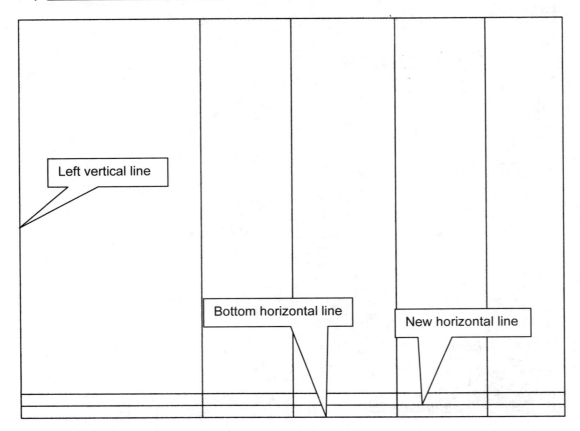

1) In the **Visible** layer, create the title block's horizontal lines.

    a) <u>Command:</u> **offset**   or   *Modify* panel:

    b) `Specify offset distance or [Through/Erase/Layer] <Through>:` **0.25**

    c) `Select object to offset or [Exit/Undo] <Exit>:` Select the bottom horizontal line of your border.

    d) `Specify point on side to offset or [Exit/Multiple/Undo] <Exit>:` **m**

    e) `Specify point on side to offset or [Exit/Undo] <next object>:` Select a point above the bottom horizontal line of your border.

    f) `Specify point on side to offset or [Exit/Undo] <next object>:` Select a point above the new horizontal line.

    g) `Specify point on side to offset or [Exit/Undo] <next object>:` **e**

2) In the **Visible** layer, create the title block's vertical lines. Use the **OFFSET** command to offset the left vertical line at distances of **3.50**, **5.25**, **7.25** and **9.00** inches.

3) **TRIM** 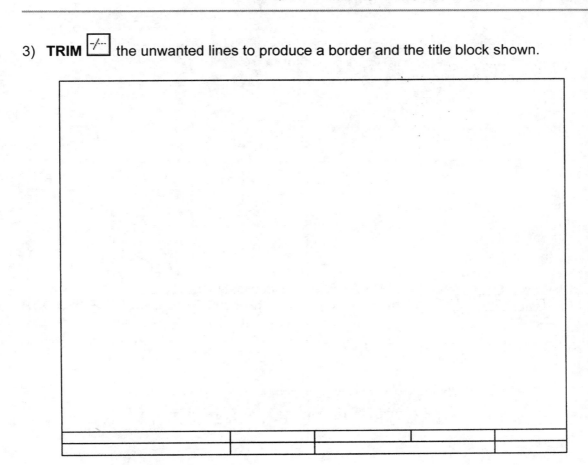 the unwanted lines to produce a border and the title block shown.

3.9.3) Filling in the title block text

1) Enter the text into the title block.
   a) Turn your **Caps Lock** on.
   b) Enter your *Dimension* layer.
   c) Use the **STYLE** command to check your text settings. Make sure that the *Annotative* toggle is selected.

   d) <u>Command:</u> **mtext**   or   *Annotation* panel:
   e) Specify first corner: Snap to the endpoint shown.

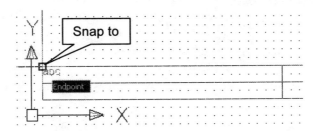

f) `Specify opposite corner or [Height/Justify/Line spacing/ Rotation/Style/Width/Columns]:` **int**
   `of` Select the intersection shown.

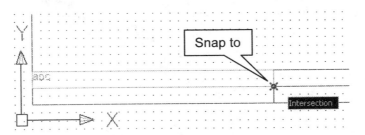

g) _Paragraph_ panel: Select the **Middle Left** justification 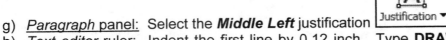.
h) _Text editor_ ruler: Indent the first line by 0.12 inch. Type **DRAWN BY: YOUR NAME**.

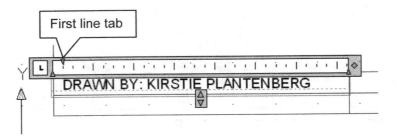

i) Click in the drawing area to exit the command.
j) Use the same procedure as above to enter the rest of the title block text.

DRAWN BY: KIRSTIE PLANTENBERG	SHEET #:	# OF SHEETS:	DATE:	SCALE:
PART NAME:	PART #:	MAT:		REQ'D:

2)

3.9.4) Blocking the title block and border

1) **BLOCK** your title block and border.

a. <u>Command:</u> **block** or *Block* panel: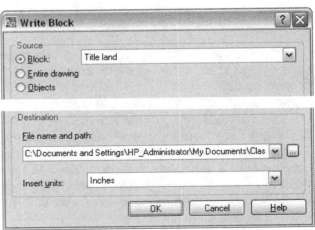

b. *Block Definition* window:
   i. Name the block **Title land**.
   ii. Enter a *Base point* of **0.00, 0.00, 0.00**
   iii. Select all objects that make up your title block and border using the **Select objects** icon.
   iv. Activate the **Retain** radio button.
   v. Activate the **Annotative** and **Allow exploding** checkboxes.
   vi. Set the *Block units* to **Inches**.
   vii. **OK**

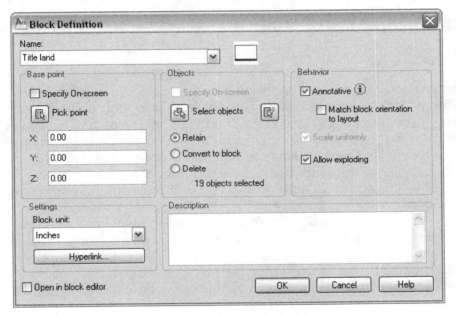

2) Write the *Title land* block to a file.
   a. <u>Command:</u> **wblock**
   b. *Write Block* window:
      i. Select the **Block** radio button.
      ii. Select the **Title land** block from the pull-down menu.
      iii. Select a location for the file by clicking on the file path icon ⬚ and name the file **Title land**.
      iv. Select **Inches** as the insert units.
      v. **OK**

In Class Student Exercise 3-2: Portrait title block

Draw a border and title block that can be used for portrait drawing.
- Open your *set-inch.dwt*.
- Set your LIMITS to 8.5,11.
- Draw a 3/8 inch border (Visible layer).
- Draw a title block like Form 1 illustrated in Figure 3.8a (Visible layer).
- Enter the TEXT (Dimension layer).
- BLOCK the border and title block as *Title port* using the same settings as in the *Title land* block.
- WBLOCK *Title port*.

3.10) MODEL AND LAYOUT SPACE

3.10.1) Model Space

In model space, you draw your design at a 1:1 scale. You specify whether one unit represents one millimeter, one centimeter, one inch, one foot, or whatever unit is most convenient. If you are going to create a 2-D orthographic projection, you can create both the model (drawing) and annotations (dimensions), and print entirely from within model space. This method is simple, but has several limitations including:
- It is suitable for drawings that are viewed from only one direction. 2-D drawings are only viewed from one direction, but 3-D drawings may have many viewing directions.
- It does not support multiple views and view dependent layer settings.
- Scaling the annotations and title block requires computation. This is because if you change the scale of the model the annotations change with it.

With this method, you always draw geometric objects at full scale (1:1) and text, dimension and other annotations at a scale that will appear at the correct size when the drawing is plotted.

3.10.2) Layout Space

In paper/layout space, you can place objects and annotations that are not part of your design such as a title block and dimensions. In paper space, you see what will be printed (usually on an 8.5 x 11 sheet of paper). Therefore, objects from the model space that are larger than the paper are scaled to fit.

You can plot objects that are in the model space from paper space using viewports. A viewport is a rectangular window that views the object from a specified line of sight. Viewports are most useful when working with a 3-D model. In this situation, you can create several viewports that view the 3-D model from several different vantage points. When looking at a 2-D drawing, you really only want to view the xy plane. A situation where you might use multiple viewports with a 2-D drawing is if you are showing part of the model at a different scale.

In paper space, each layout viewport is like a picture frame containing a photograph of the model. Each layout viewport contains a view that displays the model at an independent scale and orientation that you specify. You can also specify different layers properties in each layout viewport. The advantages of plotting from paper space are:

- You can plot multiple viewports.
- The size and location of the objects within each viewport is completely within your control.
- With annotative scaling, it is not necessary to calculate the appropriate dimension and text scale. Annotative scaling will be discussed in detail in Chapter 5. Figure 3-10 shows an example of what you would see in paper space before plotting.

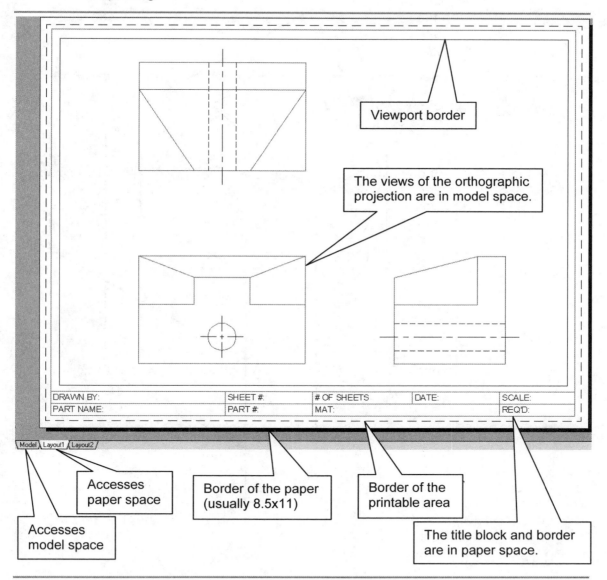

Figure 3-10: Paper space

3.11) ORTHOGRAPHIC PROJECTION TUTORIAL

By the end of this tutorial you will have created and printed an orthographic projection of the part shown using proper pen widths. We will draw the orthographic projection using the procedure explained in chapter 2. We will start by drawing the front view and use projectors to construct the top and right side views. Visible, hidden, and centerlines will be drawn on their own layer. Once the drawing is complete we will use both the model space and the layout space to plot the drawing.

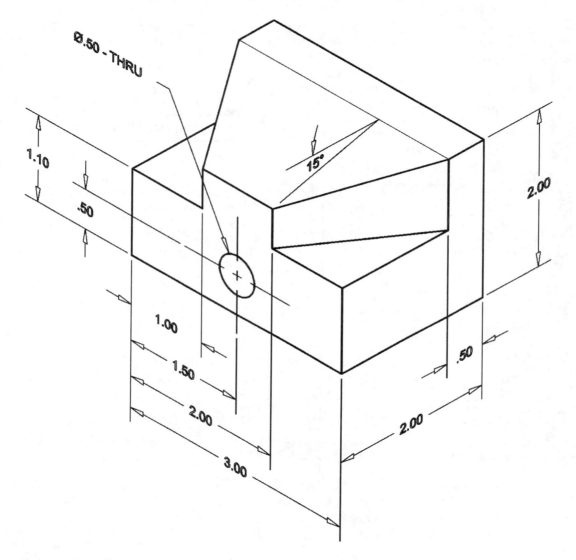

3.11.1) Draw the front view

1) View the *Model - Layout*, *Pen widths* and *Printing* videos and read section 3.10).

2) Take some time to sketch what you think the FRONT, TOP and RIGHT SIDE views of the above object will look like.

3)  *set-inch.dwt*.

4)  **Ortho Tut.dwg**, and save periodically throughout this tutorial.

5) Enter your WCS [icon].

6) If you are using *Dynamic Input*, set the *Pointer Input Format* to **Absolute coordinates**.

7) In the **Layout** layer, draw a **RECTANGLE** that indicates the edges of your limits/paper (11x8.5).

8) **ZOOM ALL**

9) In your **Visible** layer, draw the visible lines of the front view.
   a) Draw a **RECTANGLE** that is **3** inches long and **2** inches wide near the bottom left corner of your drawing area.
   b) Set your **UCS** origin [icon] to the bottom left corner of the front view.
   c) Draw the 2 **LINE**s within the rectangle.
   d) Draw the **CIRCLE**. (Note: ∅ = diameter)

> **Note:** Some visible features are missing, but this is all we can do for now.

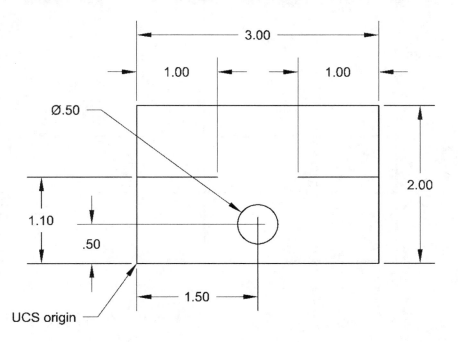

3.11.2) Drawing the right side view

1) Turn your **Object Snap** on and set the following object snaps to be automatically detected. (Endpoint, Midpoint, Center, Quadrant, Intersection, Nearest, Perpendicular, Extension). (right click – **Settings**)

2) In the **Construction** layer, draw horizontal and vertical construction lines (**XLINE**) off of every edge and boundary of the front view.
   a) Create the horizontal projectors.

       i.   <u>Command:</u> **xline**   or   <u>*Draw* panel:</u> ↗

       ii.   Specify a point or [Hor/Ver/Ang/Bisect/Offset]: **h**

       iii. Specify through point: Select every corner, edge and quadrant that should have a horizontal projector coming off of it.

       iv. Specify through point: **Enter**

   b) Move the lines of the front view above the construction lines.

       i.   <u>*Home* tab - *Modify* panel:</u> ▣▾ (Bring to Front)

       ii.   Select objects: Using a window, select all the lines of the front view.

       iii. Select objects: **Enter**

   c) Create the vertical projectors.
   d) Bring the lines of the front view above the construction lines.

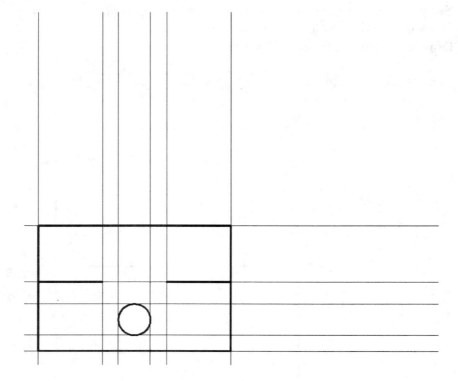

3) In the **Visible** layer, draw the visible features of the L-shaped part of the right side view.

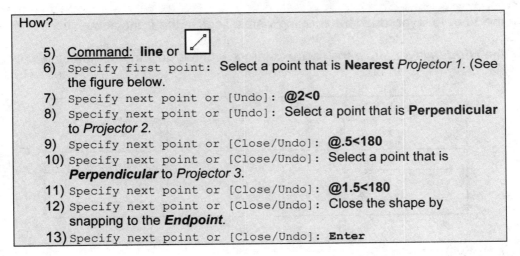

How?

5) <u>Command:</u> **line** or

6) `Specify first point:` Select a point that is **Nearest** *Projector 1*. (See the figure below.

7) `Specify next point or [Undo]:` **@2<0**

8) `Specify next point or [Undo]:` Select a point that is **Perpendicular** to *Projector 2*.

9) `Specify next point or [Close/Undo]:` **@.5<180**

10) `Specify next point or [Close/Undo]:` Select a point that is **Perpendicular** to *Projector 3*.

11) `Specify next point or [Close/Undo]:` **@1.5<180**

12) `Specify next point or [Close/Undo]:` Close the shape by snapping to the **Endpoint**.

13) `Specify next point or [Close/Undo]:` **Enter**

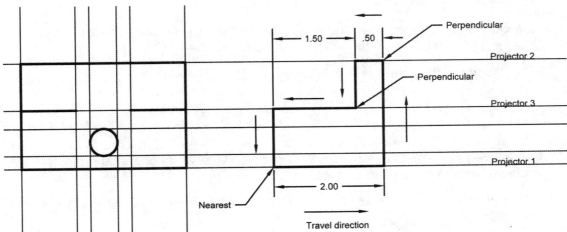

4) Draw the angled feature of the right side view using the following commands.
   a) Turn the **Polar Tracking** on and set **POLARANG** to **15** degrees.
   b) Use a polar tracking path and the **Extension** snap to construct the angled line.
   c) Connect the angled line with the L-shaped body.

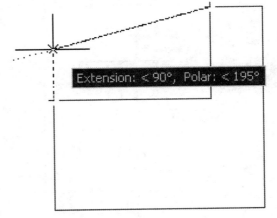

5) In the **Construction** layer, project the angled feature of the right side view back to the front view.

6) In the **Visible** layer, draw the missing visible lines in the front view.

7) In the **Hidden** layer, draw the rectangular view of the hole in the right side view.

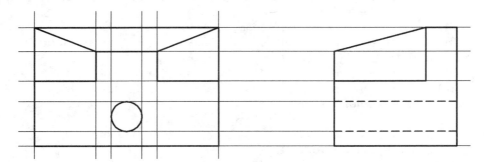

3.11.3) Drawing the top view

1) In the Construction layer, draw the projectors needed to complete the top view.
   a) Draw a 45° projector off the upper right corner of the front view.

   i.   Command: **xline**   or   *Draw* panel:
   ii. Specify a point or [Hor/Ver/Ang/Bisect/Offset]: **a**
   iii. Enter angle of xline (0) or [Reference]: **45**
   iv. Specify through point: Select the upper right corner of the front view.
   v.   Specify through point: **Enter**

   b) Draw vertical projectors up from the right side view and horizontal projectors over to where the top view will be located.

   c) Use the **Bring to Front** icon to bring the lines of the right side view to the front.

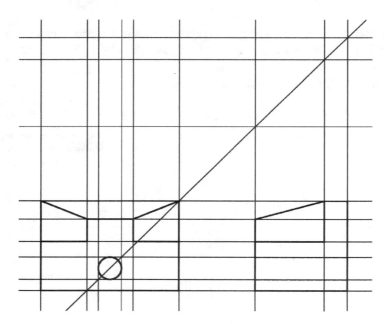

2) Draw the visible and hidden features of the top view.

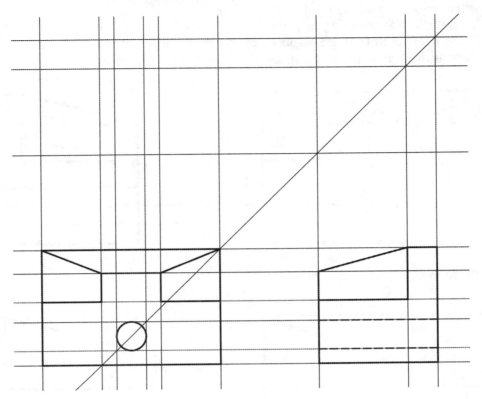

3) Turn the **Construction** layer off.

Click on the light bulb to turn the layer off.

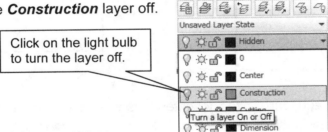

3.11.4) Drawing centerlines

1) In the **Center** layer, draw the centerlines for the hole in the front view.

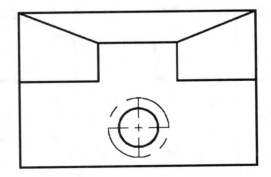

   a) Draw a concentric **CIRCLE** around the hole in the front view that is slightly larger than the hole but does not extend beyond the boundaries of the object.
   b) Draw a horizontal **LINE** from the left **Quadrant** of the new circle to the right **Quadrant**.
   c) Draw a vertical line in a similar way.
   d) **ERASE** the new circle that was drawn.

   e) Select the two center lines and enter the *Properties* window  (*View* tab). Change the line type scale to **0.7**.

2) Draw the centerline in the right side.
   a) Turn the *Polar tracking* on.
   b) Draw a **LINE** from the **Endpoint** of the horizontal centerline in the front view to **Perpendicular** to the back visible line of the right side view.

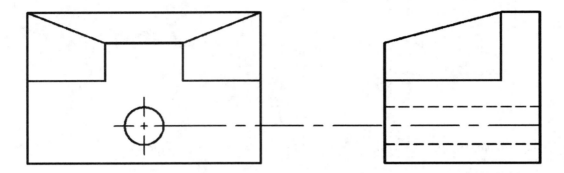

   c) **TRIM** this centerline as shown.

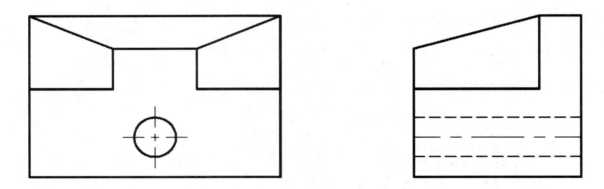

   d) Use polar tracking and grip boxes to extend each end of the centerline 0.25 inches beyond the visible lines.

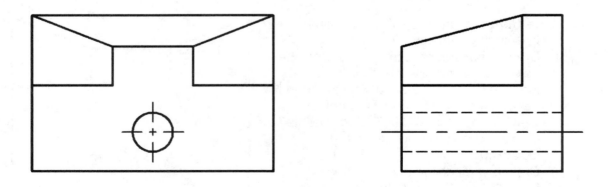

3) Follow the same steps to create the centerline in the top view.

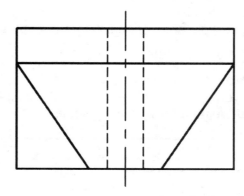

4) Use the **MOVE** command to center all three views within your limits.

5)

3.11.6) Printing the layout

1) Select the *Layout1* tab at the bottom of your drawing screen.

2) Insert your landscape title block.

   a) <u>Command:</u> **insert**   or   *Block* <u>panel:</u>

   b) *Insert* <u>widow:</u>
      i. Use the **Browse...** button to locate and open you *Title land.dwg* block.
      ii. Scale = 1 (uniform)
      iii. Rotation angle = 0
      iv. *Insertion point* <u>area:</u> Select the ***Specify On-screen*** checkbox and manually specify an insertion point that centers your title block within the printable area. The printable area is indicated by a dashed line. The size of this area depends on the type of printer being used.
      v. ***OK***

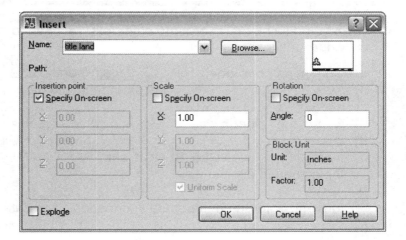

3) Notice the features of the layout (see the figure below). Don't worry about your line type scale. It will still print out correctly. At this point, you should see…
   - The border of the 8.5x11 sheet of paper.
   - The border of the printable area. The size of the printable area is printer dependent.
   - The viewport border.
   - The orthographic projection is in model space.
   - The rectangle that you drew to indicate the 11x8.5 limits. Therefore the objects in the model are not being shown at a 1:1 scale relative to paper space.

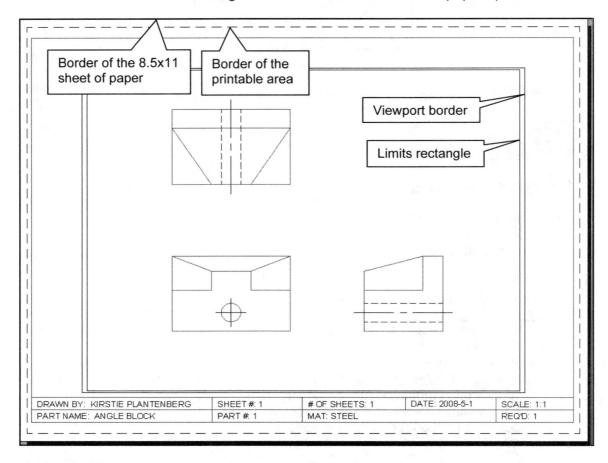

| DRAWN BY: KIRSTIE PLANTENBERG | SHEET #: 1 | # OF SHEETS: 1 | DATE: 2008-5-1 | SCALE: 1:1 |
| PART NAME: ANGLE BLOCK | PART #: 1 | MAT: STEEL | | REQ'D: 1 |

4) Fill in your title block. In order to enter text, we need to break the title block into its individual entities.

   a) Command: **explode**   or   *Modify* panel:
   b) Select objects: Select any part of the title block.
   c) Select objects: **Enter**
   d) Command: **ddedit**   or   Double click on the word to edit
   e) Select an annotation object or [Undo]: Select *PART NAME:* in your title block. Type in **ANGLE BLOCK** after PART NAME: and then click anywhere on the screen to exit the word.
   f) Select an annotation object or [Undo]: Select each title block entry in turn and enter the appropriate information. The date will be different.
   g) Select an annotation object or [Undo]: **Enter**

5) Click on the viewport border to activate its grip boxes. Using the grip boxes, resize the viewport border so that it is just inside your title block border.

6) With the view port still selected, notice that at *Viewport Scale* is added to the *Status* bar. The *Viewport Scale* indicates the scale at which object within the view port are shown relative to the paper space. If you have more than one view port, each view port may have a different scale.

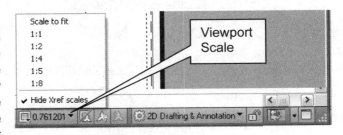

7) Click on the *Viewport Scale* and change it to **1:1**.

8) Double click inside the viewport border. This activates the model space and the viewport border will thicken. **PAN** the orthographic projection so that it is centered within the title block border. Double click outside the viewport border to re-enter paper space.

9) Change your viewport border to the **Layout** layer. Turn **OFF** your *Layout* layer.

10) Set your pen widths and prepare to print.
   a) *Menu browser.* **Print – Page Setup...**
   b) *Page Setup Manager* window: **Modify...**
   c) *Page Setup – Layout1* window:
      i. Select a printer.
      ii. Plot the Layout.
      iii. Select a 1:1 scale.
      iv. *Plot style table (pen assignments)* area: Select **monochrome.ctb** from the pull-down menu.

      v. Select the **Edit...** 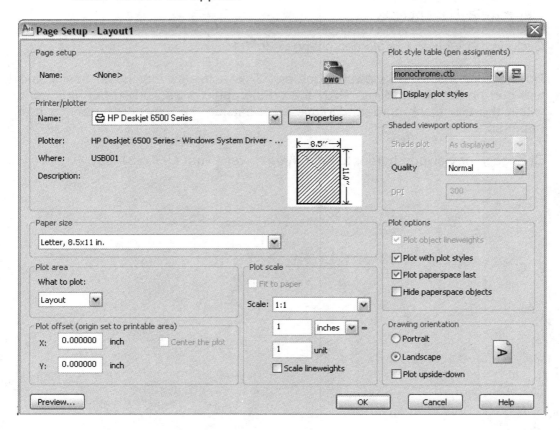 icon next to the pull-down menu. A *Plot Style Table Editor* window will appear.

d) *Plot Style Table Editor – monochrome.ctb* window:
   iii. *Plot styles* field: Select **Color 1** (red – visible line color).
   iv. *Lineweight* field: Select **0.6000 mm** from the pull-down menu.
   v. Follow the same procedure to set the widths of the other lines types.
      * **Color 5** (blue – hidden) = **0.45 mm**
      * **Color 7** (black – center and dimension lines) = **0.3 mm**
   vi. **Save & Close**
e) *Page Setup – Layout1* window: **OK**
f) *Page Setup Manager* window: **Close**

Note: Every setting except the pen widths are saved within the drawing file and will not change unless you change them. The pen widths are computer specific and will have to be re-entered if you change computers.

11) Plot your drawing.
    a) *Menu Browser:*
       Print – Plot....
    b) *Plot - Layout1*
       window:
       Preview...
    c) If the plot preview
       is what you want
       to print, hit `Esc`.
    d) *Plot - Layout1*
       window: **OK**

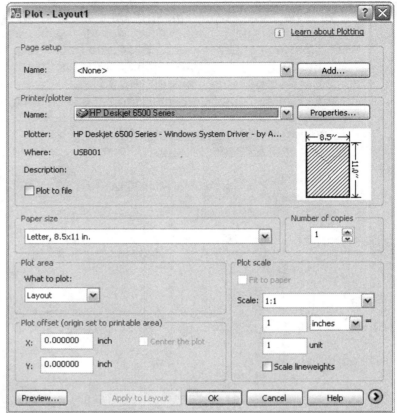

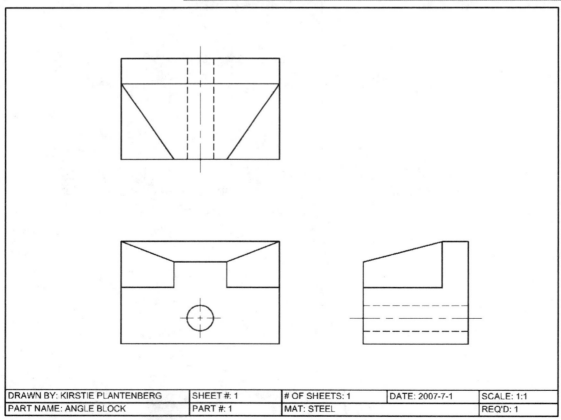

DRAWN BY: KIRSTIE PLANTENBERG	SHEET #: 1	# OF SHEETS: 1	DATE: 2007-7-1	SCALE: 1:1
PART NAME: ANGLE BLOCK	PART #: 1	MAT: STEEL		REQ'D: 1

12) Switch back to your model space by clicking the **Model** tab at the bottom of the drawing screen. Notice that your title block disappears. This is because layout objects do not appear in the model space.

13)

3.11.7) Printing a metric drawing

1)  **ortho_metric_student_2010.dwg**. This file contains a metric version of the orthographic projection completed in the previous sections.

2) 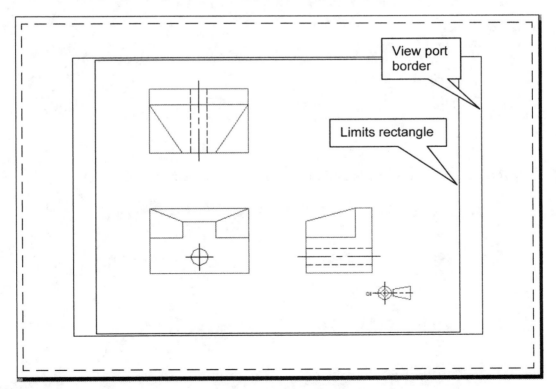 **Ortho Metric Tut.dwg**

3) Verify that the drawing is indeed metric. On the **Layout** layer, draw a limits **RECTANGLE** that is **280 x 216** mm whose lower left corner starts at **0,0**.

4) **ZOOM ALL**

5) Enter **Layout** space. Notice that the sheet does not have the same proportions as an 8.5 x 11 sheet of paper. The default metric paper size is 210 x 297 mm.

6) We will be printing out on an 8.5 x 11 sheet of paper. Enter the *Page Setup – Layout1* window (**Print – Page Setup...**) and set the following parameter.
   a) Paper size = **8.5 x 11**.
   b) Plot scale area:
      i. Scale = **Custom**
      ii. **1 inches** = **25.4** units
   c) Plot style = **monochrome.ctb**

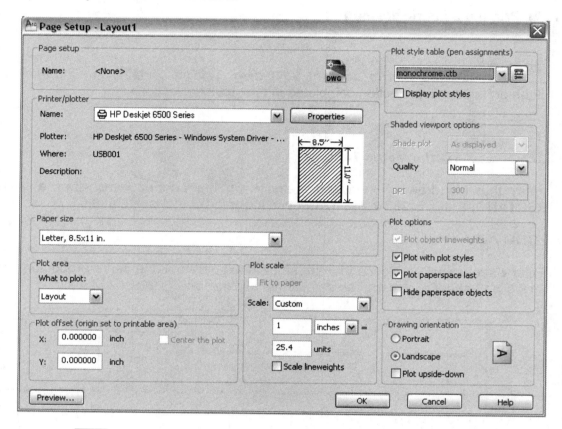

7) **INSERT** 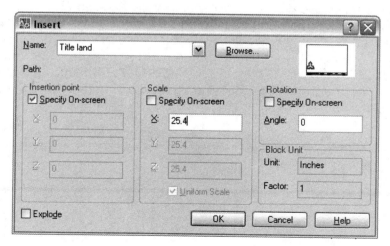 your title block and border using a **25.4** scale.

8) Fill in your title block, adjust your view port border, set the **Viewport Scale** to 1:1, center your model, change your viewport border to the *Layout* layer, turn the *Layout* layer off, save and print your drawing.

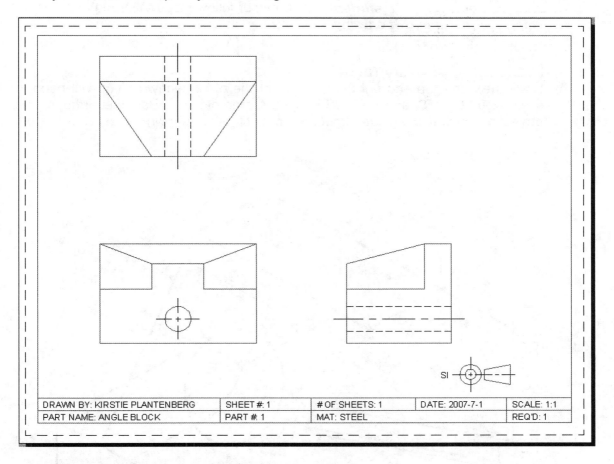

| DRAWN BY: KIRSTIE PLANTENBERG | SHEET #: 1 | # OF SHEETS: 1 | DATE: 2007-7-1 | SCALE: 1:1 |
| PART NAME: ANGLE BLOCK | PART #: 1 | MAT: STEEL | | REQ'D: 1 |

3.12) AUXILIARY VIEW TUTORIAL

The objective of this tutorial is to draw an orthographic projection with an auxiliary view. Objects often contain inclined surfaces. When the features on these inclined surfaces are not shown true size in any of the principle views (Front, Top, Right Side), an auxiliary view is used. The projection plane used to create the auxiliary view is not vertical or horizontal like those used to create the principle views, but it is parallel to the inclined surface. This allows the features on the inclined surface to be shown true size in the auxiliary view. We will draw the principle views of the orthographic projection in the usual way. The auxiliary view will be created by rotating the user coordinate system.

3.12.1) Drawing the orthographic projection

1) [Open] *auxiliary_tut_student_2010.dwg* or follow steps a) through c).

   a) Open your *set-mm.dwt* drawing template.

   b) [Save As] **Auxiliary Tut.dwg**.

   c) Draw the front, top and right side views of the object shown. You will need to scale your LIMITS and LTSCALE by a factor of 2.5. Use the orthographic projection shown as a guide. Important projectors are shown.

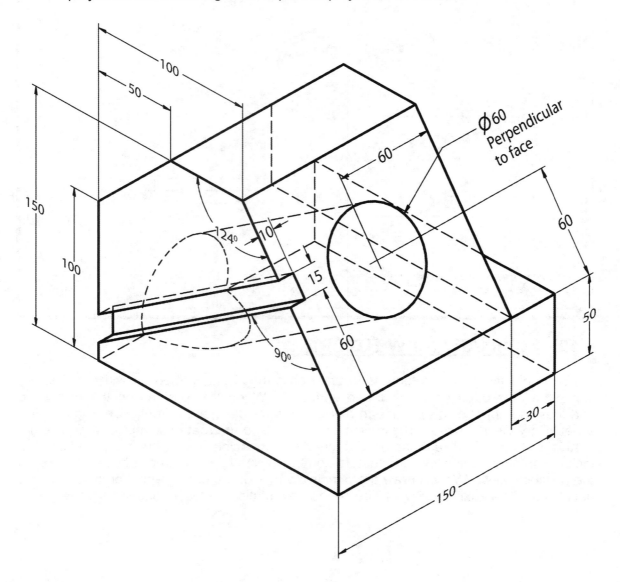

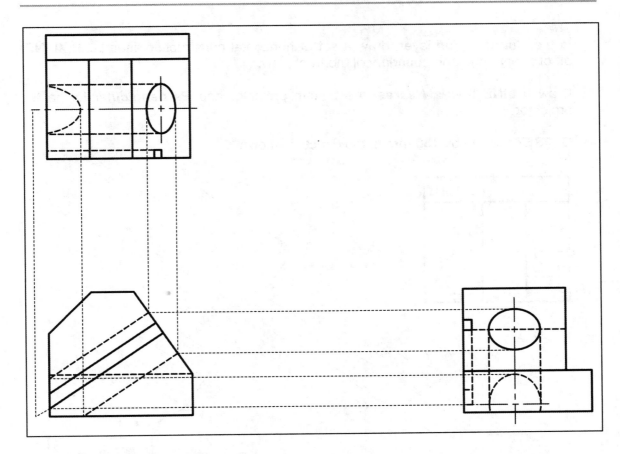

3.12.2) Creating the auxiliary view

1) Rotate your UCS so that the x axis is perpendicular to the angled face.

    a) *View* tab - *Coordinate* panel:

    b) `Specify rotation angle about Z axis <90>:` **34**

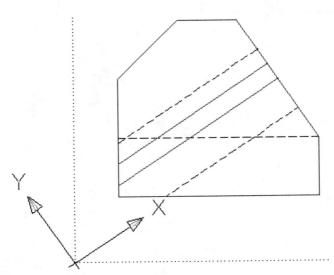

2) In the **Construction** layer, draw a set of horizontal construction lines 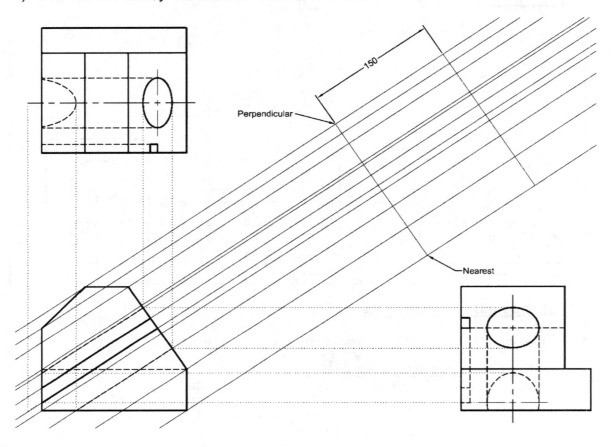 (**XLINE**) off of every edge and boundary of the front view.

3) Draw a **LINE** that is **Nearest** the bottom projector and **Perpendicular** to the top projector.

4) **OFFSET** the line by **150 mm** in the direction shown.

5) Fill in the features of the auxiliary view. Create construction lines where necessary.

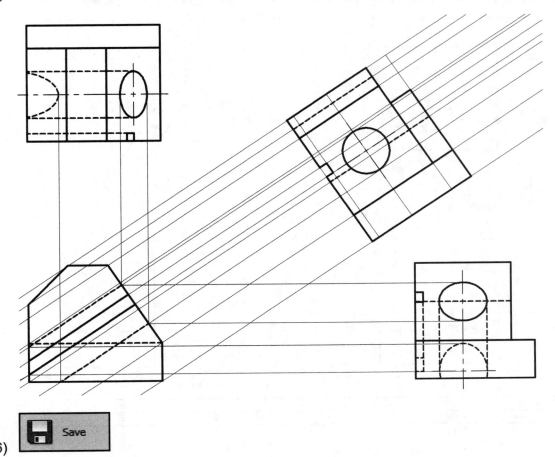

6)

7) Make the necessary preparations and print you drawing and title block.

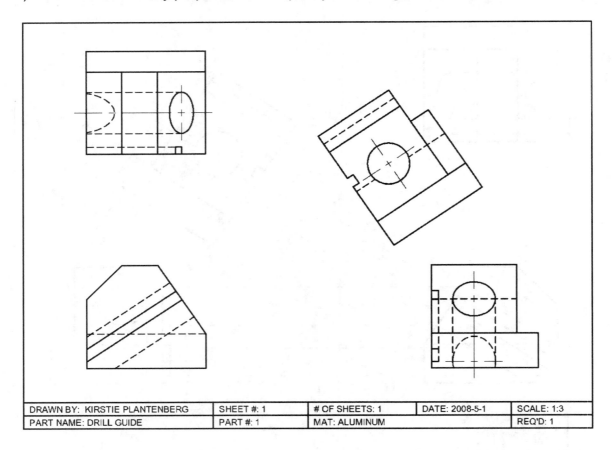

DRAWN BY: KIRSTIE PLANTENBERG	SHEET #: 1	# OF SHEETS: 1	DATE: 2008-5-1	SCALE: 1:3
PART NAME: DRILL GUIDE	PART #: 1	MAT: ALUMINUM		REQ'D: 1

CREATING ORTHOGRAPHIC PROJECTIONS IN AUTOCAD CROSSWORD PUZZLE

Name: _____ Date: _____

CP3-1)

Across

3. What pen styles table is used if you want to print in black and white?
4. The command used to break a block up into its individual components.
6. What typed command is used to write a block to a file?
8. Lines occurring on a LOCKED or OFF layer may not be selected. Which layer status still allows you to see the lines?
10. What layer property controls an entity's printed width.
11. The place/window where you can change a layers color, linetype and status.
14. To change the line type scale of an individual object, you must enter the .... window.

Down

1. The layer you are drawing on is said to be ....
2. The typed command used to edit existing text.
5. The typed command that is used to control the length of the dashes and spaces of the different line types.
7. A grouping of objects that may be reused.
9. How do you access model space from within paper space?
12. The space where you see exactly what is going to be printed.
13. The construction layer is used to create projection lines. When the orthographic projection is complete we do not need these lines anymore. The easiest way to not show the projection lines is to turn the construction layer ....

CREATING ORTHOGRAPHIC PROJECTIONS IN AUTOCAD PROBLEMS

P3-1) Use AutoCAD to create an orthographic projection of the following object. Draw the three standard views. Print using appropriate pen widths and insert a title block.

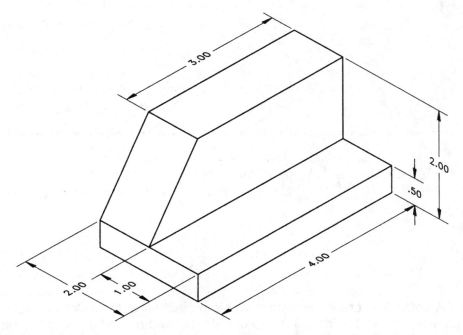

P3-2) Use AutoCAD to create an orthographic projection of the following object. Draw the three standard views. Print using appropriate pen widths and insert a title block.

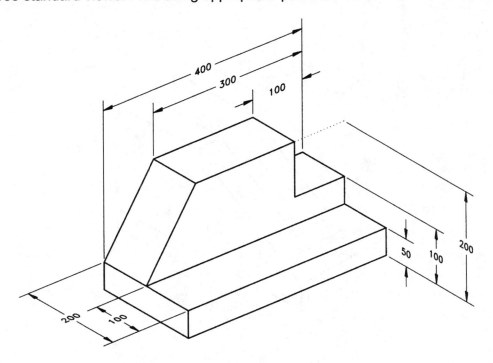

P3-3) Use AutoCAD to create an orthographic projection of the following object. Draw the three standard views. Print using appropriate pen widths and insert a title block.

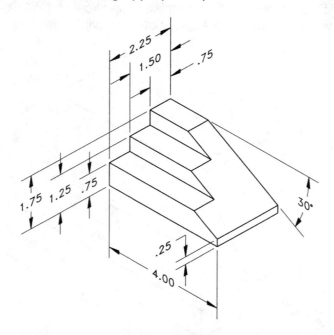

P3-4) Use AutoCAD to create an orthographic projection of the following object. Draw the three standard views. Print using appropriate pen widths and insert a title block.

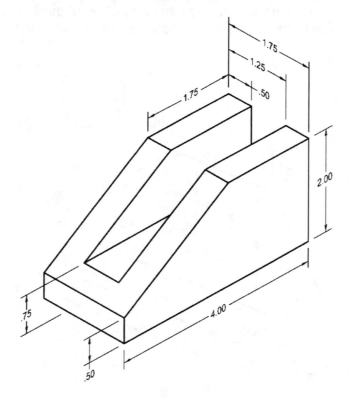

P3-9) Use AutoCAD to create an orthographic projection of the following object. Draw the three standard views. Print using appropriate pen widths and insert a title block.

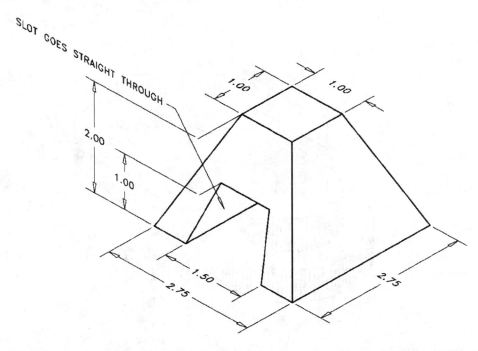

P3-10) Use AutoCAD to create an orthographic projection of the following object. Draw the three standard views. Print using appropriate pen widths and insert a title block.

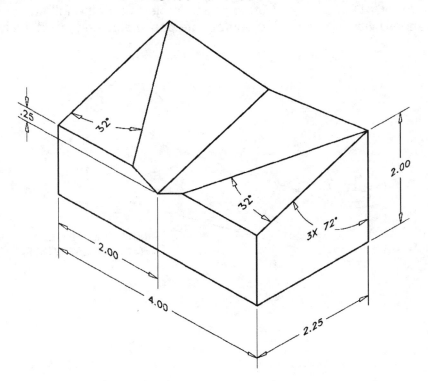

P3-11) Use AutoCAD to create an orthographic projection of the following object. Draw the three standard views. Print using appropriate pen widths and insert a title block.

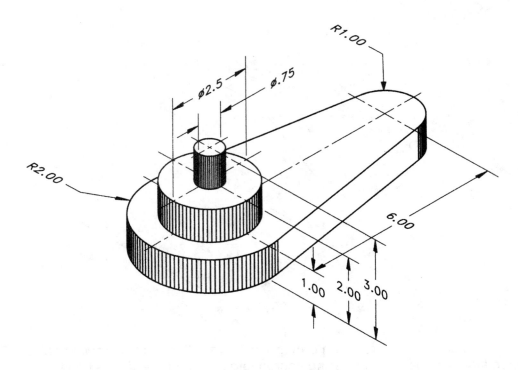

P3-12) Use AutoCAD to create an orthographic projection of the following object. Draw the three standard views. Print using appropriate pen widths and insert a title block.

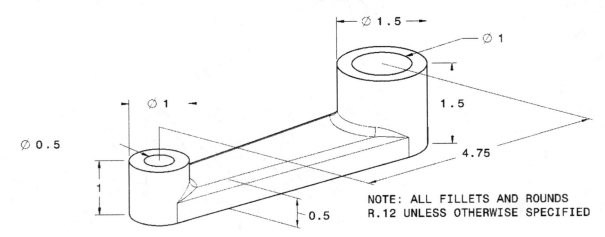

NOTE: ALL FILLETS AND ROUNDS
R.12 UNLESS OTHERWISE SPECIFIED

P3-13) Use AutoCAD to create an orthographic projection of the following object. Draw the three standard views. Print using appropriate pen widths and insert a title block.

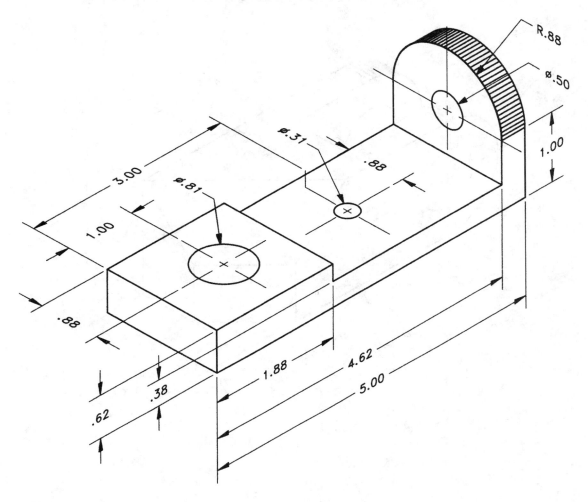

P3-14) Use AutoCAD to create an orthographic projection of the following object. Draw the three standard views. Print using appropriate pen widths and insert a title block.

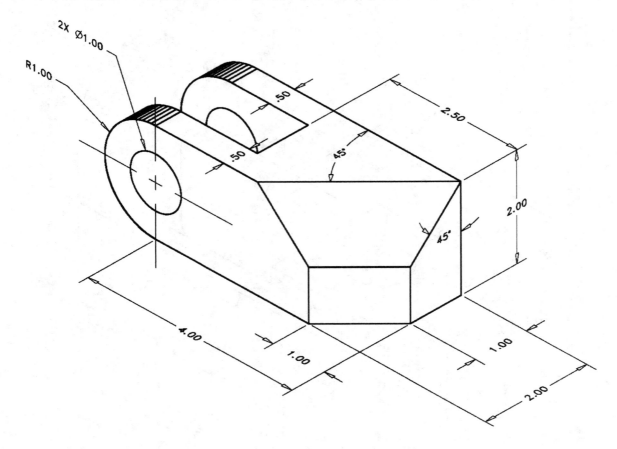

P3-15) Use AutoCAD to create an orthographic projection of the following object. Draw the three standard views. Print using appropriate pen widths and insert a title block.

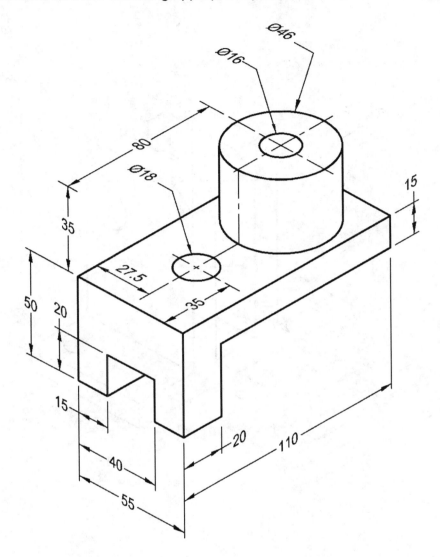

P3-16) Use AutoCAD to create an orthographic projection of the following object. Draw the three standard views. Print using appropriate pen widths and insert a title block.

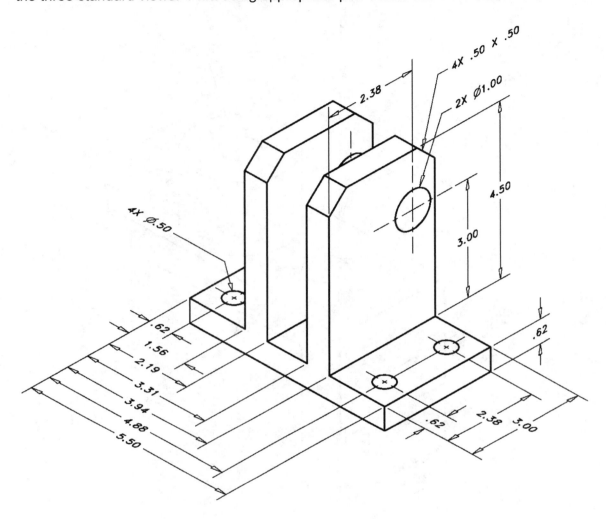

P3-17) Use AutoCAD to create an orthographic projection of the following object. Draw the three standard views. Print using appropriate pen widths and insert a title block.

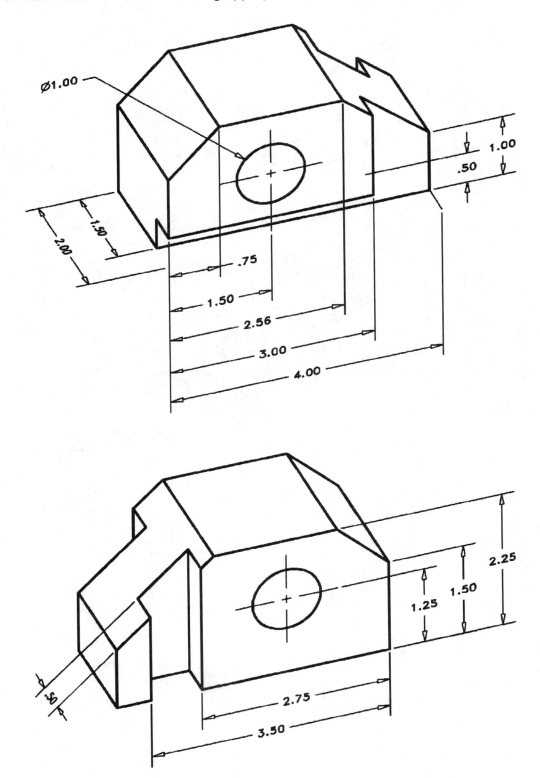

P3-18) Use AutoCAD to create an orthographic projection of the following object. Draw the three standard views. Print using appropriate pen widths and insert a title block.

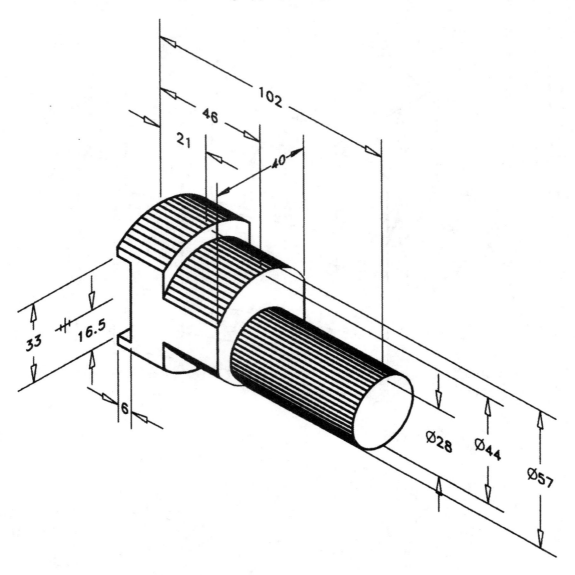

P3-19) Use AutoCAD to create an orthographic projection of the following object. Draw the three standard views. Print using appropriate pen widths and insert a title block.

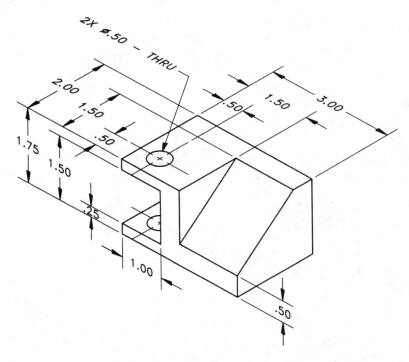

P3-20) Use AutoCAD to create an orthographic projection of the following object. Draw the three standard views. Print using appropriate pen widths and insert a title block.

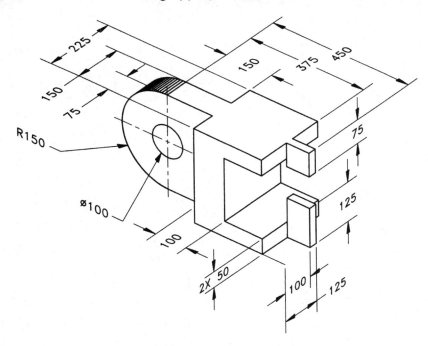

P3-21) Use AutoCAD to create an orthographic projection of the following object. Draw the three standard views. Print using appropriate pen widths and insert a title block.

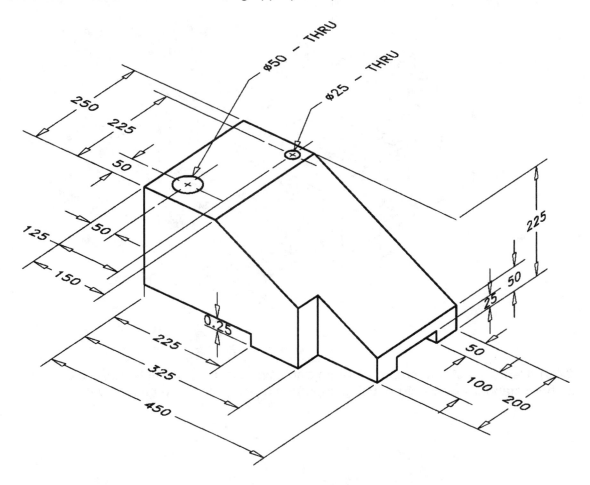

P3-22) Use AutoCAD to create an orthographic projection of the following object. Draw the three standard views. Print using appropriate pen widths and insert a title block.

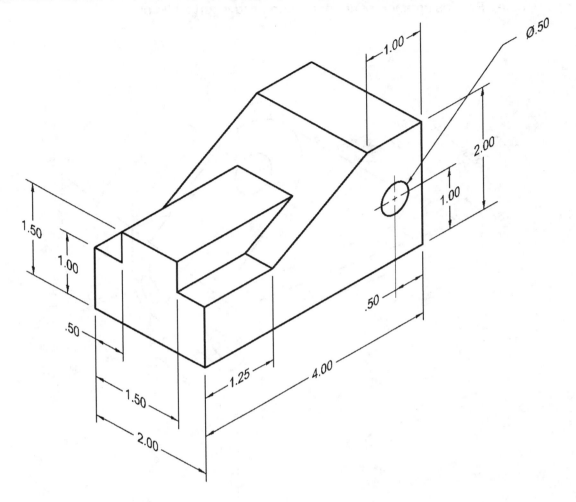

P3-23) Use AutoCAD to create an orthographic projection of the following object. Draw an auxiliary view that shows the angled surface true shape. Use partial views where appropriate. Print using appropriate pen widths and insert a title block.

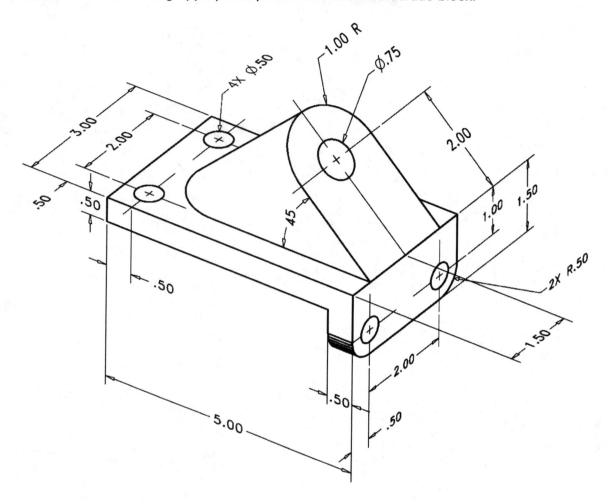

P3-24) Use AutoCAD to create an orthographic projection of the following object. Draw an auxiliary view that shows the angled surface true shape. Use partial views where appropriate. Print using appropriate pen widths and insert a title block.

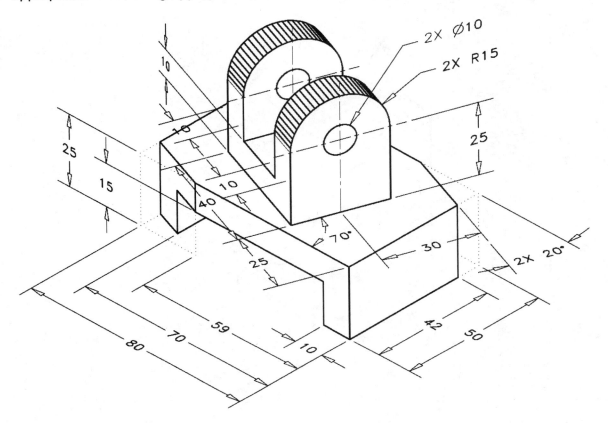

P3-25) Use AutoCAD to create an orthographic projection of the following object. Draw two auxiliary views that show the angled features true shape. Use partial views where appropriate. Print using appropriate pen widths and insert a title block.

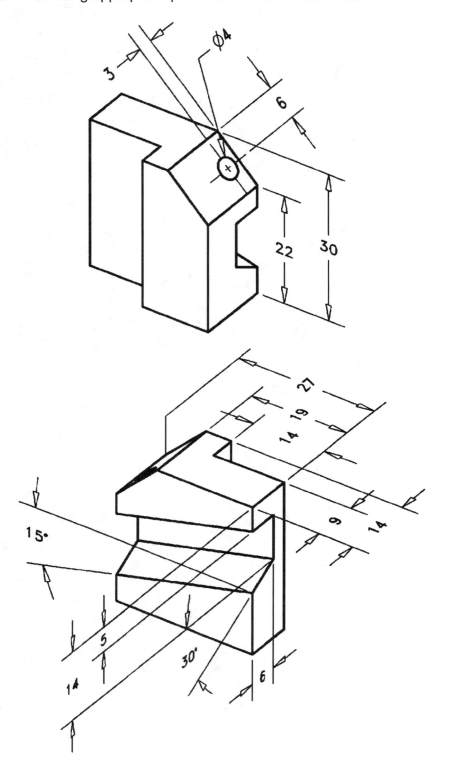

P3-26) Use AutoCAD to create an orthographic projection of the following object. Draw an auxiliary view that shows the angled feature true shape. Use partial views where appropriate. Print using appropriate pen widths and insert a title block.

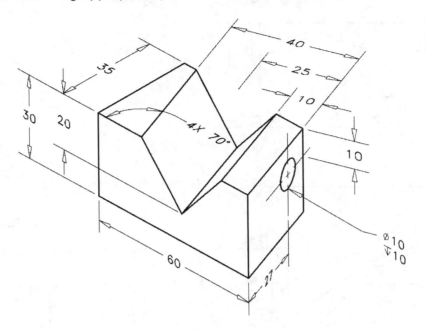

P3-27) Use AutoCAD to create an orthographic projection of the following object. Draw an auxiliary view that shows the angled surface true shape. Use partial views where appropriate. Print using appropriate pen widths and insert a title block.

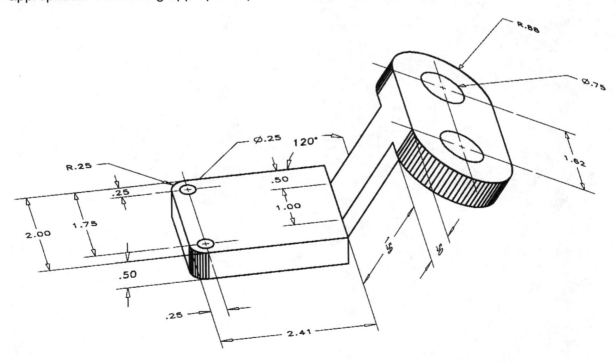

P3-28) Use AutoCAD to create an orthographic projection of the following object. Draw an auxiliary view that shows the angled surface true shape. Use partial views where appropriate. Print using appropriate pen widths and insert a title block.

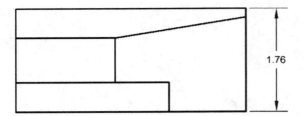

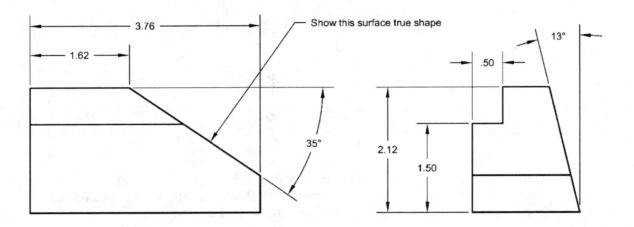

P3-29) Use AutoCAD to create an orthographic projection of the following object. Draw an auxiliary view that shows the angled surface true shape. Use partial views where appropriate. Print using appropriate pen widths and insert a title block.

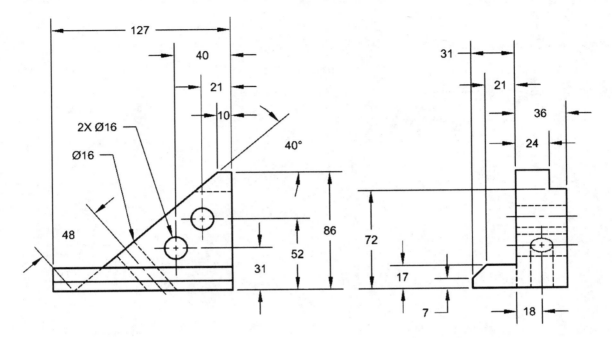

NOTES:

DIMENSIONING

In Chapter 4 you will learn how to dimension an orthographic projection using proper dimensioning techniques. This may seem like a simple task; however, dimensioning a part is not as easy as inserting the sizes used to draw the part. Dimensions affect how a part is manufactured. A small change in how an object is dimensioned may produce a part that will not pass inspection. The type and placement of the dimensions and the dimension text is highly controlled by ASME standards (American Society of Mechanical Engineers). By the end of this chapter, you will be able to dimension a moderately complex part using proper dimensioning techniques. CAUTION! Dimensioning complex/production parts require the knowledge of GD&T (Geometric Dimensioning & Tolerancing).

4.1) DETAILED DRAWINGS

In addition to the shape description of an object given by an orthographic projection, engineering drawings must also give a complete size description using dimensions. This enables the object to be manufactured. **An orthographic projection, complete with all the dimensions and specifications needed to manufacture the object is called a *detailed drawing*.** Figure 4-1 shows an example of a detailed drawing.

Dimensioning a part correctly entails conformance to many rules. It is very tempting to dimension an object using the measurements needed to draw the part. But, these are not necessarily the dimensions required to manufacture it. Generally accepted dimensioning standards should be used when dimensioning any object. Basically, the dimensions should be given in a clear and concise manner and should include all the information needed to produce and inspect the part exactly as intended by the designer. There should be no need to measure the size of a feature directly from the drawing.

The dimensioning standards presented in this chapter are in accordance with the ASME Y14.5M-1994 standard. Other common sense practices will also be presented.

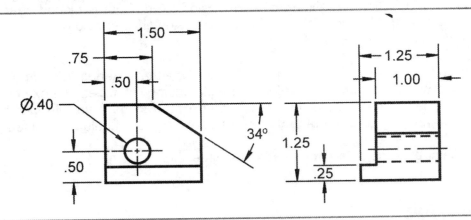

Figure 4-1: Detailed drawing

4.2) **LEARNING TO DIMENSION**

Proper dimensioning techniques require the knowledge of the following three areas.

1) <u>Dimension Appearance and Techniques:</u> Dimensions use special lines, arrows, symbols and text. In Section 4.3 (Dimension Appearance and Techniques) we will learn:

   a) The lines used in dimensioning.
   b) Types of dimensions.
   c) Dimension symbols.
   d) Dimension spacing and readability.
   e) Dimension placement.

2) <u>Dimensioning and Locating Features:</u> Different types of features require unique methods of dimensioning.

3) <u>Dimension Choice:</u> Your choice of dimensions will directly influence the method used to manufacture a part. Learning the following topics will guide you when choosing your dimension units, decimal places and the dimension's starting point:

   a) Units and decimal places.
   b) Locating features using datums.
   c) Dimension accuracy and error build up.

4.3) **DIMENSION APPEARANCE AND TECHNIQUES**

4.3.1) **Lines Used in Dimensioning**

Dimensioning requires the use of *dimension*, *extension* and *leader lines*. **All lines used in dimensioning are drawn thin so that they will not be confused with visible lines.** Thin lines should be drawn at approximately 0.3 mm or 0.016 inch.

- <u>Dimension line:</u> A dimension line is a thin solid line terminated by arrowheads, which indicates the direction and extent of a dimension. A number is placed near the mid point to specify the feature's size. Ideally, dimension lines should be broken to allow for the insertion of the feature's size.

- <u>Extension line:</u> An extension line is a thin solid line that extends from a point on the drawing to which the dimension refers. The dimension line meets the extension lines at right angles, except in special cases. **There should be a visible gap between the extension line and the object**. Long extension lines should be avoided.

Figure 4-2 illustrates the different features of a dimension.

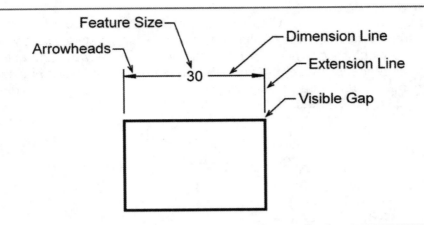

Figure 4-2: Features of a dimension.

- Leader line: A leader line is a straight inclined thin solid line that is usually terminated by an arrowhead. It is used to direct a dimension, note, symbol, item number, or part number to the intended feature on a drawing. The leader is not vertical or horizontal, except for a short horizontal portion extending to the first or last letter of the note. The horizontal part should not underline the note and may be omitted entirely.

The leader may be terminated:
  a) with an arrow, if it ends on the outline of an object.
  b) with a dot (Ø1.5 mm, minimum), if it ends within the outline of an object.
  c) without an arrowhead or dot, if it ends within the outline of an object.

When creating leader lines, the following should be avoided:
  a) Crossing leaders.
  b) Long leaders.
  c) Leaders that are parallel to adjacent dimension, extension or section lines.
  d) Small angles between the leader and the terminating surface.

Figure 4-3 illustrates different leader line configurations.

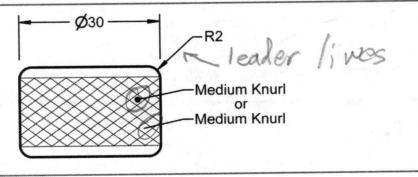

Figure 4-3: Leader line configurations.

- Arrowheads: The length and width ratio of an arrowhead should be 3 to 1 and the width should be proportional to the line thickness. A single style of arrowhead should be used throughout the drawing. Arrowheads are drawn between the extension lines if possible. If space is limited, they may be drawn on the outside. Figure 4-4 shows the most common arrowhead configurations.

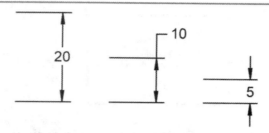

Figure 4-4: Arrowhead and feature size placement.

4.3.2) Types of Dimensions

Dimensions are given in the form of *linear distances*, *angles*, and *notes*.

- Linear distances: A linear dimension is used to give the distance between two points. They are usually arranged horizontally or vertically, but may also be aligned with a particular feature of the part.

- Angles: An angular dimension is used to give the angle between two surfaces or features of a part.

- Notes: Notes are used to dimension diameters, radii, chamfers, threads, and other features that can not be dimensioned by the other two methods.

Instructor Led Exercise 4-1: Dimension types

In Figure 4-1, count the different types of dimensions.

- How many linear horizontal dimensions are there?
- How many linear vertical dimensions are there?
- How many angular dimensions are there?
- How many leader line notes are there?

4.3.3) Lettering

Lettering should be legible, easy to read, and uniform throughout the drawing. **Upper case** letters should be used for all lettering unless a lower case is required. **The minimum lettering height is 0.12 in (3 mm).**

4.3.4) Dimensioning Symbols

Dimensioning symbols replace text and are used to minimize language barriers. Many companies produce parts all over the world. A print made in the U.S.A. may have to be read in several different countries. The goal of using dimensioning symbols it to eliminate the need for language translation. Table 4-1 shows some commonly used dimensioning symbols. These symbols will be used and explained throughout the chapter.

Term	Symbol	Term	Symbol
Diameter	∅	Depth / Deep	∇
Spherical diameter	S∅	Dimension not to scale	10
Radius	R	Square (Shape)	□
Spherical radius	SR	Arc length	$\hat{5}$
Reference dimension	(8)	Conical Taper	▷
Counterbore / Spotface	⊔	Slope	◁
Countersink	∨	Symmetry	⩦
Number of places	4X		

Table 4-1: Dimensioning symbols.

4.3.5) Dimension Spacing and Readability

Dimensions should be easy to read and minimize the possibility for conflicting interpretations. Dimensions should be given clearly and in an organized fashion. They should not be crowded or hard to read. The following is a list of rules that control dimension spacing and readability:

a) The spacing between dimension lines should be uniform throughout the drawing. The space between the first dimension line and the part should be at least 10 mm; the space between subsequent dimension should be at least 6 mm. However, the above spacing is only intended as a guide.

b) Do not dimension inside an object or have the dimension line touch the object unless clearness is gained.

c) Dimension text should be horizontal which means that it is read from the bottom of the drawing.

d) Dimension text should not cross dimension, extension or visible lines.

Instructor Led Exercise 4-2: Spacing and readability 1

Consider the incorrectly dimensioned object shown. There are 5 types of dimensioning mistakes. List them and then dimension the object correctly.

1)   4)
2)   5)
3)

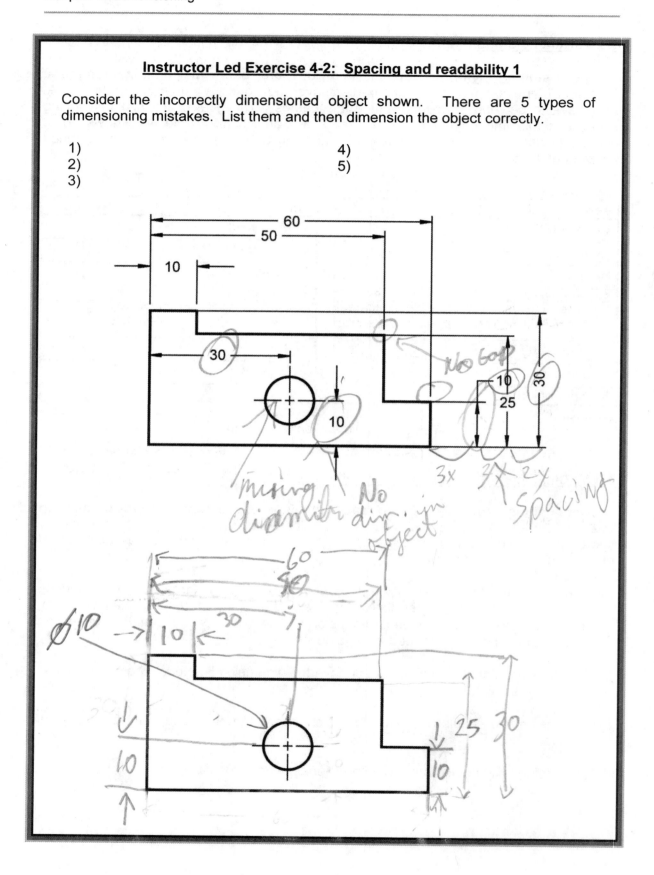

e) Dimension lines should not cross extension lines or other dimension lines. To avoid this, shorter dimensions should be placed before longer ones. Extension lines can cross other extension lines or visible lines. However, this should be minimized. Where extension lines cross other lines, the extension lines are not broken. If an extension line crosses an arrowhead or is near an arrowhead, a break in the extension line is permitted.

f) Extension lines and centerlines should not connect between views.

g) Leader lines should be straight, not curved, and point to the center of the arc or circle at an angle between 30°-60°. The leaders should *float* or, in other words, lead from the arrow up to the text.

Try Exercise 4-3.

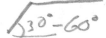

h) Dimensions should not be duplicated or the same information given in two different ways. The use of reference (duplicated) dimensions should be minimized. Duplicate dimensions may cause needless trouble. If a change is made to one dimension, the reference dimension may be overlooked causing confusion. If a reference dimension is used, the size value is placed within parentheses (e.g. (10)).

Try Exercise 4-4.

4.3.6) Dimension Placement

Dimensions should be placed in such a way as to enhance the communication of your design. The following are rules that govern the logical and practical arrangement of dimensions to insure maximum legibility:

a) Dimensions should be grouped whenever possible.

b) Dimensions should be placed between views, unless clearness is promoted by placing some outside.

c) Dimensions should be attached to the view where the shape is shown best.

d) Do not dimension hidden lines.

Try Exercise 4-5.

Instructor Led Exercise 4-3: Spacing and readability 2

Consider the incorrectly dimensioned object shown. There are 4 types of dimensioning mistakes. List them and then dimension the object correctly.

1)   3)

2)   4)

Instructor Led Exercise 4-4: Duplicate dimensions

Find the duplicate dimensions and cross out the ones that you feel should be omitted.

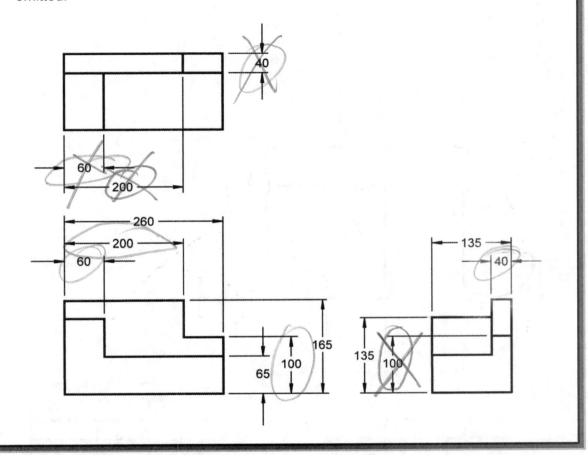

Instructor Led Exercise 4-5: Dimension placement

Consider the incorrectly dimensioned object shown. There are 6 types of dimensioning mistakes. List them and then dimension the object correctly.

1)   4)

2)   5)

3)   6)

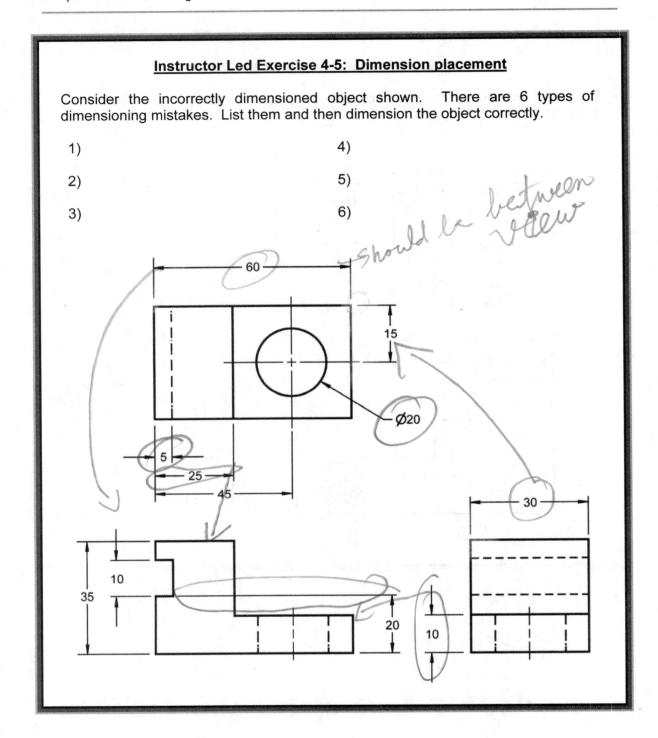

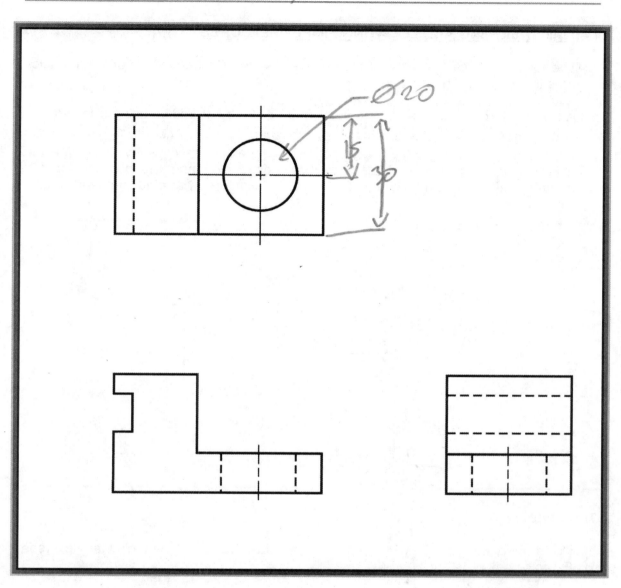

4.4) **DIMENSIONING AND LOCATING SIMPLE FEATURES**

The following section illustrates the standard ways of dimensioning different basics features that occur often on a part.

a) A circle is dimensioned by its diameter and an arc by its radius using a leader line and a note. A diameter dimension is preceded by the symbol "∅", and a radial dimension is preceded by the symbol "R". On older drawings you may see the abbreviation "DIA" placed after a diameter dimension and the abbreviation "R" following a radial dimension. Figure 4-5 illustrates the diameter and radius dimensions.

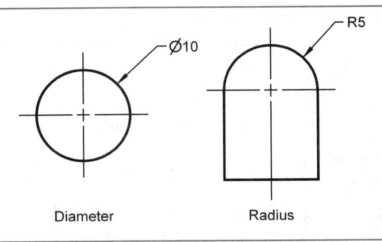

Diameter   Radius

Figure 4-5: Diameter and radius dimensions

Try Exercise 4-6

b) Holes are dimensioned by giving their diameter and location in the circular view (see Exercise 4-6).

c) A cylinder is dimensioned by giving its diameter and length in the rectangular view, and is located in the circular view. By giving the diameter of a cylinder in the rectangular view, it is less likely to be confused with a hole (see Exercise 4-6).

Instructor Led Exercise 4-6: Circular and rectangular views

Below is shown the front and top view of a part. Consider the hole and cylinder features of the part when answering the following questions.
- Which view is considered the circular view and which is considered the rectangular view?
- Looking at just the top view, can you tell the difference between the hole and the cylinder?

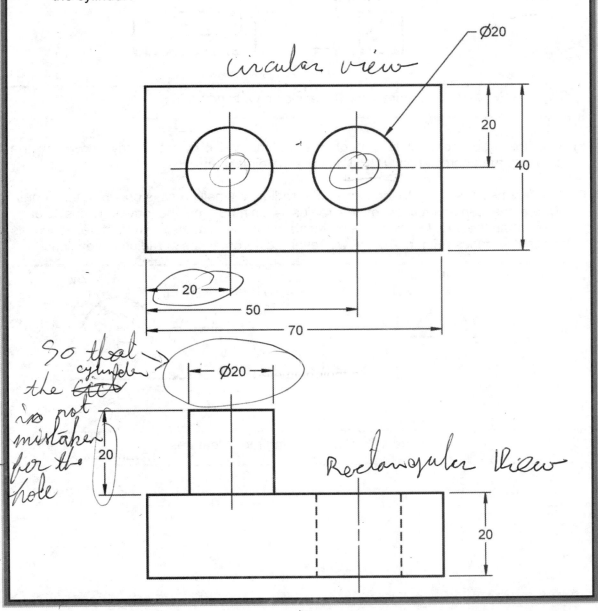

d) The depth of a blind hole may be specified in a note and is the depth of the full diameter from the surface of the object. Figure 4-6 illustrates how to dimension a blind hole (i.e. a hole that does not pass completely through the object).

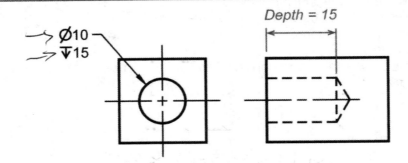

Figure 4-6: Dimensioning a blind hole.

e) If a hole goes completely through the feature and it is not clearly shown on the drawing, the abbreviation "THRU" follows the dimension.

f) If a dimension is given to the center of a radius, a small cross is drawn at the center. Where the center location of the radius is unimportant, the drawing must clearly show that the arc location is controlled by other dimensioned features such as tangent surfaces. Figure 4-7 shows several different types of radius dimensions.

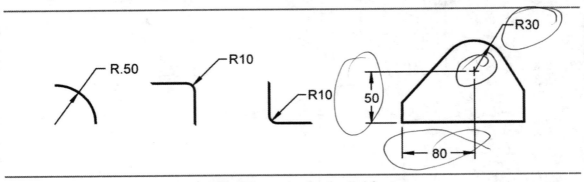

Figure 4-7: Dimensioning radial features.

g) A complete sphere is dimensioned by its diameter and an incomplete sphere by its radius. A spherical diameter is indicated by using the symbol "S∅" and a spherical radius by the symbol "SR". Figure 4-8 illustrates the spherical diameter and spherical radius dimensions.

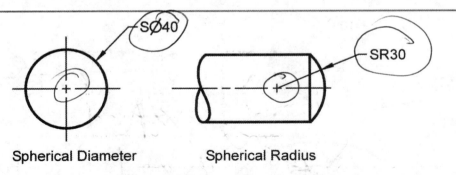

Spherical Diameter   Spherical Radius

Figure 4-8: Dimensioning spherical features.

h) Repetitive features or dimensions may be specified by using the symbol "X" along with the number of times the feature is repeated. There is no space between the number of times the feature is repeated and the "X" symbol, however, there is a space between the symbol "X" and the dimension (i.e. 8X ∅10).

Instructor Led Exercise 4-7: Dimensioning and locating features

Dimension the following object.

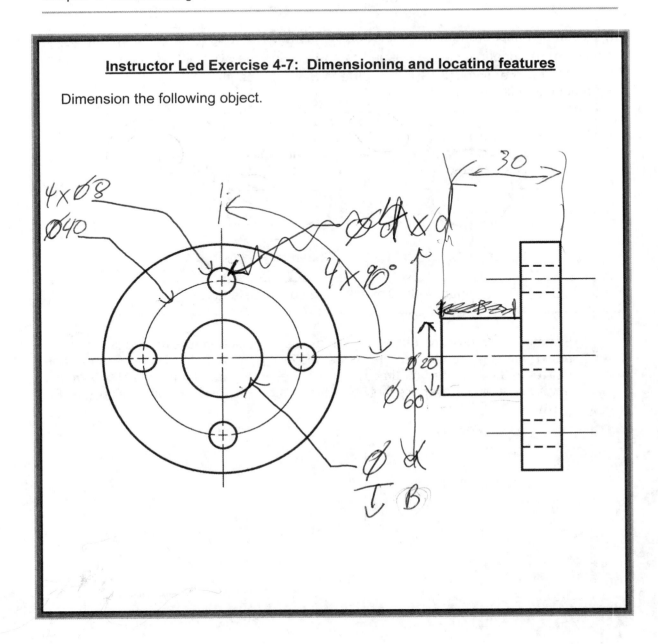

4.5) **DIMENSIONING AND LOCATING ADVANCED FEATURES**

The following section will illustrate the standard ways of dimensioning different features that occur often on a part.

a) If the center of a radius is outside the drawing or interferes with another view, the dimension lines may be foreshortened. In this case, a false center and jogged dimensions are used to give the size and location from the false center as shown in Figure 4-9. The false center is indicated by a small cross.

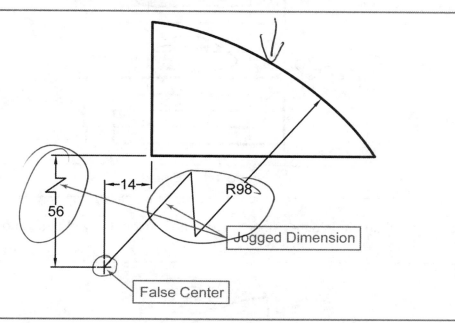

Figure 4-9: Jogged radius

b) Solid parts that have rounded ends are dimensioned by giving their overall dimensions (see Figure 4-10). If the ends are partially rounded, the radii are also given. For fully rounded ends, the radii are indicated but the value is not given.

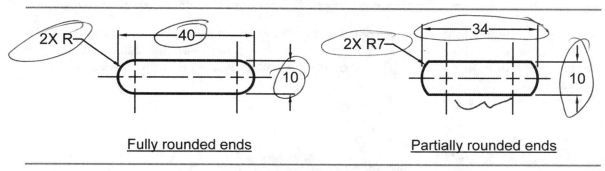

Fully rounded ends   Partially rounded ends

Figure 4-10: Rounded ends

c) Slots are dimensioned by giving their overall dimensions or by giving the overall width and the distance between centers as shown in Figure 4-11. The radii are indicated but the value is not given.

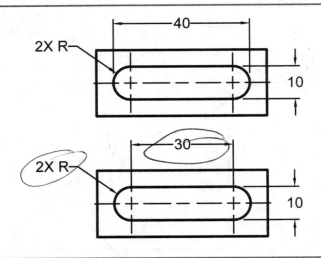

Figure 4-11: Slots

d) The length of an arc is dimensioned using the arc length symbol as shown in Figure 4-12.

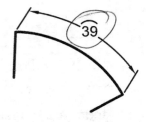

Figure 4-12: Arc length

e) Equally spaced features are specified by giving the number of spaces followed by the repeated feature symbol "X", a space, and then the dimension value of the space as shown in Figure 4-13. One space may be dimensioned and given as a reference value.

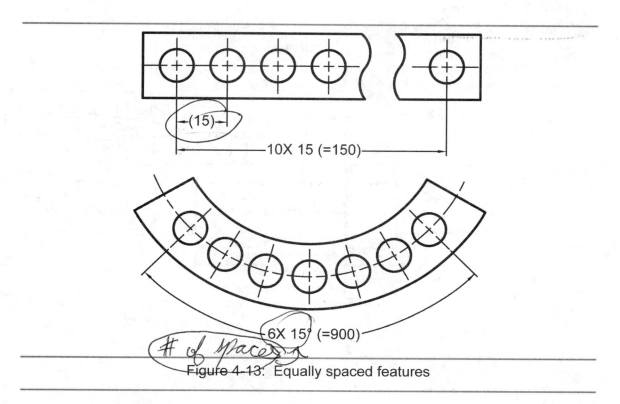

Figure 4-13: Equally spaced features

f)   If a part is symmetric, it is only necessary to dimension to one side of the center line of symmetry. The center line of symmetry is indicated by using the symbol "—". On older drawings you might see the symbol "℄" used instead. Figure 4-14 illustrates the use of the symmetry symbol.

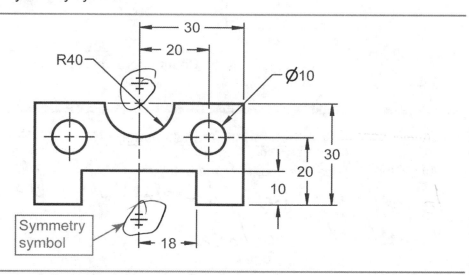

Figure 4-14: Center line of symmetry.

g) Counterbored holes are specified by giving the diameter ($\emptyset$) of the drill (and depth if appropriate), the diameter ($\emptyset$) of the counterbore ($\sqcup$), and the depth ($\overline{\vee}$) of the counterbore in a note as shown in Figure 4-15. If the thickness of the material below the counterbore is significant, this thickness rather than the counterbore depth is given.

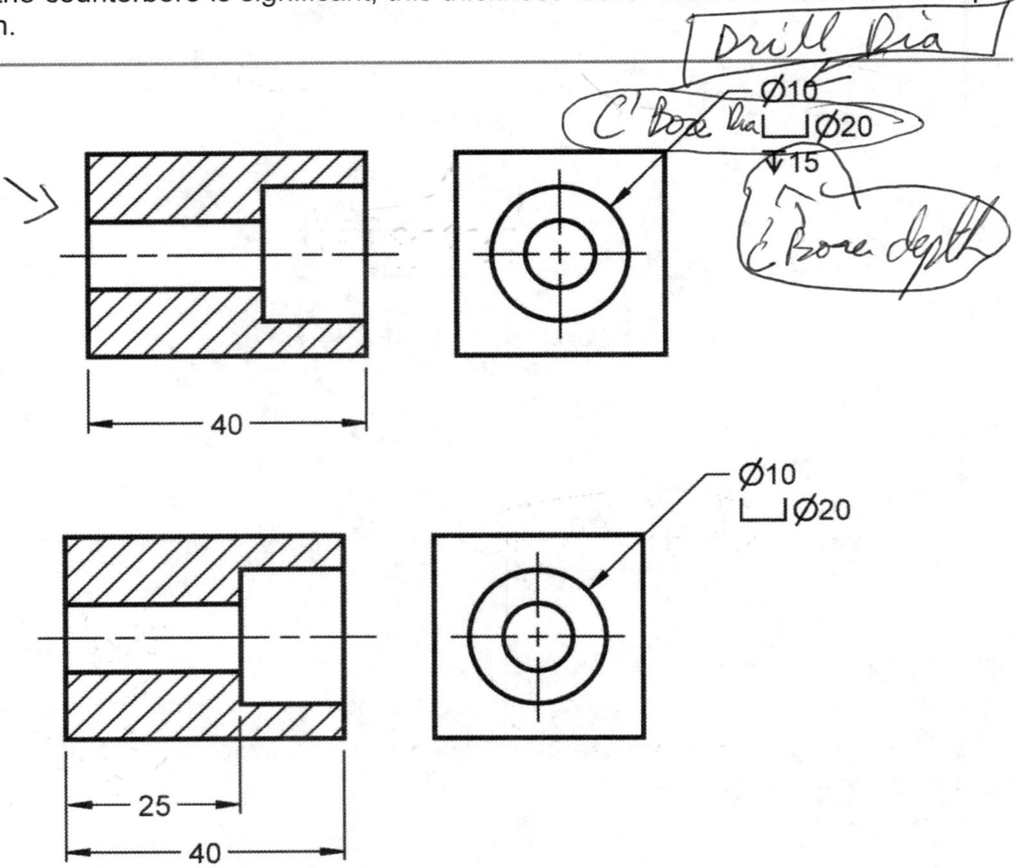

Drill Dia

C'Bore Dia

C'Bore depth

$\emptyset10$
$\sqcup \emptyset20$
$\overline{\vee}15$

$\emptyset10$
$\sqcup \emptyset20$

Figure 4-15: Counterbored holes.

Application Question 4-1

What is the purpose of a counterbored hole?

to recess a bolt so that it's flush with the surface.

h) Spotfaced holes are similar to counterbored holes. The difference is that the machining operation occurs on a curved surface. Therefore, the depth of the counterbore drill cannot be given in the note. It must be specified in the rectangular view as shown in Figure 4-16.

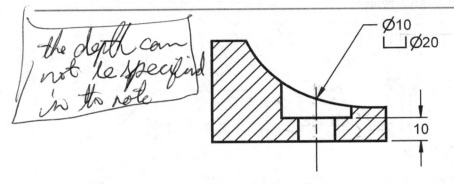

the depth can not be specified in the note

Ø10
⌴Ø20

10

Figure 4-16: Spotfaced holes.

i) Countersunk holes are specified by giving the diameter (Ø) of the drill (and depth if appropriate), the diameter (Ø) of the countersink (⌵), and the angle of the countersink in a note as shown in Figure 4-17.

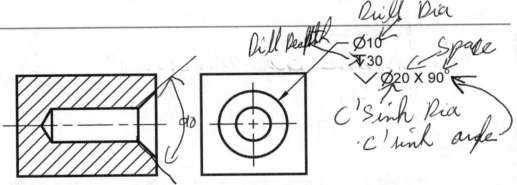

Drill Dia
Drill Depth
Ø10
▽30
Space
⌵ Ø20 X 90°
C'sink Dia
c'sink angle

Figure 4-17: Countersunk holes.

Application Question 4-2

What is the purpose of a countersunk hole?

Bolt = recess

---

j) Chamfers are dimensioned by a linear dimension and an angle, or by two linear dimensions. A note may be used to specify 45 degree chamfers because the linear value applies in either direction (see Figure 4-18). Notice that there is a space between the 'X' symbol and the linear dimension. The space is inserted so that it is not confused with a repeated feature.

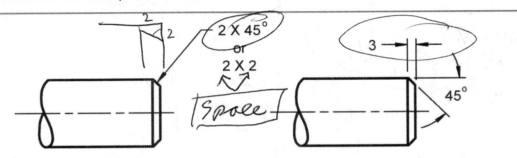

Figure 4-18: Chamfers.

Application Question 4-3

What is the purpose of a chamfer?

1) safety

2) improve engagement of mating parts.

4.5.1) Drawing Notes

Drawing notes give additional information that is used to complement conventional dimension. Drawing notes provide information that clarify the manufacturing requirements for the part. They cover information such as treatments and finishes among other manufacturing processes. A note may also be used to give blanket dimensions, such as the size of all rounds and fillets on a casting or a blanket tolerance. Notes may apply to the entire drawing or to a specific area. A general note applies to the entire drawing. A local note is positioned near and points to the specified area to which it applies. The note area is identified with the heading "NOTE:".

Instructor Led Exercise 4-8: Advanced features

Consider the incorrectly dimensioned object shown. There are 7 types of dimensioning mistakes. List them and then dimension the object correctly.

1) use the symbols
2) Spaces
3) angle up
4) Dim where feature is shown best

5) Radius
6) Dont dim hidden
7) locate center pt.

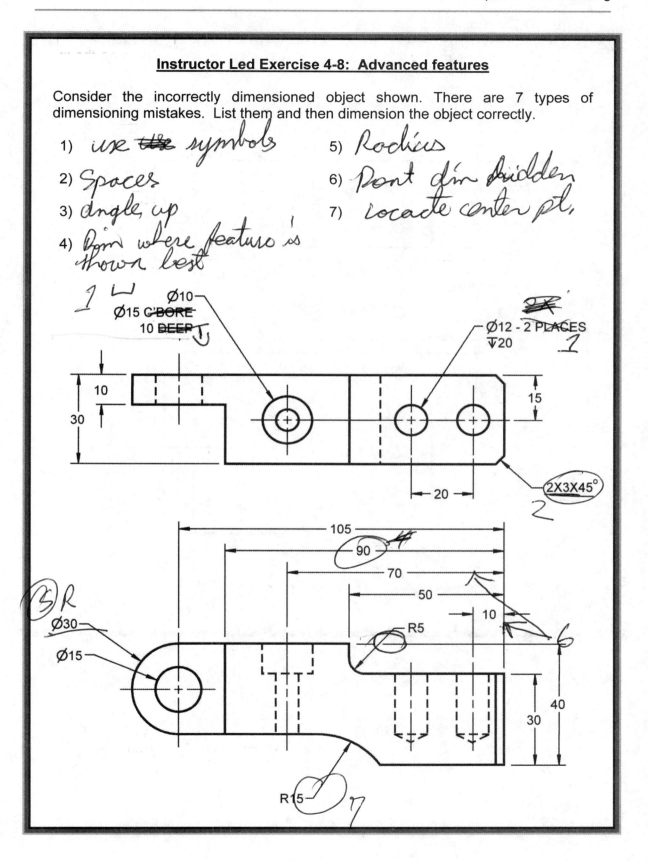

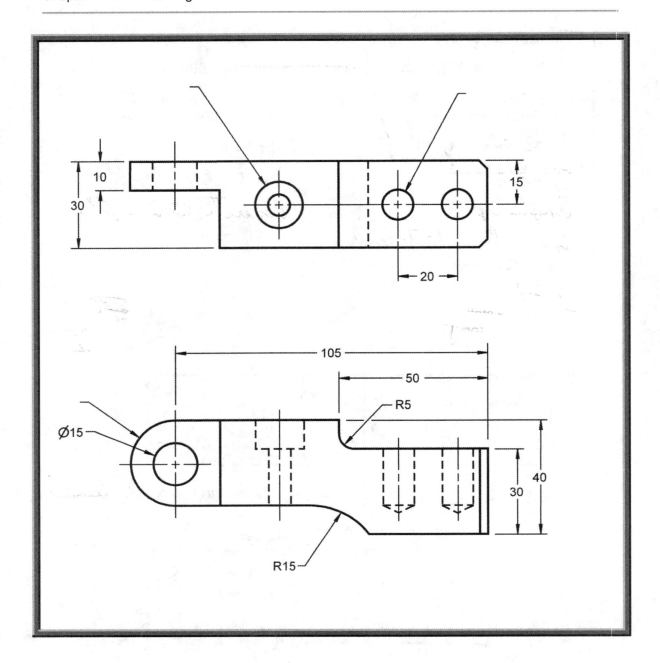

4.6) **DIMENSION CHOICE**

Dimension placement and dimension text influences the manufacturing process used to make the part. However, your **choice of dimensions should depend on the function and the mating relationship of the part**, and then on manufacturing. Even though dimensions influence how the part is made, the manufacturing process should not be specifically stated on the drawing.

4.6.1) **Units and Decimal Places**

a) Decimal dimensions should be used for all machining dimensions. Sometimes you may encounter a drawing that specifies standard drills, broaches, and the like by size. For drill sizes that are given by number or letter, a decimal size should also be given.

b) On drawing where all the dimensions are given either in millimeters or inches, individual identification of the units is not necessary. However, the drawing should contain a note stating UNLESS OTHERWISE SPECIFIED, ALL DIMENSION ARE IN MILLIMETERS (or INCHES). If some inch dimensions are used on a millimeter drawing or visa versa, the abbreviations **IN** or **mm** shall follow the dimension value.

c) Metric dimensions are given in 'mm' and to 0 or 1 decimal place (e.g. 10, 10.2). When the dimension is less than a millimeter, a zero should proceed the decimal point (e.g. 0.5).

d) English dimensions are given in 'inches' and to 2 decimal places (e.g. 1.25). A zero is not shown before the decimal point for values less than one inch (e.g. .75).

e) Metric 3rd angle drawings should be designated by the SI projection symbol shown in Figure 4-19.

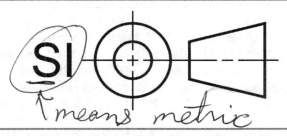

Figure 4-19: SI projection symbol.

4.6.2) Locating Features Using Datums

Consider three mutually perpendicular datum planes as shown in Figure 4-20. These planes are imaginary and theoretically exact. Now, consider a part that touches all three datum planes. The surfaces of the part that touch the datum planes are called datum features. **Most of the time, features on a part are located with respect to a datum feature.** In some cases, it is necessary to locate a feature with respect to another feature that is not the datum feature.

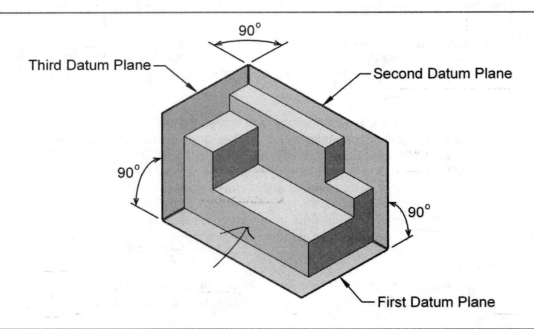

Figure 4-20: Datums and datum features.

Datum feature selection is based on the function of the part. When selecting datum features, think of the part as a component of an assembly. Functionally important surfaces and features should be selected as datum features. For example, to ensure proper assembly, mating surfaces should be used as datum features. A datum feature should be big enough to permit its use in manufacturing the part. If the function of the part is not known, take all possible measures to determine its function before dimensioning the part. In the process of learning proper dimensioning techniques, it may be necessary to make an educated guess as to the function of the part. Figure 4-21 shows a dimensioned part. Notice how all the dimensions originate from the datum features.

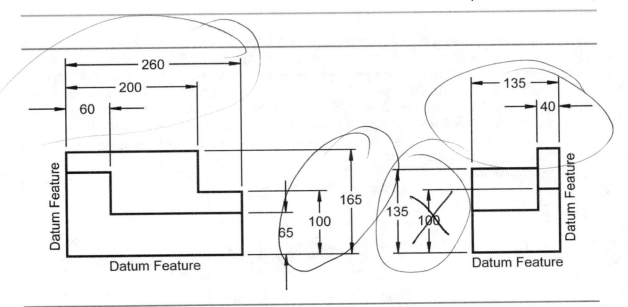

Figure 4-21: Dimensioning using datum features.

a) Datum dimensioning is preferred over continuous dimensioning (see Figure 4-22). Features should be located with respect to datum features.

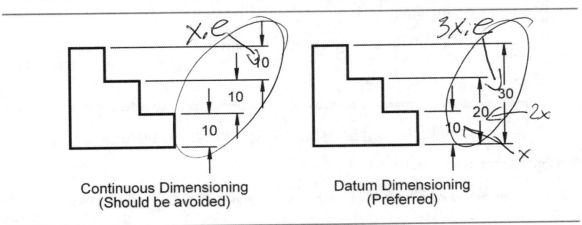

Continuous Dimensioning
(Should be avoided)

Datum Dimensioning
(Preferred)

Figure 4-22: Continuous versus datum dimensioning.

b) Dimensions should be given between points or surfaces that have a functional relation to each other (slots, mating hole patterns, etc...). Figure 4-23 shows a part that has two holes that are designed to mate up with two pins on another part. Therefore, the distance between the holes is more important than the distance of the second hole from the datum feature. There would be a similar dimension on the other part specifying the distance between the pins to ensure proper mating.

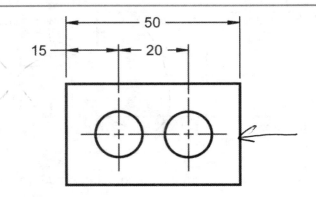

Figure 4-23: Dimensioning functionally important features.

4.6.3) Dimension Accuracy

There is no such thing as an "exact" measurement. Every dimension has an implied or stated tolerance associated with it. A tolerance is the amount a dimension is allowed to vary.

Instructor Led Exercise 4-9: Dimension accuracy

Consider the figure shown below.

- Which dimensions have implied tolerances and which have stated tolerances?

- Does the arrow indicate an increasing or decreasing accuracy?

- Write down the range in which the dimension values are allowed to vary.

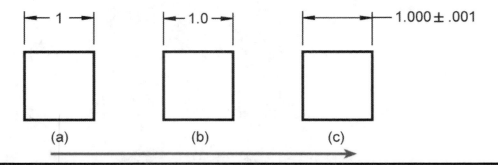

4.6.4) Rounding off

The more accurate the dimension the more expensive it is to manufacture. To cut costs it is necessary to round off fractional dimensions. If, for example, we are rounding off to the second decimal place and the third decimal place number is less than 5, we truncate after the second decimal place. If the number in the third decimal place is greater than 5, we round up and increase the second decimal place number by 1. If the number is exactly 5, whether or not we round up depends on if the second decimal place number is odd or even. If it is odd, we round up and if it is even, it is kept the same.

Instructor Led Exercise 4-10: Rounding off

Round off the following fractions to two decimal places according to the rules stated above.

(5/16) .3125 →   (1/8) .125 →

(5/32) .1562 →   (3/8) .375 →

4.6.5) Cumulative Tolerances (Error Buildup)

Figure 4-24 shows two different styles of dimensioning. One is called *Continuous Dimensioning,* the other *Datum Dimensioning.* Continuous dimensioning has the disadvantage of accumulating error. **It is preferable to use datum dimensioning to reduce error buildup.**

Consider the part shown in Figure 4-24. It is dimensioned using both continuous and datum dimensioning. The implied tolerance of all the dimensions is on the first decimal place. If we look at the continuous dimensioning case, the actual dimensions are x.e, where 0.e is the error associated with each dimension. Adding up the individual dimensions, we get an overall dimension of $3x + 3*(0.e)$. The overall dimension for the datum dimensioning case is $3x + 0.e$. As this example shows, continuous dimensioning accumulates error.

Another advantage of using datum dimensioning is the fact that many manufacturing machines are programmed using a datum or origin. Therefore, it makes it easier for the machinist to program the machine if datum dimensioning is used.

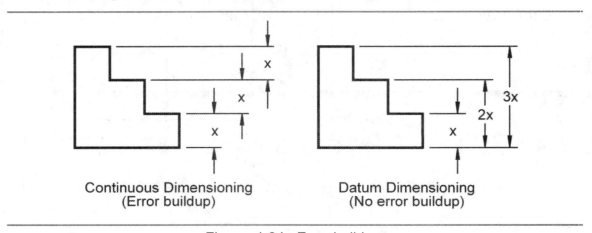

Continuous Dimensioning
(Error buildup)

Datum Dimensioning
(No error buildup)

Figure 4-24: Error buildup.

6-1
6-7
8-1
8-1

Instructor Led Exercise 4-11: Dimension choice

Consider the incorrectly dimensioned object shown.   There are 6 types of dimensioning mistakes. List them and then dimension the object correctly.

1)   4)

2)   5)

3)   6)

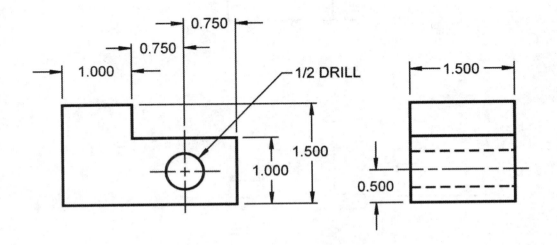

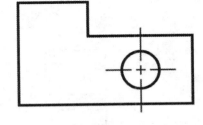

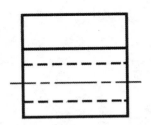

Video Exercise 4-12: Beginning Dimensioning

This video exercise will take you through dimensioning the following objects using proper dimensioning techniques.

<u>Video Exercise 4-13: Intermediate Dimensioning</u>

This video exercise will take you through dimensioning the following objects using proper dimensioning techniques.

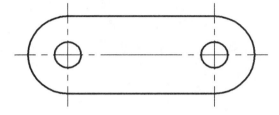

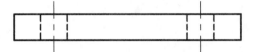

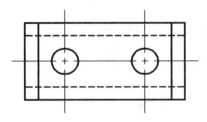

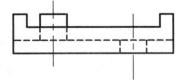

NOTES:

In Class Student Exercise 4-14: Dimensioning 1

Name: _____ Date: _____

Dimension the following object using proper dimensioning techniques. Did we need to draw the right side view?

This way is up

NOTES:

In Class Student Exercise 4-15: Dimensioning 2

Name: _____ Date: _____

Dimension the following object using proper dimensioning techniques.

This way is up

<u>NOTES:</u>

In Class Student Exercise 4-16: Dimensioning 3

Name: _____ Date: _____

Dimension the following object using proper dimensioning techniques.

This way is up

<u>NOTES:</u>

In Class Student Exercise 4-17: Dimensioning 4

Name: _____ Date: _____

Dimension the following object using proper dimensioning techniques.

NOTES:

Video Exercise 4-18: Advanced Dimensioning 1

This video exercise will take you through dimensioning the following objects using proper dimensioning techniques.

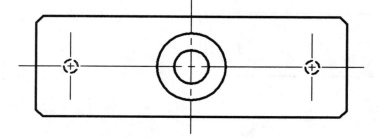

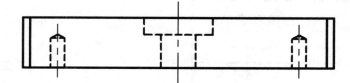

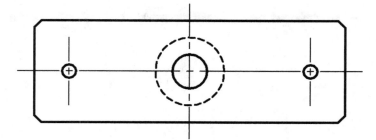

Video Exercise 4-19: Advanced Dimensioning 2

This video exercise will take you through dimensioning the following objects using proper dimensioning techniques.

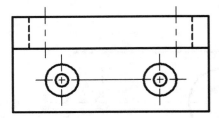

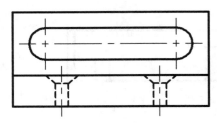

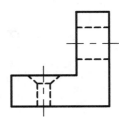

DIMENSIONING CROSSWORD PUZZLE

Name: _____   Date: _____

CP4-1)

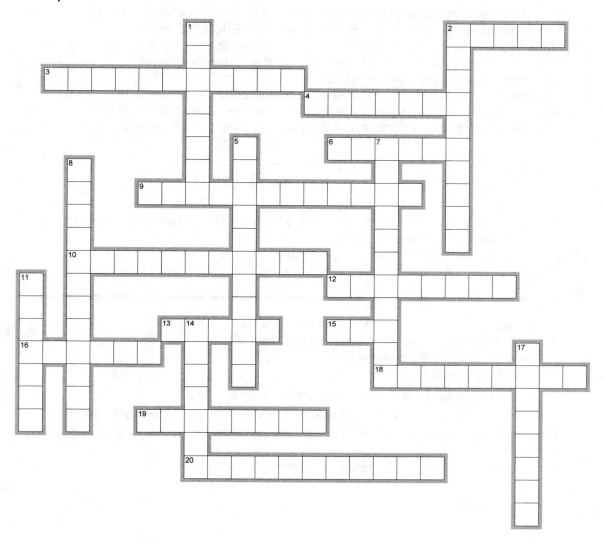

Across

2. What is this symbol? ⟱
3. What is this symbol? ⟍⟋
4. Dimension and extension lines are thin so that they will not be mistaken for .... lines.
6. What unit of measure is most commonly used on English drawing?
9. Datum dimensioning is preferred over continuous dimensions because it reduces ....
10. What unit of measure is most commonly used on a metric drawing?
12. Leader lines should not be horizontal or ....
13. Dimensioning hidden lines under some circumstances is allowed. (true, false)
15. How many zeros to the right of the decimal does two thousandths of an inch have?
16. The following symbol indicates that the drawing uses this unit of measure?

18. Which line type does not have arrowheads? (dimension, extension, leader)
19. A .... is located in the circular view.
20. A cylinder's diameter is given in the .... view.

Down

1. A circular hole's diameter is placed in the .... view.
2. A detailed drawing is an orthographic projection with ....
5. A reference dimension is given within ....
7. What is this symbol? ⌐‾⌐
8. A surface of the part that touches the datum plane.
11. X is the symbol used for repeated features. What else is this symbol used for?
14. Dimensions generally take the form of linear dimensions, notes and leaders and .... dimensions.
17. A complete circle such as a hole is dimensioned by its ....

Name: _____   Date: _____

P4-2) The following object is dimensioned incorrectly. Identify the incorrect dimensions and list all mistakes associated with them. Then, dimension the object correctly using proper dimensioning techniques. There are four mistakes.

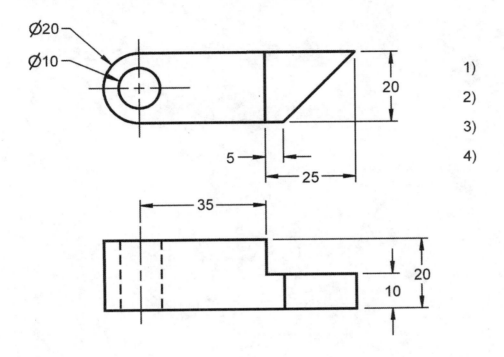

1)

2)

3)

4)

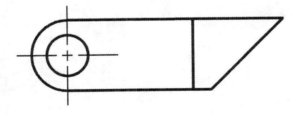

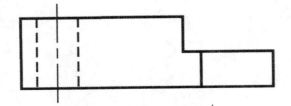

NOTES:

Name: _____   Date: _____

P4-3) The following object is dimensioned incorrectly. Identify the incorrect dimensions and list all mistakes associated with them. Then, dimension the object correctly using proper dimensioning techniques. There are six mistakes.

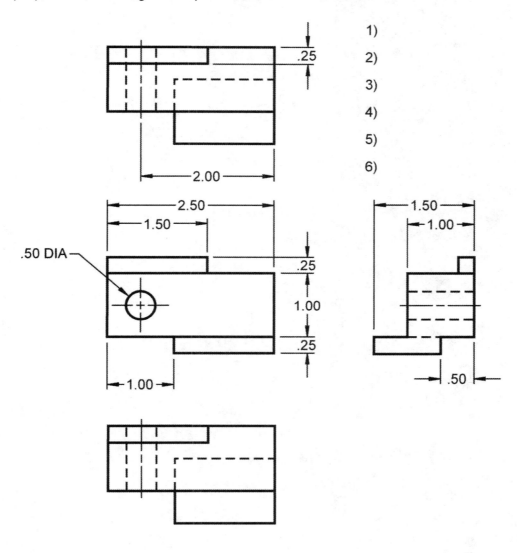

1)

2)

3)

4)

5)

6)

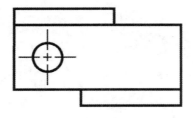

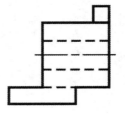

NOTES:

Name: _____ Date: _____

P4-4) The following object is dimensioned incorrectly. Identify the incorrect dimensions and list all mistakes associated with them. Then, dimension the object correctly using proper dimensioning techniques. There are four mistakes.

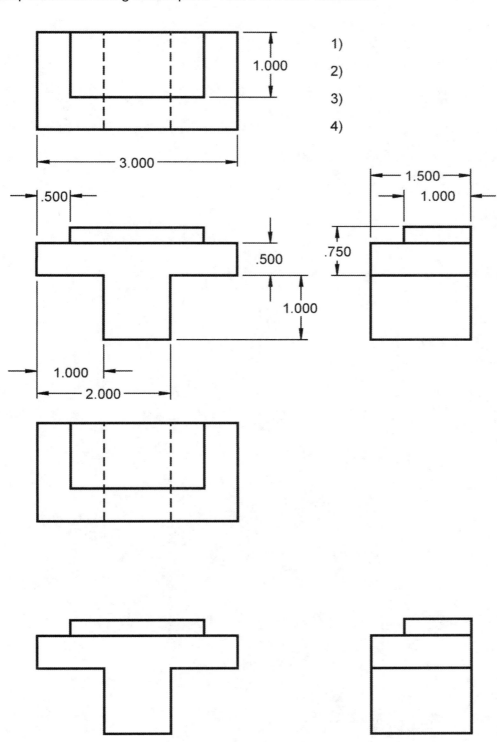

1)

2)

3)

4)

NOTES:

Name: _____   Date: _____

P4-6) Completely dimension the objects shown (by hand) using proper dimensioning techniques. Wherever a numerical dimension value is required, place an 'x'. Use dimensioning symbols where necessary.

NOTES:

Name: _____   Date: _____

P4-7) Completely dimension the objects shown (by hand) using proper dimensioning techniques. Wherever a numerical dimension value is required, place an 'x'. Use dimensioning symbols where necessary.

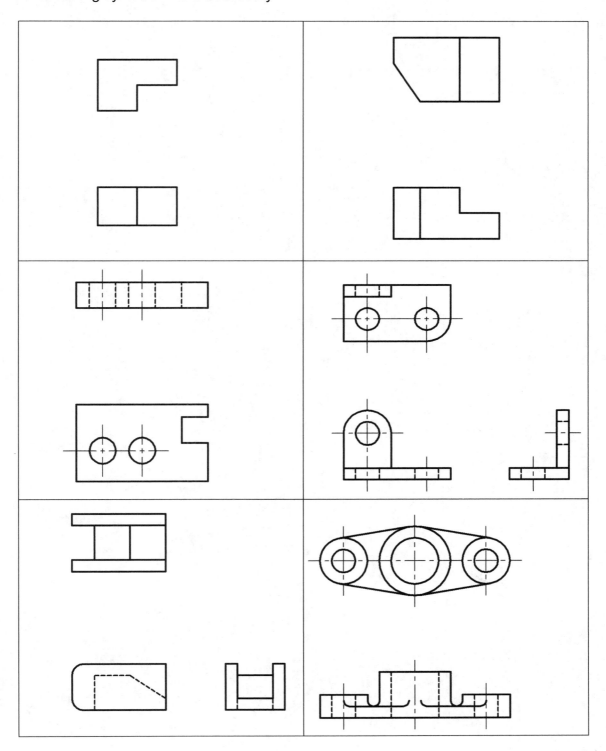

NOTES:

Name: _____   Date: _____

P4-8) Completely dimension the objects shown (by hand) using proper dimensioning techniques. Wherever a numerical dimension value is required, place an 'x'. Use dimensioning symbols where necessary.

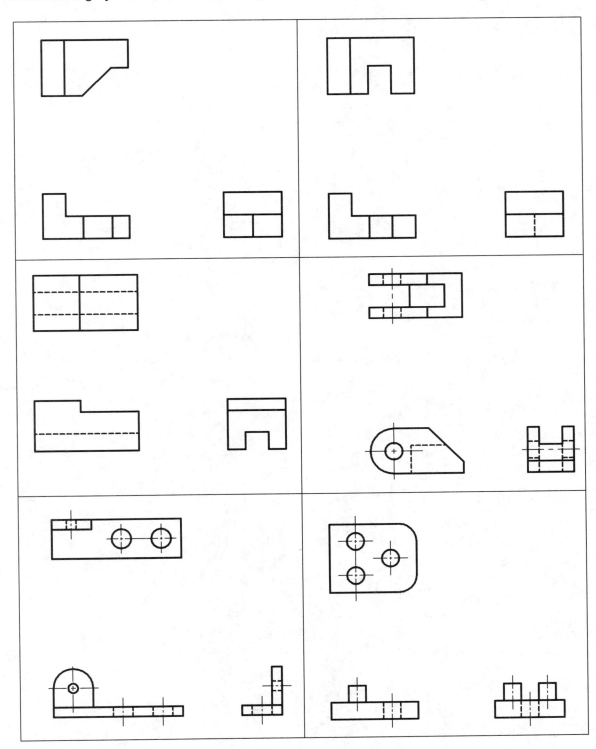

NOTES:

Name: _____   Date: _____

P4-9) Completely dimension the objects shown (by hand) using proper dimensioning techniques. Wherever a numerical dimension value is required, place an 'x'. Use dimensioning symbols where necessary.

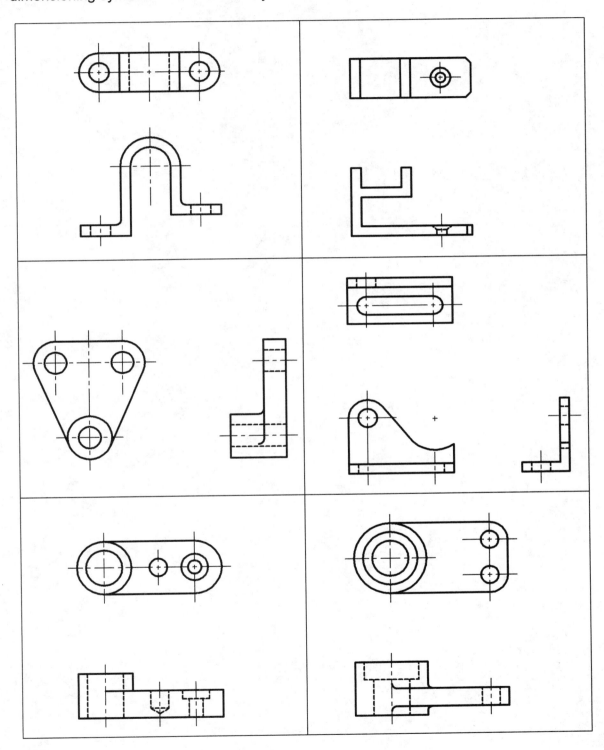

NOTES:

DIMENSIONING IN AUTOCAD

In Chapter 5 you will learn how to dimension a part in AutoCAD. AutoCAD makes creating linear, angular, diameter and radius dimensions quite easy. By default, these dimensions are associative. This means that the dimension values change if the geometry they are attached to changes. In order to maintain the associativity between dimension and geometry, it is often necessary to edit the dimension text of more complex features after the dimension has been created. By the end of this chapter, you will be able to create, place and edit dimensions using a predefined dimensioning style.

5.1) INTRODUCTION

Dimensioning a part in AutoCAD is quite automated. It is as easy as selecting the geometry you wish to dimension and then selecting the dimension's location. AutoCAD will create the dimension lines, extension lines, arrow heads and dimension text. This is both good and bad. It makes dimensioning an object very fast. However, new users may find it frustrating when trying to fine tune the dimension settings to achieve dimensions that look just the way they want them to look. Dimension appearance and properties may be adjusted in the *Dimension Styles Manager* window. Some experimentation with these dimension settings may be required.

There are several ways to access AutoCAD's dimensioning commands. The *Dimension* pull-down menu, dashboard and toolbar contain commands that allow you to create a variety of dimension types. Dimensioning commands may also be typed in at the *Command* prompt or the *Dim* prompt. The *Dim* prompt is similar to the *Command* prompt except that it is used solely for creating and modifying dimensions using keyed in commands. One disadvantage with this method is that you are unable to draw or modify objects from the *Dim* prompt.

Dimensions are created as single entities and, with the exception of multileaders, are associated with the geometries used to create them. They are similar to blocks. If, for some reason, you need to edit the individual line and arrows of a dimension, it must be EXPLODED first. However, the associativity or connection to the geometry is broken if the dimension is exploded.

In this chapter annotative objects will be introduced. If an object is annotative, its scale or size will change with the view port scale. For example, using annotative text allows your printed text to always remain 1/8 of an inch high (or what ever value you set it to) no matter what scale you are using to print. AutoCAD will automatically adjust the height of the text. Objects that may be defined as annotative include text, dimensions, multileaders, hatches and blocks.

5.2) **DIMENSION COMMANDS**

5.2.1) Dimensions panel

Figure 5-1 shows the *Dimensions* panel which is located in the *Annotate* tab.

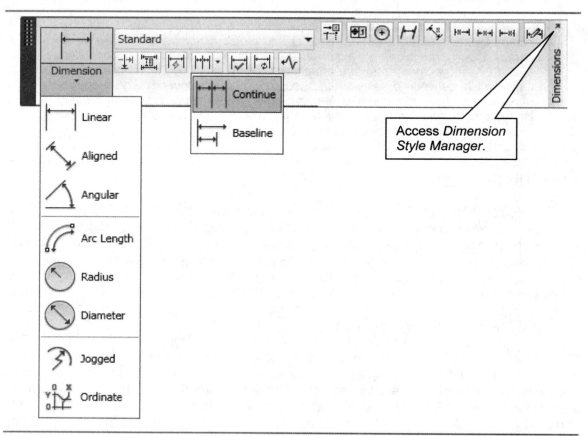

Figure 5-1: The *Dimensions* panel

The commands located in the *Dimensions* panel are:

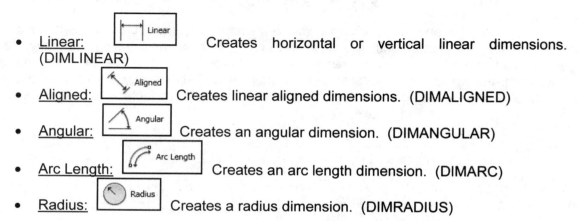

- **Linear:** Creates horizontal or vertical linear dimensions. (DIMLINEAR)

- **Aligned:** Creates linear aligned dimensions. (DIMALIGNED)

- **Angular:** Creates an angular dimension. (DIMANGULAR)

- **Arc Length:** Creates an arc length dimension. (DIMARC)

- **Radius:** Creates a radius dimension. (DIMRADIUS)

- Diameter: Creates a diameter dimension. (DIMDIAMETER)

- Jogged: Creates jogged dimensions for circles and arcs. (DIMJOGGED)

- Ordinate: Creates ordinate point dimensions. (DIMORDINATE)

- Dimension Style:

- Current Dimension Style: Standard Allows you to select a defined dimension style. Dimension Styles can be created and modified in the *Dimension Styles Manager*. To access the *Dimension Styles Manager* window click on the little arrow in the corner of the *Dimensions* panel or type **DIMSTYLE**.

- Break: Allows you to specify whether or not you want a dimension to break if it crosses a selected object. (DIMBREAK)

- Adjust Space: Allows you to define a uniform spacing between dimensions. (DIMSPACE)

- Quick Dimension: Creates a linear, radius or diameter dimension by selecting the object and not two points as with the other linear dimension commands. (QDIM)

- Baseline: Creates a series of baseline dimensions using an existing dimension to define the baseline. (DIMBASELINE) The command **DIMDLI** controls the spacing of the dimension lines in baseline dimensions.

- Continue: Creates a series of continuous dimensions using an existing dimension to continue from. (DIMCONTINUE)

- Inspection: Allows you to add or remove an inspection dimension from a selected dimension. (DIMINSPECT)

- Update: Redraws the dimensions with the current dimension style settings. (-DIMSTYLE)

- Jogged Line: Adds a jog to a linear dimension. (DIMJOGLINE)

- Reassociate: Associates or reassociates a selected dimension to an object or a point on an object. (DIMREASSOCIATE)

- Tolerance: Allows you to create a GD&T feature control frame. (TOLERANCE)

- Center Mark: Places a mark identifying the center of a circle or arc. (DIMCENTER) The size of the mark is controlled by the **DIMCEN** variable. If the center mark interferes with the centerline break, DIMCEN should be set to 0.

- Oblique: Makes the extension lines of a linear dimension oblique. This is useful when dimensioning pictorials. (DIMEDIT)

- <u>Text Angle:</u> [icon] Allows you to rotate the dimension text to a specified angle. (DIMTEDIT)
- <u>Left Justify:</u> [icon] Places the dimension text on the left side. (DIMTEDIT)
- <u>Center Justify:</u> [icon] Places the dimension text in the center. (DIMTEDIT)
- <u>Right Justify:</u> [icon] Places the dimension text on the right side. (DIMTEDIT)
- <u>Override:</u> [icon] Allows you to override dimension style variables. (DIMOVERRIDE)

5.2.2) **The Leaders Panel**

Figure 5-2 shows the *Leaders* panel which is located in the *Annotate* tab.

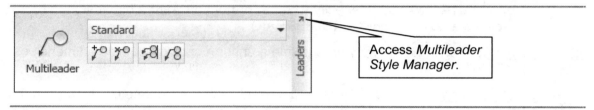

Figure 5-2: The *Leaders* panel

The commands located in the *Leaders* panel are:

- <u>Multileader:</u> [icon] Creates various types of leaders and notes. (MLEADER)
- <u>Current Multileader Style:</u> [Standard ▼] Allows you to select a defined multileader style. Multileader Styles can be created and modified in the *Multileader Styles Manager*. To access the *Multileader Styles Manager* window click on the little arrow in the corner of the *Leaderss* panel or type **MLEADERSTYLE**.
- <u>Add Leader:</u> [icon] Adds a leader(s) to an existing multileader. (MLEADEREDIT)
- <u>Remove Leader:</u> [icon] Removes a leader from an existing multileader. (MLEADEREDIT)
- <u>Align:</u> [icon] Aligns several existing multileaders with a line created within the command. (MLEADERALIGN)
- <u>Collect:</u> [icon] Collects the content of several multileaders and creates a single multileader. (MLEADERCOLLECT)

The *multileader* command may be accessed in the following way.

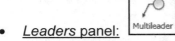

- *Leaders* panel:
- *Command* window: **mleader**

Multileader options (`Specify leader arrowhead location or [leader Landing first/Content first/Options] <Options>:`).
- leader Landing first: Allows you to specify the location of the short horizontal line at the end of a leader first.
- Content first: Allows you to specify the leader note first.
- Options: `Enter an option [Leader type/leader lAnding/Content type/Maxpoints/First angle/Second angle/eXit options] <eXit options>:`
  - Leader type: The leader may be constructed from a straight line or a spline.
  - leader lAnding: Allows you to specify whether or not you want a short horizontal line at the end of the leader.
  - Content type: Allows you to specify whether your content is a block or mtext.
  - Maxpoints: Allows you to create leader lines that consist of several straight line segments, or specify how many defining points you want for your spline.
  - First angle / Second angle: Allows you to specify at least 2 angles that you wish to use to draw your leader lines.

5.3) DIMENSION STYLES

5.3.1) Dimension Style Manager

The *Dimension Style Manager* (Figure 5-3) is used to create new dimension styles, set the current style, modify styles, set overrides on the current style, and compare styles. The *Dimension Style Manager* window may be accessed using the **DDIM** or **DIMSTYLE** commands. It may also be accessed from the *Dimensions* panel. The features of the *Dimension Style Manager* window are (see figure 5-3):

- Current dimension style: The current dimension style is the style that is applied to dimensions you create.
- Styles: This is a list of styles that are available.
- List: Allows you to display all styles or only the styles that are in use.
- Preview of: Shows a preview of what the dimensions will look like.
- Set Current: Sets a selected style to be current.
- New...: Allows you to create a new style.
- Modify...: Allows you to modify the current style.
- Override...: Allows you to set temporary override settings to the current style.
- Compare...: Allows you to compare styles.

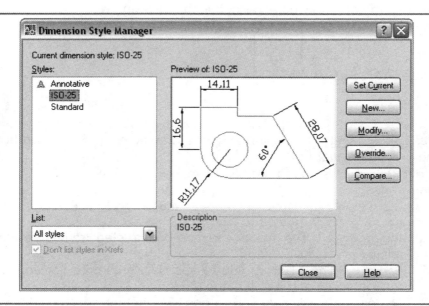

Figure 5-3: The *Dimension Style Manager* window

The default metric drawing dimension style is ISO-25. ISO stands for 'International Standards Organization'. The United States follows ASME's standards. ASME stands for 'American Society of Mechanical Engineers'. The ASME standard related to dimensioning is close to the ISO standard; therefore, we can use the ISO standard as a starting point when we create a new ASME dimension style.

5.3.2) Multileader Style Manager

The *Multileader Style Manager* (Figure 5-4) is used to create new multileader styles, set the current style and modify styles. The *Multileader Style Manager* window may be accessed using the **MLEADERSTYLE** command. It may also be accessed from the *Leaders* panel. The features of the *Multileader Style Manager* window are (see Figure 5-4):

- Current multileader style: The current multileader style is the style that is applied to multileaders that you create.
- Styles: This is a list of styles that are available.
- List: Allows you to display all styles or only the styles that are in use.
- Preview of: Shows a preview of what the multileader will look like.
- Set Current: Sets a selected style to be current.
- New...: Allows you to create a new style.
- Modify...: Allows you to modify the current style.

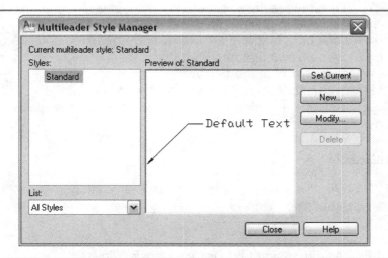

Figure 5-4: The *Multileader Style Manager* window

5.4) DIMENSION VARIABLES

Dimension appearance may be modified by changing the value of the following dimension variables. Only the most commonly used variables are listed. These variables may also be set in the *Dimension Styles Manager*. However, it is not uncommon to change some of these variables on the fly.

5.4.1) Dimension Scale

- **DIMSCALE:** This command sets the overall size or scale factor of the dimensions. The following variables are controlled directly by the DIMSCALE variable. There is usually no need to change them individually.
  - **DIMASZ:** Controls the size of the arrows.
  - **DIMEXE:** Controls the length of the extension lines beyond dimension lines.
  - **DIMEXO:** Controls the gap between the extension line and the object.
  - **DIMGAP:** Controls the space between the dimension text and the dimension line.
  - **DIMTXT:** Controls the height of the dimension text unless the current style has a fixed height.

5.4.2) Dimension and Extension Lines

- **DIMSOXD:** Suppresses the placement of dimension lines outside of the extension lines.
  - 0 = Off
  - 1 = On
- **DIMTOFL:** Draws dimension lines between extension lines even if the text is placed outside the extension lines.
  - 0 = Off
  - 1 = On

- **DIMATFIT:** Determines how dimension text and arrows are arranged when space is not sufficient to place both within the extension lines.
  - 0 = Places both text and arrows outside the extension lines.
  - 1 = Moves arrows first and then text.
  - 2 = Moves text first, then arrows.
  - 3 = Moves either text or arrows, whichever fits best.
- **DIMCLRD:** Assigns a color to dimension lines, arrowheads and dimension leader lines.

5.4.3) Dimension Text

- **DIMTIH**: Forces the dimension text inside the extension lines to be positioned horizontally, rather than aligned.
  - 0 = Off
  - 1 = On
- **DIMTIX**: Forces dimension text inside extension lines.
  - 0 = Off
  - 1 = On
- **DIMDEC**: Sets the number of decimal places displayed for the primary units.
- **DIMJUST**: Controls the horizontal positioning of the dimension text.
  - 0 = Above the dimension line and center justifies it between the extension lines.
  - 1 = Next to the first extension line.
  - 2 = Next to the second extension line.
  - 3 = Above the dimension line and next to the first extension line.
  - 4 = Above the dimension line and next to the second extension line.
- **DIMTAD**: Controls the vertical position of the text relative to the dimension lines.
  - 0 = Centered between the extension lines.
  - 1 = Above the dimension line except when the dimension line is not horizontal and DIMTIH = 1. The distance from the dimension line to the bottom of the text is controlled by DIMGAP.
  - 2 = On the side of the dimension line farthest away from the dimension origin(s).
  - 3 = According to the JIS (Japanese Industrial Standards).
- **DIMTMOVE**: Sets dimension text movement rules.
  - 0 = Moves the dimension line with the dimension text.
  - 1 = Adds a leader when the dimension text is moved.
  - Allows text to be moved freely without a leader.
- **DIMTOH**: Controls the position of the dimension text outside the extension lines.
  - 0 or Off= Aligns the text with the dimension line.
  - 1 or On= Draws the text horizontally.
- **DDEDIT**: Edits single line text, dimension text and feature control frames.
- **DIMTEDIT**: Moves and rotates dimension text.
- **DIMCLRT**: Assigns colors to dimension text.

5.4.4) Diameter and Radial Dimensions

- **DIMCEN**: Controls size of the center marks drawn by diameter and radial dimensions.

- **DIMJOGANG:** Determines the angle of the transverse segment of the dimension line in a jogged radius dimension.

5.4.5) Angular Dimensions

- **DIMADEC:** Controls the number of decimal places displayed in angular dimensions.
- **DIMAUNIT:** Sets the units format for angular dimensions.

5.4.6) Alternative Units

- **DIMALT**: Adds an additional dimension text in an alternative unit.
  - 0 = Off
  - 1 = On
- **DIMALTD**: Controls the number of decimal places in the alternative unit.
- **DIMALTF**: Controls the conversion factor of the alternative unit. For example, the conversion factor from inches to millimeters is 25.4.

5.4.7) Toleranced Dimensions

- **DIMLIM**: Presents dimensions in limit form.
- **DIMTOL**: Presents dimensions in tolerance form.
- **DIMTM**: Sets the negative tolerance value.
- **DIMTP**: Sets the positive tolerance value.

5.4.8) Miscellaneous

- **DIMARCSYM:** Controls whether or not an arc symbol will be placed above an arc length dimension.
  - 0 = Before the dimension text.
  - 1 = Above the dimension text.
  - 2 = Will not display the arc length symbol.

5.5) THE DIM PROMPT

Within the *Dim* prompt (the dimension mode), you can type in dimensioning commands that allow you to create and modify dimensions. This is convenient for users that are more comfortable typing commands than they are using icons. To access the *Dim* prompt type **DIM** in the *Command* window. A *Dim* prompt will replace the *Command* prompt. To get out of the *Dim* prompt type the command **EXIT** or **E**.

The *Dim* prompt does not work in combination with the *Dimension* toolbar or the *Dimension* pull-down menu. Selecting a command within the toolbar or the pull-down menu automatically exits the user from the *Dim* prompt.

5.5.1) Creating Dimensions from the *Dim* Prompt

Within the *Dim* prompt you may type commands that allow you to create and modify preset dimension types. The types of dimensions that you can create range from linear dimensions to diameter dimensions to dimensions that are aligned with a particular feature of the drawing. The dimension commands used to create and modify dimensions are listed below. The capitalized letters are the minimum amount you must type in order to invoke the command.

- **HORizontal**: Used to create a linear dimension that measures a distance in the x direction.
- **VERtical**: Used to create a linear dimension that measures a distance in the y direction.
- **ALigned**: Used to create a linear dimension that is aligned with the extension line origins.
- **ANgular**: Used to create an angular dimension. AutoCAD will automatically place the degree symbol after the angular value. If you are manually typing in the dimension, type **%%D** after the numerical value to invoke the degree symbol.
- **Diameter**: Used to create a diameter dimension. AutoCAD will automatically place the diameter symbol $\emptyset$ in front of the dimension value. If you are manually typing in the dimension, type **%%C** before the numerical value to invoke the diameter symbol.
- **RAdius**: Used to create a radius dimension.
- **Leader**: Used to create a leader – note.
- **Newtext**: Used to edit existing dimension text.
- **TEdit**: Used to change the position of the dimension and the dimension text.
- **UPdate**: Redraws the dimensions with the current dimension style settings.

5.6) ASSOCIATIVE DIMENSIONS

Associative dimensions are dimensions that are associated with a geometric object or a particular feature of your part. This means that if the feature is changed, the associated dimension value will change. For example, if the diameter of a circle is 10 mm then the diameter dimension value will read $\emptyset$10. If you subsequently change the diameter of the circle to 20 mm within the *Properties* window, the dimension value will automatically change to $\emptyset$20. Associativity is broken if you manually type in the dimension text, replace the dimension text or EXPLODE the dimension. Leader dimensions are not associative. The dimension commands that are related to associativity are:

- **DIMDISASSOCIATE:** Removes associativity from a selected dimension.
- **DIMREASSOCIATE:** Associates a selected dimension to geometric objects.
- **DIMREGEN:** Updates the locations of all associative dimensions.
- **DIMASSOC:** Controls the associativity of dimensions and whether dimensions are exploded.

5.7) ANNOTATIVE OBJECTS

Annotative objects are objects that can support multiple viewport scales. Consider the following situation. I start a metric drawing and set my text height to 3 mm. If I print at a 1:1 scale, my text height will measure 3 mm on the printed page. However, if I print at a 1:2 scale my text height will only measure 1.5 mm. Annotative text adjusts its height so that no matter what viewport scale you select, the text will always measure 3 mm on the printed page. Figure 5-5 shows an example of regular text and annotative text at three different viewport scales. Notice that the regular text height increases or decreases depending on the viewport scale, and the annotative text height never changes.

How does this work? If you select the annotative text, you will see not just one instance of the text, but three or however many viewport scales it supports. Figure 5-6 shows the selected annotative text and the instances that it supports. Objects that may be defined as annotative include text, dimensions, multileaders, hatches and blocks. The principle is the same for all annotative objects.

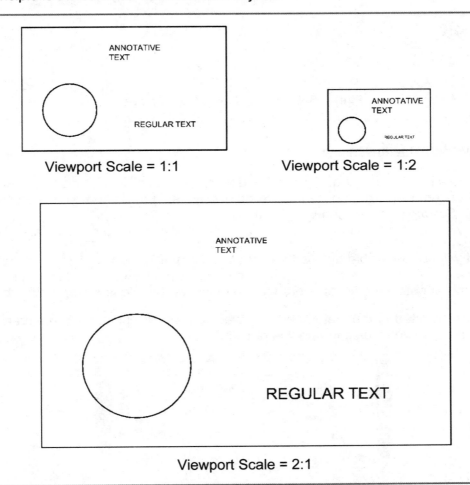

Figure 5-5: Annotative text

ANNOTATIVE TEXT

Figure 5-6: Annotative text instances

5.7.1) Annotative Object Scale

An annotative object, by default, only supports a 1:1 scale. Supported scales may be added or removed from an annotative object by using the commands located in the *Annotation Scaling* panel as shown in Figure 5-7.

If the view port scale is changed to a scale that the annotative object does not support, it will not be visible unless the *Annotative Visibility* icon is turned on. This icon is located in the status bar. You may choose to have AutoCAD automatically add scales to the annotative objects every time the view port scale is change by turning this icon on (located in the status bar). However, every supported scale increases the size of your file. I would discourage this practice.

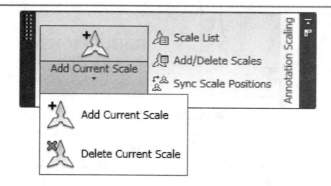

Figure 5-7: *Annotation Scaling* panel

The commands located in the *Annotation Scaling* panel are:

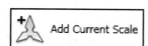

- <u>Add Current Scale:</u> Allows you to add a scale that the object will support.

- <u>Delete Current Scale:</u>  Allows you to delete a supported scale from an object.

- <u>Scale List:</u> Brings up the *Edit Scale List* window which list all scales available. It also allows you to add or delete scales. (SCALELISTEDIT)

- <u>Add/Delete Scales:</u> Brings up the *Annotation Object Scale* window which list all scales supported by the selected object(s). It also allows you to add or delete supported scales. (OBJECTSCALE)

- <u>Synchronize Scale Positions:</u> Resets the positions of all scale representations.

5.8) <u>DIMENSIONING TUTORIAL</u>

The objective of this tutorial is to familiarize the user with creating a variety of dimension types. This tutorial will also take the user through the steps required to create a new dimension style. We will first dimension the object using the ISO-25 standard. The differences between the ISO standard and the ASME standard will be pointed out and then we will create an ASME dimension style and use that style to dimension the object. The last section of this tutorial will illustrate the dimensions associativity and annotative properties.

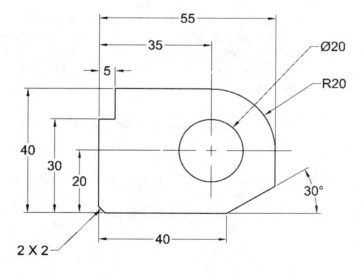

5.8.1) <u>Drawing the object</u>

1) View the *Creating Dimension*, *Multileaders*, *Associativity* and *Annotative Objects* videos and read section 5.1) through 5.7).

2) **Open** **set-mm.dwt** drawing template. Verify the following settings...
   - STYLE: Text style = Arial, Text height = 3 mm, Annotative.
   - LIMITS = 280, 216

3)  **Dim Tut.dwg**

4) Draw the above object (without the dimensions) using the appropriate layers. Make sure to include the centerlines.

5) Turn your **Object Snap** on and have it automatically detect, at minimum, *Endpoint* and *Intersection*.

6) Zoom in to better view your drawing.

5.8.2) Drawing linear dimensions

1) Set the **Dimension** layer as current and activate the **Annotate** tab.

2) Add the linear dimensions.

   a) <u>Command:</u> **dimlinear**   or   *Dimensions* <u>panel:</u>
   b) `Specify first extension line origin or <select object>:` **Select** *Point1*.
   c) `Specify second extension line origin:` **Select** *Point2*.
   d) `Specify dimension line location or [Mtext/Text/Angle/ Horizontal/Vertical/Rotated]:` **Pull the dimension out and away from the** object and left click when the dimension is in the approximate location shown.
   e) Add the other linear dimensions shown in a similar manner. When adding the 35 mm and 20 mm dimension, select the end of the center line. When adding the 55 mm dimension, select the end of the radius.

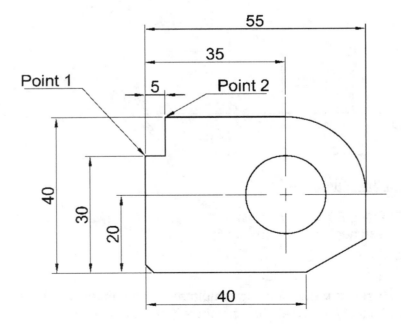

3) Evenly space the linear dimensions.

a) <u>Command:</u> **dimspace** or *Dimensions* panel:
b) `Select base dimension:` Select the 5 mm dimension.
c) `Select dimensions to space:` Select the 35 mm and then the 55 mm dimension.
d) `Select dimensions to space:` **Enter**
e) `Enter value or [Auto] <Auto>:` **a**
f) Notice that the AUTO option spaces the dimensions too close. **UNDO**.
g) Repeat the above process using **8** mm as the spacing
h) Evenly space the vertical linear dimensions.

5.8.3) Drawing diameter and radius dimensions

1) Dimension the radius.

a) <u>Command:</u> **dimradius** or *Dimensions* panel:
b) `Select arc or circle:` Select the radius.
c) `Specify dimension line location or [Mtext/Text/Angle]:` Pull the dimension out and away from the object and left click when the dimension is in the approximate position shown. Notice that the radius symbol "R" is automatically placed in front of the dimension value.

2) Dimension the hole.

a) <u>Command:</u> **dimdia** or *Dimensions* panel:
b) `Select arc or circle:` Select the circle.
c) `Specify dimension line location or [Mtext/Text/Angle]:` Pull the dimension out and away from the object and left click when the dimension is in the approximate position shown. Notice that the diameter symbol "∅" is automatically placed in front of the dimension value.

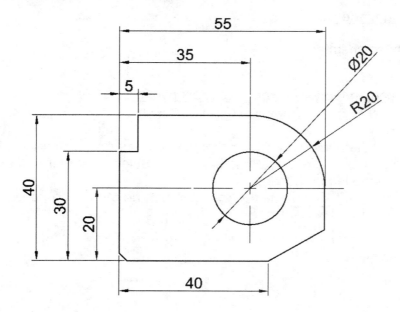

5.8.4) Drawing angular dimensions

1) Dimension the angled feature.

   a) Command: **dimangular**   or   *Dimensions* panel:
   b) Select arc, circle, line, or <specify vertex>: Select *Line 1*.
   c) Select second line: Select *Line 2*.
   d) Specify dimension arc line location or [Mtext/Text/Angle]: Pull the dimension out and away from the object and left click when the dimension is in the approximate position shown. Notice that the degree symbol "°" is automatically placed behind the dimension value.

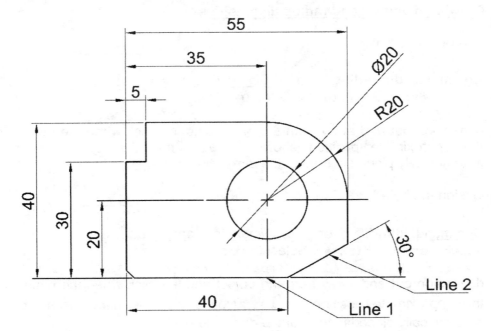

5.8.5) Drawing leaders

1) Dimension the chamfer.

   a) Command: **mleader**   or   *Leaders* panel:
   b) Specify leader arrowhead location or [leader Landing first/Content first/Options] <Options>: **mid**
      of Select the angled line of the chamfer near the middle. (see the figure below)
   c) Specify leader landing location: Select the point where the angled portion of the leader will end.
   d) *Text Editor* tab: Set the text height to **3** mm (In the ribbon), enter the text **2 X 2**

   and then select ⊠ Close Text Editor.

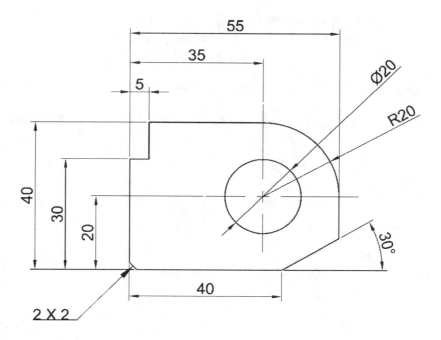

5.8.6) Creating a new dimension style

The ISO-25 standard used to create the above drawing is different from the ASME standard that we need to use. Notice the following:
- The dimension text is not always horizontal.
- The dimension text is next to or above the dimension line (there is no break allowing space for the text).
- The diameter and radius dimension text is aligned with the leader line.
- The diameter dimension leader line goes through the circle.
- The multileader arrow is bigger than the other dimension arrows and the leader landing underlines the text.

1) Create a new ASME dimension style.

    a) <u>Command:</u> **ddim**   or   *Dimensions* panel:
    b) *Dimension Style Manager* window: **New…**
    c) *Create New Dimension Style* window:
       i. *New Style Name* field: **ASME**
      ii. *Start With* field: **ISO-25**
     iii. *Use for* field: **All dimensions**
     iv. Activate the **Annotative** checkbox.
      v. **Continue**

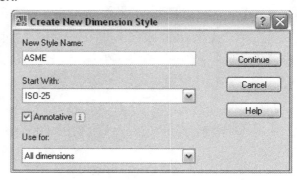

d) *New Dimension Style: ASME* window – *Symbols and Arrows* tab:
   i. *Center marks* area: Select the **None** radio button. The center mark often obscures centerline breaks. If you need to place a center mark, you can use the command DIMCENTER.
   ii. *Arc length symbol* area: Select the **Above** dimension text radio button.

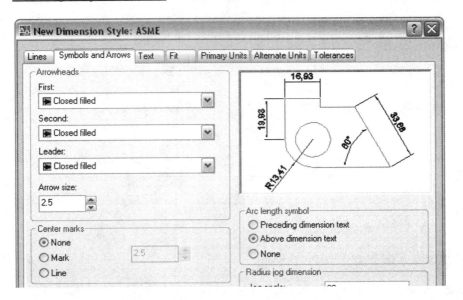

e) *New Dimension Style: ASME* window – *Text* tab:
   i. *Text placement* area – *Vertical* field: **Centered**
   ii. *Text alignment* area: Select the **Horizontal** radio button. Notice the preview area changes as you change the settings.

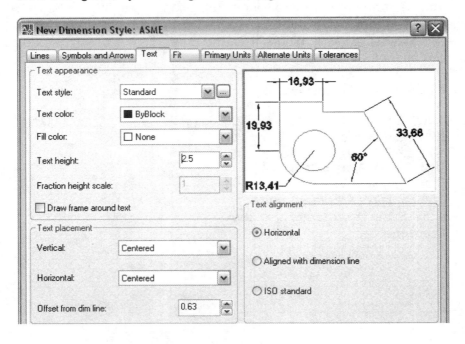

f) *New Dimension Style: ASME* window – *Fit* tab:
   i. *Fine tuning* area: Deselect the **Draw dim line between ext lines** checkbox.

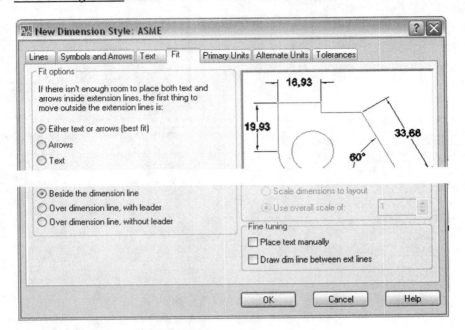

g) *New Dimension Style: ASME* window – *Primary Units* tab:
   i. *Linear dimensions* area - *Precision* field: Set the precision to **0**.
   ii. *Linear dimensions* area - *Decimal separator* field: Select **'.'(Period)**.
   iii. *Zero suppression* area: Deselect the **Trailing** checkbox.

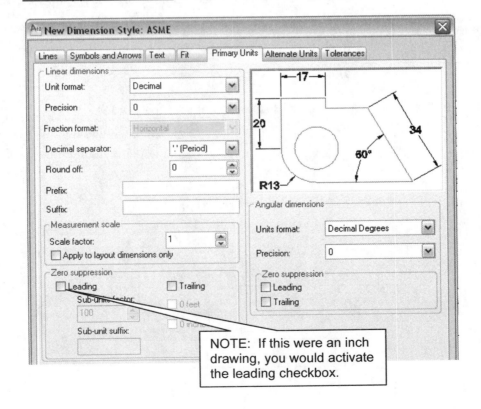

NOTE: If this were an inch drawing, you would activate the leading checkbox.

h) *New Dimension Style: ASME* window: **OK**

i) *AutoCAD Alert* window: **OK**

j) *Dimension Style Manager* window: Notice that the ASME style has been added to the *Styles* field.
  i. Select the **ASME** style and then select the **Set Current** button.
  ii. **Close**

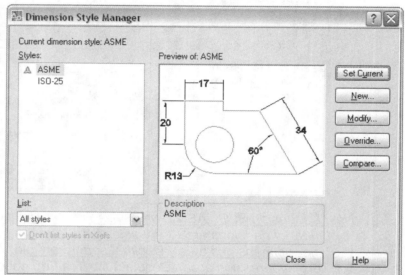

2) Update your dimensions to the ASME style.

a) *Dimensions* panel:

b) `Select objects:` **all**

c) `Select objects:` **Enter**

d) Notice that all the dimensions change except for the leader.

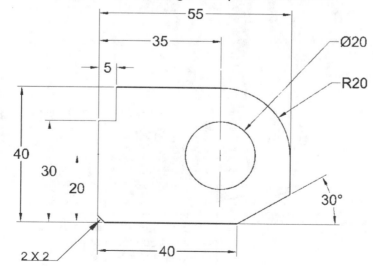

3) Create a new multileader style.

   a) <u>Command:</u> **mleaderstyle**   or   <u>*Leaders* panel:</u>

   b) <u>*Multileader Style Manager* window:</u> **New …**

   c) <u>*Create New Multileader Style* window:</u>
      i. <u>*New style name* field:</u> **ASME**
      ii. <u>*Start with* field:</u> ***Standard***
      iii. Select the **Annotative** check box.
      iv. ***Continue***

   d) <u>*Modify Multileader Style: ASME* window – *Leader Format* tab:</u> Set the *Arrowhead Size* to **2.5**. This size matches the size of the arrowheads defined in the *Dimension Style Manager*.

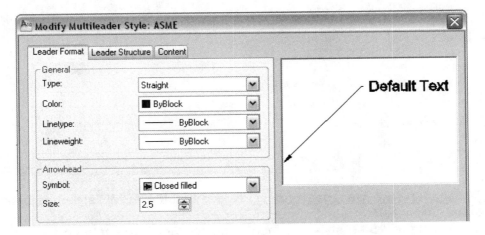

   e) <u>*Modify Multileader Style: ASME* window – *Leader Structure* tab:</u> Set the *landing distance* to **2.5**. This is the length of the horizontal segment.

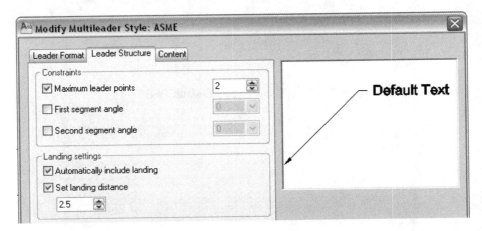

f) *Modify Multileader Style: ASME* window – *Content* tab: Set the *Right Horizontal attachment* to **Middle of top line** and then select **OK**. This defines how the text is placed relative to the landing.

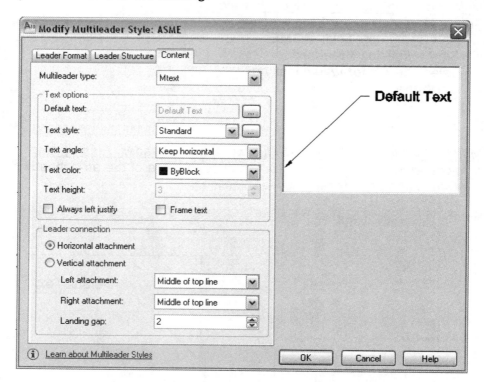

g) *Multileader Style Manager* window: Notice that the ASME style has been added to the *Styles* field.
    i. Select the **ASME** style and then select the **Set Current** button.
    ii. **Close**

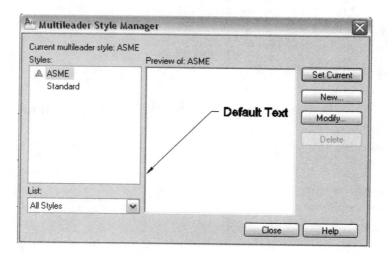

4) Try to update 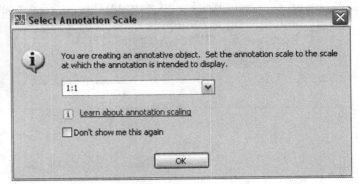 the chamfer dimension. Notice that multileaders do not update. **ERASE** the dimension and create a new one. If a *Select Annotation Scale* window appears select **OK**.

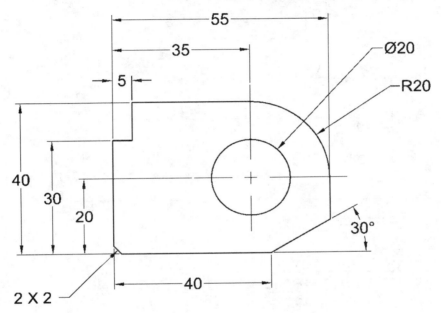

5.8.7) Annotative objects

1) Enter paper space (*Layout1*) and prepare your drawing to print 1:1 scale on an 8.5 x 11 inch sheet of paper.

> How?
>
> 1) Enter **Layout1**. Notice that the sheet does not have the same proportions as an 8.5 x 11 sheet of paper. The default metric paper size is 210 x 297 mm.
> 1) We will be printing out on an 8.5 x 11 sheet of paper. Enter the *Page Setup – Layout1* window (**Print – Page Setup...**) and set the following parameter.
>   a) Paper size = **8.5 x 11**.
>   b) *Plot scale* area:
>   i. Scale = **Custom**
>   ii. **1 inches** = **25.4** units
>   c) Plot style = **monochrome.ctb**

2) Insert your title block and border using a **25.4** scale. **EXPLODE** the title block and fill in the following information:
    - Part name = **DIMENSIONING TUT**
    - Scale = **1:1**

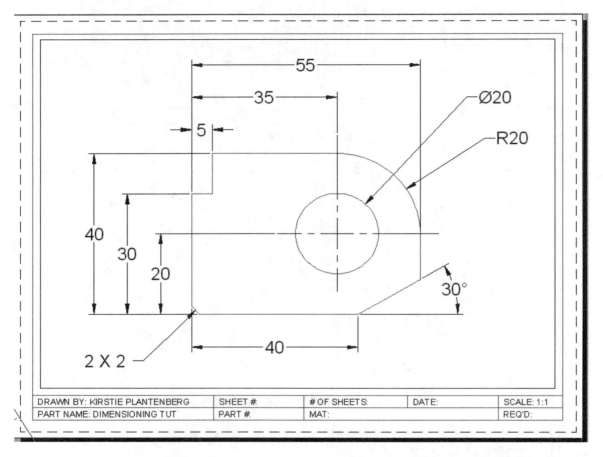

| DRAWN BY: KIRSTIE PLANTENBERG | SHEET #: | # OF SHEETS: | DATE: | SCALE: 1:1 |
| PART NAME: DIMENSIONING TUT | PART #: | MAT: | | REQ'D: |

3) Adjust your view port border so that it just fits in your title block, but it is still accessible. We will need to click on it later.

4) Place the view port border on the *Layout* layer.

5) Click on the view port border and set the *Viewport Scale* to *1:1*, center your model, turn the *Layout* layer OFF, and print your drawing.

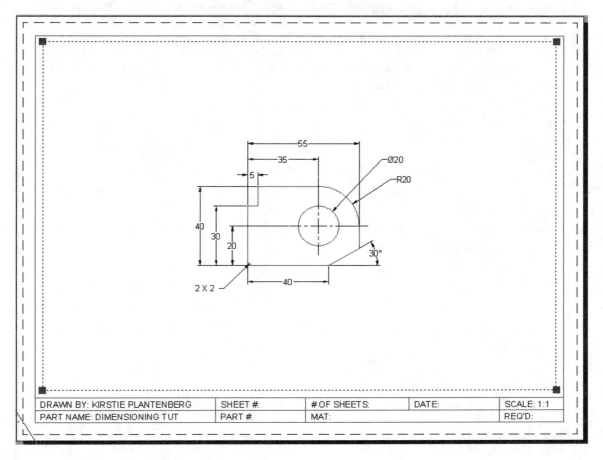

| DRAWN BY: KIRSTIE PLANTENBERG | SHEET #: | # OF SHEETS: | DATE: | SCALE: 1:1 |
| PART NAME: DIMENSIONING TUT | PART #: | MAT: | | REQ'D: |

6) Measure the size of the text and confirm that it is 3 mm high.

7) Turn the *Layout* layer ON.

8) Click on your view port border and change the *Viewport Scale:* to **2:1**. Your dimensions may disappear. This is because they are annotative objects and they do not, as of yet, support a 2:1 scale. To see your dimensions, click on the **Annotation Visibility** 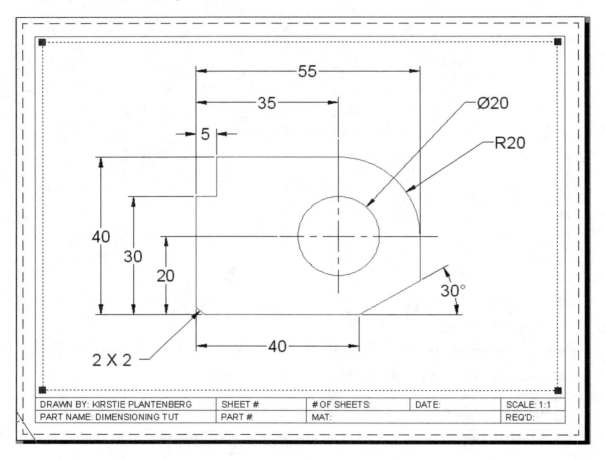 icon in the status bar. Notice that your model and dimension size has doubled. If you where to print your drawing now, the text height would measure 6 mm on the paper. However, we would like the text to always be 3 mm high no matter what the view port scale is.

| DRAWN BY: KIRSTIE PLANTENBERG | SHEET # | # OF SHEETS: | DATE: | SCALE: 1:1 |
| PART NAME: DIMENSIONING TUT | PART #: | MAT: | | REQ'D: |

9) Add a 2:1 scale support to the annotative dimensions.
   a) Double click inside your view port border to enter model space.
   b) Select all of your dimensions.

   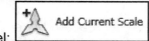

   c) *Annotation Scaling* panel:
   d) Click on one of the dimensions. Notice that is now shows two instances of the dimension. One instance for the 1:1 scale and one for the 2:1 scale.

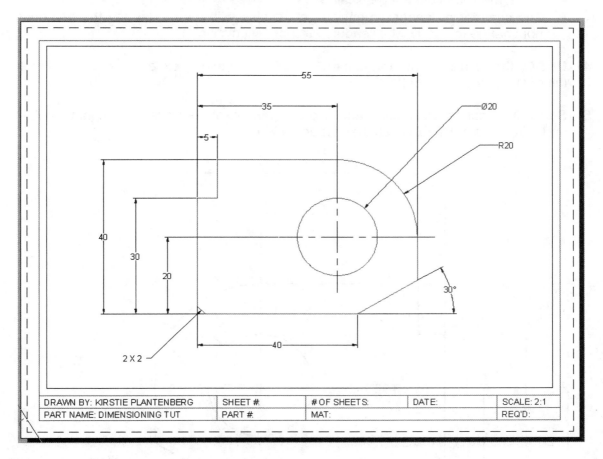

| DRAWN BY: KIRSTIE PLANTENBERG | SHEET #: | # OF SHEETS: | DATE: | SCALE: 2:1 |
| PART NAME: DIMENSIONING TUT | PART #: | MAT: | | REQ'D: |

10) Get back to the paper space by double clicking outside of the view port border.

11) Switch back and forth between a 1:1 scale and a 2:1 scale. Notice that the text height remains the same. Now the text will print out at 3 mm whether your view port scale is 1:1 or 2:1.

12) Set your view port scale to *2:1*, turn OFF the *Layout* layer, change the SCALE field in your title block to **2:1** and print your drawing. Measure the height of the text to confirm that it printed at 3 mm.

5.8.8) **Dimension scale and associativity**

1) Set your view port scale to *1:1*.

2) Enter model space from within paper space, select all the objects in your drawing, including the dimensions, and **SCALE** them by a factor of **2**.

3) You should notice three things.
   - The dimension values have increased by a factor of two. This is called associativity. The dimensions are associated with the object and the dimension values will change when the object changes.
   - The dimensions did not get scaled.
   - The chamfer or leader dimension gets scaled with the model and the text does not change to 4 X 4. Multileaders are not associative.

4) **UNDO** the scaling and this time **SCALE** everything, except for the chamfer dimension, by a scale of 2.

5) Select the chamfer dimension and use the grip boxes to move it back into position and edit the text (**DDEDIT**) so that it reads **4 X 4**.

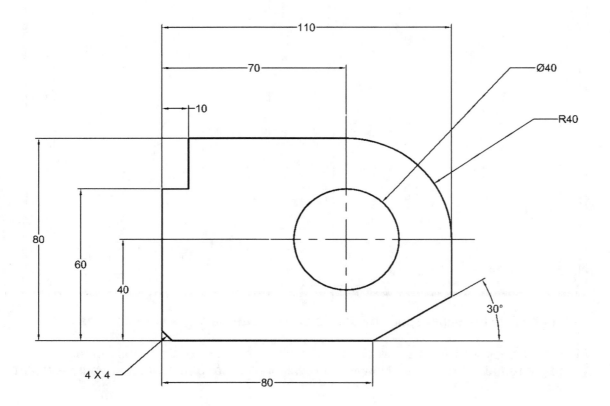

6) Notice that the 10 mm dimension value is outside the extension lines. Sometimes it is desirable to force the text between the extension lines.
   a) <u>Command:</u> **dimtix**
   b) Enter new value for DIMTIX <OFF>: **on**
   c) Update ⊞ only the 10 mm dimension.
   d) Turn your **DIMTIX** off.

7) Set the spacing between the linear dimensions to 10 mm 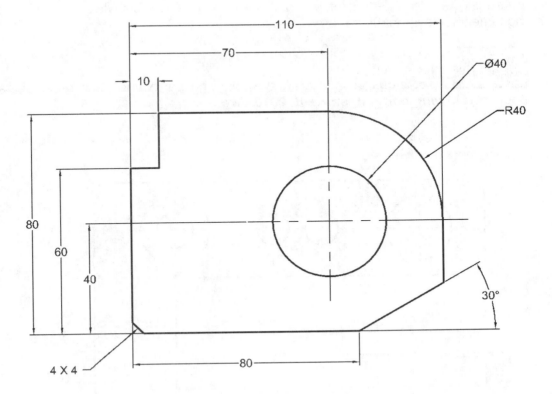. If necessary, use grip boxes to move the other dimensions to a more appropriate location.

8) Enter the appropriate scale in your title block, save and print your drawing.

In Class Student Exercise 5-1: Dimension styles

Create an annotative ASME dimension and multileader styles (as in the above tutorial) in your *set-mm.dwt* and your *set-inch.dwt*. Once the style is created and set to be the current dimension style, resave your template file. For the *set-inch.dwt*, use a 0.00 precision and suppress the leading zero. For the inch multileader, use the same setting as the *Standard* style.

5.9) <u>EDITING DIMENSION TEXT TUTORIAL</u>

The objective of this tutorial is to familiarize the user with editing dimension text. We will be adding text to a dimension without influencing its associativity. We will also be adding dimension symbols.

1) [Open] **set-inch.dwt** and draw the following part without the dimensions, or open the file **dim_edit_tut_student_2010.dwg**.

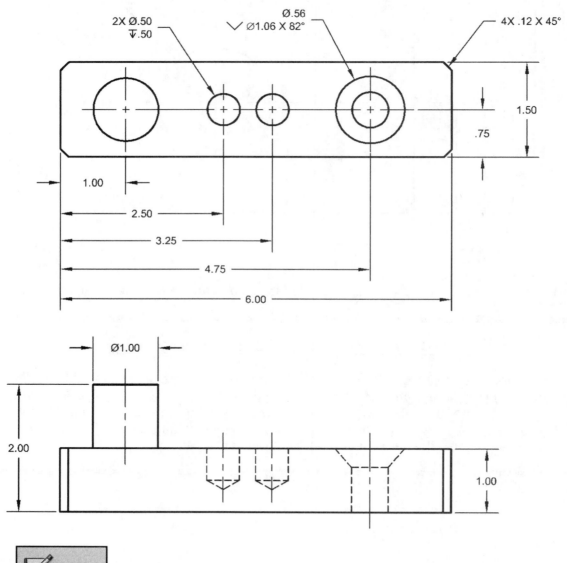

2) [Save As] **Dim Edit Tut.dwg**

3) Dimension the part as shown. To force the dimension text between the extension lines use the dimension variable **DIMTIX**. Remember that the `Space` bar repeats the last command used.

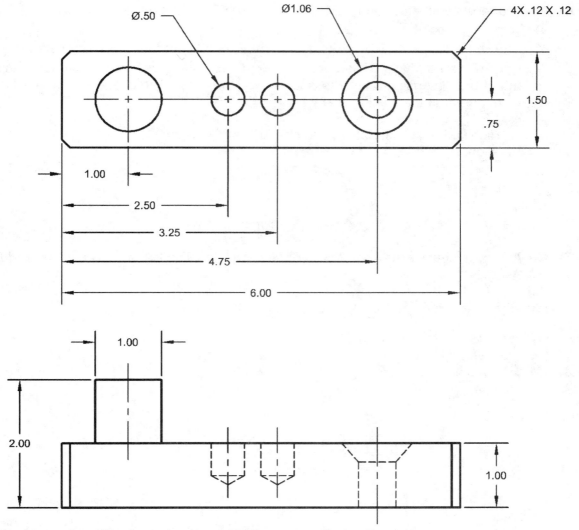

4) Add a diameter symbol to the 1.00 diameter cylinder dimension.
   a) <u>Command:</u> **ddedit**
   b) `Select an annotation object or [Undo]:` Select the 1.00 dimension text of the cylinder. Move the cursor to the front of the text.
   c) *Text Editor* tab:
      i. The symbols menu is available by selecting the @ icon. Select *Diameter* from the menu.

      ii.

   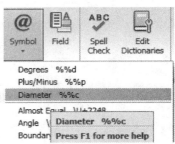

   d) `Select an annotation object or [Undo]:` **Enter**
   e) The dimension text should now read ⌀**1.00**.

5) On your own, change the chamfer dimension from 4X .12 X .12 to **4X .12 X 45°**. Insert a degree symbol in the same way that you inserted a diameter symbol.

6) Add the repeated feature and depth text to the ⌀.50 dimension text.
   a) Command: **ddedit**
   b) Select an annotation object or [Undo]: Select the ⌀.50 dimension text. Type **2X** and a space. Then use the **Right arrow** to position your cursor at the end of the dimension text. Press **Enter** to start a new line of text and type **x.50**. Make sure that the **x** is in lower case.
   c) *Text Editor* tab:
      i. Highlight the lower case **x** and change its font to **gdt**.
      ii. Align the text to the right.
      iii.
   d) Select an annotation object or [Undo]: **Enter**

7) On your own, change the countersink dimension text. The following is a list of useful *gdt* symbols.

8)

9) Print your drawing indicating your print scale in the title block. Your dimensions text should print out as 0.12 inch high.

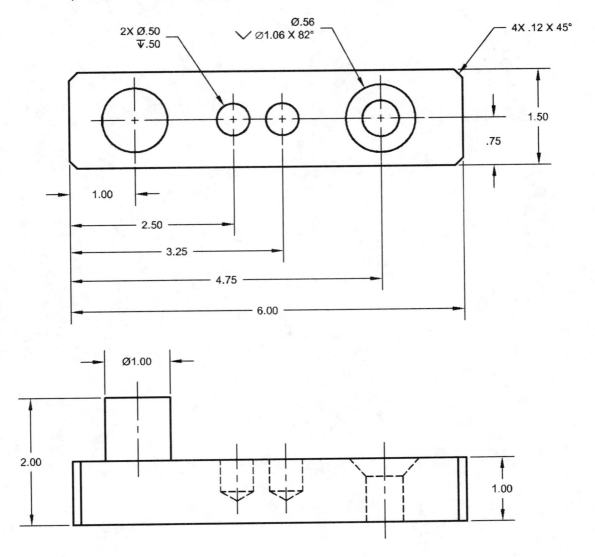

NOTES:

DIMENSIONING IN AUTOCAD CROSSWORD PUZZLE

Name: _____ Date: _____

CP5-1)

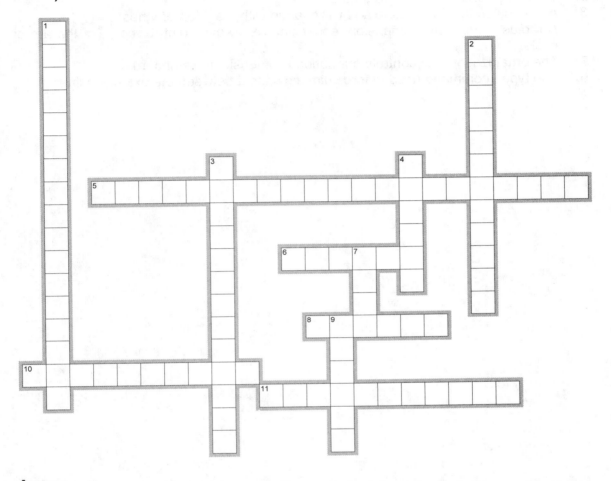

Across

5. The name of the window used to create and modify dimension styles.
6. The name of the command that allows you to apply any changes made to the current dimension style.
8. The typed command is used to edit dimension text.
10. An object that will adjust its scale as the viewport scale changes.
11. A dimension type that does not have associativity.

Down

1. The ribbon panel that contains commands that allow you to add and remove an annotative object's supported scales.
2. Dimension text should be aligned ...
3. A dimension that is linked to and will change with the geometry has ...
4. A radius or diameter dimension leader should always point to the ... of the arc or circle.
7. The organization that controls our national dimensioning standard.
9. The typed command used to force dimension text between the extension lines.

DIMENSIONING IN AUTOCAD PROBLEMS

Print each drawing using the appropriate pen widths and insert your titleblock.

P5-1) Using AutoCAD, draw the necessary views and completely dimension the part shown. Do not base your 2-D dimension placement on the 3-D dimensions shown. Use proper dimensioning techniques to dimension your object.

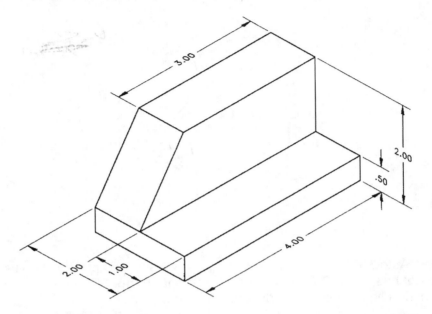

P5-2) Using AutoCAD, draw the necessary views and completely dimension the part shown. Do not base your 2-D dimension placement on the 3-D dimensions shown. Use proper dimensioning techniques to dimension your object.

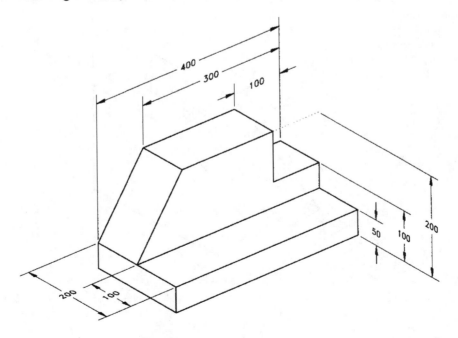

P5-3) Using AutoCAD, draw the necessary views and completely dimension the part shown. Do not base your 2-D dimension placement on the 3-D dimensions shown. Use proper dimensioning techniques to dimension your object.

2. 27

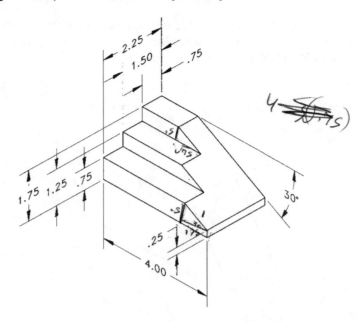

P5-4) Using AutoCAD, draw the necessary views and completely dimension the part shown. Do not base your 2-D dimension placement on the 3-D dimensions shown. Use proper dimensioning techniques to dimension your object.

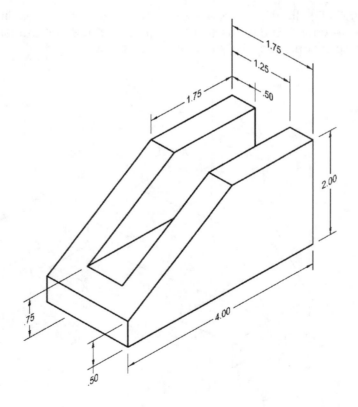

P5-5) Using AutoCAD, draw the necessary views and completely dimension the part shown. Do not base your 2-D dimension placement on the 3-D dimensions shown. Use proper dimensioning techniques to dimension your object.

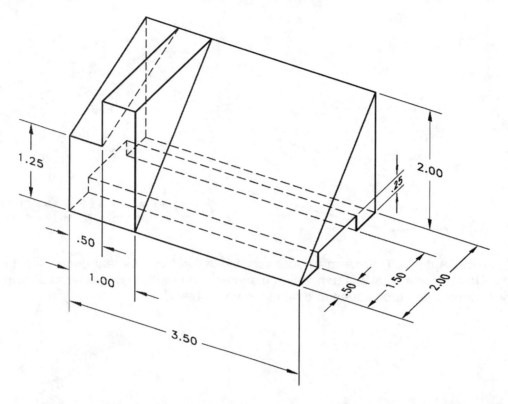

P5-6) Using AutoCAD, draw the necessary views and completely dimension the part shown. Do not base your 2-D dimension placement on the 3-D dimensions shown. Use proper dimensioning techniques to dimension your object.

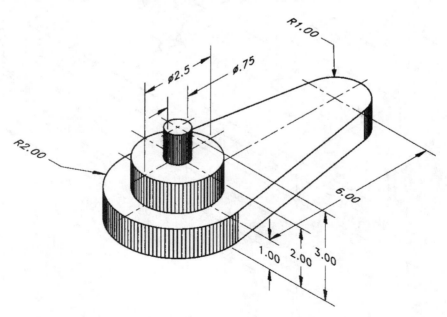

P5-7) Using AutoCAD, draw the necessary views and completely dimension the part shown. Do not base your 2-D dimension placement on the 3-D dimensions shown. Use proper dimensioning techniques to dimension your object.

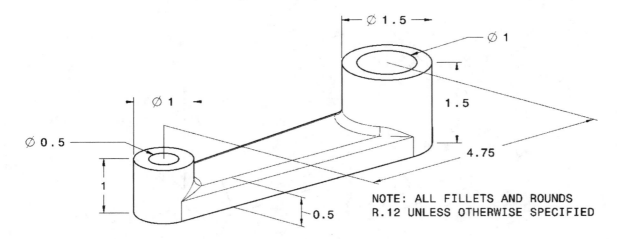

NOTE: ALL FILLETS AND ROUNDS R.12 UNLESS OTHERWISE SPECIFIED

P5-8) Using AutoCAD, draw the necessary views and completely dimension the part shown. Do not base your 2-D dimension placement on the 3-D dimensions shown. Use proper dimensioning techniques to dimension your object.

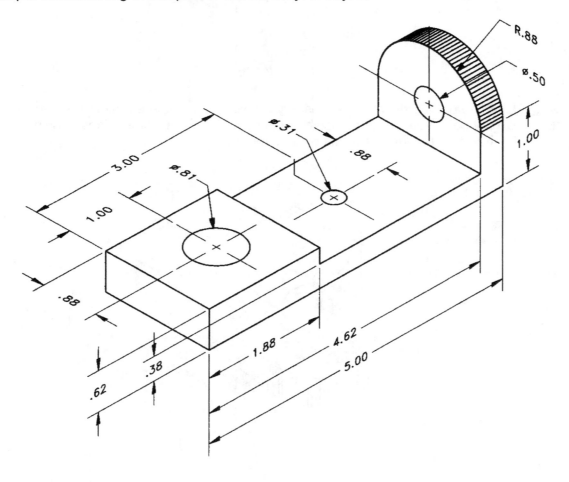

P5-9) Using AutoCAD, draw the necessary views and completely dimension the part shown. Do not base your 2-D dimension placement on the 3-D dimensions shown. Use proper dimensioning techniques to dimension your object.

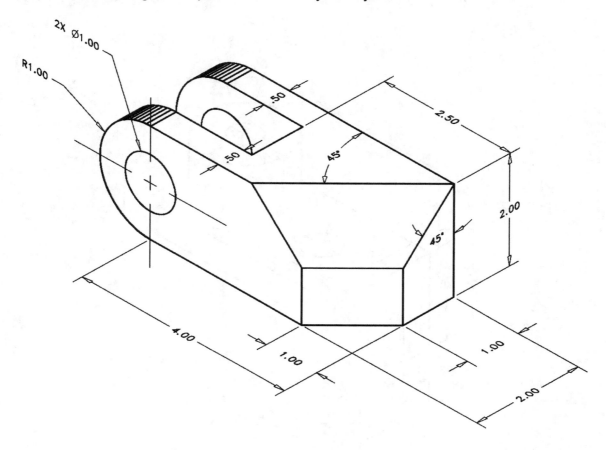

P5-10) Using AutoCAD, draw the necessary views and completely dimension the part shown. Do not base your 2-D dimension placement on the 3-D dimensions shown. Use proper dimensioning techniques to dimension your object.

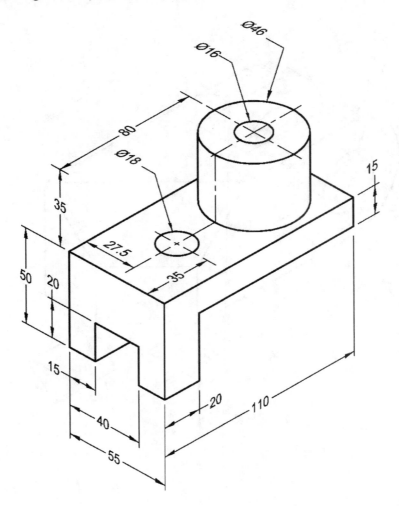

P5-11) Using AutoCAD, draw the necessary views and completely dimension the part shown. Do not base your 2-D dimension placement on the 3-D dimensions shown. Use proper dimensioning techniques to dimension your object.

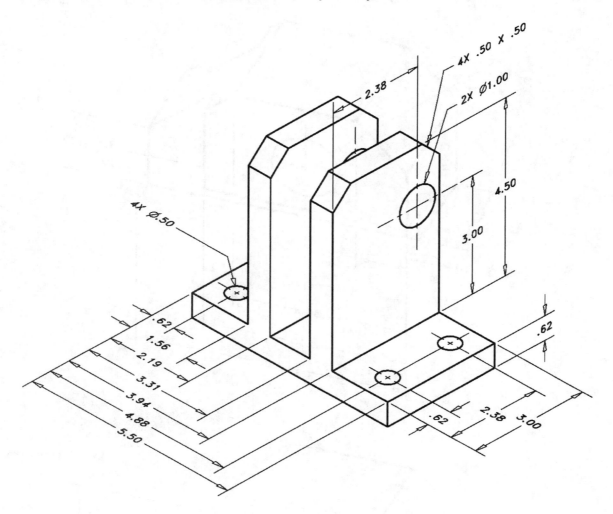

P5-12) Using AutoCAD, draw the necessary views and completely dimension the part shown. Do not base your 2-D dimension placement on the 3-D dimensions shown. Use proper dimensioning techniques to dimension your object.

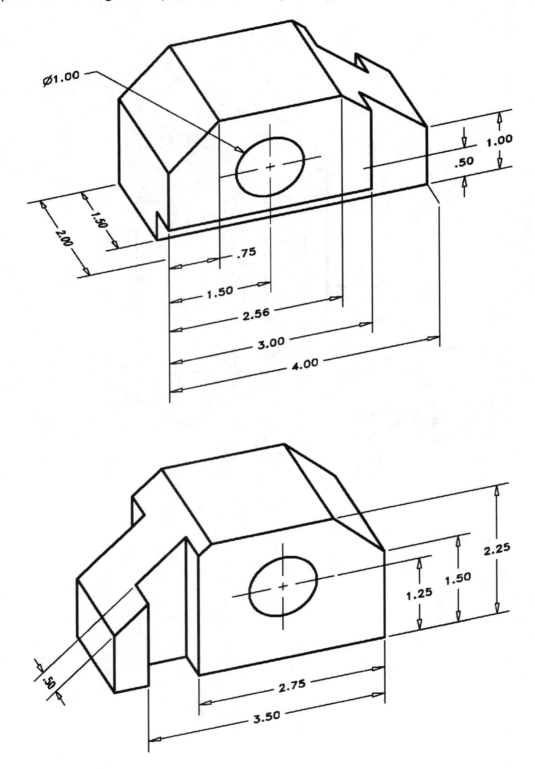

P5-13) Using AutoCAD, draw the necessary views and completely dimension the part shown. Do not base your 2-D dimension placement on the 3-D dimensions shown. Use proper dimensioning techniques to dimension your object.

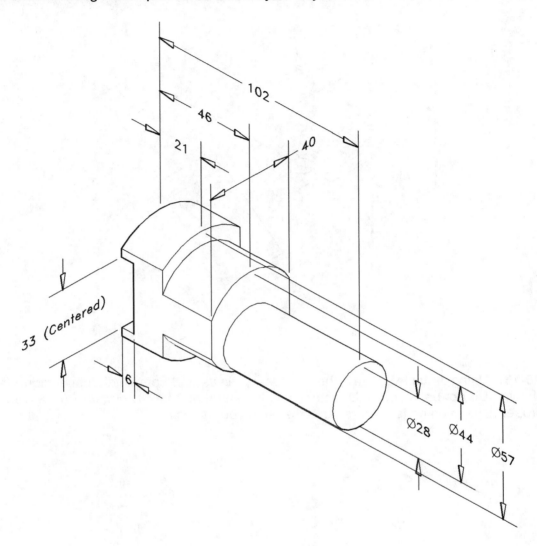

P5-14) Using AutoCAD, draw the necessary views and completely dimension the part shown. Do not base your 2-D dimension placement on the 3-D dimensions shown. Use proper dimensioning techniques to dimension your object.

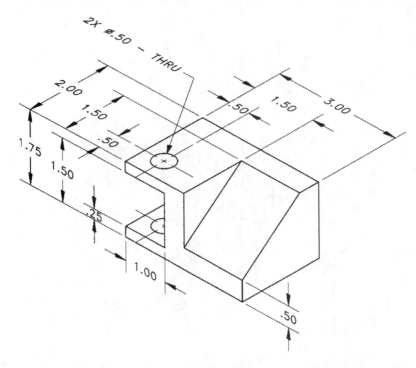

P5-15) Using AutoCAD, draw the necessary views and completely dimension the part shown. Do not base your 2-D dimension placement on the 3-D dimensions shown. Use proper dimensioning techniques to dimension your object.

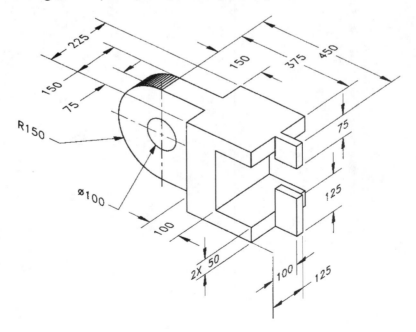

P5-16) Using AutoCAD, draw the necessary views and completely dimension the part shown. Do not base your 2-D dimension placement on the 3-D dimensions shown. Use proper dimensioning techniques to dimension your object.

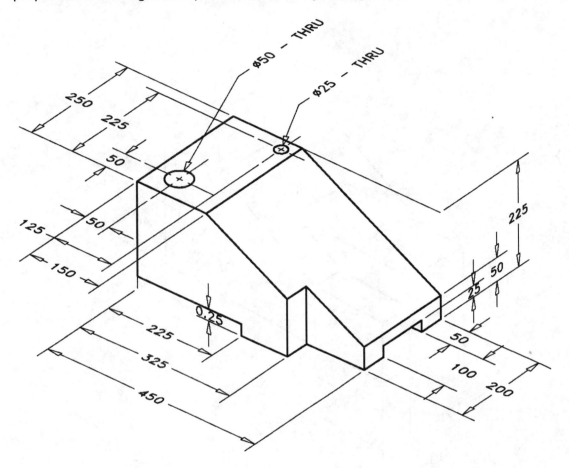

P5-17) Using AutoCAD, draw the necessary views and completely dimension the part shown. Do not base your 2-D dimension placement on the 3-D dimensions shown. Use proper dimensioning techniques to dimension your object.

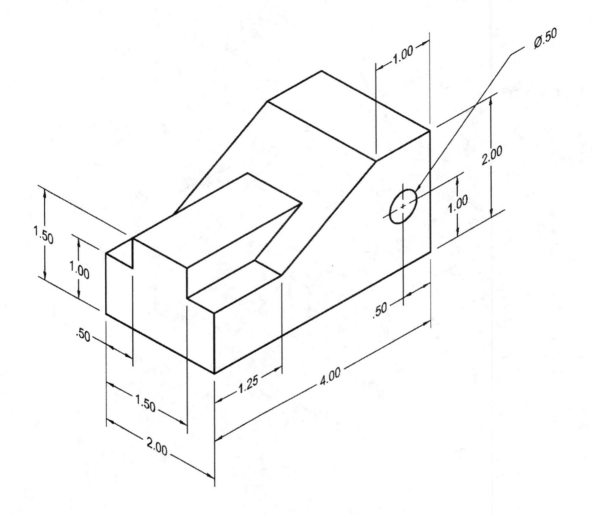

P5-18) Using AutoCAD, draw the necessary views and completely dimension the part shown. Do not base your 2-D dimension placement on the 3-D dimensions shown. Use proper dimensioning techniques to dimension your object.

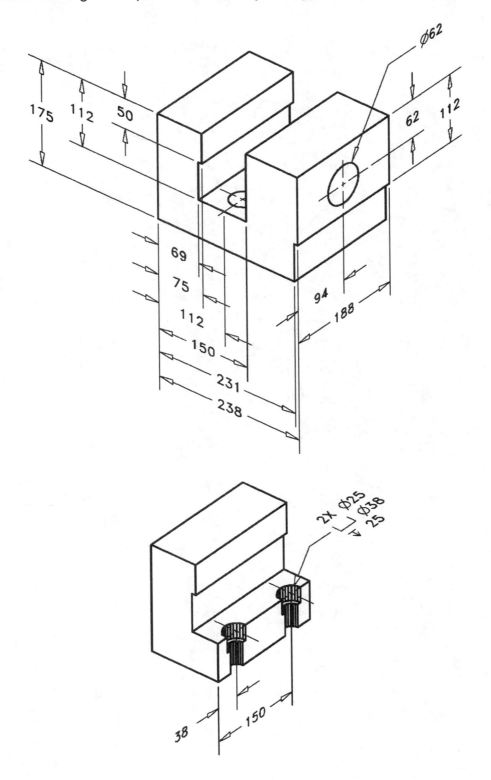

P5-19) Using AutoCAD, draw the necessary views and completely dimension the part shown. Do not base your 2-D dimension placement on the 3-D dimensions shown. Use proper dimensioning techniques to dimension your object.

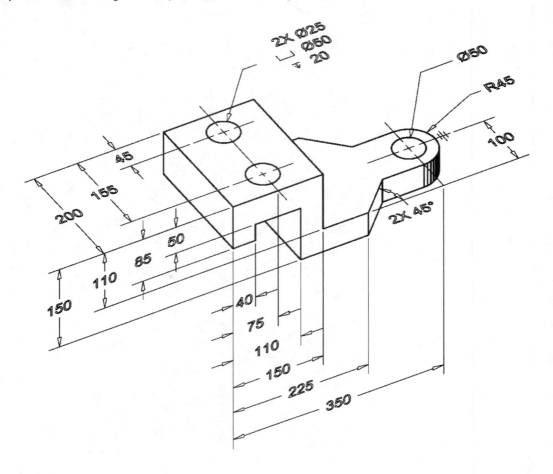

P5-20) Using AutoCAD, draw the necessary views and completely dimension the part shown. Do not base your 2-D dimension placement on the 3-D dimensions shown. Use proper dimensioning techniques to dimension your object.

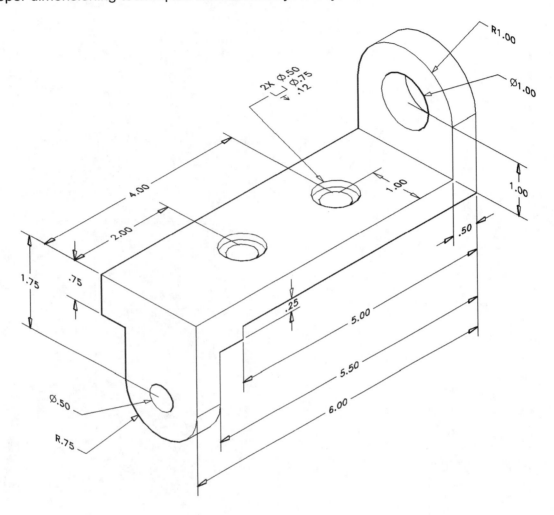

P5-21) Using AutoCAD, draw the necessary views and completely dimension the part shown. Do not base your 2-D dimension placement on the 3-D dimensions shown. Use proper dimensioning techniques to dimension your object.

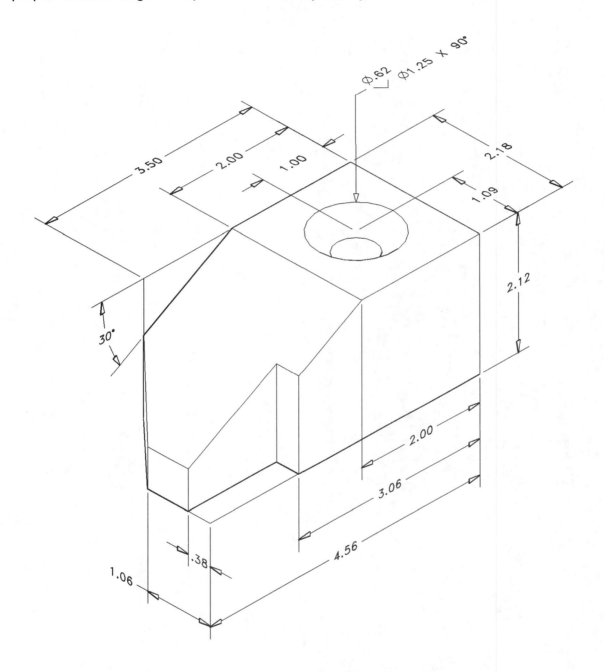

P5-22) Using AutoCAD, draw the necessary views and completely dimension the part shown. Do not base your 2-D dimension placement on the 3-D dimensions shown. Use proper dimensioning techniques to dimension your object.

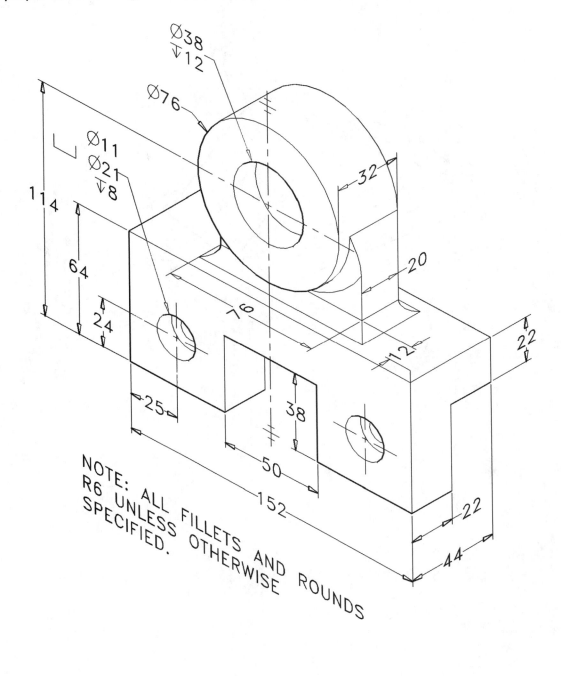

NOTE: ALL FILLETS AND ROUNDS R6 UNLESS OTHERWISE SPECIFIED.

P5-23) Using AutoCAD, draw the necessary views and completely dimension the part shown. Do not base your 2-D dimension placement on the 3-D dimensions shown. Use proper dimensioning techniques to dimension your object.

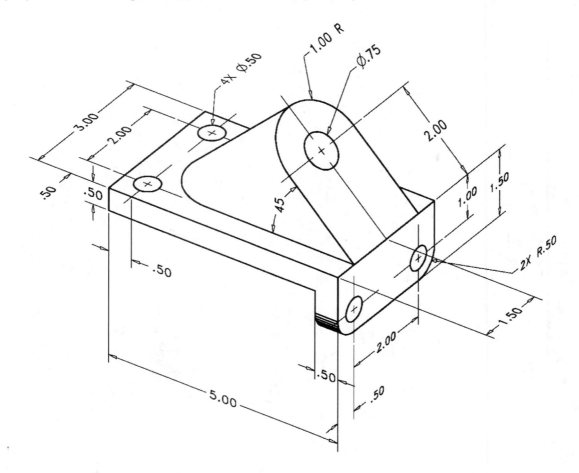

P5-24) Using AutoCAD, draw the necessary views and completely dimension the part shown. Do not base your 2-D dimension placement on the 3-D dimensions shown. Use proper dimensioning techniques to dimension your object.

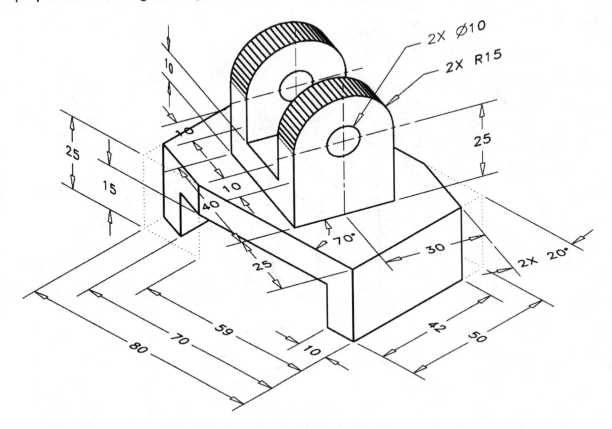

P5-25) Using AutoCAD, draw the necessary views and completely dimension the part shown. Do not base your 2-D dimension placement on the 3-D dimensions shown. Use proper dimensioning techniques to dimension your object.

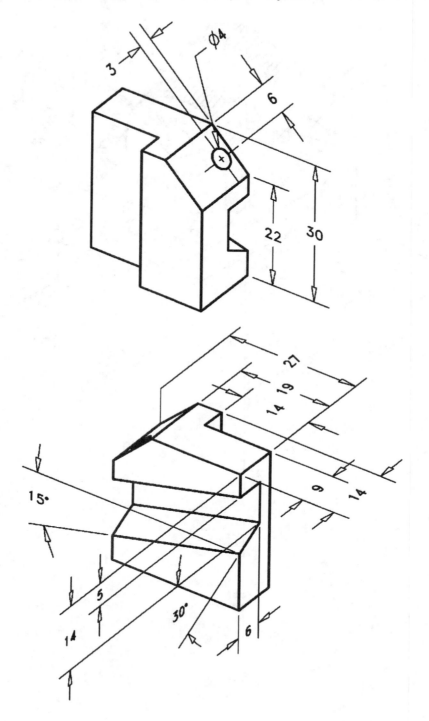

P5-26) Using AutoCAD, draw the necessary views and completely dimension the part shown. Do not base your 2-D dimension placement on the 3-D dimensions shown. Use proper dimensioning techniques to dimension your object.

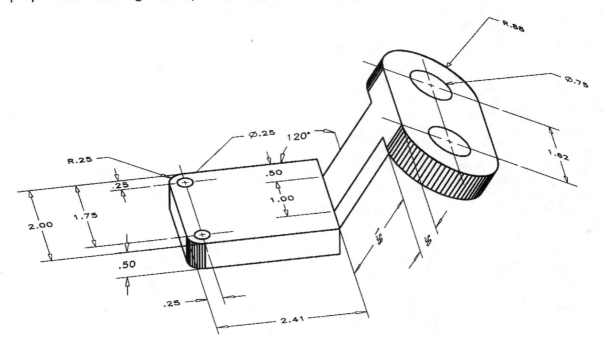

NOTES:

SECTIONING

In Chapter 6 you will learn how to create various types of sectional views. Sectional views allow you to see inside an object. Using a sectional view within an orthographic projection can be very useful for parts that have complex interior geometry. By the end of this chapter, you will be able to create several different types of sectional views. You will also be able to choose which type of section is the most appropriate for a given part.

6.1) SECTIONAL VIEWS

A sectional view or section looks inside an object. Sections are used to clarify the interior construction of a part that cannot be clearly described by hidden lines in exterior views. It is a cut away view of an object. Often, objects are more complex and interesting on the inside than on the outside. **By taking an imaginary cut through the object and removing a portion, the inside features may be seen more clearly.** For example, a geode is a rock that is very plain and featureless on the outside, but cut into it and you get an array of beautiful crystals.

6.1.1) Creating a Section View

To produce a section view, the part is cut using an imaginary cutting plane. The portion of the part that is between the observer and the cutting plane is mentally discarded exposing the interior construction as shown in Figure 6-1.

A sectional view should be projected perpendicular to the cutting plane and conform to the standard arrangement of views. If there are more than one section, they should be labeled with capital letters such as A, B or C. These letters are placed near the arrows of the cutting plane line. The sectional view is then labeled with the corresponding letter (e.g. SECTION A-A) as shown in Figure 6-2. Letters that should not be used to label sections are I, O, Q, S, X and Z. These letters may lead to misinterpretation. They are often used for other purposes.

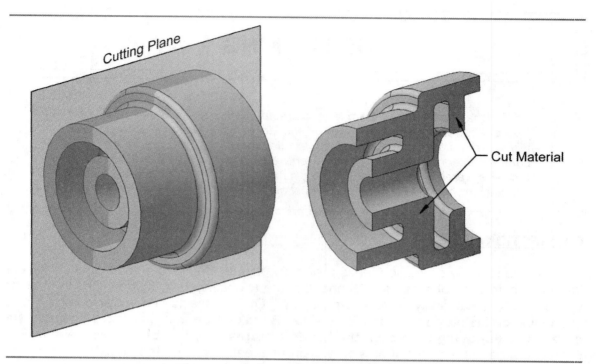

Figure 6-1: Creating a section view.

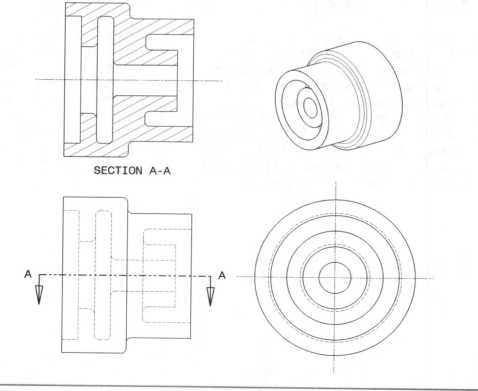

SECTION A-A

Figure 6-2: Sectional view.

6.1.2) <u>Lines used in Sectional Views</u>

• <u>Cutting Plane Line</u>

A cutting plane line is used to show where the object is being cut and represents the edge view of the cutting plane. Arrows are placed at the ends of the cutting plane line to indicate the direction of sight. The arrows point to the portion of the object that is kept. Cutting plane lines are thick (0.6 to 0.8 mm) and take precedence over centerlines. Figure 6-3 shows the two different types of cutting plane lines that are used on prints and Figure 6-2 illustrates its use.

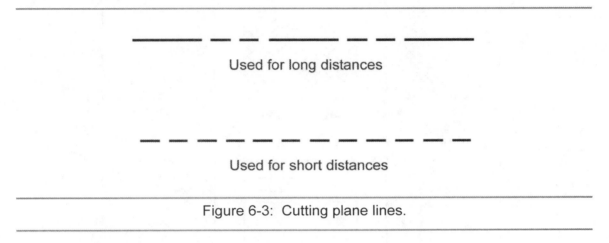

Used for long distances

Used for short distances

Figure 6-3: Cutting plane lines.

• <u>Section Lines</u>

Section lines are used to indicate where the cutting plane cuts the material (see Figure 6-2). Cut material is that which makes contact with the cutting plane. Section lines have the following properties:

√ Section lines are thin lines (0.3 mm).
√ Section line symbols (i.e. line type and spacing) are chosen according to the material from which the object is made. Figure 6-4 shows some of the more commonly used section line symbols.
√ Section lines are drawn at a 45° angle to the horizontal unless there is some advantage in using a different angle.

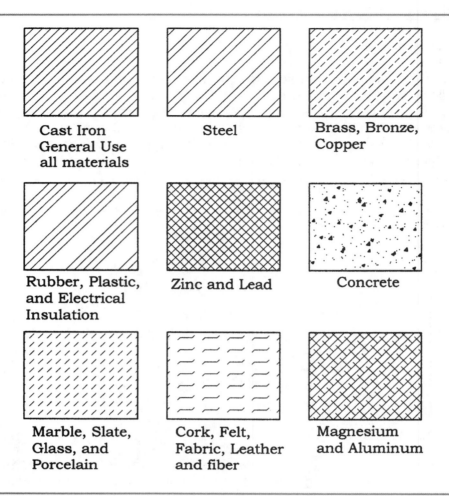

Figure 6-4: Section line symbols.

6.1.3) Rules of Sectioning

Rule 1.   A section lined area is always completely bounded by a visible outline.

Rule 2.   The section lines in all sectioned areas should be parallel. Section lines shown in opposite directions indicate a different part.

Rule 3.   All the visible edges behind the cutting plane should be shown.

Rule 4.   Hidden features should be omitted in all areas of a section view. Exceptions include threads and broken out sections.

6.2) BASIC SECTIONS

Many types of sectioning techniques are available to use. The type chosen depends on the situation and what information needs to be conveyed.

6.2.1) Full Section

To create a full section, the cutting plane passes fully through the object. The half of the object that is between the observer and the cutting plane is mentally removed exposing the cut surface and visible background lines of the remaining portion. Full sections are used in many cases to avoid having to dimension hidden lines as shown in Figure 6-5.

View Video Exercise 6-1 and Try Exercise 6-2

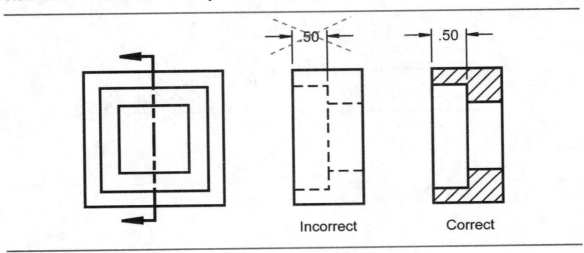

.50   .50

Incorrect   Correct

Figure 6-5: Full section.

6.2.2) Half Section

A half section has the advantage of exposing the interior of one half of an object while retaining the exterior of the other half. Half sections are used mainly for symmetric, nearly symmetric objects or assembly drawings. The half section is obtained by passing two cutting planes through the object, at right angles to each other, such that the intersection of the two planes coincides with the axis of symmetry. Therefore, only a quarter of the object is mentally removed. On the sectional view, a centerline is used to separate the sectioned and unsectioned halves. Hidden lines should not be shown on either half. Figure 6-6 shows an example of a half section.

View Video Exercise 6-3 and Try Exercise 6-4

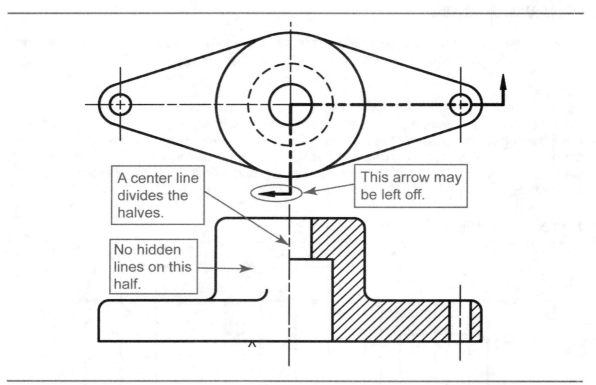

Figure 6-6: Half section.

6.2.3) Offset Section

An offset section is produced by bending the cutting plane to show features that don't lie in the same plane. The section is drawn as if the offsets in the cutting plane were in one plane. Figure 6-7 shows an offset section.

Try Exercise 6-5

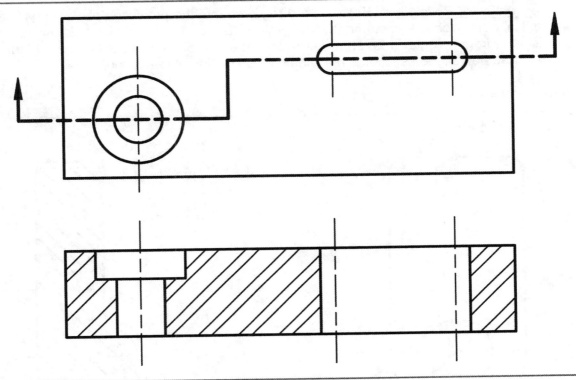

Figure 6-7: Offset section.

6.3) **ADVANCED SECTIONS**

6.3.1) **Aligned Section**

In order to include angled elements in a section, the cutting plane may be bent so that it passes through those features. The plane and features are then revolved, according to the convention of revolution, into the original plane.

o Convention of Revolution: Features are revolved into the projection plane, usually a vertical or horizontal plane, and then projected. The purpose of this is to show a true distance from a center or to show features that would otherwise not be seen. Figure 6-8 shows an aligned section employing the convention of revolution.

View Video Exercise 6-6 and Try Exercise 6-7

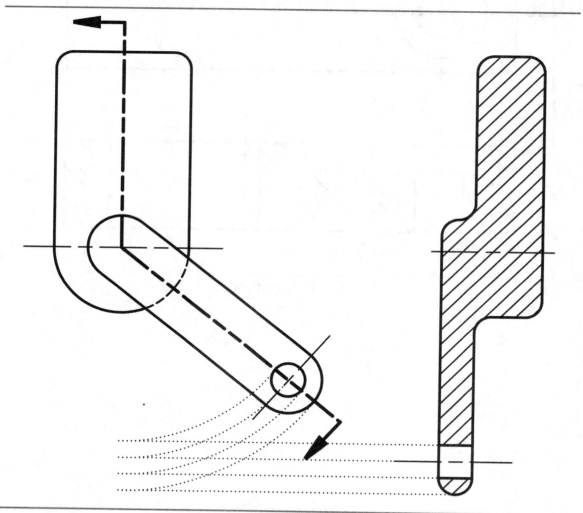

Figure 6-8: Aligned section.

6.3.2) <u>Rib and Web Sections</u>

To avoid a false impression of thickness and solidity, ribs and webs and other similar features are not sectioned even though the cutting plane passes along the center plane of the rib or web. However, if the cutting plane passes crosswise through the rib or web, the member is shown in section as indicated in Figure 6-9.

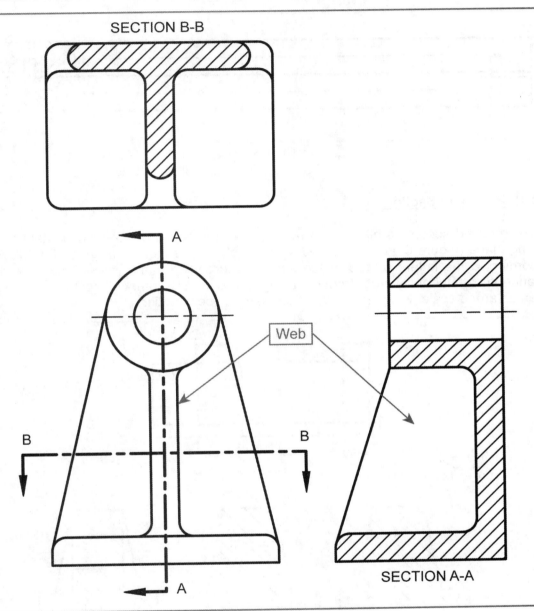

Figure 6-9: Rib and web sections.

6.3.3) Broken Section

Sometimes only a portion of the object needs to be sectioned to show a single feature of the part. In this case, the sectional area is bound on one side by a break line. Hidden lines are shown in the unsectioned area of a broken section. Figure 6-10 shows an example of a broken section.

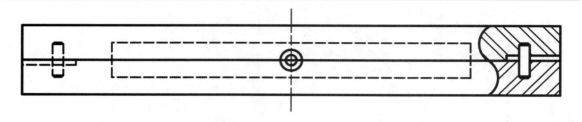

Figure 6-10: Broken section.

6.3.4) Removed Section

A removed section is one that is not in direct projection of the view containing the cutting plane (Figure 6-11). Removed sections should be labeled (e.g. SECTION A-A) according to the letters placed at the ends of the cutting plane line. They should be arranged in alphabetical order from left to right. Frequently, removed sections are drawn to an enlarged scale, which is indicated beneath the section title.

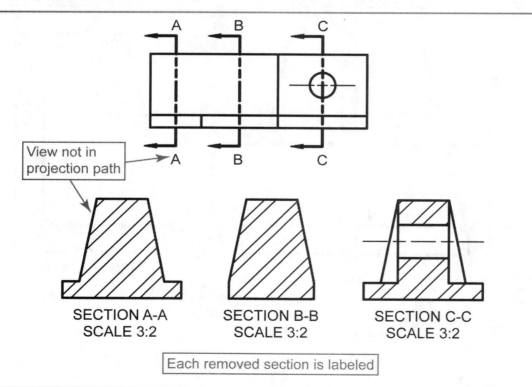

Figure 6-11: Removed section.

6.3.5) Revolved Section

The cross sectional shape of a bar, arm, spoke or other elongated objects may be shown in the longitudinal view by means of a revolved section. The visible lines adjacent to a revolved section may be broken out if desired. The super imposition of the revolved section requires the removal of all original lines covered by the section as shown in Figure 6-12. The true shape of a revolved section should be retained after the revolution regardless of the direction of the lines in the view.

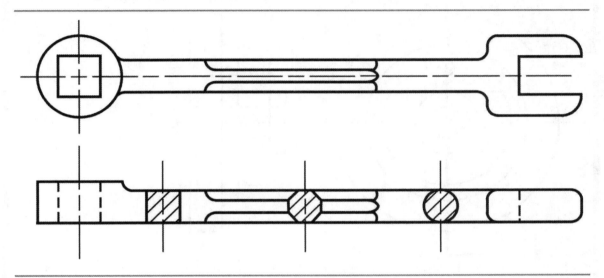

Figure 6-12: Revolved section.

6.3.6) Non-Sectioned Parts

It is common practice to show standard parts like nuts, bolts, rivets, shafts and screws 'in the round' or un-sectioned. This is done because they have no internal features. Other non-sectioned parts include bearings, gear teeth, dowels, and pins.

6.3.7) Thin Sections

For extremely thin parts of less than 4 mm thickness, such as sheet metal, washers, and gaskets, section lines are ineffective; therefore, the parts should be shown in solid black or without section lines.

Video Exercise 6-1: Full Section

The following video exercise will take you through creating a full section of the objects shown.

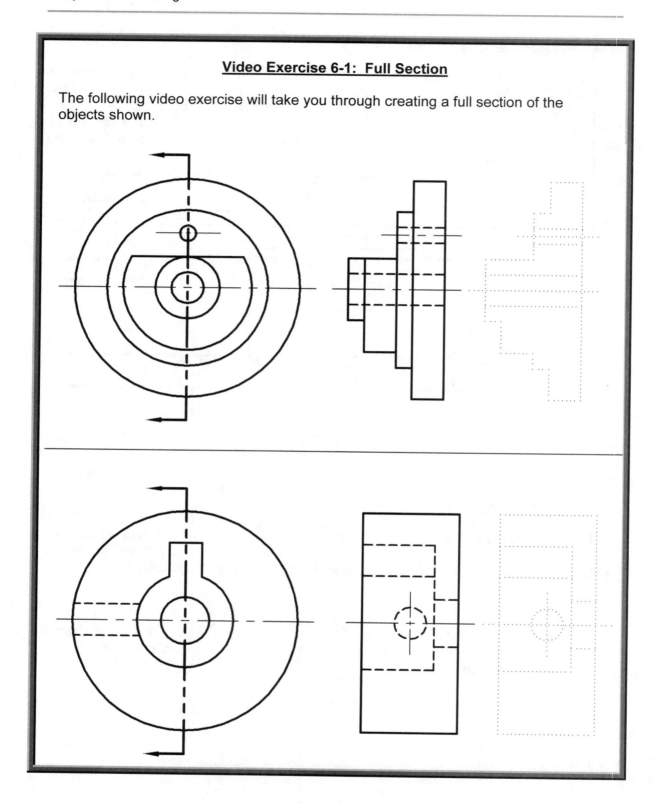

Instructor Led Exercise 6-2: Full section

Given the top and right side views, sketch the front view as a full section. The material used is steel.

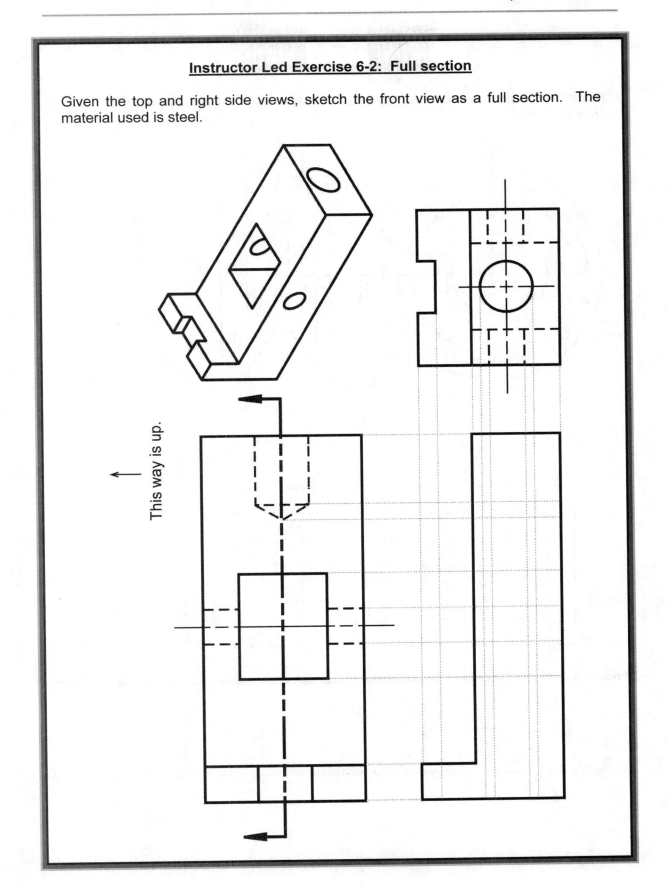

This way is up.

Video Exercise 6-3: Half Section

The following video exercise will take you through creating a half section of the objects shown.

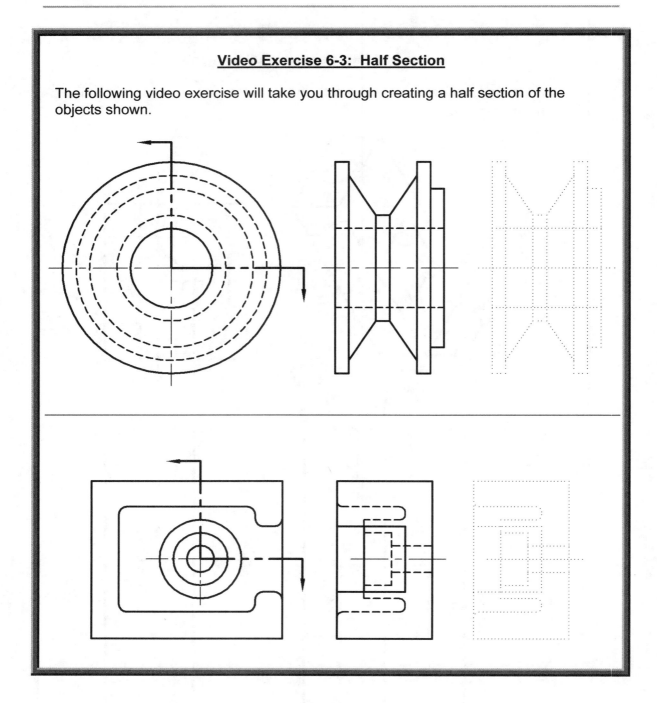

Instructor Led Exercise 6-4: Half section

Given the front and right side views, sketch the top view as a full section and create a half sectioned front view. The material is brass.

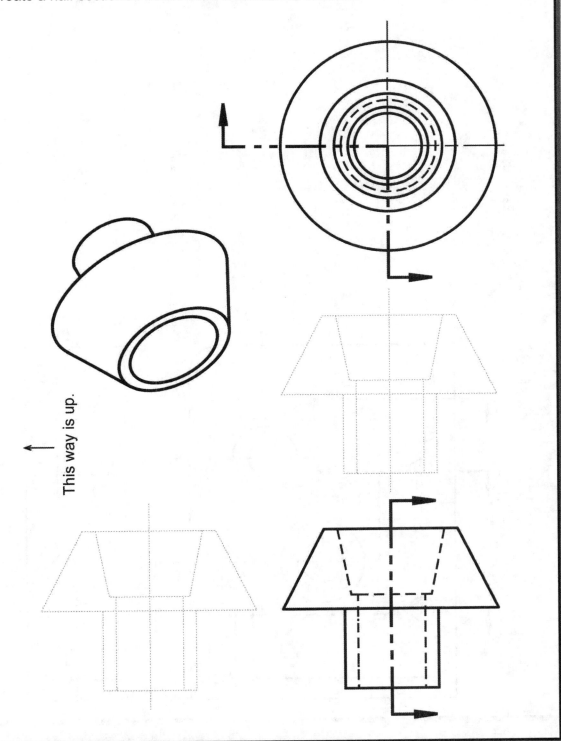

This way is up.

Instructor Led Exercise 6-5: Offset section

Given the front and top views, sketch the three missing section views in their appropriate places. The material is cast iron.

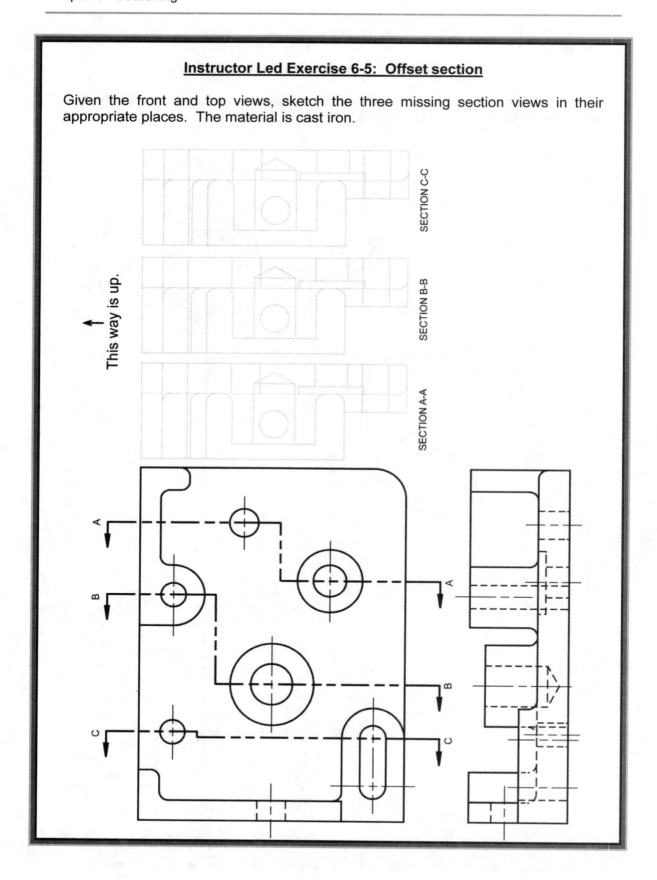

Video Exercise 6-6: Aligned Section

The following video exercise will take you through creating an aligned section of the object shown.

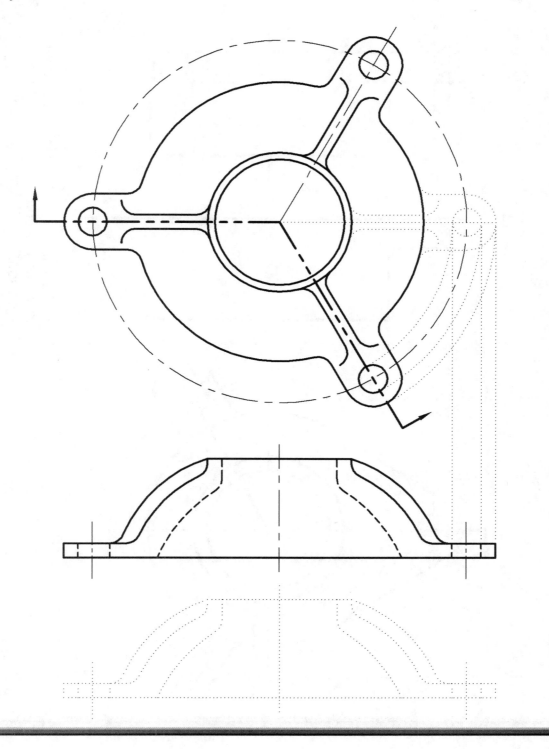

Instructor Led Exercise 6-7: Aligned section

Given the front and unrevolved right side views, sketch the right side view as an aligned section using the conventions of revolution. The material is cast iron.

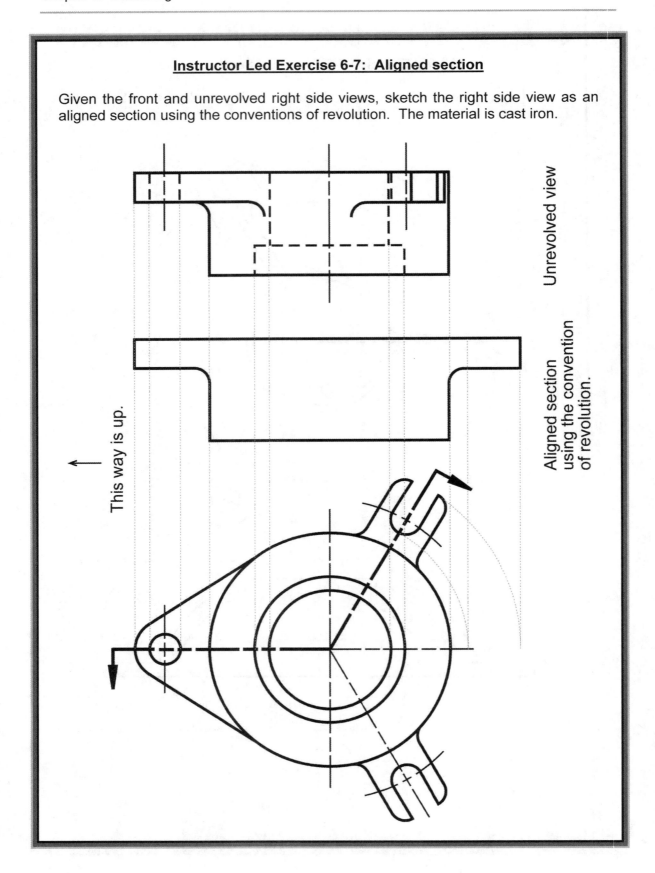

Unrevolved view

Aligned section using the convention of revolution.

This way is up.

SECTIONING CROSSWORD PUZZLE

Name: _____   Date: _____

CP6-1)

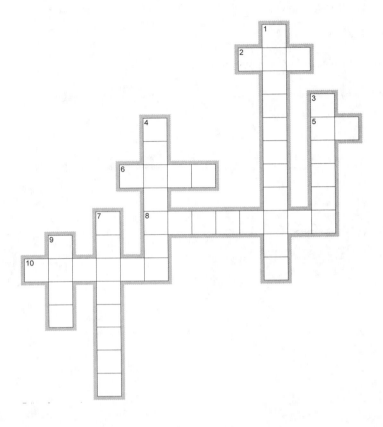

Across

2. A cutting plane line indicates where the part is being ....
5. Is it permissible to show hidden lines on some portion of a half section?
6. A full section removes one .... of the object.
8. The convention of revolution is used when creating an aligned section so that the angle features may be shown ....
10. The sectioned and non-sectioned halves of a half section are separated by a .... line.

Down

1. Section lines are used to indicate ....
3. The purpose of a section view is to see what is on the .... of a part.
4. A half section removes one .... of the object.
7. Section line symbols or patterns depend on a part's ....
9. The arrows at the end of a cutting plane line point to the part of the object that is being ....

NOTES:

SECTIONING PROBLEMS

Name: _____ Date: _____

P6-1) Sketch the sectional view as indicated. The material of the part is Steel.

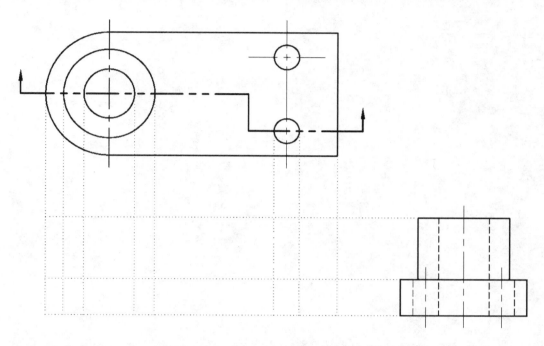

P6-2) Sketch the sectional view as indicated. The material of the part is Aluminum.

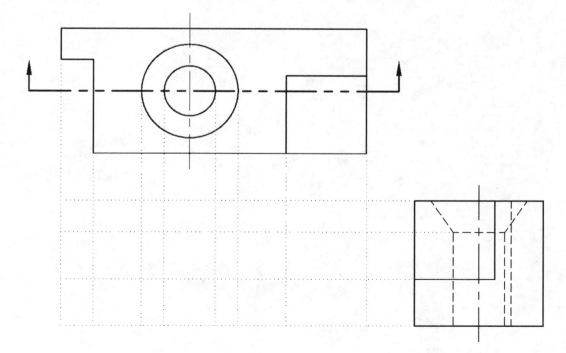

NOTES:

Name: _____ Date: _____

P6-3) Sketch the sectional view as indicated. The material of the part is Rubber.

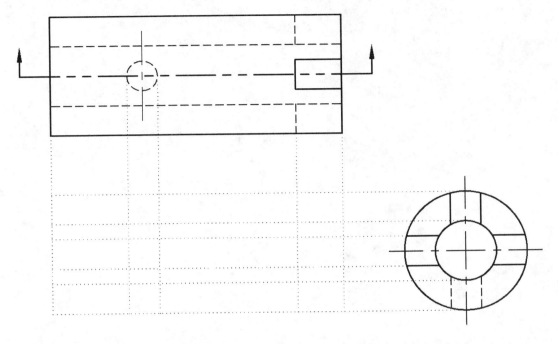

P6-4) Sketch the sectional view as indicated. The material of the part is Brass.

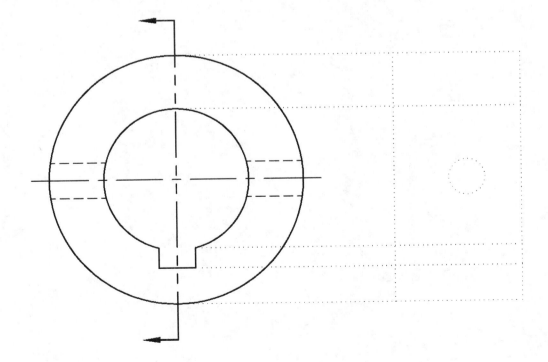

NOTES:

Name: _____ Date: _____

P6-5) Sketch the sectional view as indicated. The material of the part is Aluminum.

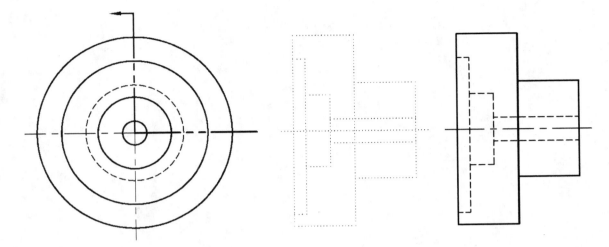

P6-6) Sketch the sectional view as indicated. The material of the part is Cast Iron.

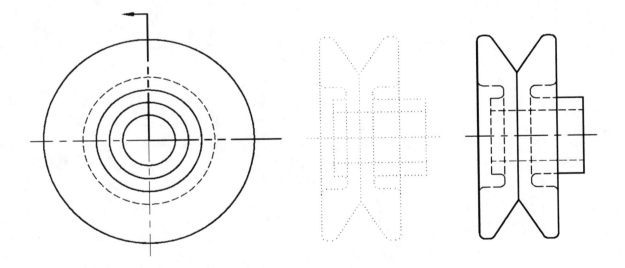

NOTES:

Name: _____   Date: _____

P6-7) Sketch the sectional view as indicated. The material of the part is Cast Iron.

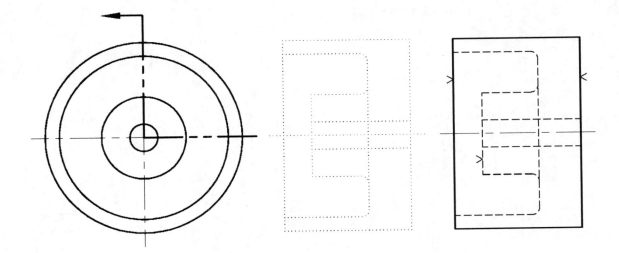

P6-8) Sketch the sectional view as indicated. The material of the part is Brass.

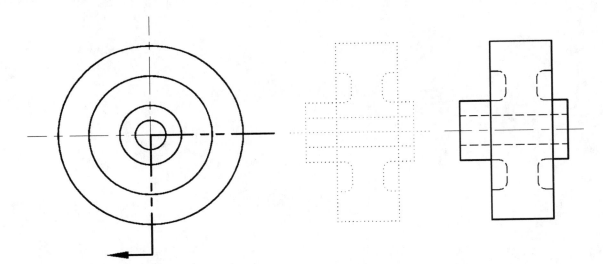

NOTES:

Name: _____ Date: _____

P6-9) Sketch the sectional view as indicated. The material of the part is Rubber.

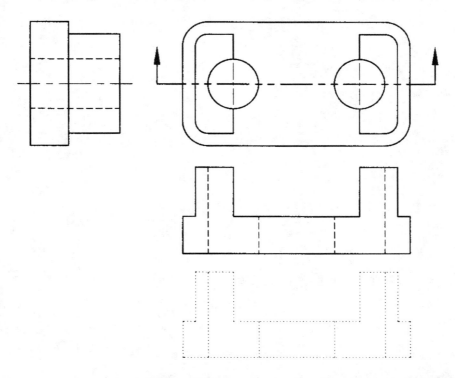

P6-10) Sketch the sectional view as indicated. The material of the part is Steel.

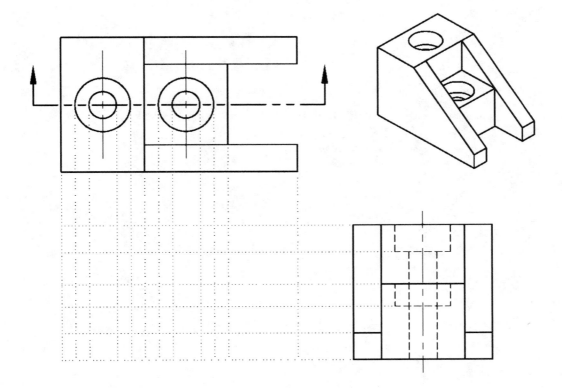

NOTES:

Name: _____ Date: _____

P6-11) Sketch the sectional view as indicated. The material of the part is Rubber.

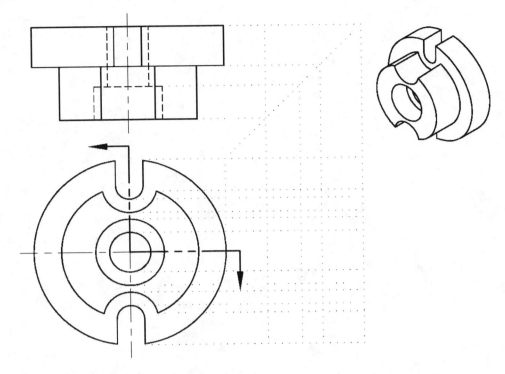

P6-12) Sketch the sectional view as indicated. The material of the part is Steel.

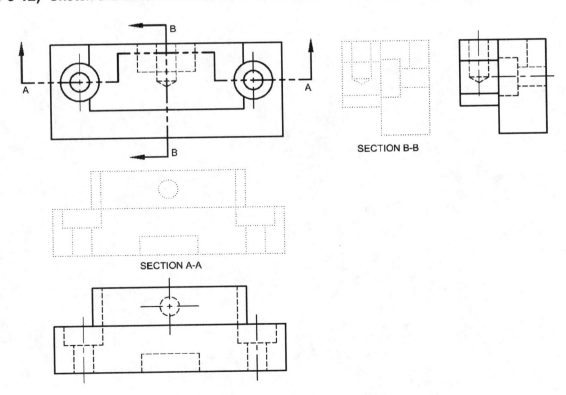

SECTION B-B

SECTION A-A

NOTES:

Name: _____ Date: _____

P6-13) Sketch the sectional view as indicated. The material of the part is Steel.

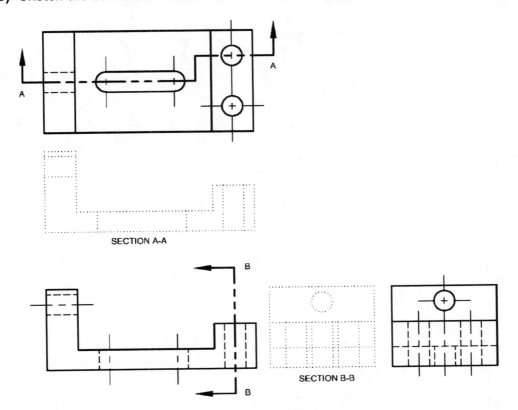

P6-14) Sketch the sectional view as indicated. The material of the part is Aluminum.

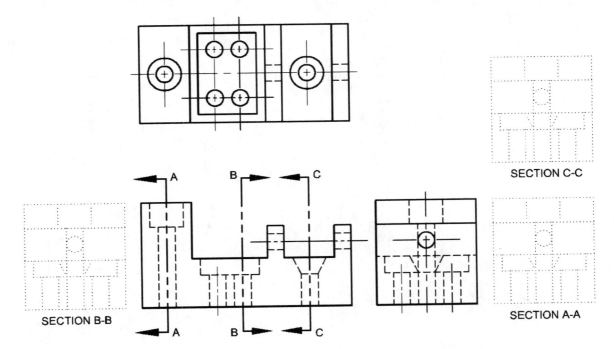

NOTES:

Name: _____   Date: _____

P6-15) Sketch the sectional view as indicated. The material of the part is Cast Iron.

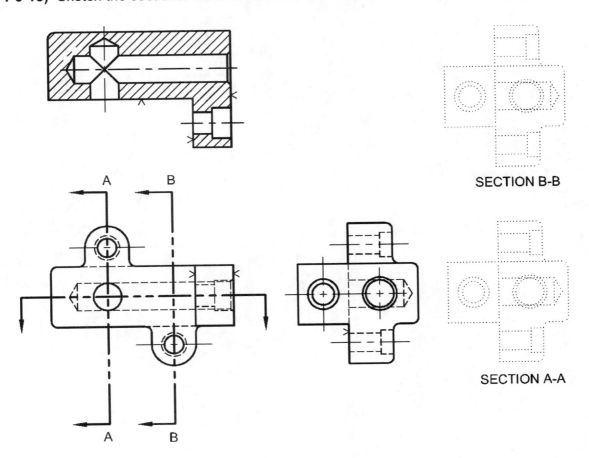

SECTION B-B

SECTION A-A

NOTES:

Name: _____   Date: _____

P6-16) Sketch the sectional view as indicated. The material of the part is Steel.

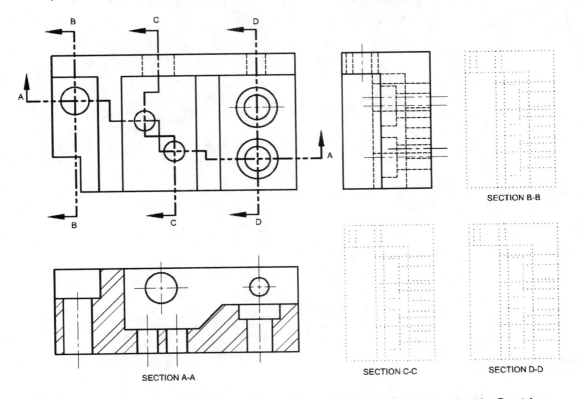

SECTION B-B

SECTION A-A

SECTION C-C   SECTION D-D

P6-17) Sketch the sectional view as indicated. The material of the part is Cast Iron.

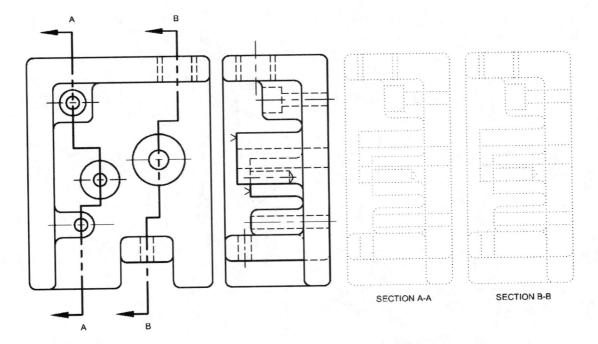

SECTION A-A   SECTION B-B

<u>NOTES:</u>

Name: _____ Date: _____

P6-18) Sketch the sectional view as indicated. The material of the part is Steel.

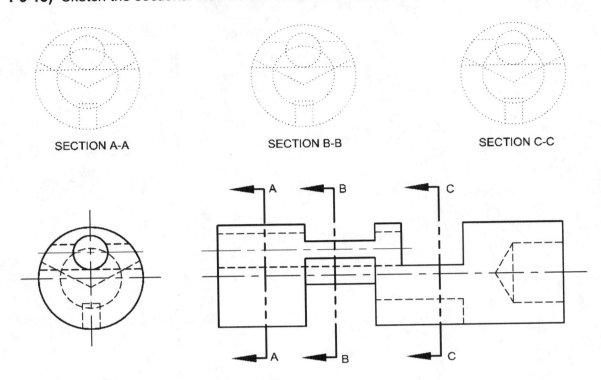

P6-19) Sketch the sectional view as indicated. The material of the part is Aluminum.

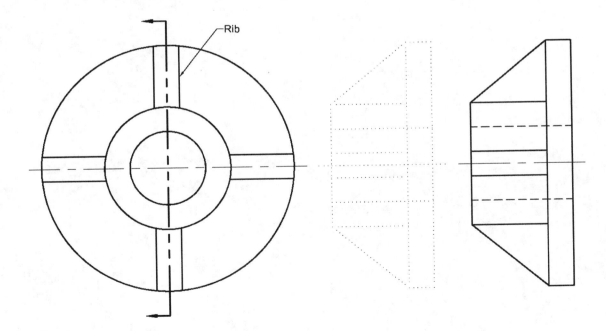

NOTES:

Name: _____ Date: _____

P6-20) Sketch an aligned section view using the conventions of revolution. The unsectioned right side view is shown true shape. The material of the part is Cast Iron.

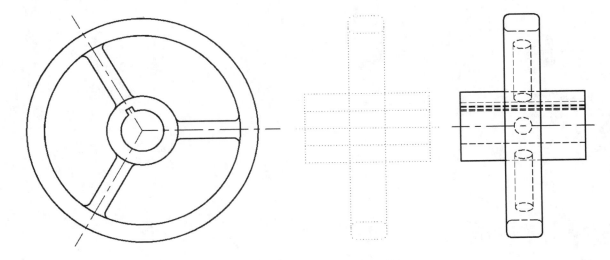

P6-21) Sketch an aligned section view using the conventions of revolution. The unsectioned right side view is shown true shape. The material of the part is Cast Iron.

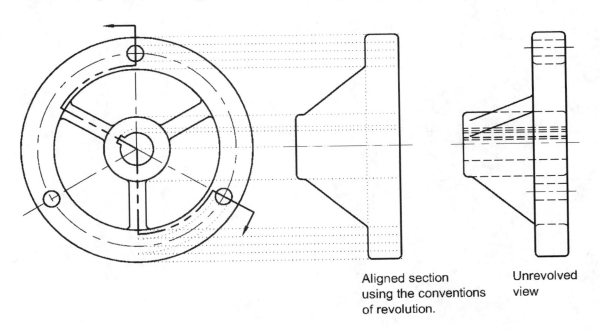

Aligned section
using the conventions
of revolution.

Unrevolved
view

NOTES:

CREATING SECTION VIEWS IN AUTOCAD

In Chapter 7 you will learn how to create section views in AutoCAD. Creating a section view in AutoCAD's 2-D environment consists of creating section lines, or hatches as they are called in AutoCAD, and drawing a cutting plane line. There are many different predefined hatch patterns available. By the end of this chapter, you will be able to draw cutting plane lines and place sections lines within a bounded area.

7.1) INTRODUCTION

When drawing a section view, it is necessary to draw cutting plane lines and section lines. The *Phantom* line type is used to create the cutting plane line and it is printed thick. Cutting plane lines are thicker than visible lines. Therefore, they are placed on their own layer. Section lines on the other hand are thin and may be placed on the dimension layer. AutoCAD makes drawing section lines very easy. The command used to create section lines is **HATCH**. Section lines or hatch symbols are predefined and may be drawn at different angles and at different scales. The scale controls the distance between the parallel hatch lines.

7.2) CUTTING PLANE LINES

Figure 7-1 shows an example of a cutting plane line. The cutting plane line is placed on its own layer and the layer line type is *Phantom*. The thickness of the cutting plane line is between 0.6 and 0.8 mm. The procedure for drawing a cutting plane line is simple. A line is drawn indicating where the part is to be cut and multileaders are used to indicate the view direction. The cutting plane line arrows are usually larger than the arrowheads used in dimensioning, therefore a new multileader style will be created that has a large arrow and no landing.

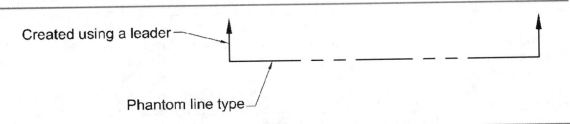

Created using a leader

Phantom line type

Figure 7-1: Cutting plane line

7.3) HATCHES

Section lines are created using hatches. AutoCAD has many predefined hatches. Some of these are shown in Figure 7-2. Several of them are labeled by material. However, the most commonly used hatches are labeled by their standard number.

- ANSI31 = Cast Iron or general use
- ANSI32 = Steel
- ANSI33 = Brass, Bronze, Copper
- ANSI34 = Rubber, Plastic, Electrical Insulation
- ANSI37 = Zinc, Lead
- ANSI38 = Magnesium, Aluminum

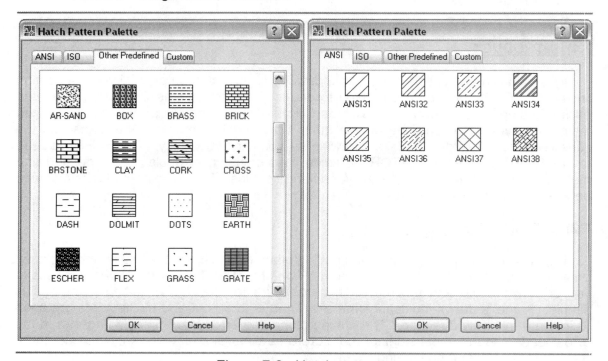

Figure 7-2: Hatch patterns

The angle and scale at which the hatches are drawn may be controlled within the *Hatch and Gradient* window (Figure 7-3). Section lines are usually drawn at 45 degrees. For the ANSI standard hatches, the default angle is 45 degrees. This is indicated by a 0 in the *Angle* field. Any non-zero angle specified in this field is either added to or subtracted from 45 degrees. The scale of the hatch controls the space between the parallel lines. It will be increased or decreased depending on the size of the part.

The hatched area is usually bounded by lines, circles or arcs. The two easiest ways to specify a hatch boundary are:

- Pick points: Specify a point within an area that is enclosed by objects. AutoCAD will automatically select all objects that bound the area.
- Select objects: Manually select the objects that bound the area. If you want to hatch an area whose boundary is not quite closed, you can set the **HPGAPTOL** system variable to bridge gaps between lines and arcs.

Hatches, by default, are associative. That means that they will be updated when the boundary is changed. Associativity is automatically removed if HPGAPTOL is set to 0 and a change in the boundary results in a gap. Associativity is reapplied if the boundary is mended.

Hatches may also be defined as annotative. That is, they will change their scale depending on the viewport scale used to view the drawing.

The *Hatch and Gradient* window may be accessed in the following ways:

- *Draw* panel: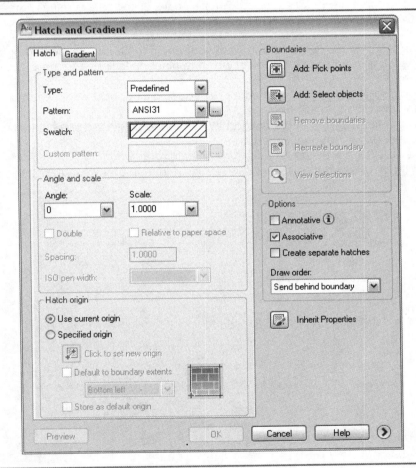
- *Command* window: **HATCH**

Figure 7-3: The *Hatch and Gradient* window

Creating hatches

1) Command: **hatch** or   *Draw* panel:
2) *Hatch and Gradient* window:
   a) *Type and pattern* area - *Pattern* field: Select a hatch pattern. You may view all the predefined patterns by selecting the *Hatch Pattern* icon
   b) *Angle and scale* area – *Angle* field: Enter an angle. This angle is either added to (positive angle) or subtracted from (negative angle) the patterns default angle. The default angle is usually 45 degrees.
   c) *Angle and scale* area – *Scale* field: Enter a scale. The scale is usually the same as your DIMSCALE; however, it also depends on the size of the part and the size of the cut areas.
   d) *Options* area: Select whether you want your hatch to be annotative and/or associative.
   e) *Boundaries* area: Select the area in which to place hatches. This may be done in two ways.
      • *Add: Pick points*: This method allows you to pick a point within each bounded area that you wish to place hatches.
      • *Add:* Select objects: This method allows you to select the objects that will create the boundaries of your sectioned area.
   f) Press **Enter** or **Space** to end boundary selection.
   g) Select the **Preview** button to view the results and then press **Esc** to exit the preview.
   h) **OK**

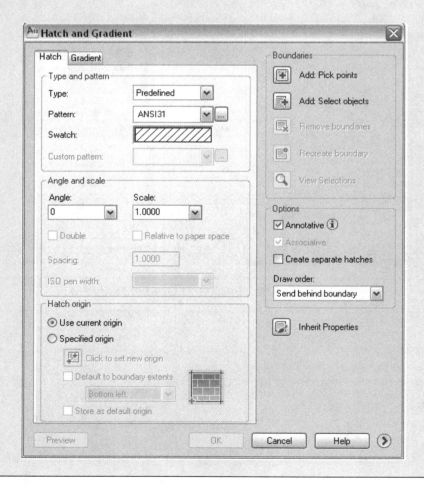

7.4) <u>CREATING HATCHES TUTORIAL</u>

The objective of this tutorial is to familiarize the user with the different methods and options available when creating hatches. It will take you through the different ways of choosing the hatch boundary and show you the affect of changing the hatch angle and scale.

7.4.1) <u>Creating hatches</u>

1) View the sectioning video and read section 7.1) though 7.3).

2)  *set-mm.dwt*

3)  **Creating hatches Tut.dwg**.

4) Draw the following object in your *Visible* layer. Use annotative text to write your name inside the object. It is not necessary to include the dimensions.

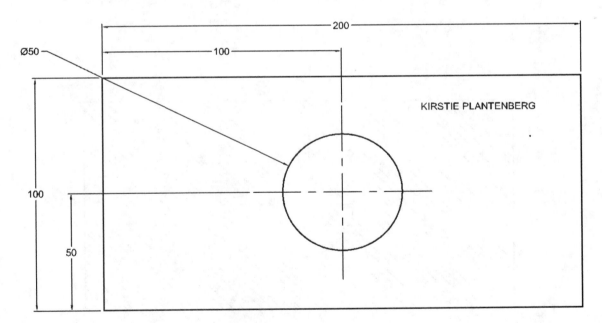

5) Draw section lines using the *Select Boundary* method.
   a) Make your **Dimension** layer current.
   b) <u>Command:</u> **hatch**   or   *Draw* <u>panel:</u>

c) *Hatch and Gradient* window
  i. *Pattern* field: **ANSI31** (Cast iron)
  ii. *Options* area: Select the **A̲nnotative** checkbox.
  iii. Select the **Add: Select objects** icon.
  iv. Select every line of your rectangle and then hit **Enter** or the **Space bar**.
  v. Select **Preview** to see how the hatches will look and then **Esc**.
  vi. **OK** (Notice that everything inside the selected boundary is hatched.)

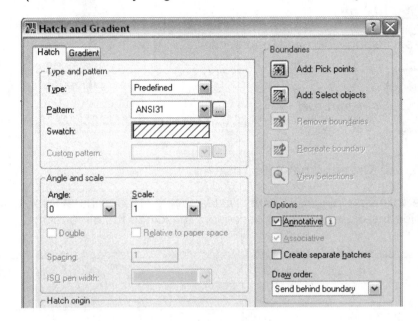

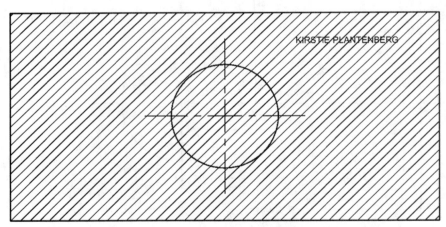

6) Double click on the hatch and add the text and the circle to the boundary. Notice the difference.

7) Draw section lines using the *Pick Point* method.
  a) **ERASE** the previous hatch.
  b) Command: **hatch**   or   *Draw* panel:

c) *Hatch and Gradient* window
   i. *Pattern* field: **ANSI31** (Cast iron)
   ii. *Options* area: Select the **A̲nnotative** checkbox.
   iii. Select the **Add: Pick points** icon.
   iv. Select a point that is inside the rectangle but outside the circle and then hit **Enter** or the **Space bar**.
   v. Select **Preview** to see how the hatches will look and then **Esc**.
   vi. **OK** (Notice that the area you indicated is hatched. The hatch stops at any boundary.)

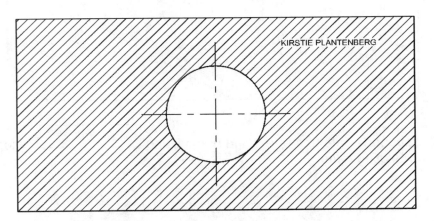

7.4.2) Changing hatch properties

1) Change the hatch symbol to **ANSI32**.
   a) Double click on the hatch that you have drawn.
   b) *Hatch Edit* window:
      i. *Pattern* field: **ANSI32** (Steel)
      ii. **OK**

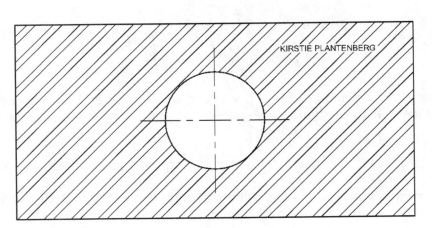

2) On your own edit the hatch and change the pattern to **ANSI33** (Brass), the scale to **2** and the angle to be **-15** (this is an actual angle of 45-15 = 30).

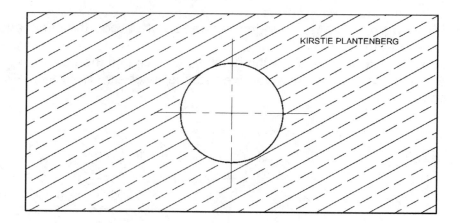

3) Add a 1:2 support scale to the text and hatch using 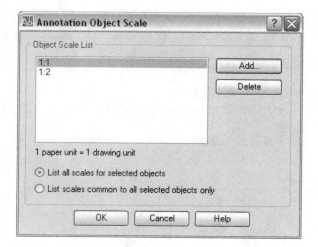 Add/Delete Scales located in the *Annotation Scaling* panel.

4) Enter paper space and change the viewport scale back and forth between 1:1 and 1:2. Notice that the text and hatch pattern adjusts their scale as the view port scale changes.

5) Save your drawing and print a 1:1 drawing using the appropriate pen widths.

6) On your own, change the shape of the rectangle and notice that the hatch, due to its associativity, changes to match the boundary.

7.5) HALF SECTION TUTORIAL

In this tutorial we will create a section view from an existing orthographic projection. It will take you through placing a cutting plane line in the top view and changing the front view into a half section. The mechanics of changing a non-sectioned view into a sectioned view is relatively easy. It is the visualization that is the challenging part. The procedure consists of inserting a cutting plane line and changing the line type of some lines from hidden to visible, trimming and erasing unwanted lines, and then HATCHING or placing section lines in the areas that have been cut.

7.5.1) Inserting the cutting plane line

1) Open the drawing **half_section_tut_student_2010.dwg**. This is a drawing of a casting. The little V shapes on the part are finish marks. These marks indicate where the casting will be machined. You will be changing the original drawing into the half section shown below.

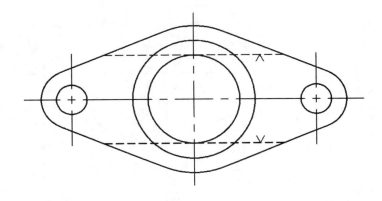

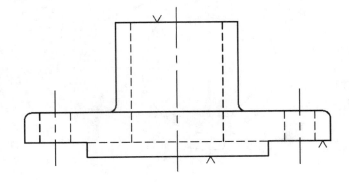
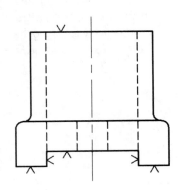

2) Make the **Cutting** layer current.

3) **Half Section Tut.dwg**

4) Get rid of the centerlines where the cutting plane line will be placed. Remember, cutting plane lines take precedence over other lines. In the top view, **ERASE/TRIM** the horizontal centerline to the right of the middle vertical centerline and **TRIM** the vertical centerline below the horizontal centerline.

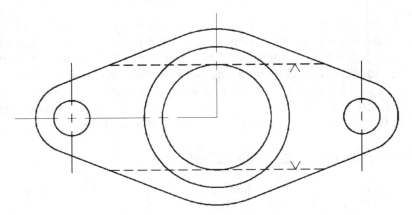

5) In the top view, draw a phantom **LINE** from the **CENTER** to the **QUADRANT** of the right side radius. Then draw a phantom **LINE** from the **CENTER** to the **QUADRANT** of the bottom radius. (See figure below.)

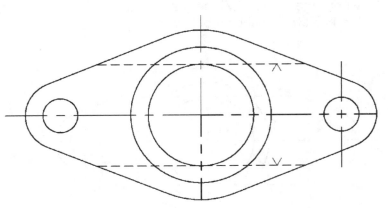

6) Extend the cutting plane lines **0.40** inches past the edge of the part using grip boxes and *POLAR* tracking.

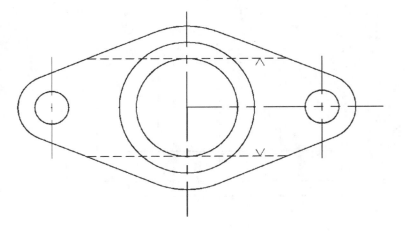

7) Create a new multileader style.

   a) Command: **mleaderstyle**   or   *Leaders* panel:

   b) *Multileader Style Manager* window: **New ...**

   c) *Create New Multileader Style* window:

      i. *New style name* field: **Cutting**

      ii. *Start with* field: ***Standard***

      iii. Select the **Annotative** check box.

      iv. **Continue**

   d) *Modify Multileader Style: ASME* window – *Leader Format* tab: Set the *Arrowhead Size* to **0.36**. This is twice the size of a dimension arrowhead.

   e) *Modify Multileader Style: ASME* window – *Leader Structure* tab: Deactivate the ***Automatically include landing*** checkbox.

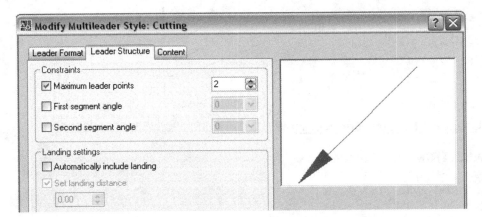

   f) *Modify Multileader Style: ASME* window – *Content* tab – *Multileader type* field: Select **None** and then select **OK**.

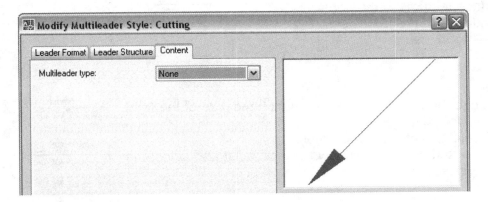

   g) *Multileader Style Manager* window:

      i. Select the ***Cutting*** style and then select the **Set Current** button.

      ii. **Close**

8) Draw two **Mutileaders** that are approximately 0.75 inch long. One should be horizontal and the other vertical (as shown). These will be placed at the end cutting plane lines to indicate direction of sight.

9) Move the multileaders to the positions shown in the figure.

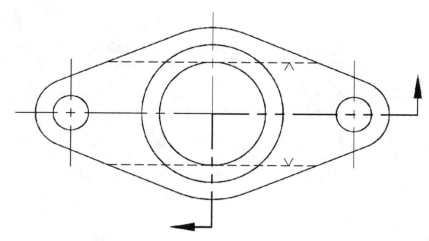

7.5.2) Creating the half section view

1) **ERASE/TRIM** the hidden lines and any centerline associated with a hidden feature in the left hand side of the front view.

2) **ERASE/TRIM** any visible lines associated with surface features in the right hand side of the front view. (See figure below.)

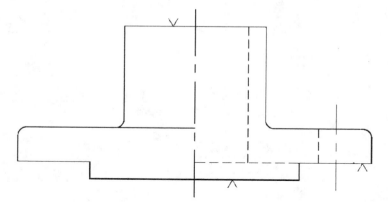

3) Change the hidden lines in the right hand side of the front view into visible lines.
   a) Select all of the hidden lines.
   b) Go to the Layer pull down selection list and select the **Visible** layer.

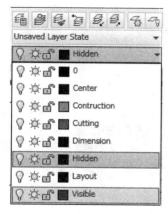

4) In your **Dimension** layer, place section lines in the areas that are cut using an annotative **ANSI31** hatch pattern. Use the *pick point* method and select all the cut areas.

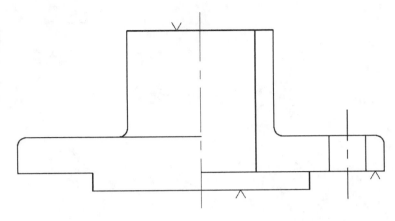

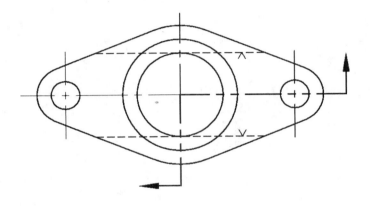

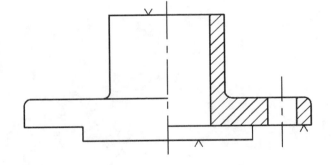

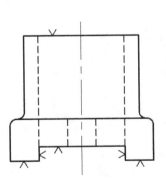

5) Save your drawing and print it at a 1:1 scale. Include your title block with the appropriate information filled in.

NOTES:

CREATING SECTION VIEWS IN AUTOCAD CROSSWORD PUZZLE

Name: _____ Date: _____

CP7-1)

Across

2. The typed command used to create section lines.
5. The section line angle resulting when a value of -10 degrees is entered into the angle field.
6. Cutting plane line *linetype*.
9. ANSI31
11. The boundary selection method that would be used if you want to fill everything inside the boundary.

Down

1. The boundary selection method used to create a hatch that stops when it encounters a boundary.
3. The cutting plane line arrowheads are created using ...
4. A line that is drawn thicker than the visible line.
7. The system variable used to bridge gaps in the hatch boundary.
8. ANSI33
10. ANSI32

CREATING SECTION VIEWS IN AUTOCAD PROBLEMS

P7-1) Draw the following object converting the front view into an offset section. It is not necessary to include the dimensions. The material of the part is Steel.

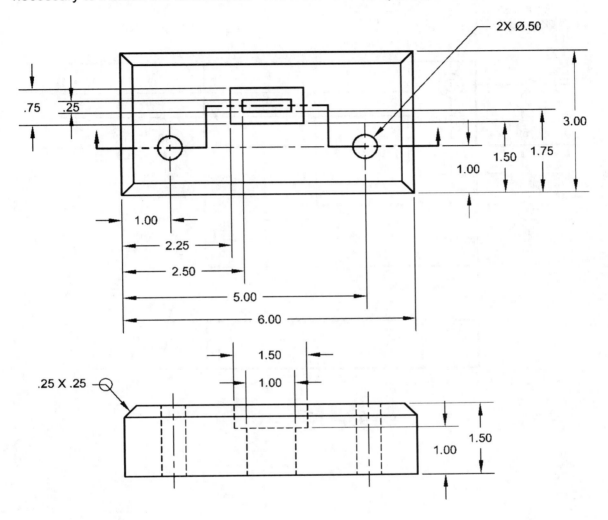

P7-2) Draw the following object converting the front view into an offset section. Capture as many features as possible. Draw the appropriate cutting plane line. It is not necessary to include the dimensions. The material of the part is Aluminum.

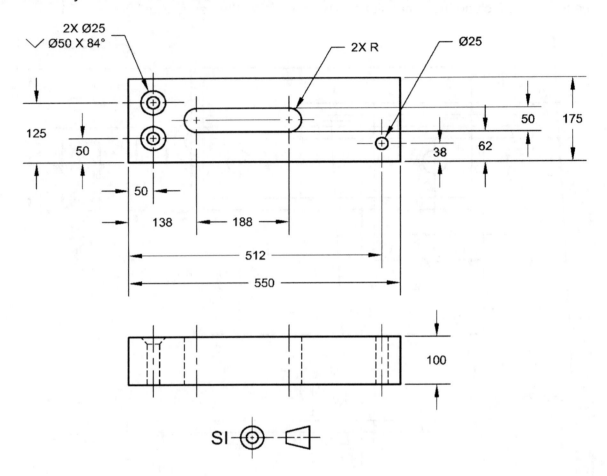

P7-3) Draw the following object converting the front view into an offset section. Capture as many features as possible. Draw the appropriate cutting plane line. It is not necessary to include the dimensions. The material of the part is Plastic.

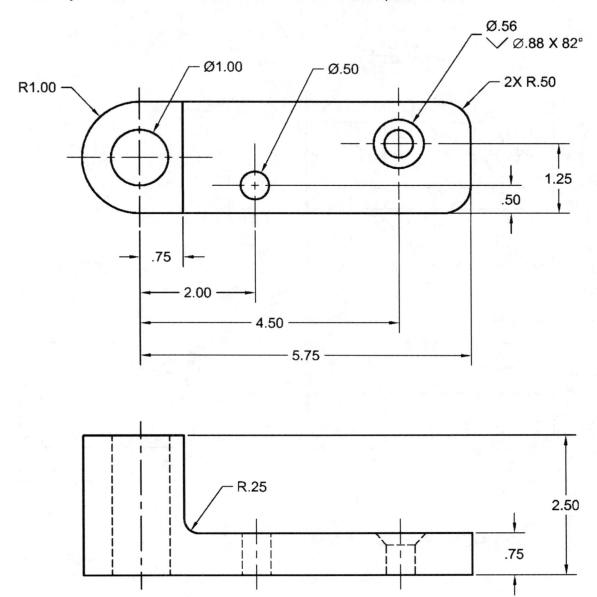

Ø.56

∨ Ø.88 X 82°

Ø1.00

Ø.50

R1.00

2X R.50

1.25

.50

.75

2.00

4.50

5.75

R.25

2.50

.75

P7-4) Draw all three views of the following object converting the front view into a full section. Draw the appropriate cutting plane line. It is not necessary to include the dimensions. The material of the part is Steel.

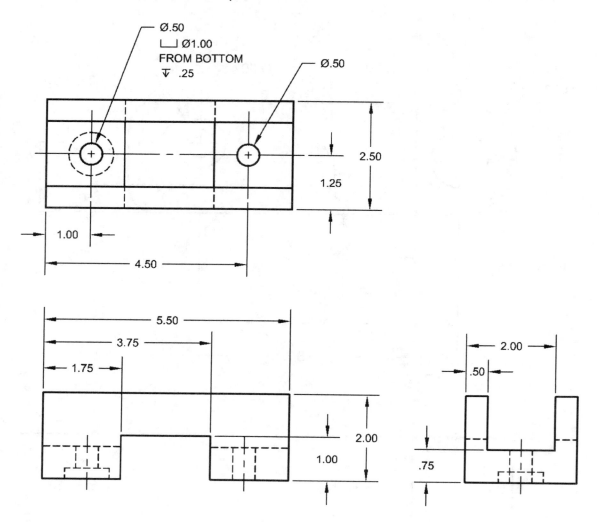

P7-7) Draw the following object converting the front view into an offset section. Capture as many features as possible. Draw the appropriate cutting plane line. It is not necessary to include the dimensions. The material of the part is Cast Iron.

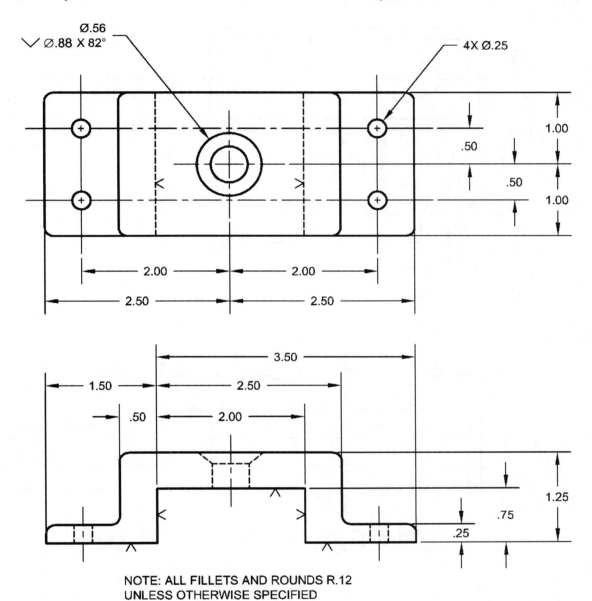

NOTE: ALL FILLETS AND ROUNDS R.12
UNLESS OTHERWISE SPECIFIED

P7-8) Draw the following object converting the front view into a full section. It is not necessary to include the dimensions. The material of the part is Cast Iron.

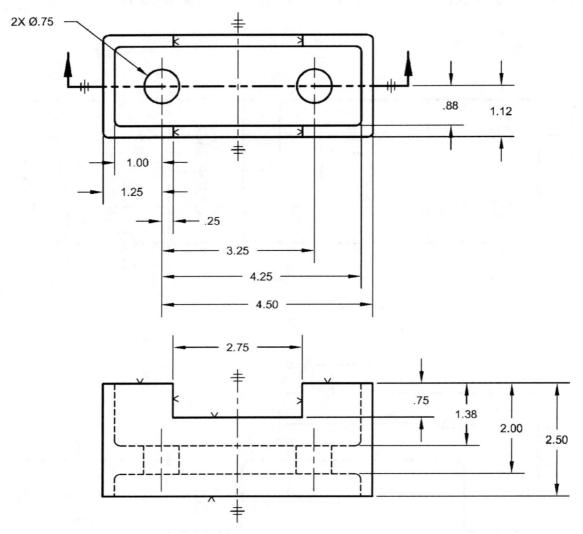

NOTE: ALL FILLETS AND ROUNDS R.12
UNLESS OTHERWISE SPECIFIED

P7-9) Draw the following object converting the front view into a full section. It is not necessary to include the dimensions. The material of the part is Cast Iron.

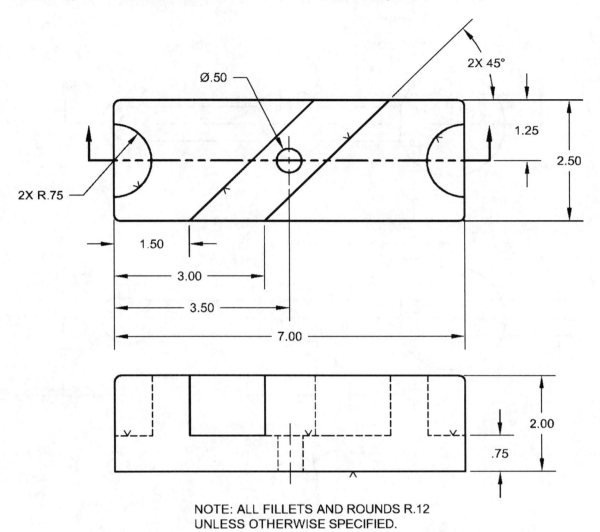

NOTE: ALL FILLETS AND ROUNDS R.12
UNLESS OTHERWISE SPECIFIED.

P7-10) Draw the following object converting the front view into a full section. It is not necessary to include the dimensions. The material of the part is Plastic.

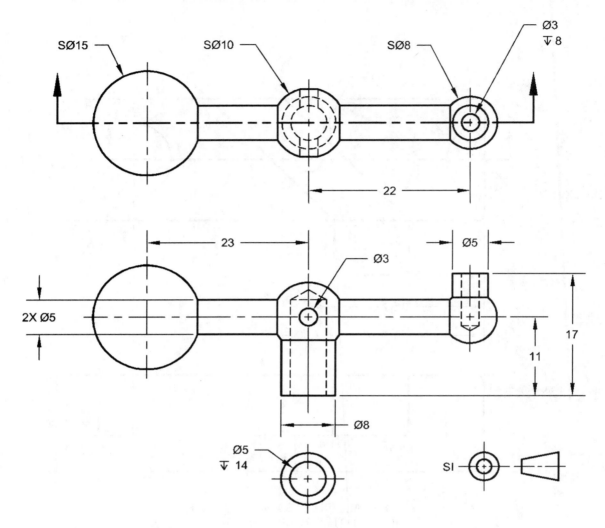

P7-11) Draw the following object converting the right side view into a half section. Draw the appropriate cutting plane line. It is not necessary to include the dimensions. The material of the part is Brass.

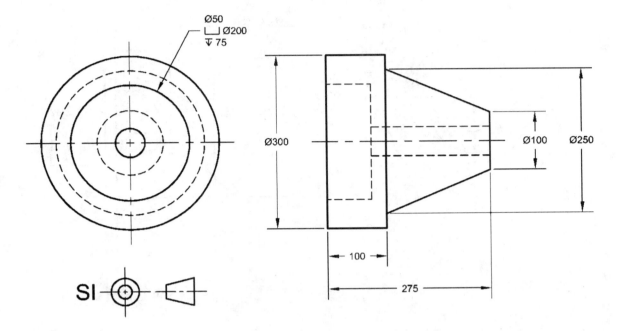

P7-12) Draw the following object converting the right side view into a half section. It is not necessary to include the dimensions. The material of the part is Steel.

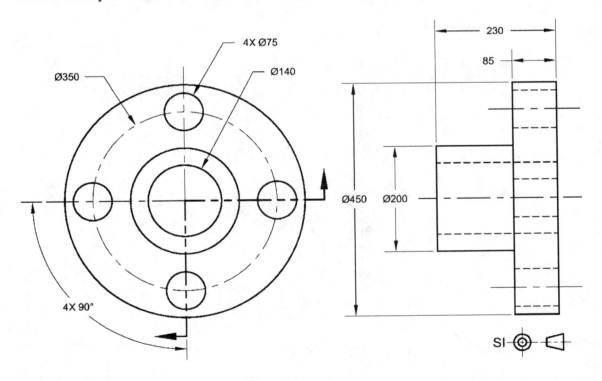

P7-13) Draw the following object converting the right side view into a half section. It is not necessary to include the dimensions. The material of the part is Aluminum.

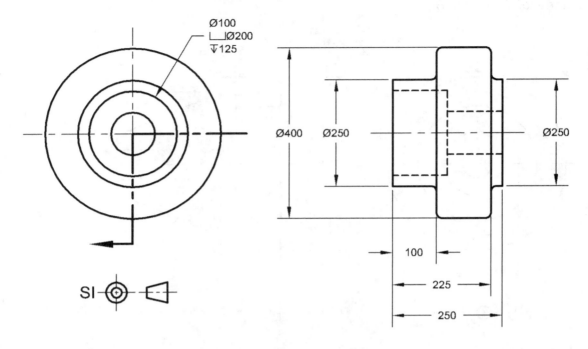

P7-14) Draw the following object converting the right side view into a half section. Draw the appropriate cutting plane line. It is not necessary to include the dimensions. The material of the part is Steel.

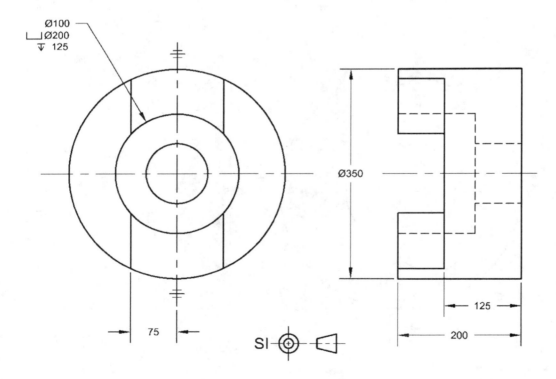

P7-15) Draw the following object converting the left side view into a half section. Draw the appropriate cutting plane line. It is not necessary to include the dimensions. The material of the part is Steel.

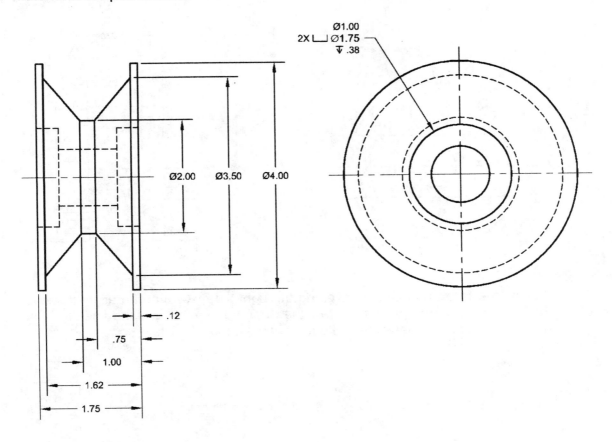

P7-16) Draw the following object converting the right side view into a half section. It is not necessary to include the dimensions. The material of the part is Aluminum.

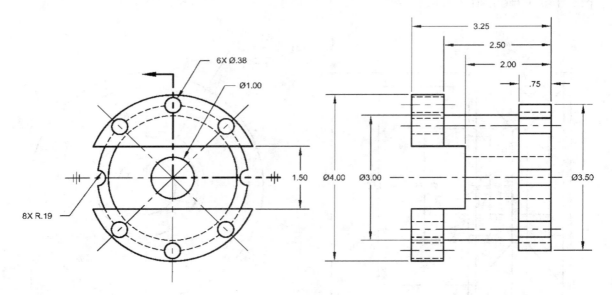

P7-17) Draw the following object converting the right side view into an aligned section using the conventions of revolution. Draw the appropriate cutting plane line. It is not necessary to include the dimensions. The material of the part is Steel.

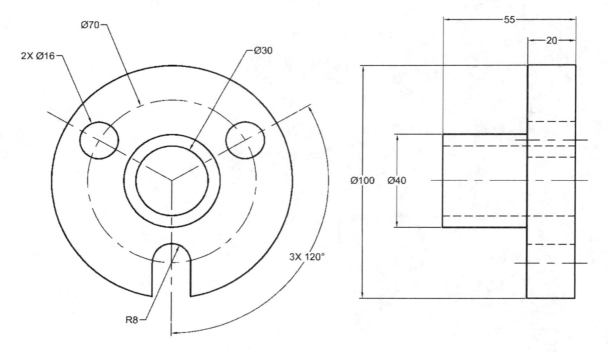

P7-18) Draw the following object converting the right side view into an aligned section using the conventions of revolution. Draw the appropriate cutting plane line. It is not necessary to include the dimensions. The material of the part is Cast iron.

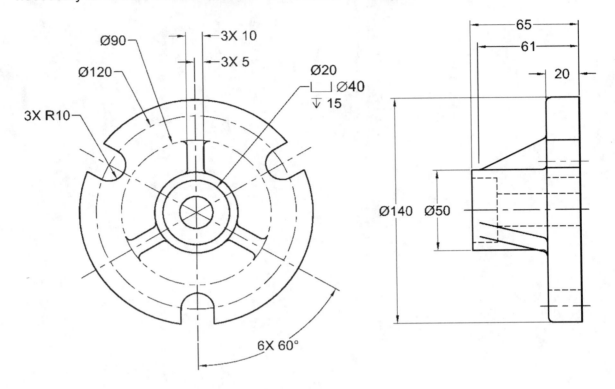

<u>NOTES:</u>

TOLERANCING

In Chapter 8 you will learn about tolerancing and how important this technique is to mass production. Tolerancing enables an engineer to design interchangeable or replacement parts. If a feature's size is toleranced, it is allowed to vary within a range of values or limits. It is no longer controlled by a single size. By the end of this chapter, you will be able to apply tolerances to a basic dimension and calculate a feature's limits.

8.1) TOLERANCING AND INTERCHANGEABILITY

Tolerancing is dimensioning for interchangeability. An interchangeable part is a part that possesses functional and physical characteristics equivalent in performance to another part for which it is intended to replace. When dimensioning an interchangeable part, the dimension is not a single value but a range of values that the part must fall within.

Interchangeability is achieved by imposing tolerances or limits on a dimension. **A tolerance is the total amount of dimensional variation permitted.** In other words, it is the difference between the maximum and minimum size of the feature. Tolerancing enables similar parts to be near enough alike so that any one of them will fit properly into the assembly. For example, you would like to replace your mountain bike's seat post with a seat post that contains a shock absorber. You expect that all seat posts designed for mountain bikes will be interchangeable.

Tolerancing and interchangeability are an essential part of mass production. **Tolerances are necessary because it is impossible to manufacture parts without some variation.** A key component of mass production is the ability to buy replacement parts that are interchangeable or can substitute for the part being replaced.

Tolerancing gives us the means of specifying dimensions with whatever degree of accuracy we may require for our design to work properly. We would like to choose a tolerance that is not unnecessarily accurate or excessively inaccurate. Choosing the correct tolerance for a particular application depends on the design intent (end use) of the part, cost, how it is manufactured, and experience.

8.2) TOLERANCING STANDARDS

Standards are needed to establish dimensional limits for parts that are to be interchangeable. Standards make it possible for parts to be manufactured at different times and in different places with the assurance that they will meet assembly requirements. The two most common standards agencies are the American National Standards Institute (ANSI) and the International Standards Organization (ISO). The ANSI standards are now being compiled and distributed by the American Society of Mechanical Engineers (ASME). The information contained in this chapter is based on the following standards: ASME Y14.5 - 1994, ANSI B4.1 – 1967 (R1994), and ANSI B4.2 – 1978 (R1984).

8.3) <u>TOLERANCE TYPES</u>

The tolerancing methods presented in this chapter include *limit* dimensions, *plus-minus* tolerances, and *page* or *block* tolerances.

- <u>Limit Dimensions:</u> Limits are the maximum and minimum size that a part can obtain and still function properly. For example, the diameter of a shaft may vary between .999 inch and 1.001 inches. On a drawing, you would see this dimension specified as one of the following:

$$\varnothing^{1.001}_{.999} \quad \text{or} \quad \varnothing.999 - 1.001$$

The upper limit is placed above the lower limit. When both limits are placed on one line, the lower limit precedes the upper limit. Limit dimensions provide the blueprint reader with the limits of allowable variation without any calculation. It eliminates potential calculation mistakes.

- <u>Plus-Minus Tolerances:</u> Plus-minus tolerances give a basic size and the variation that can occur around that basic size. On a drawing, a plus-minus tolerance dimension would look like the following:

$$10.0^{+0.1}_{-0.2}$$

When the positive and negative variations are the same, it is referred to as an equal bilateral tolerance. When they are not the same, the specification is called an unequal bilateral and when one of the variances is zero, the tolerance is unilateral. The type of tolerance chosen depends on the direction in which variation is most detrimental. Plus-minus tolerances are convenient because a design may be initially drawn and dimensioned using basic sizes. As the design progresses, tolerances may be added.

- <u>Page or Block Tolerances:</u> Page tolerances, also called block tolerances, get their name from their location on the drawing. Page tolerances are generally placed in the lower right hand corner of the page in or near the title block. The page tolerance is actually a general note that applies to all dimensions not covered by some other tolerancing type. The format of a page tolerance note may look like the following.

> UNLESS OTHERWISE SPECIFIED ALL:
> .XX = ± .010 inch
> .XXX = ± .005 inch
> .XXXX = ± .002 inch

Page tolerances are used for two reasons. First, they act as a default tolerance for any dimensions that may have been overlooked when tolerances were assigned. Second, they are often used to quickly tolerance non-critical dimensions.

8.4) <u>SHAFT-HOLE ASSEMBLY</u>

In the intervening sections, a simple shaft and hole assembly will be used to illustrate different concepts and definitions. Figure 8-1 shows a shaft that is designed to fit into a hole. Both the shaft and the hole are allowed to vary between a maximum and minimum diameter.

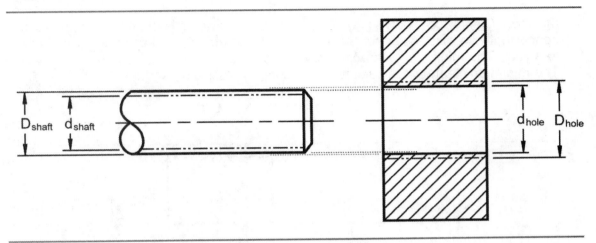

Figure 8-1: Shaft and hole assembly.

8.5) <u>INCH TOLERANCES</u>

Consider a simple shaft and hole assembly, like that shown in Figure 8-2, when reading the following definitions relating to tolerancing in inches. Both the diameter of the shaft and hole are allowed to vary between a maximum and minimum value.

- <u>Limits:</u> The limits are the maximum and minimum size that the part is allowed to be.

- <u>Basic Size:</u> The basic size is the size from which the limits are calculated. It is common for both the hole and the shaft and is usually the value of the closest fraction.

- <u>Tolerance:</u> The tolerance is the total amount a specific dimension is permitted to vary.

- <u>Maximum Material Condition (MMC):</u> The MMC is the size of the part when it consists of the most material.

- <u>Least Material Condition (LMC):</u> The LMC is the size of the part when it consists of the least material.

- Maximum Clearance: The maximum clearance is the maximum amount of space that can exist between the hole and the shaft. Don't let the word clearance fool you. The maximum clearance may be positive (a space) or negative (no space). The maximum clearance is calculated by using the following equation:

$$\text{Max. Clearance} = \text{LMC}_{hole} - \text{LMC}_{shaft}$$

- Minimum Clearance (Allowance): The minimum clearance is the minimum amount of space that can exist between the hole and the shaft. Don't let the word clearance fool you. The minimum clearance may be positive (a space) or negative (no space). The minimum clearance is calculated by using the following equation:

$$\text{Min. Clearance} = \text{MMC}_{hole} - \text{MMC}_{shaft}$$

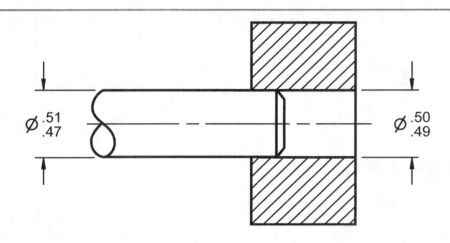

Figure 8-2: Toleranced shaft and hole pair (English).

Instructor Led Exercise 8-1: Inch tolerance definitions

Referring to Figure 8-2, fill in the following table.

	Shaft	Hole
Limits		
Basic Size		
Tolerance		
MMC		
LMC		
Max. Clearance		
Min. Clearance (Allowance)		

8.5.1) Types of Fits

Within the set of inch tolerances, there are four major types of fits. Within each fit there are several degrees or classes. The type of fit and class that you choose to implement depends on the function of your design. The major categories of fits are: *clearance*, *interference*, *transition*, and *line*. Table 8-1 lists and defines each of the four types of fits.

Type of Fit	Definition	When it exists
Clearance Fit	The internal member (shaft) fits into the external member (hole) and always leaves a space or clearance between the parts.	Min. Clear > 0
Interference Fit	The internal member is larger than the external member such that there is always an actual interference of metal.	Max. Clear ≤ 0
Transition Fit	The fit might result in either a clearance or interference fit condition.	Min. Clear < 0 Max. Clear > 0
Line Fit	The limits of size are specified such that a clearance or surface contact may result.	Min. Clear = 0 Max. Clear > 0

Table 8-1: Types of fits.

Instructor Led Exercise 8-2: Types of fits

From everyday life, list some examples of clearance and interference fits.

Fit	Examples
Clearance	
Interference	

Instructor Led Exercise 8-3: Determining fit type

Determine the basic size and type of fit given the limits for the shaft and hole.

Shaft Limits	Hole Limits	Basic Size	Type of Fit
1.498 - 1.500	1.503 – 1.505		
.751 - .755	.747 - .750		
.373 - .378	.371 - .375		
.247 - .250	.250 - .255		

8.5.2) ANSI Standard Limits and Fits (English)

The following fit types and classes are in accordance with the ANSI B4.1-1967 (R1994) standard.

- Running or Sliding Clearance Fits (RC)

Running and sliding clearance fits are intended to provide running performance with suitable lubrication. Table 8-2 lists the different classes of running and sliding clearance fits and their design uses.

- Locational Fits (LC, LT, LN)

Locational fits are intended to determine only the location of the mating parts. They are divided into three groups: clearance fits (LC), transition fits (LT), and interference fits (LN). Table 8-3 lists the different classes of locational fits and their design uses.

- FN: Force Fits:

Force fits provide a constant bore pressure throughout the range of sizes. The classes are categorized from FN1 to FN5. Table 8-4 lists the different classes of force fits and their design uses.

Class of Fit	Description	Design use
RC9 -RC8	Loose running fit	Used with material such as cold rolled shafting and tubing made to commercial tolerances.
RC7	Free running fit	Used where accuracy is not essential, or where large temperature variations occur.
RC6 -RC5	Medium running fit	Used on accurate machinery with higher surface speeds where accurate location and minimum play is desired.
RC4	Close running fit	Used on accurate machinery with moderate surface speeds where accurate location and minimum play is desired.
RC3	Precision running fit	This is the closest fit, which can be expected to run freely. Intended for slow speeds. Not suitable for appreciable temperature changes.
RC2	Sliding fit	Used for accurate location. Parts will move and turn easily but are not intended to run freely. Parts may seize with small temperature changes.
RC1	Close Sliding fit	Used for accurate location of parts that must be assembled without perceptible play.

Table 8-2: Running and sliding clearance fit classes.

Class of Fit	Description	Design use
LC	Locational clearance fit	Intended for parts that are normally stationary, but which can be freely assembled or disassembled. They run from snug fits (parts requiring accuracy of location), through the medium clearance fits (parts where freedom of assembly is important). The classes are categorized from LC1 being the tightest fit to LC11 being the loosest.
LT	Locational transition fit	Used where accuracy of location is important, but a small amount of clearance or interference is permissible. The classes are categorized from LT1 to LT6.
LN	Locational interference fit	Used where accuracy of location is of prime importance, and for parts requiring rigidity and alignment with no special requirements for bore pressure. The classes are categorized from LN1 to LN3.

Table 8-3: Locational fit classes.

Class of Fit	Description	Design use
FN1	Light drive fit	This fit produces a light assembly pressure and, a more or less, permanent assembly.
FN2	Medium drive fit	Suitable for ordinary steel parts or for shrink fits on light sections. About the tightest fit that can be used with high-grade cast iron.
FN3	Heavy drive fit	Suitable for heavier steel parts or for shrink fit in medium sections.
FN4 - FN5	Force fit	Suitable for parts that can be heavily stressed, or for shrink fits where the heavy pressing forces required are impractical.

Table 8-4: Force fit classes.

Instructor Led Exercise 8-4: Limits and fits

Given a basic size of .50 inches and a fit of RC8, calculate the limits for both the hole and the shaft. Use the ANSI limits and fit tables given in the Appendix A.

Shaft:

Hole:

In Class Student Exercise 8-5: Milling Jack assembly tolerances

Name: _____ Date: _____

Consider the *Milling Jack* assembly shown. Notice that there are many parts that fit into or around other parts. Each of these parts are toleranced to ensure proper fit and function.

Milling Jack assembled and exploded views.

In Class Student Exercise 8-5 Cont.: Milling Jack assembly tolerances

The *V-Anvil* fits into the *Sliding Screw* (see assembly drawing) with a RC4 fit. The basic size is .375 (3/8). Determine the limits for both parts.

- V – Anvil limits:

- Sliding Screw limits:

Part#3: V - Anvil   Part#2: Sliding Screw

In Class Student Exercise 8-5 Cont.: Milling Jack assembly tolerances

Name: _____ Date: _____

The *Sliding Screw* fits into the *Base* (see next page) with a RC5 fit. The basic size is .625 (5/8). Determine the limits for both parts.

- Sliding Screw limits:

- Base limits:

Part#1: Base

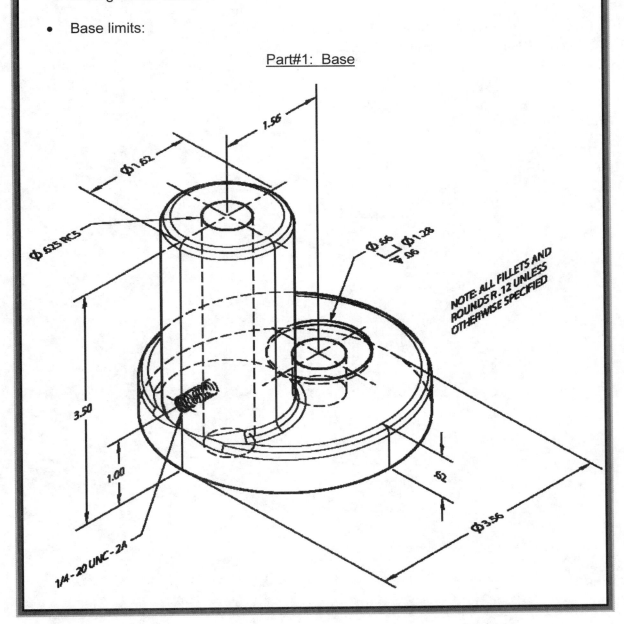

NOTE: ALL FILLETS AND ROUNDS R .12 UNLESS OTHERWISE SPECIFIED

NOTES:

8.6) METRIC TOLERANCES

Consider a simple shaft and hole assembly, like that shown in Figure 8-3, when reading the following definitions relating to tolerancing in millimeters. The dimensions of both are shown in Figure 8-3. Both the diameter of the shaft and hole are allowed to vary between a maximum and minimum value.

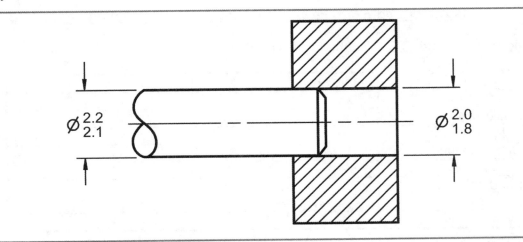

Figure 8-3: Toleranced shaft and hole pair (metric).

- **Basic Size:** The basic size is the size from which the limits are calculated.

- **Tolerance:** The tolerance is the total amount a dimension is permitted to vary.

- **Upper deviation:** The upper deviation is the difference between the basic size and the permitted maximum size of the part.

    UD = | basic size – max size |

- **Lower deviation:** The lower deviation is the difference between the basic size and the minimum permitted size of the part.

    LD = | basic size – min size |

- **Fundamental deviation:** The fundamental deviation is the closest deviation to the basic size. To determine the fundamental deviation, compare the upper deviation and the lower deviation. The fundamental deviation is the smaller of the two. A letter in the fit specification represents the fundamental deviation. If the letter is capital, it is referring to the hole's fundamental deviation and a lower case letter refers to the shaft. Refer to Table 8-5 for metric fit designations.

- **International tolerance grade number (IT#):** The IT#'s are a set of tolerances that vary according to the basic size and provide the same relative level of accuracy within a given grade. The number in the fit specification represents the IT#. A smaller number provides a smaller tolerance.

- Tolerance zone: The fundamental deviation in combination with the IT# defines the tolerance zone. The IT# establishes the magnitude of the tolerance zone or the amount that the dimension can vary. The fundamental deviation establishes the position of the tolerance zone with respect to the basic size.

Instructor Led Exercise 8-6: Millimeter tolerance definitions

Referring to Figure 8-3, fill in the following table.

	Shaft	Hole
Limits		
Basic Size		
Tolerance		
Upper deviation		
Lower deviation		
Fundamental deviation		
Type of fit		

8.6.1) __ANSI Standard Limits and Fits__ (Metric)

The following fit types are in accordance with the ANSI B4.2-1978 (R1994) standard. Available metric fits and their descriptions are summarized in Table 8-5.

FIT SYMBOL			
Hole Basis	**Shaft Basis**	**Fit**	**Description**
H11/c11	C11/h11	Loose running fit	For wide commercial tolerances or allowances.
H9/d9	D9/h9	Free running fit	Good for large temperature variations, high running speeds, or heavy journal pressures.
H8/f7	F8/h7	Close running fit	For accurate location at moderate speeds and journal pressures.
H7/g6	G7/h6	Sliding fit	Not intended to run freely, but to move and turn freely and locate accurately.
H7/h6	H7/h6	Locational clearance fit	For locating stationary parts but can be freely assembled and disassembled.
H7/k6 and H7/n6	K7/h6 and N7/h6	Locational transition fit	For accurate location.
H7/p6	P7/h6	Locational interference fit	For parts requiring rigidity where accuracy of location is important, but without special bore pressure requirements.
H7/s6	S7/h6	Medium drive fit	For ordinary steel parts or shrink fits on light sections, the tightest fit usable with cast iron.
H7/u6	U7/h6	Force fit	Suitable for parts that can be highly stressed.

Table 8-5: Metric standard fits.

8.6.2) __Tolerance Designation__

Metric fits are specified using the fundamental deviation (letter) and the IT#. When specifying the fit for the hole, an upper case letter is used. A lower case letter is used when specifying the fit for the shaft. As stated before, the IT# establishes the magnitude of the tolerance zone or the amount that the dimension can vary. The fundamental deviation establishes the position of the tolerance zone with respect to the basic size.

Instructor Led Exercise 8-7: Metric fit designation

Fill in the appropriate name for the fit component.

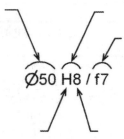

8.6.3) Basic Hole and Basic Shaft Systems

Notice that Table 8-5 gives two different tolerance designations for each type of fit. Metric limits and fits are divided into two different systems: the basic hole system and the basic shaft system. Each system has its own designation.

- Basic hole system: The basic hole system is used when you want the basic size to be attached to the hole dimension. For example, if a standard drill, reamer, broach, or another standard tool is used to produce a hole, you would want to use the hole system. In this system, the minimum hole diameter is taken as the basic size.

- Basic shaft system: The basic shaft system is used when you want the basic size to be attached to the shaft dimension. For example, you would use the shaft system if you need to tolerance a hole based on the size of a purchased standard drill rod. In this system, the maximum shaft diameter is taken as the basic size.

Instructor Led Exercise 8-8: Systems

Identify the type of fit and the system used to determine the limits of the following shaft and hole pairs.

Shaft	Hole	Type of Fit	System
9.987 – 9.972	10.000 – 10.022		
60.021 - 60.002	60.000 - 60.030		
40.000 – 39.984	39.924 – 39.949		

Instructor Led Exercise 8-9: Metric limits and fits.

Find the limits, tolerance, type of fit, and type of system for a ⌀30 H11/c11 fit. Use the tolerance tables given in Appendix A.

	Shaft	Hole
Limits		
Tolerance		
System		
Fit		

Find the limits, tolerance, type of fit, and type of system for a ⌀30 P7/h6 fit.

	Shaft	Hole
Limits		
Tolerance		
System		
Fit		

8.7) SELECTING TOLERANCES

Tolerances will govern the method of manufacturing. **When tolerances are reduced, the cost of manufacturing rises very rapidly.** Therefore, specify as generous a tolerance as possible without interfering with the function of the part.

Choosing the most appropriate tolerance depends on many factors. As stated before it depends on design intent, cost and how the part will be manufactured. Choosing a tolerance that will allow the part to function properly is the most important. Things to consider are: length of engagement, bearing load, speed, lubrication, temperature, humidity, and material. Experience also plays a significant role.

Table 8-6 may be used as a general guide for determining the machining processes that will under normal conditions, produce work within the tolerance grades indicated. As the tolerance grade number decreases the tolerance becomes smaller. Tolerance grades versus actual tolerances may be found in any Machinery's Handbook.

Machining Operation	IT Grades							
	4	5	6	7	8	9	10	11
Lapping & Honing	░	░						
Cylindrical Grinding		░	░	░				
Surface Grinding		░	░	░	░			
Diamond Turning		░	░	░				
Diamond Boring		░	░	░				
Broaching		░	░	░	░			
Reaming			░	░	░	░	░	
Turning				░	░	░	░	░
Boring					░	░	░	░
Milling							░	░
Planing & Shaping							░	░
Drilling							░	░
Punching							░	░
Die Casting								░

Table 8-6: Relation of machining processes to international tolerance grades.

8.8) TOLERANCE ACCUMULATION

The tolerance between two features of a part depends on the number of controlling dimensions. A distance can be controlled by a single dimension or multiple dimensions. The maximum variation between two features is equal to the sum of the tolerances placed on the controlling dimensions. As the number of controlling dimensions increases, the tolerance accumulation increases. Remember, even if the dimension does not have a stated tolerance, it has an implied tolerance.

Instructor Led Exercise 8-10: Tolerance accumulation

What is the tolerance accumulation for the distance between surface A and B for the three different dimensioning methods?

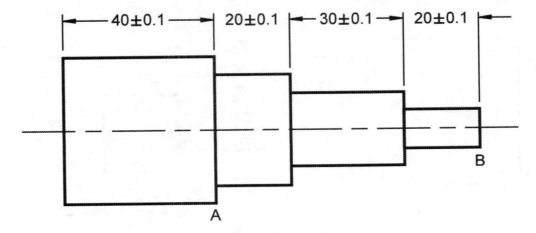

Tolerance accumulation between surface A and B =

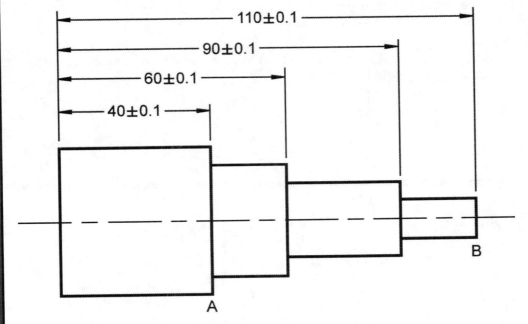

Tolerance accumulation between surface A and B =

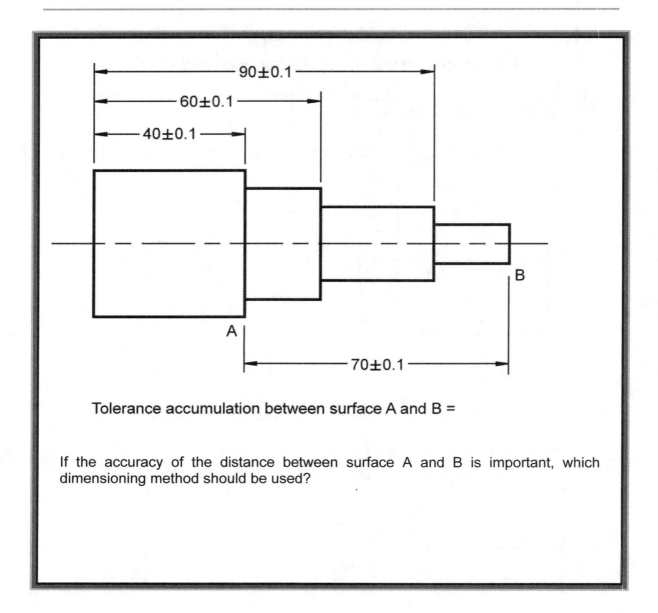

Tolerance accumulation between surface A and B =

If the accuracy of the distance between surface A and B is important, which dimensioning method should be used?

Instructor Led Exercise 8-11: Over dimensioning

Assuming that the diameter dimensions are correct, explain why this object is dimensioned incorrectly.

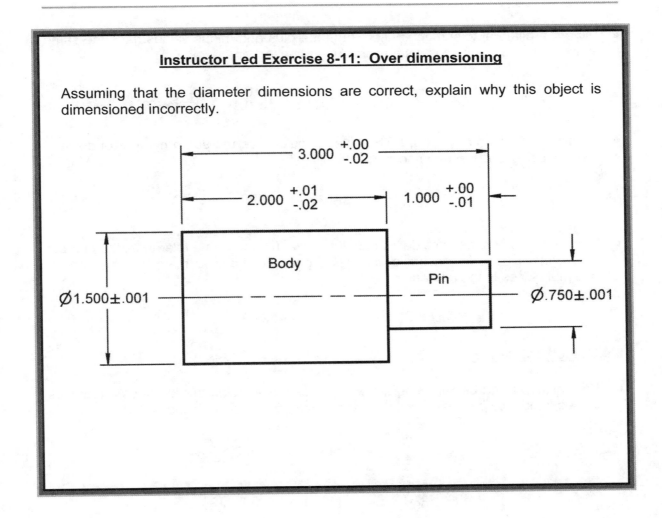

8.9) FORMATTING TOLERANCES

The conventions that are presented in this section pertain to the number of decimal places and format of tolerance dimensions, and are in accordance with the ASME Y14.5M standard.

8.9.1) Metric Tolerances

- If a tolerance is obtained from a standardized fit table, the limits plus the basic size and tolerance symbol should be given in one of the following three ways. It is preferred to use the forms that directly state the limits.

$$\emptyset^{20.240}_{20.110} \; (\emptyset 20 \; C11) \qquad \text{or} \qquad \emptyset 20 \; C11 \left(\emptyset^{20.240}_{20.110}\right) \qquad \text{or} \qquad \emptyset 20 \; C11$$

- Where a unilateral tolerance exists, a single zero without a plus-minus sign is shown.

$$40^{\;\;\;0}_{-0.02} \qquad \text{or} \qquad 40^{+0.02}_{\;\;\;0}$$

- Where a bilateral tolerance is used, both the plus and minus values have the same number of decimal places, using zeros where necessary.

$$10 \begin{array}{l} +0.25 \\ -0.10 \end{array} \quad \text{not} \quad 10 \begin{array}{l} +0.25 \\ -0.1 \end{array}$$

- If limit dimensions are used, both values should have the same number of decimal places, using zeros where necessary.

$$\begin{array}{l} 15.45 \\ 15.00 \end{array} \quad \text{not} \quad \begin{array}{l} 15.45 \\ 15 \end{array}$$

- Basic dimensions are considered absolute. When used with a tolerance, the number of decimal places in the basic dimension does not have to match the number of decimal places in the tolerance.

$$45 \pm 0.15 \quad \text{not} \quad 45.00 \pm 0.15$$

8.9.2) Inch Tolerances

- For unilateral and bilateral tolerances, the basic dimension and the plus and minus values should be expressed with the same number of decimal places.

$$.500 \begin{array}{l} +.000 \\ -.002 \end{array} \quad \text{not} \quad .500 \begin{array}{l} 0 \\ -.002 \end{array}$$

$$.500 \begin{array}{l} +.001 \\ -.002 \end{array} \quad \text{not} \quad .50 \begin{array}{l} +.001 \\ -.002 \end{array}$$

- If limit dimensions are used, both values should have the same number of decimal places, using zeros where necessary.

$$\begin{array}{l} .252 \\ .250 \end{array} \quad \text{not} \quad \begin{array}{l} .252 \\ .25 \end{array}$$

- When basic dimensions are used, the number of decimal places should match the number of decimal places in the tolerance.

$$2.000 \pm 0.015 \quad \text{not} \quad 2.0 \pm 0.015$$

8.9.3) Angular Tolerances

- Where angle dimensions are used, both the angle and the plus and minus values have the same number of decimal places.

$$30.0° \pm .2° \quad \text{not} \quad 30° \pm .2°$$

TOLERANCING CROSSWORD PUZZLE (Inch)

Name: _____   Date: _____

CP8-1)

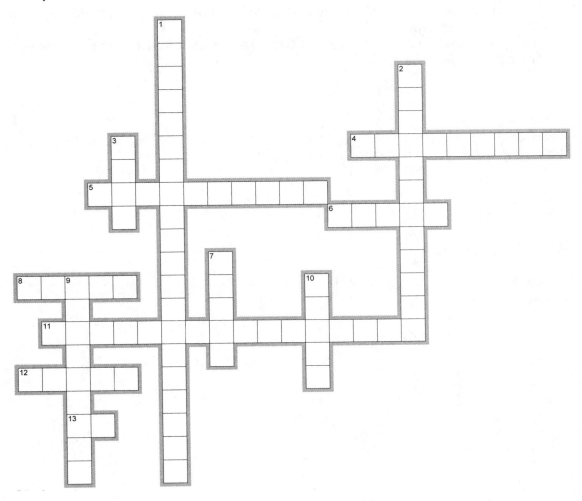

Across

4. A fit that always leaves space between the mating parts.
5. A fit the sometimes leaves a space between the mating parts.
6. When specifying a limit dimension, the .... limit goes first.
8. When specifying a limit dimension, the .... limit goes on top.
11. RC
12. This type of dimension has the advantage of providing the print reader with the allowable variation without any calculation.
13. Is it possible to machine a part to an exact size?

Down

1. LT
2. The fit that never leaves a space between the mating parts.
3. A tolerance is the maximum amount a part is allowed to ....
7. This type of tolerance applies a tolerance to all dimensions not covered by some other tolerancing type.
9. This type of tolerancing is convenient because a design may be initially drawn and dimensioned using basic sizes.
10. FN

TOLERANCING CROSSWORD PUZZLE (Metric)

Name: _____   Date: _____

CP8-2)

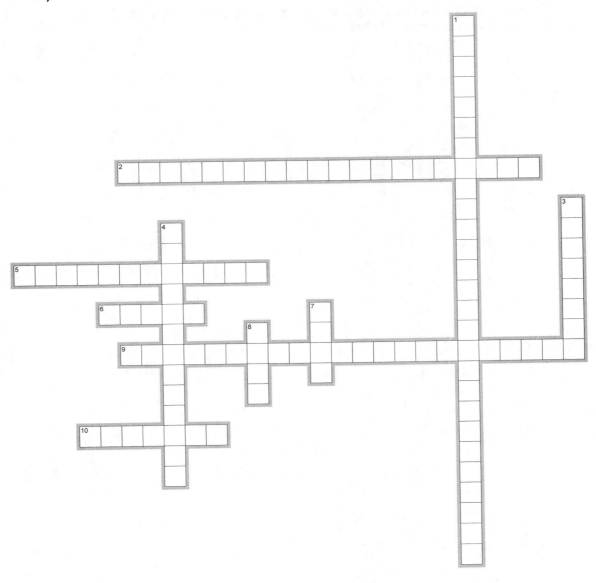

Across

2. When designating a metric fit, what does the letter represent?
5. A factor that influences tolerance choice.
6. One of the two systems used in the metric tolerance tables.
9. P7/h6
10. H7/g6

Down

1. When designating a metric fit, what does the number represent?
3. Tightening a tolerance will .... the manufacturing costs.
4. A factor that influences tolerance choice.
7. When specifying the tolerance zone, a capital letter represents the fit for the ....
8. A factor that influences tolerance choice.

Name: _____   Date: _____

P8-2) Find the limits of the shaft and hole for the following basic size – fit combinations.

	(a)	(b)	(c)	(d)	(e)	(f)	(g)
Basic Size	.25	.5	.75	1	1.375	2	2.125
Fit 1	RC3	RC5	RC1	RC9	RC7	RC4	RC6
Fit 2	LC2	LC7	LC11	LC6	LC1	LC9	LC4
Fit 3	LT1	LT2	LT3	LT4	LT5	LT6	LT3
Fit 4	LN2	LN1	FN1	FN5	LN3	FN4	FN2

	Shaft	Hole
Basic Size		
Limits		

	Shaft	Hole
Basic Size		
Limits		

	Shaft	Hole
Basic Size		
Limits		

	Shaft	Hole
Basic Size		
Limits		

	Shaft	Hole
Basic Size		
Limits		

	Shaft	Hole
Basic Size		
Limits		

	Shaft	Hole
Basic Size		
Limits		

	Shaft	Hole
Basic Size		
Limits		

NOTES:

Name: _____ Date: _____

P8-3) Fill in the given table for the following shaft and hole limits.

	(a)	(b)	(c)	(d)	(e)	(f)	(g)	(h)
Shaft Limits	5.970	79.990	16.029	25.061	120.000	2.000	30.000	8.000
	5.940	79.971	16.018	25.048	119.780	1.994	29.987	7.991
Hole Limits	6.030	80.030	16.018	25.021	120.400	2.012	30.0062	7.978
	6.000	80.000	16.000	25.000	120.180	2.002	9.985	7.963

	Shaft	Hole
Limits		
Basic size		
Tolerance		
Upper Deviation		
Lower Deviation		
Fundamental Deviation		
IT Grade		
System (hole, shaft)	
Fit	

	Shaft	Hole
Limits		
Basic size		
Tolerance		
Upper Deviation		
Lower Deviation		
Fundamental Deviation		
IT Grade		
System (hole, shaft)	
Fit	

	Shaft	Hole
Limits		
Basic size		
Tolerance		
Upper Deviation		
Lower Deviation		
Fundamental Deviation		
IT Grade		
System (hole, shaft)	
Fit	

<u>NOTES:</u>

Name: _____ Date: _____

P8-4) Find the limits of the shaft and hole for the following basic size – fit combinations.

	(a)	(b)	(c)	(d)	(e)	(f)	(g)
Basic Size	5	10	12	16	20	25	30
Fit 1	H11/c11	H7/k6	H7/p6	H7/u6	H8/f7	H7/n6	H7/s6
Fit 2	U7/h6	N7/h6	G7/h6	C11/h11	S7/h6	H7/h6	K7/h6

	Shaft	**Hole**
Basic Size		
Limits		

	Shaft	**Hole**
Basic Size		
Limits		

	Shaft	**Hole**
Basic Size		
Limits		

	Shaft	**Hole**
Basic Size		
Limits		

	Shaft	**Hole**
Basic Size		
Limits		

	Shaft	**Hole**
Basic Size		
Limits		

	Shaft	**Hole**
Basic Size		
Limits		

	Shaft	**Hole**
Basic Size		
Limits		

NOTES:

TOLERANCING IN AUTOCAD

In Chapter 9 you will learn how to apply tolerances to existing dimensions. The tolerance parameters may be set in the Tolerancing tab of the Dimension Styles Manager window. By the end of this chapter, you will be able to create toleranced dimensions using the limit and plus-minus tolerance forms.

9.1) INTRODUCTION

AutoCAD gives you the ability to add toleranced dimensions to a detailed drawing. You can specify the tolerance form (limit or plus-minus) in the *Dimension Styles Manager* window.

There are three different procedures for adding toleranced dimensions to your drawing. The method you choose depends on the degree of forethought and the number of toleranced dimensions required.

5) You can change an existing dimension to a toleranced dimension using the **Override** button in the *Dimension Styles Manager* window and the **Dimension Update** command. This method is used if you only have a few toleranced dimensions and each dimension has a different plus and minus tolerance values.

6) You can add new toleranced dimensions using the **Override** button in the *Dimension Styles Manager* window. This method is used if you have a number of toleranced dimensions.

7) You can add toleranced dimensions by creating and using a *Tolerance* dimension style. This is most useful if you have many toleranced dimensions that have the same plus and minus tolerance values.

9.2) TOLERANCE PARAMETERS

The parameters used to control the values and look of your toleranced dimensions are set in the *Tolerance* tab of the *Dimension Styles Manager* window. To enter the *Dimension Styles Manager* window use the command **DDIM**, **DIMSTYLE** or it can be access through the *Dimensions* panel.

Setting tolerance parameters

1) Command: **dimstyle**   or   *Dimensions* panel: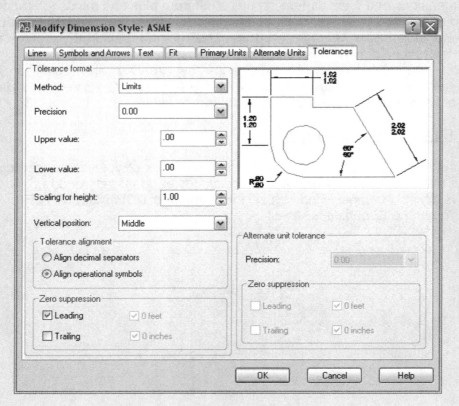
2) *Dimension Styles Manager* window: **Override...** (Select **New...** if you want to create a *Tolerance* dimension style.)
3) *Override Current Style: ASME* window – *Tolerance* tab - *Tolerance format* area:
   a) *Method* field: Select the tolerance form.
      - None = No tolerance
      - Symmetric = A plus-minus tolerance that is symmetric.
      - Deviation = A plus-minus tolerance.
      - Limits = A limit tolerance
      - Basic = Places a box around the dimension indicating a basic (non-toleranced) dimension.
   b) *Precision* field: Select the number of decimal places that your dimension will have.
   c) *Upper value* field: Enter the value that will be added to the basic or nominal size.
   d) *Lower value* field: Enter the value that will be subtracted from the basic or nominal size. (Note: If a negative number is placed in this box, the value will be added to the basic size.)
   e) *Vertical position field:* Select the position of the dimension symbols such as ∅ and R.
   f) **OK**
4) *Dimension Styles Manager* window: **Close**
5) Newly created dimensions will have the override properties. To change an existing dimension, use the *update* icon located in the *Dimensions* panel.

9.3) <u>TOLERANCING TUTORIAL</u>

The objective of this tutorial is to familiarize the user with the different tolerance settings and how to apply them.

9.3.1) <u>Drawing the object</u>

1) View the *Tolerancing* video and read sections 9.1) and 9.2).

2)  *set-inch.dwt*. Your default dimension style should be the ASME style.

3) 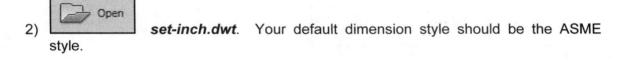 **Tolerancing Tut.dwg**.

4) Set your **LIMITS** to *22 x 17*, **ZOOM ALL**, and draw the necessary views and dimension the object as shown.

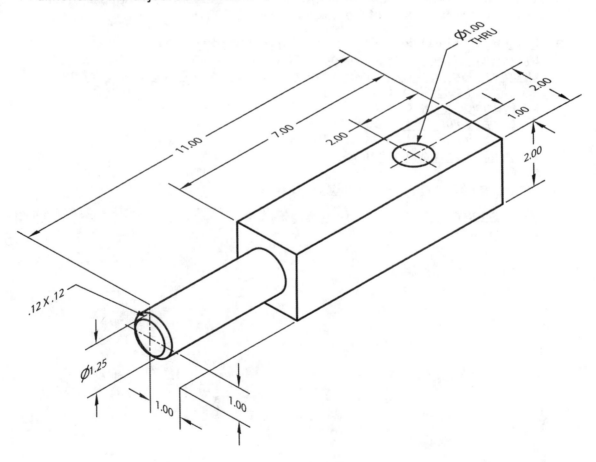

9.3.2) Tolerancing

Your detailed drawing should look something like the figure shown. There may be slight differences in the dimension placement. Your dimensions will look smaller when viewed in *Model* space. When working on an individual dimension, you may want to zoom in to get a better view.

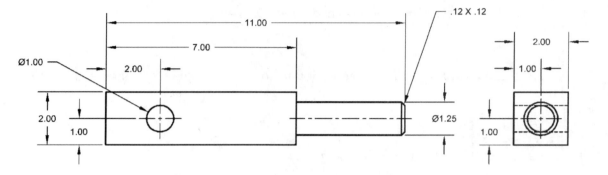

1) Change the dimension of the hole to a limit form dimension using a locational clearance fit of LC6. Looking at the fit tables, the amount that is added and subtracted to the basic size of the hole (1.00) is +0.002 and 0.

 a) Command: **dimstyle**   or   *Dimensions* panel:
 b) *Dimension Styles Manager* window: **Override...**
 c) *Override Current Style: ASME* window – *Tolerance* tab – *Tolerance format* area:
   i. *Method* field: **Limits**
   ii. *Precision* field: **0.000**
   iii. *Upper value* field: **0.002**
   iv. *Lower value* field: **0**
   v. *Vertical position* field: **Middle**
   vi. **OK**
 d) *Dimension Styles Manager* window: **Close**
 e) *Dimensions* panel:
 f) Select objects:
   Select the ∅1.00
   dimension of the hole.
 g) Select objects: **Enter**

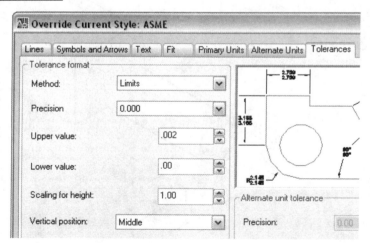

2) On your own, change the diameter of the shaft to a limit dimension using a RC3 clearance fit. Looking at the fit tables, the amount that is added to and subtracted from the basic size of the shaft (1.25) is -0.0010 and 0.0016.

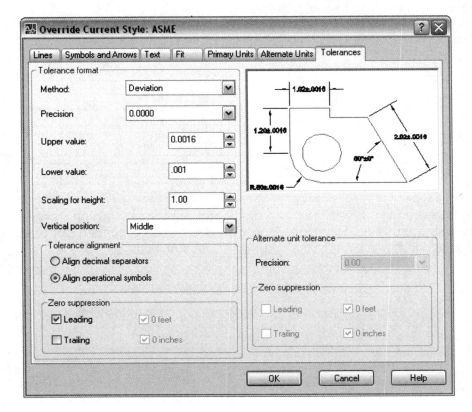

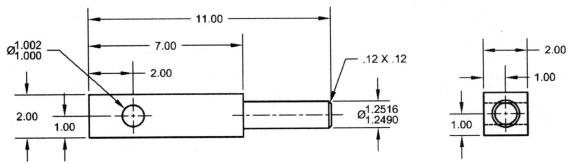

(Don't worry; your dimensions will look much smaller.)

3) Apply a ±0.001 tolerance to the dimensions that locates the shaft and a +0.0005 and -0.001 tolerance to the 2.00 hole location dimension. The basic size and tolerance values should have the same number of decimal places and the leading zero on the tolerance values should be suppressed.

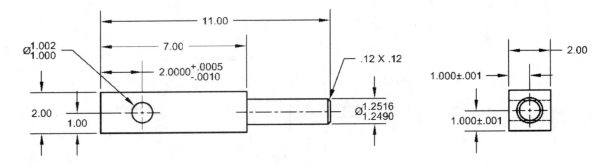

4) Save your drawing, insert your title block and print your drawing using a 1:3 scale. By default, there is no 1:3 scale. You will have to add a custom scale and then you need to add that scale support to your annotative objects.

TOLERANCING IN AUTOCAD CROSSWORD PUZZLE

Name: _____   Date: _____

CP9-1)

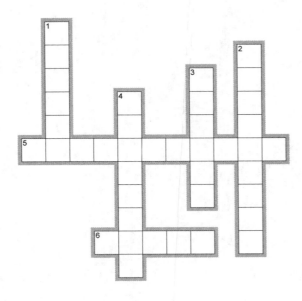

Across

5. This dimension was created using the ... tolerancing method.   10.0 ±0.1
6. If -0.001 is typed into the lower value field, then 0.001 will be ... to/from the basic size.

Down

1. This option allows you to change the settings of your current dimension style and apply those changes.

2. This dimension was created using the ... tolerancing method. $10.0\ {}^{+0.1}_{-0.2}$

3. This dimension was created using the ... tolerancing method. $\emptyset\ {}^{1.001}_{.999}$

4. This option allows you to change the settings of your current dimension style and apply those changes without corrupting the original style.

<u>NOTES:</u>

TOLERANCING IN AUTOCAD PROBLEMS

P9-1) Draw the following object including dimensions. Apply a H7/g6 Sliding clearance fit to the ∅20 hole and shaft. Apply a U7/h6 force fit to the ∅10 hole and shaft. Insert your title block and print.

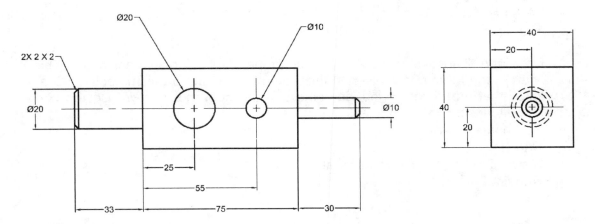

P9-2) Draw and dimension the *Drive Pulley* using proper dimensioning techniques. This *Drive Pulley* is part of the *Pulley Assembly* given in the Assembly chapter problem section (Chapter 13). Notice that the dimensioned isometric drawing does not always use the correct symbols or dimensioning techniques. This object is part of the *Pulley Assembly* given in the Assembly chapter problem section.
- Part name = Drive Pulley
- Part No. = 2
- Material = Steel
- Required = 1

P9-3) Draw and dimension the *Follower Pulley* using proper dimensioning techniques. This *Follower Pulley* is part of the *Pulley Assembly* given in the Assembly chapter problem section (Chapter 13). Notice that the dimensioned isometric drawing does not always use the correct symbols or dimensioning techniques.
- Part name = Follower Pulley
- Part No. = 3
- Material = Steel
- Required = 1

P9-4) Draw and dimension the *Shaft* using proper dimensioning techniques. This *Shaft* is part of the *Pulley Assembly* given in the Assembly chapter problem section (Chapter 13). Notice that the dimensioned isometric drawing does not always use the correct symbols or dimensioning techniques.
- Part name = Shaft
- Part No. = 4
- Material = Hardened Steel
- Required = 1

P9-5) Draw and dimension the *Bushing* using proper dimensioning techniques. This *Bushing* is part of the *Pulley Assembly* given in the Assembly chapter problem section (Chapter 13). Notice that the dimensioned isometric drawing does not always use the correct symbols or dimensioning techniques.

- Part name = Bushing
- Part No. = 5
- Material = Brass
- Required = 1

P9-6) Draw and dimension the *V-Anvil* using proper dimensioning techniques. This *V-Anvil* is part of the *Milling Jack* given in the Assembly chapter problem section (Chapter 13). Notice that the dimensioned isometric drawing does not always use the correct symbols or dimensioning techniques.

- Part name = V-Anvil
- Part No. = 3
- Material = SAE 1045 – Heat Treat
- Required = 1

THREADS AND FASTENERS

In Chapter 10 you will learn about fasteners. Fasteners give us the means to assemble parts and to later disassemble them if necessary. Most fasteners have threads; therefore, it is important to understand thread notation when learning about fasteners. By the end of this chapter, you will be able to draw and correctly annotate threads on an orthographic projection. You will also be able to calculate an appropriate bolt or screw clearance hole.

10.1) FASTENERS

Fasteners include items such as bolts, nuts, set screws, washers, keys, and pins, just to name a few. Fasteners are not a permanent means of assembly, such as, welding or adhesives. They are used in the assembly of machines that, in the future, may need to be taken apart and serviced. The most common type of fastener is the screw. There are many types of screws and many types of screw threads or thread forms.

Fasteners and threaded features must be specified on your engineering drawing. If the fastener is purchased, specifications must be given to allow the fastener to be ordered correctly. If the fastener is to be manufactured, a detailed drawing must be produced. The majority of this chapter will focus on how to draw and dimension threaded features.

10.2) SCREW THREAD DEFINITIONS

- Screw Thread: A screw thread is a ridge of uniform section in the form of a helix (see Figure 10-1).

- External Thread: External threads are on the outside of a member. A chamfer on the end of the screw thread makes it easier to engage the nut. An external thread is cut using a die or lathe.

- Internal Thread: Internal threads are on the inside of a member. An internal thread is cut using a tap.

- Major DIA (D): The major diameter is the largest diameter for both internal and external threads. Sometimes referred to as the nominal or basic size.

- Minor DIA (d): The minor diameter is the smallest diameter.

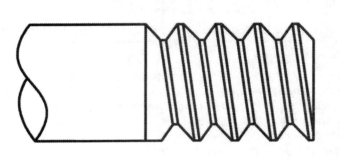

External Threads   Internal Threads

Figure 10-1: External and internal threads.

- Pitch DIA (d_P): Consider a line that cuts across the threads such that the distance on the line that cuts the thread space equals the distance of the line that cuts the actual thread. The pitch diameter is the location of this line.

- Crest: The crest is the top surface of the thread.

- Root: The root is the bottom surface of the thread.

- Side: The side is the surface between the crest and root.

- Depth of thread: The depth of thread is the perpendicular distance between the crest and the root and is equal to (D-d)/2.

- Pitch (P): The pitch is the distance from a point on one thread to the corresponding point on the next thread. The pitch is given in inches per threads or millimeters per thread.

- Angle of Thread (A): The angle of thread is the angle between the sides of the threads.

- Screw Axis: The screw axis is the longitudinal centerline.

- Lead: The lead is the distance a screw thread advances axially in one turn.

- Right Handed Thread: Right handed threads advance when turned clockwise (CW). Threads are assumed RH unless specified otherwise.

- <u>Left Handed Thread:</u> Left handed threads advance when turned counter clockwise (CCW).

Application Question 10-1

Name an example of a left handed thread.

Instructor Led Exercise 10-1: Screw thread features

Identify the screw thread features using the preceding definitions as a guide.

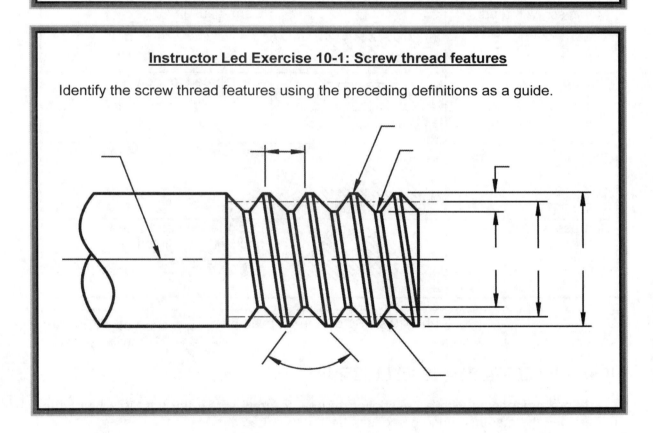

10.3) <u>TYPES OF THREAD</u>

There are many different types of threads or thread forms available. The thread form is the shape of the thread. The choice of thread form used for a particular application depends on length of engagement and load among other factors. *Unified* and *Metric* threads are the most widely used thread forms. Table 10-1 describes just a few of the different thread forms available and their uses.

Thread Name	Figure	Uses
Unified screw thread		General use.
Metric screw thread		General use.
Square		Ideal thread for power transmission.
ACME		Stronger than square thread.
Buttress		Designed to handle heavy forces in one direction (e.g. truck jack).

Table 10-1: Screw thread examples

10.4) <u>MANUFACTURING SCREW THREADS</u>

Before proceeding with a description of how to draw screw threads, it is helpful to understand the manufacturing processes used to produce threads.

To cut internal threads, a tap drill hole is drilled first and then the threads are cut using a tap. The tap drill hole is a little bigger than the minor diameter of the mating external thread to allow engagement. The depth of the tap drill is longer than the length of the threads to allow the proper amount of threads to be cut as shown in Figure 10-2. There are approximately three useless threads at the end of a normal tap. A bottom tap has useful threads all the way to the end, but is more expensive than a normal tap. If a bottom tap is used, the tap drill depth is approximately the same as the thread length.

To cut external threads, you start with a shaft the same size as the major diameter. Then, the threads are cut using a die or on a lathe. For both internal and external threads, a chamfer is usually cut at the points of engagement to allow easy assembly.

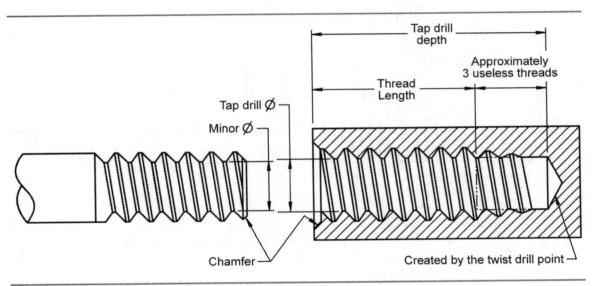

Figure 10-2: Manufacturing screw threads.

10.5) DRAWING SCREW THREADS

There are three methods of representing screw threads on a drawing: *detailed*, *schematic*, and *simplified*. The screw thread representations and standards presented in this chapter are in accordance with the ASME Y14.6-2001 standard. The physical dimension of a particular thread may be obtained in Appendix B.

10.5.1) Detailed Representation

A detailed representation is a close approximation of the appearance of an actual screw thread. The form of the thread is simplified by showing the helix structure with straight lines and the truncated crests and roots as a sharp 'V' similar to that shown in Figure 10-1. This method is comparatively difficult and time consuming.

10.5.2) Schematic Representation

The schematic representation is nearly as effective as the detailed representation and is much easier to draw. Staggered lines are used to represent the thread roots and crests (see Figures 10-3 and 10-4). This method should not be used for hidden internal threads or sections of external threads.

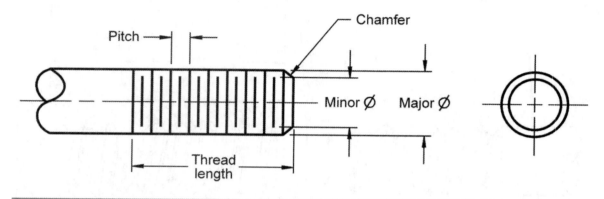

Figure 10-3: Schematic representation of external threads.

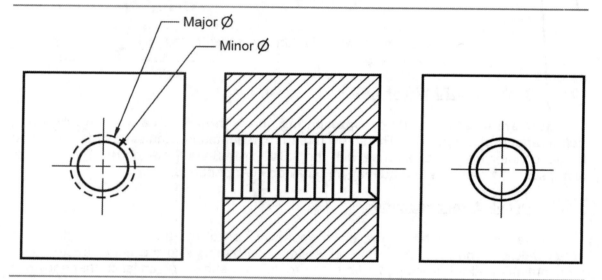

Figure 10-4: Schematic representation of internal threads.

10.5.3) Simplified Representation

In the simplified representation, the screw threads are drawn using visible and hidden lines to represent the major and minor diameters. Line choice depends on whether the thread is internal or external and the viewing direction (see Figures 10-5 and 10-6). Simplified threads are the simplest and fastest to draw. This method should be used whenever possible.

The major, minor, and tap drill diameters may be looked up in Appendix B. If screw thread tables are not available for reference, the minor diameter can be approximated as 75% of the major diameter.

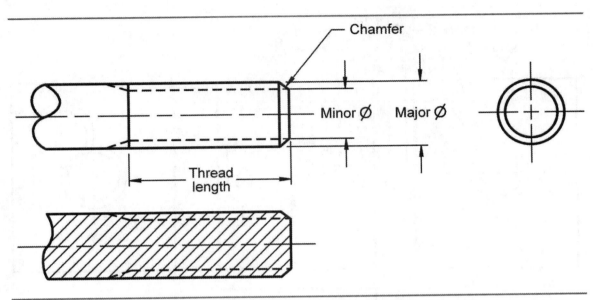

Figure 10-5: Simplified representation of external threads.

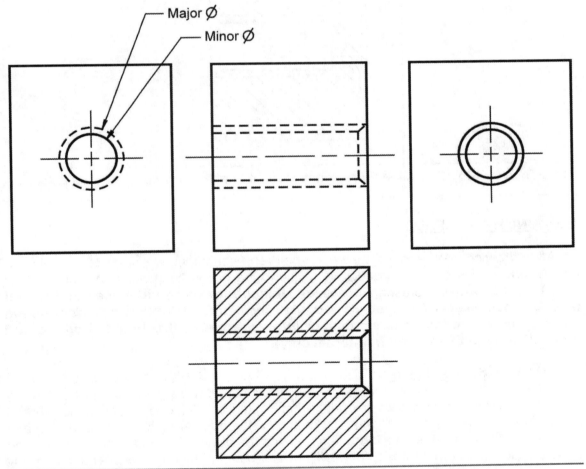

Figure 10-6a: Simplified representation of internal threads.

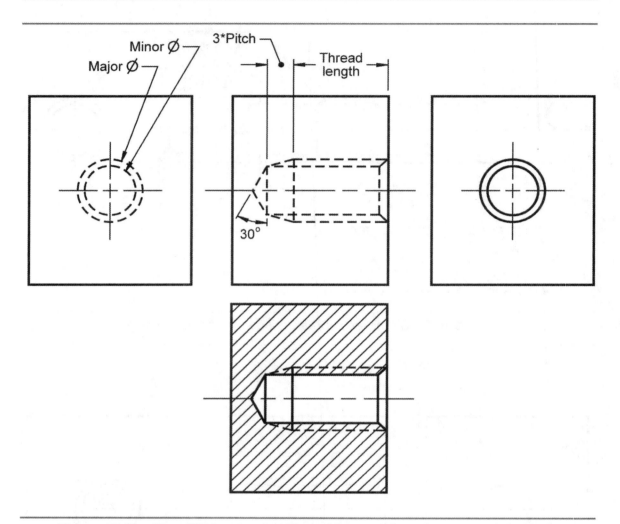

Figure 10-6b: Simplified representation of internal threads cut on a blind hole.

10.6) UNIFIED THREADS

After drawing a thread using the proper representation, we need to identify the thread form and size in a thread note. Each type of thread (Unified, Metric, ACME, etc…) has its own way of being identified. **Unified threads are identified in a thread note by their *major diameter*, *threads per inch*, *thread form* and *series*, *thread class*, whether the thread is *external* or *internal*, whether the thread is *right* or *left* handed, and the thread *depth* (internal only).**

10.6.1) Unified Thread Note

The following is a list of components that should be included in the Unified thread note. The first three components (major diameter, threads per inch, and thread form and series) should be included in all thread notes and the depth of thread should be included for all applicable internal thread notes. The other components are optional and are only used if additional refinement is needed.

1. Major Diameter: The major diameter is the largest diameter for both internal and external threads.

2. Threads per Inch: The number of threads per inch is equal to one over the pitch.

3. Thread Form and Series: The thread form is the shape of the thread cut (Unified) and the thread series is the number of threads per inch for a particular diameter (coarse, fine, extra fine).

    • UNC: UNC stands for *Unified National coarse*.   Coarse threads are the most commonly used thread.

    • UNF: UNF stands for *Unified National fine*.   Fine threads are used when high degree of tightness is required.

    • UNEF: UNEF stands for *Unified National extra fine*.   Extra fine threads are used when the length of engagement is limited (e.g. sheet metal).

4. Thread Class: The thread class indicates the closeness of fit between the two mating threaded parts.   There are three thread classes.   A thread class of "1" indicates a generous tolerance and used when rapid assembly and disassembly is required.   A thread class of "2" is a normal production fit.   This fit is assumed if none is stated.   A thread class of "3" is used when high accuracy is required.

5. External or Internal Threads: An "A" (external threads) or "B" (internal threads) is placed next to the thread class to indicate whether the threads are external or internal.

6. Right handed or left handed thread: Right handed threads are indicated by the symbol "RH" and left handed threads are indicated by the symbol "LH".   Right handed threads are assumed if none is stated.

7. Depth of thread: The thread depth is given at the end of the thread note and indicates the thread depth for internal threads.   The stated depth is not the tap drill depth.   Remember the tap drill depth is longer that the thread depth.

Instructor Led Exercise 10-2: Unified National thread note components

Identify the different components of the following Unified National thread notes.

1/4 – 20 UNC – 2A – RH

1/4	
20	
UNC	
2	
A	
RH	

10.6.2) Unified Thread Tables

Standard screw thread tables are available in order to look up the major diameter, threads per inch, tap drill size, and minor diameter for a particular thread. These thread tables are given in the ASME B1.1-2003 standard which are restated in Appendix B.

Instructor Led Exercise 10-3: Unified National thread note

Write the thread note for a #10 fine thread.

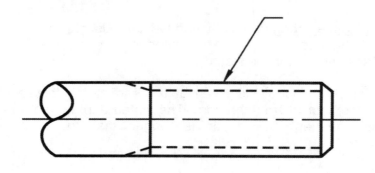

What are the major and minor diameters in inches?

Major DIA	
Minor DIA	

10.7) <u>METRIC THREADS</u>

Metric threads are identified, in a thread note, by "M" for Metric thread form, the *major diameter* followed by a lower case "x", *pitch*, *tolerance class*, whether the thread is *right* or *left* handed, and *thread depth* (internal only).

10.7.1) <u>Metric thread note</u>

The following is a list of components that should be included in a Metric thread note. The first three components (Metric form, major diameter, and pitch) should be included in all thread notes and the depth of thread should be included for all applicable internal thread notes. The other components are optional and are only used if additional refinement is needed.

1. <u>Metric Form:</u> Placing an "M" before the major diameter indicates the Metric thread form.

2. <u>Major Diameter:</u> This major diameter is the largest diameter for both internal and external.

3. <u>Pitch:</u> The pitch is given in millimeters per thread.

4. <u>Tolerance Class:</u> The tolerance class describes the looseness or tightness of fit between the internal and external threads. The tolerance class contains both a tolerance grade given by a number and tolerance position given by a letter. In a thread note, the minor or pitch diameter tolerance is stated first followed by the major or crest diameter tolerance if it is different. Two classes of Metric thread fits are generally recognized. For general purpose, the fit "6H/6g" should be used. This fit is assumed if none is stated. For a closer fit, use "6H/5g6g".

   - <u>Tolerance Grade:</u> The tolerance grade is indicated by a number. The smaller the number the tighter the fit. The number "5" indicates good commercial practice. The number "6" is for general purpose threads and is equivalent to the thread class "2" used for Unified National threads.

   - <u>Tolerance Position:</u> The tolerance position specifies the amount of allowance and is indicated by a letter. Upper case letters are used for internal threads and lower case letters for external threads. The letter "e" is used for large allowances, "g" and "G" are used for small allowances, and "h" and "H" are used for no allowance.

5. <u>Right handed or left handed thread:</u> Right handed threads are indicated by the symbol "RH" and left handed threads are indicated by the symbol "LH". Right handed threads are assumed if none is stated.

6. <u>Depth of thread:</u> The thread depth is given at the end of the thread note and indicates the thread depth for internal threads, not the tap drill depth.

Instructor Led Exercise 10-4: Metric thread note components

Identify the different components of the following Metric thread notes.

M10 x 1.5 – 4h6h – RH

M	
10	
1.5	
4h	
6h	
Internal or External	
RH	

10.7.2) Metric Thread Tables

Standard screw thread tables are available in order to look up the major diameter, threads per inch, tap drill size, and minor diameter for a particular thread. These thread tables are given in the ASME B1.13M-2001 standard which are given in Appendix B.

Instructor Led Exercise 10-5: Metric thread tables

For a ⌀16 internal Metric thread, what are the two available pitches and the corresponding tap drill diameter and the corresponding minor diameter for the mating external thread?

Pitch	Tap drill size	Minor DIA

Which has the finer thread?

The finer thread is M16x(   )

Instructor Led Exercise 10-5 Cont.: Metric thread tables

Write the thread note for a 16 mm diameter coarse thread.

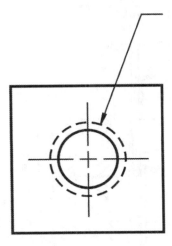

10.8) DRAWING BOLTS

Figure 10-7 illustrates how to draw bolts. The variable D represents the major or nominal diameter of the bolt. Nuts are drawn in a similar fashion.

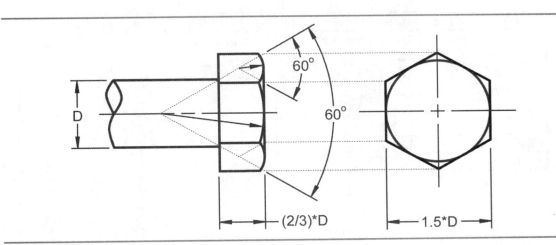

Figure 10-7: Drawing bolts.

10.9) BOLT AND SCREW CLEARANCES

Bolts and screws attach one material with a clearance hole to another material with a threaded hole. The size of the clearance hole depends on the major diameter of the fastener and the type of fit that is required for the assembly to function properly.

Clearance holes can be designed to have a *normal, close* or *loose* fit. Table 10-2 gives the normal fit clearances which are illustrated in Figure 10-8. For detailed information on clearances for bolts and screws, refer to the ASME B18.2.8-1999 standard also given in Appendix B.

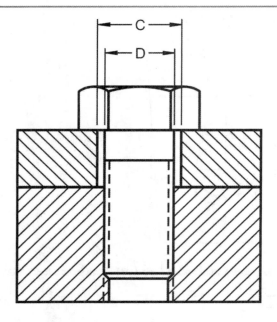

Figure 10-8: Bolt clearance.

Inch clearances	
Nominal screw size (D)	Clearance hole (C)
#0 - #4	D + 1/64
#5 – 7/16	D + 1/32
1/2 – 7/8	D + 1/16
1	D + 3/32
1 1/8, 1 1/4	D + 3/32
1 3/8, 1 1/2	D + 1/8

Metric clearances	
Nominal screw size (D)	Clearance hole (C)
M1.6	D + 0.2
M2, M2.5	D + 0.4
M4, M5	D + 0.5
M6	D + 0.6
M8, M10	D + 1
M12 – M16	D + 1.5
M20, M24	D + 2
M30 – M42	D + 3
M48	D + 4
M56 – M90	D + 6
M100	D + 7

Table 10-2: Bolt and screw normal fit clearance holes.

Sometimes bolt or screw heads need to be flush with the surface. This can be achieved by using either a counterbore or countersink depending on the fasteners head shape. Counterbores are holes that are designed to recess bolt or screw heads below the surface of a part as shown in Figure 10-9. Countersinks are angled holes that are designed to recess screws with angled heads as shown in Figure 10-10. Appendix B gives the clearance hole diameters illustrated in Figure 10-9 and 10-10. Typically CH = H + 1/16 (1.5 mm) and C1 = D1 + 1/8 (3 mm).

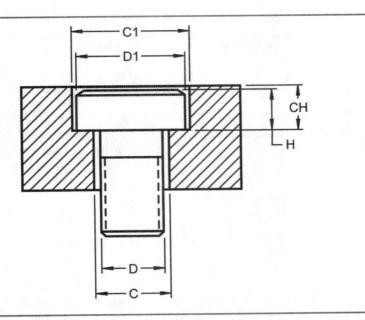

Figure 10-9: Counterbore clearances.

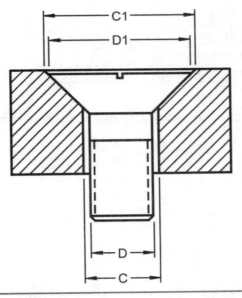

Figure 10-10: Countersink clearances.

Instructor Led Exercise 10-6: Fastener tables and clearance holes

What is the normal fit clearance hole diameter for the following nominal bolt sizes?

Nominal size	Clearance hole
1/4	
3/4	

A 5/16 - 18 UNC – Socket Head Cap Screw needs to go through a piece of metal in order to screw into a plate below. The head of the screw should be flush with the surface. Fill in the following table for a normal fit clearance hole. Refer to Appendix B.

Max. Head diameter	
Max. Height of head	
Clearance hole diameter	
Counterbore diameter	
Counterbore depth	

An M8x1.25 Flat Countersunk Head Metric Cap Screw needs to go through a piece of metal in order to screw into a plate below. The clearance hole needs to be close and the head needs to go below the surface. What should the countersink diameter and clearance hole diameter be?

Major diameter	
Head diameter	
Countersink diameter	
Clearance hole diameter	

THREAD AND FASTENER CROSSWORD PUZZLE

Name: _____ Date: _____

CP10-1)

Across

4. 1/4 - 20 UNC. What is 20?
7. The simplified thread symbol uses a .... line to represent the minor diameter on external threads.
10. A bolt or screw clearance hole diameter depends on what factor?
11. A bolt or screw clearance hole diameter depends on what factor?

Down

1. How much longer is the tap drill depth than the thread depth? (.... times the pitch)
2. The schematic thread symbol draws lines at every crest and ....
3. Unified National Coarse. What is the thread form?
5. The units of pitch are mm or inches per ....
6. The tap drill size is closest in size to the .... diameter.
8. Unified National Coarse. What is the thread series?
9. M5 x 0.8. What is 0.8?

NOTES:

THREAD AND FASTENER PROBLEMS

Name: _____ Date: _____

P10-1) Write the thread notes for the following external threads. Also, what are the minor diameter and the pitch? Thread class = 2.

	(a)	(b)	(c)	(d)	(e)	(f)	(g)
Major ⌀	1/4	7/8	3/4	1/2	1	3/8	5/16
Series	Fine	Coarse	Fine	Coarse	Fine	Extra Fine	Coarse

Thread Note	
Minor diameter	
Pitch	

Thread Note	
Minor diameter	
Pitch	

Thread Note	
Minor diameter	
Pitch	

P10-2) Write the thread notes for the following internal threads. Also, what are the tap drill size and/or diameter and the pitch? Thread class = 3.

	(a)	(b)	(c)	(d)	(e)	(f)	(g)
Major ⌀	7/16	1/4	5/8	1 ¼	3/8	1/2	1
Series	Fine	Coarse	Fine	Coarse	Fine	Extra Fine	Coarse

Thread Note	
Tap drill size and/or diameter	
Pitch	

Thread Note	
Tap drill size and/or diameter	
Pitch	

Thread Note	
Tap drill size and/or diameter	
Pitch	

P10-3) Write the thread notes for the following threads. Also, what is the major diameter in inches?

	(a)	(b)	(c)	(d)	(e)	(f)	(g)
Major ⌀	#0	#2	#4	#5	#6	#8	#10
Series	Fine	Coarse	Fine	Coarse	Fine	Fine	Coarse

Thread note	
Major diameter	

Thread note	
Major diameter	

Thread note	
Major diameter	

Name: _____   Date: _____

P10-4) Write the thread notes for the following external threads. Also, what are the minor diameter and the number of threads per mm?

	(a)	(b)	(c)	(d)	(e)	(f)	(g)
Major ∅	M3	M4	M8	M10	M12	M20	M24
Series	Coarse	Coarse	Fine	Coarse	Fine	Fine	Coarse

Thread Note	
Minor diameter	
# of threads per mm	

Thread Note	
Minor diameter	
# of threads per mm	

Thread Note	
Minor diameter	
# of threads per mm	

P10-5) Write the thread notes for the following internal threads. Also, what are the tap drill size and/or diameter and the number of threads per mm?

	(a)	(b)	(c)	(d)	(e)	(f)	(g)
Major ∅	M1.6	M5	M6	M12	M18	M22	M27
Series	Coarse	Coarse	Coarse	Coarse	Fine	Fine	Coarse

Thread Note	
Tap drill size and/or diameter	
# of threads per mm	

Thread Note	
Tap drill size and/or diameter	
# of threads per mm	

Thread Note	
Tap drill size and/or diameter	
# of threads per mm	

<u>NOTES:</u>

Name: _____   Date: _____

10-6) Fill in the given table for a hex head bolt with the following major diameters.

	(a)	(b)	(c)	(d)	(e)	(f)	(g)	(h)
Major ⌀	1/4	5/16	1/2	7/8	1	9/16	3/8	7/16

Major diameter	
Width across flats	
Max. width across corners	
Head height	
Normal clearance hole	

Major diameter	
Width across flats	
Max. width across corners	
Head height	
Normal clearance hole	

Major diameter	
Width across flats	
Max. width across corners	
Head height	
Normal clearance hole	

P10-7) Fill in the given table for a hexagon (socket) head cap screw with the following major diameters.

	(a)	(b)	(c)	(d)	(e)	(f)	(g)	(h)
Major Ø	1/4	5/16	1/2	#8	#5	9/16	3/8	#10

Major diameter	
Max. head diameter	
Max. head height	
Normal clearance hole	
Counterbore diameter	
Counterbore depth	

Major diameter	
Max. head diameter	
Max. head height	
Normal clearance hole	
Counterbore diameter	
Counterbore depth	

10-8) Fill in the given table for a slotted flat countersunk head cap screw with the following major diameters.

	(a)	(b)	(c)	(d)	(e)	(f)	(g)	(h)
Major Ø	1/4	5/16	3/8	7/16	1/2	9/16	5/8	3/4

Major diameter	
Max. head diameter	
Max. head height	
Normal clearance hole	
Countersink diameter	
Countersink angle	

Major diameter	
Max. head diameter	
Max. head height	
Normal clearance hole	
Countersink diameter	
Countersink angle	

Name: _____ Date: _____

P10-9) Fill in the given table for a hex head bolt with the following major diameters.

	(a)	(b)	(c)	(d)	(e)	(f)	(g)	(h)
Major ⌀	M5	M12	M20	M30	M36	M48	M14	M24

Major diameter	
Max. width across flats	
Max. width across corners	
Max. head height	
Thread length for a screw that is shorter than 125 mm	
Normal clearance hole	

Major diameter	
Max. width across flats	
Max. width across corners	
Max. head height	
Thread length for a screw that is shorter than 125 mm	
Normal clearance hole	

P10-10) Fill in the given table for a socket head cap screw with the following major diameters.

	(a)	(b)	(c)	(d)	(e)	(f)	(g)	(h)
Major ⌀	M1.6	M2.5	M4	M6	M12	M16	M24	M42

Major diameter	
Max. head diameter	
Max. head height	
Normal clearance hole	
Counterbore diameter	
Counterbore depth	

Major diameter	
Max. head diameter	
Max. head height	
Normal clearance hole	
Counterbore diameter	
Counterbore depth	

Name: _____   Date: _____

P10-11) Fill in the given table for a flat countersunk head cap screw with the following major diameters.

	(a)	(b)	(c)	(d)	(e)	(f)	(g)	(h)
Major ⌀	M16	M3	M12	M5	M6	M8	M10	M4

Major diameter	
Head diameter	
Head height	
Normal clearance hole	
Countersink diameter	
Countersink angle	

Major diameter	
Head diameter	
Head height	
Normal clearance hole	
Countersink diameter	
Countersink angle	

DRAWING THREADS IN AUTOCAD

In Chapter 11 you will learn how to represent threads using the simplified thread symbol. You will also be taken through a procedure that will enable you to draw realistic looking hexagonal nuts and bolts. By the end of this chapter, you will be able to represent threads on a drawing and identify them using a thread note.

11.1) INTRODUCTION

There are three ways to represent threads on a drawing. The detailed representation of a thread is visually very striking, but time consuming to draw. The schematic representation is nearly as effective at indicating a thread, but it does require the use of arrays and other techniques that make it more time consuming to draw than the simplified representation. The simplified representation of a thread is very simple and easy to draw. It doesn't look much like a thread. However, after you become accustom to looking at simplified threads on a drawing, you will begin to see real threads. The simplified representation consists of nothing more than straight visible and hidden lines.

Bolts and nuts are usually specified on a standard parts sheet and do not require a detailed drawing. However, they do need to be drawn and included as part of an assembly drawing. AutoCAD has a limited selection of predefined nuts and bolts available in the *Mechanical Tool* palette. If your nut or bolt is among one of the predefined shapes, then it is easiest to use it. You will probably have to EXPLODE and modify the bolt or nut block to fit your purposes. However, it is more likely that you will have to draw your own nut, bolt or screw. After it is drawn, you can then add it to the *Tool* palette and reuse it from there.

11.2) EXTERNAL THREADS TUTORIAL

Upon completion of this tutorial you will be able to draw and identify external threads using the simplified thread representation. You will be drawing the shaft shown below. This shaft has a different thread at each end.

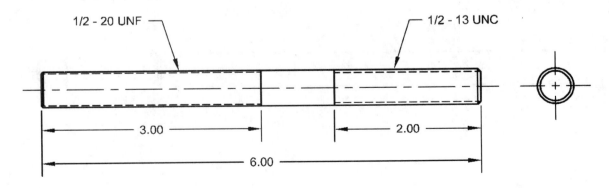

11.2.1) Drawing external Unified National threads

1) View the *Drawing Threads* video and read section 11.1).

2)  *set-inch.dwt*.

3)  **External Threads Tut.dwg**.

4) In your **Visible** layer, draw the front and side views of a cylindrical shaft that has a diameter of 0.50 inch and a length of 6 inches.

5) In your **Center** layer, add the appropriate centerlines.

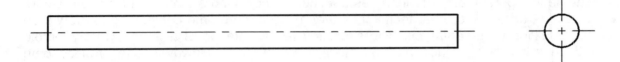

6) Draw a 1/2 - 13 UNC – 2 LONG thread on the right end of the shaft.
   a) Draw a vertical line 2 inches from the right end of the shaft to mark the end of the threads. (A fast way to do this is to OFFSET the right vertical line by 2 inches. If you used a RECTANGLE to draw the shaft, you will need to EXPLODE it before you can OFFSET the end.)
   b) Using the formula given in Appendix B, the minor diameter is calculated to be 0.42.
   c) Draw the minor diameter lines by **OFFSET**ting the top and bottom horizontal lines of the shaft by the thread depth (D-d)/2. (D = 0.5, d = 0.42).
   d) Change the minor diameter lines from the *Visible* layer to the *Hidden* layer.
   e) **TRIM** the minor diameter lines to get rid of the part that is to the left of the line marking the end of the thread.
   f) **CHAMFER** the end of the thread. The chamfer distance is usually equal to the thread depth and the angle is 45 degree.
   g) Draw the chamfer lines as shown in the figure.

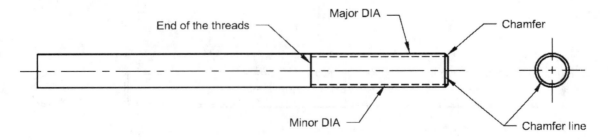

7) Use a similar procedure as above to draw a 1/2 - 20 UNF – 3 LONG thread on the left end of the shaft. Calculate the following…
   a) Minor dia =
   b) Thread depth =

   > **Note:** The hidden lines representing the minor diameter are very close to the visible lines. This may be a case where you would want to draw the minor diameter at 75% of the major diameter.

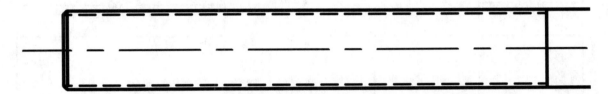

8) In your dimension layer, dimension the shaft as shown. Use an **MLEADER** and the **NEAR** *OSNAP* to create the thread notes.

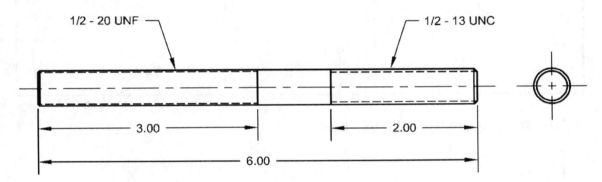

9) Insert your title block, save your drawing and print at a 1:1 scale.

11.3) INTERNAL THREADS TUTORIAL

Upon completion of this tutorial you will be able to draw internal threads using the simplified thread representation. You will be drawing the internal thread shown.

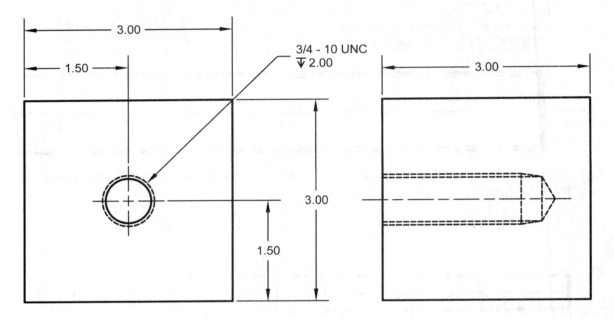

11.3.1) Drawing Unified National internal threads

1) ___ set-inch.dwt and ___ **Internal Threads Tut.dwg**.

2) In your **Visible** layer, draw the boundaries of the front and right side views. Both will be 3-inch squares.

3) Draw the circular view of a 3/4 - 10 UNC internal thread in the center of the cube.

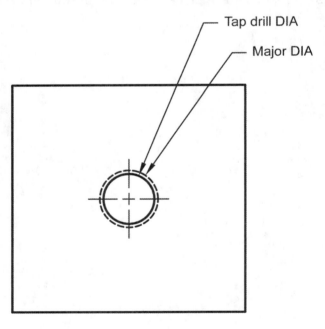

a) In your **Hidden** layer, draw a 3/4 inch diameter circle in the center of the front view. (This is your major diameter.)

b) Look up the tap drill diameter in Appendix B. It should be 21/32 inch.

c) In your **Visible** layer draw a 0.6562 inch diameter circle in the center of the front view. (This is your tap drill diameter.)

d) In your **Center** layer add the appropriate centerlines.

4) Draw the rectangular view of the 3/4 - 10 UNC – ▽2.00 internal threads in the right side view.
    a) In your **Hidden** layer, draw the rectangular view of the major diameter at a depth of 2 inches.
    b) Draw the rectangular view of the tap drill at a depth equal to the thread depth plus three times the pitch (2 + 3P = 2+ 3(1/10) = 2.3).
    c) Draw the 30° twist drill point at the end of the tap drill and the tap lines that connect the major diameter to the end of the tap drill.
    d) Add the appropriate centerline.

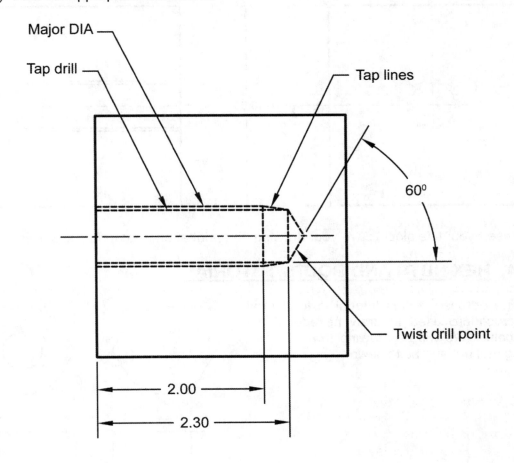

5) In your dimension layer, dimension the drawing. Dimension the internal thread as shown. Use the **Diameter** ⊘ Diameter command and edit (**DDEDIT**) the dimension text to create the thread note. If AutoCAD prompts you, disable the automatic fraction stacking.

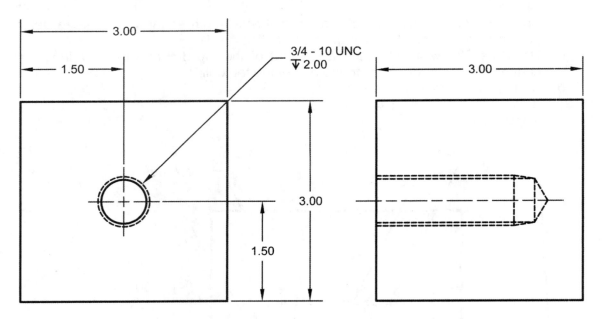

6) Insert your title block, save your drawing and print at an appropriate scale.

11.4) HEX NUTS AND BOLTS TUTORIAL

The purpose of this tutorial is to illustrate the procedure used to draw hexagonal nuts and bolts. We will be drawing the 1/4 - UNC hexagonal nut and bolt shown.

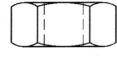

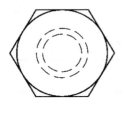

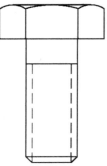

11.4.1) Drawing a hex head bolt

1)  **set-inch.dwt** and **Hex Nuts and Bolts Tut.dwg**.

2) From Appendix B look up the bolt dimensions that we will need:
   - *D* = Major diameter = 0.25
   - *H* = Head height = 0.17
   - *F* = Width across the flats = 0.44

3) In the *Visible* layer draw a **CIRCLE** that has a diameter equal to *F*.

4) Draw a hexagon (**POLYGON**) that is circumscribed about the circle.

5) In the *Construction* layer, draw vertical **CONSTRUCTION LINES** off of every corner of the hexagon.

6) Using the construction lines as a guide, draw a box that is *H* high in the *Visible* layer.

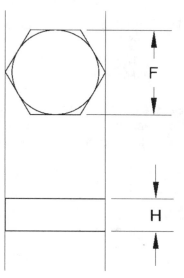

7) In the *Construction* layer, draw **LINES** at a 60 degree angle off of the top 4 intersections of the bolt head (see figure).

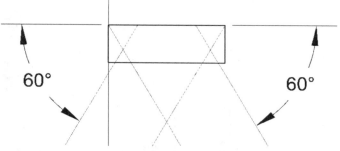

8) In the Visible layer draw three **CIRCLES** that have the centers indicated and are tangent to the top surface of the bolt.

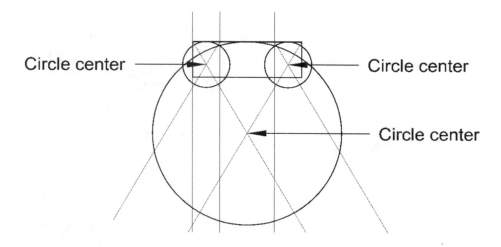

9) Finish the bolt by **TRIM**ming the circles and lines in the bolt head as shown, add a bolt body of length 5/8 inches and a thread length of 1/2 inch. Then add the major and minor diameter circles in the hexagonal view.

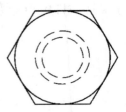

11.4.2) Drawing a hex head nut

1) From Appendix B look up the nut dimensions that we will need:
   - D = Major diameter = 0.25
   - H = Thickness = 0.22

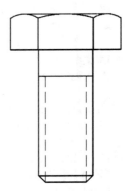

2) **COPY** the head of the bolt, **ERASE** the bottom line of the head in the front view and change the minor diameter circle in the top view from hidden to visible.

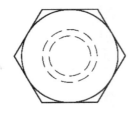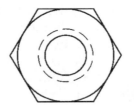

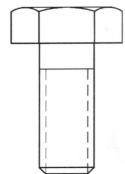

3) **OFFSET** the top line of the nut by $H/2$ = 0.11.

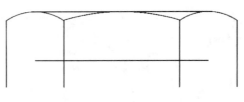

4) **MIRROR** the nut using the offset line as the mirror line.

5) **ERASE** the mirror line and add the threads.

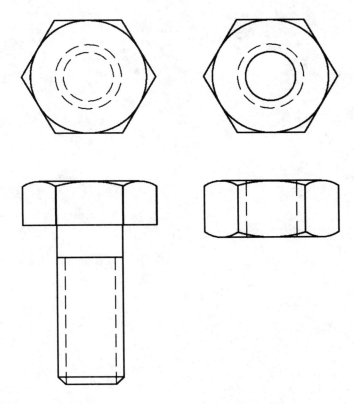

6) Insert your title block, save your drawing and print at an appropriate scale.

<u>NOTES:</u>

DRAWING THREADS IN AUTOCAD PROBLEMS

P11-1) Draw and dimension the *Bracket* using proper dimensioning techniques. This *Bracket* is part of the *Pulley Assembly* given in the Assembly chapter problem section (Chapter 13). Notice that the dimensioned isometric drawing does not always use the correct symbols or dimensioning techniques.
- Part name = Bracket
- Part No. = 1
- Material = Cast Iron
- Required = 1

P11-2) Draw and dimension the *Base* using proper dimensioning techniques. This *Base* is part of the *Milling Jack* given in the Assembly chapter problem section (Chapter 13). Notice that the dimensioned isometric drawing does not always use the correct symbols or dimensioning techniques.
- Part name = Base
- Part No. = 1
- Material = Cast Iron
- Required = 1

P11-3) Draw and dimension the *Knurled Nut* using proper dimensioning techniques. This *Knurled Nut* is part of the *Milling Jack* given in the Assembly chapter problem section (Chapter 13). Notice that the dimensioned isometric drawing does not always use the correct symbols or dimensioning techniques.
- Part name = Knurled Nut
- Part No. = 4
- Material = SAE 1045 – Heat Treat
- Required = 1

P11-4) Draw and dimension the *Pad* using proper dimensioning techniques. This *Pad* is part of the *Milling Jack* given in the Assembly chapter problem section (Chapter 13). Notice that the dimensioned isometric drawing does not always use the correct symbols or dimensioning techniques.
- Part name = Pad
- Part No. = 5
- Material = Phosphor Bronze - FAO
- Required = 1

P11-5) Draw and dimension the *Clamp Bolt* using proper dimensioning techniques. This *Clamp Bolt* is part of the *Milling Jack* given in the Assembly chapter problem section (Chapter 13). Notice that the dimensioned isometric drawing does not always use the correct symbols or dimensioning techniques.
- Part name = Clamp Bolt
- Part No. = 6
- Material = SAE 1020 – Case Hardened
- Required = 1

P11-6) Draw and dimension the *Sliding Screw* using proper dimensioning techniques. This *Sliding Screw* is part of the *Milling Jack* given in the Assembly chapter problem section (Chapter 13). Notice that the dimensioned isometric drawing does not always use the correct symbols or dimensioning techniques.

- Part name = Sliding Screw
- Part No. = 2
- Material = SAE 1045 – Heat Treat
- Required = 1

ASSEMBLY DRAWINGS

In Chapter 12 you will learn how to create an assembly drawing. An assembly drawing is a drawing of an entire machine with each part located and identified. After each part of a machine is manufactured, the assembly drawing shows us how to put these parts together. You will also learn how to generate a standard parts sheet. This sheet contains information about purchased items. The assembly drawing together with all the detailed part drawings and the standard parts sheet is called a working drawing package. By the end of this chapter, you will be able to create a working drawing package which contains all the information necessary to manufacture a machine or system.

An assembly drawing is a drawing of an entire machine or system with all of its components located and identified.

12.1) DEFINITIONS

- Detail Drawing: A detail drawing is a drawing of an individual part, which includes an orthographic projection and dimensions. One detail/part per sheet.

- Assembly Drawing: An assembly consists of a number of parts that are joined together to perform a specific function (e.g. a bicycle). The assembly may be disassembled without destroying any part of the assembly. An assembly drawing shows the assembled machine or structure with all of the parts in their functional position. Figures 12-1 and 12-2 are examples of assembly drawings.

- Subassembly Drawing: A subassembly is two or more parts that form a portion of an assembly (e.g. the drive train of a bicycle). A subassembly drawing shows only one unit of a larger machine.

- Working Drawing Package: A typical working drawing package includes an assembly drawing, detailed drawings, and a standard parts sheet. The drawing package contains the specifications that will enable the design to be manufactured.

12.1.1) Drawing Order

Drawings included in a working drawing package should be presented in the following order:

      1) Assembly drawing (first sheet)
      2) Part Number 1
      3) Part Number 2
      4) ....
      5) Standard parts sheet (last sheet)

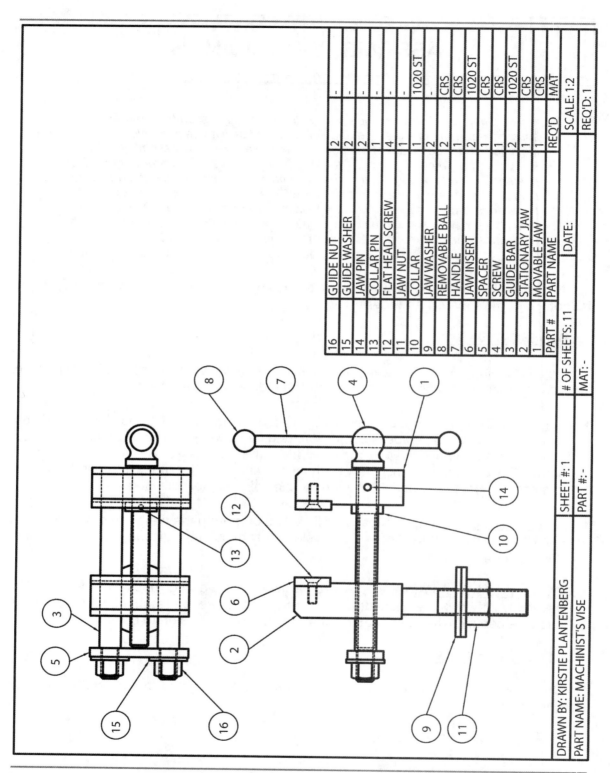

Figure 12-1: Machinist's Vise assembly drawing.

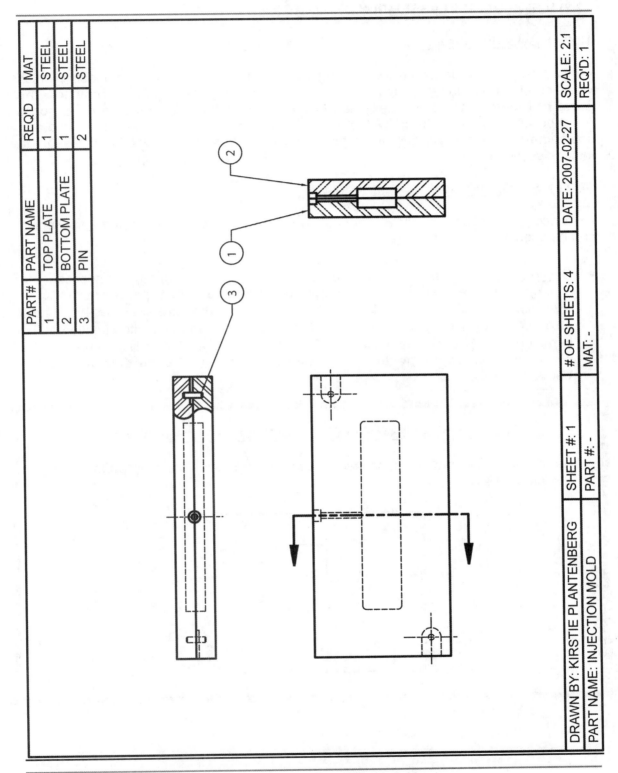

PART#	PART NAME	REQ'D	MAT
1	TOP PLATE	1	STEEL
2	BOTTOM PLATE	1	STEEL
3	PIN	2	STEEL

DRAWN BY: KIRSTIE PLANTENBERG	SHEET #: 1	# OF SHEETS: 4	DATE: 2007-02-27	SCALE: 2:1
PART NAME: INJECTION MOLD	PART #: -	MAT: -		REQ'D: 1

Figure 12-2: Injection Mold assembly drawing.

12.2) <u>VIEWS USED IN ASSEMBLY DRAWINGS</u>

12.2.1) <u>Selecting Views</u>

The purpose of an assembly drawing must be kept in mind when choosing which views need to be included. **The purpose of an assembly drawing is to show how the parts fit together** and to suggest the function of the entire unit. Its purpose is not to describe the shapes of the individual parts. Sometimes only one view is needed and sometimes it is necessary to draw all three principle views. It may also be necessary to include sectional views.

12.2.2) <u>Sectional Views</u>

Since assemblies often have parts fitting into or overlapping other parts, sectioning can be used to great advantage.

- <u>Section Lines:</u> When using sectional views in assembly drawings, it is necessary to distinguish between adjacent parts. **Section lines in adjacent parts are drawn in opposing directions.** In the largest area, the section lines are drawn at 45°. In the next largest area, the section lines are drawn at 135° (in the opposite direction of the largest area). Section line angles of 30° and 60° are used for additional parts. **The distance between the section lines may also be varied to further distinguish between parts.**

Instructor Led Exercise 12-1: Section lines in assemblies

The following assembly is sectioned. Draw in the section lines according to the rules stated above.

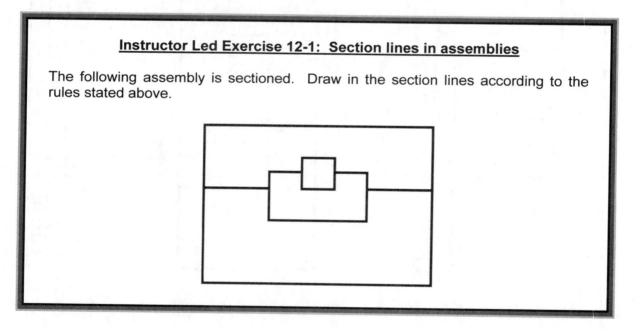

12.3) THINGS TO INCLUDE/NOT INCLUDE

The purpose of an assembly drawing is to show how the individual parts fit together. Therefore, each individual part must be identified. It is not; however, used as a manufacturing print. Some lines that are included and necessary in the detailed drawing may be left off the assembly drawing to enhance clearness. The assembly drawing should not look overly cluttered.

12.3.1) Hidden Lines

Hidden lines are often not needed. However, they should be used wherever necessary for clearness. It is left to the judgment of the drafter whether or not to include hidden lines. When a section view is used, hidden lines should not be used in the sectional view.

12.3.2) Dimensions

As a rule, dimensions are not given on assembly drawings. If dimensions are given, they are limited to some function of the object as a whole.

12.3.3) Identification

A part is located and identified by using a circle or balloon containing a part number and a leader line that points to the corresponding part. A balloon containing a part number is placed adjacent to the part. A leader line, starting at the balloon, points to the part to which it refers. Balloons identifying different parts are placed in orderly horizontal or vertical rows. The leader lines are never allowed to cross and adjacent leader lines should be as parallel to each other as possible (see Figure 12-3).

12.3.4) Parts List/ Bill of Material

The parts list is an itemized list of the parts that make up the assembled machine. **A parts list contains the *part number*, *part name*, the *number required* and the *material* of the part.** Other information may be included, such as, stock sizes of materials and weights of the parts. Parts are listed in order of their part number. Part numbers are usually assigned based on the size or importance of the part. The parts list is placed either in the upper right corner of the drawing, with part number 1 at the top, or lower right corner of the drawing, with part number 1 at the bottom (see Figures 12-1 through 12-3).

PART #	PART NAME	REQ'D	MAT
1	FRONT PLATE	1	3003 ALUMINUM
2	REAR PLATE	1	3003 ALUMINUM
3	SCREW	1	1020 STEEL
4	GUIDE ROD	2	1020 STEEL
5	CENTER PLATE	1	1020 STEEL
6	HANDLE	1	1020 STEEL
7	THREAD INSERT	1	3003 ALUMINUM
8	HEX SOC SET SCREW	1	STEEL
9	PLUNGER	1	1020 STEEL
10	DRILL BUSHING	4	1120 STEEL
11	SPRING	1	4015 STEEL
12	HEX HD SCREW	2	STEEL
13	WASHER	2	3003 ALUMINUM

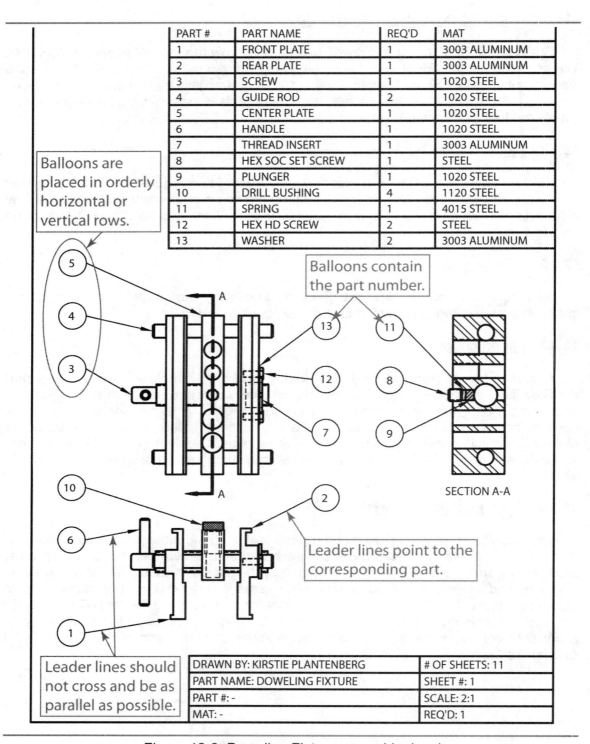

Balloons are placed in orderly horizontal or vertical rows.

Balloons contain the part number.

Leader lines point to the corresponding part.

Leader lines should not cross and be as parallel as possible.

SECTION A-A

DRAWN BY: KIRSTIE PLANTENBERG	# OF SHEETS: 11
PART NAME: DOWELING FIXTURE	SHEET #: 1
PART #: -	SCALE: 2:1
MAT: -	REQ'D: 1

Figure 12-3: Doweling Fixture assembly drawing.

12.4) <u>STANDARD PARTS</u>

Standard parts include any part that can be bought off the shelf. **Standard parts do not need to be drawn.** This could include bolts, nuts, washers, keys, etc. Purchasing information is specified on a standard parts sheet attached to the back of a working drawing package. Figure 12-4 shows an example of a standard parts sheet. This standard parts sheet lists four different items. The circle/balloon next to the item contains the part number.

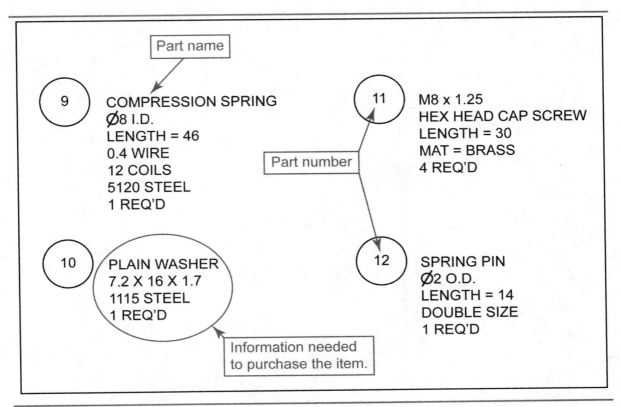

Figure 12-4: Standard parts sheet.

12.4.1) <u>General Fastener Specifications</u>

The information that should be specified on a standard parts sheet for a general fastener is listed below.

1. Thread specification (only if the fastener contains threads)
2. Head/point style or shape and name of the fastener
3. Fastener length or size
4. Fastener series
5. Material
6. Special requirements (coatings, finishes, specifications to meet)
7. REQ'D (i.e. number required)

<u>NOTES:</u>

In Class Student Exercise 12-2: Working drawing package

Consider the *Clamp* shown. Sheets of an incomplete working drawing package are given in the following pages. Complete/draw the assembly drawing, the detailed drawings of the individual parts and create a standard parts sheet.

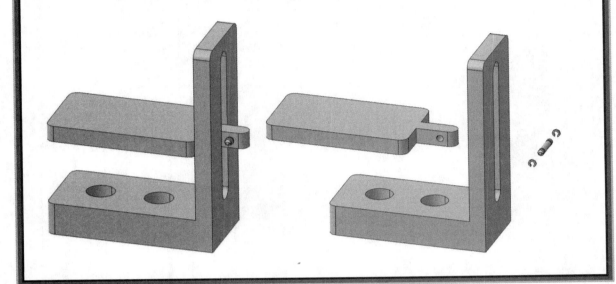

In Class Student Exercise 12-2: Working drawing package cont.

<u>Part#1:</u> The *Base* is made of steel.

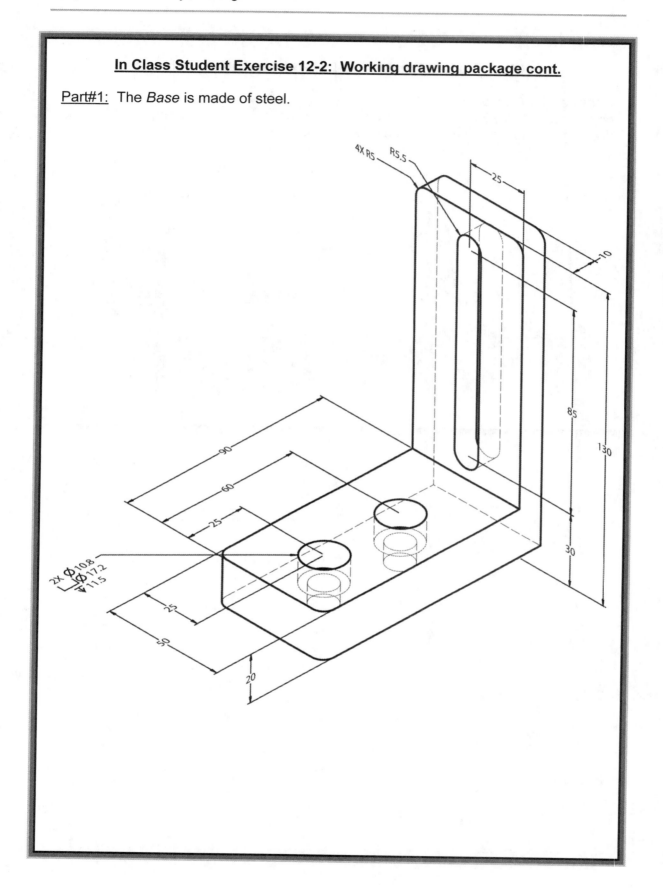

In Class Student Exercise 12-2: Working drawing package cont.

Part#2: The *Weight Plate* is made of steel.

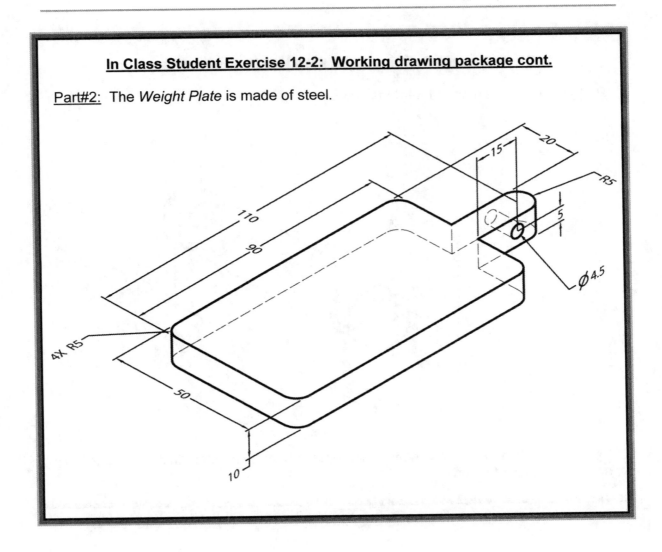

In Class Student Exercise 12-2: Working drawing package cont.

Part#3: The *Pin* is made of hardened steel.

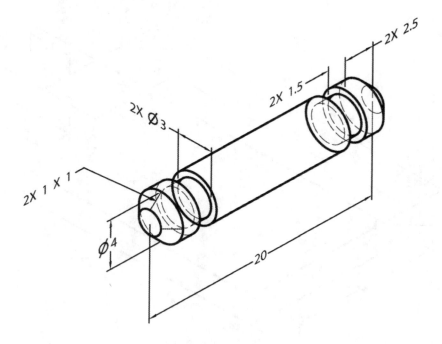

Part#4: The *Snap Ring* has an inner diameter of 3 mm, an outer diameter of 5 mm, and a thickness of 1 mm.

In Class Student Exercise 12-2: Working drawing package cont.

Name: _____ Date: _____

Balloon the assembly and fill in the parts list and title block.

PART #	PART NAME	REQ'D	MATERIAL			

	DATE:	SCALE:
# OF SHEETS:		REQ'D:
	MAT:	
SHEET #:		
PART #:		
DRAWN BY:		
PART NAME:		

In Class Student Exercise 12-2: Working drawing package cont.

Fill in the title block.

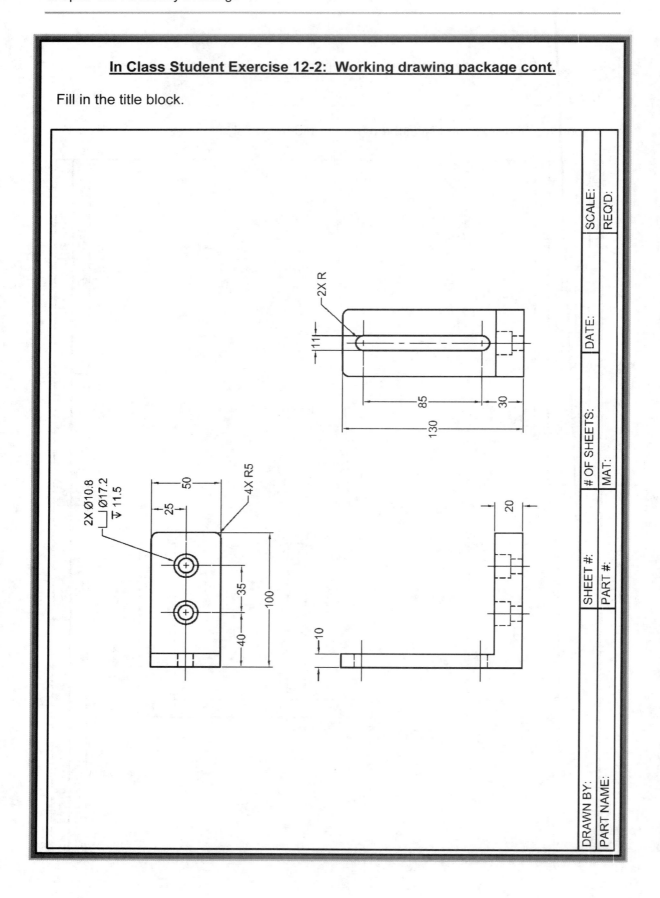

In Class Student Exercise 12-2: Working drawing package cont.

Name: _____ Date: _____

Dimension the part and fill in the title block.

In Class Student Exercise 12-2: Working drawing package cont.

Draw and dimension Part#3 and fill in the title block.

		SHEET #:	# OF SHEETS:	SCALE:
		PART #:	MAT:	REQ'D:
		DRAWN BY:	DATE:	
		PART NAME:		

In Class Student Exercise 12-2: Working drawing package cont.

Name: _____ Date: _____

Create a standard parts sheet.

				SCALE:	REQ'D:
			DATE:		
		# OF SHEETS:		MAT:	
	SHEET #:				
	PART #:				
DRAWN BY:					
PART NAME:					

NOTES:

ASSEMBLY CROSSWORD PUZZLE

Name: _____   Date: _____

CP12-1)

Across

2. The purpose of an assembly drawing is to show how the individual parts ....
4. What is always included on a detailed drawing but rarely included on an assembly drawing?
6. A standard parts sheet contains enough information about the standard parts so that they may be ....
8. Section lines are drawn in opposing directions when there are ....
10. The method used to identify and locate the parts in an assembly.

Down

1. The last sheet in a working drawing package is the .... sheet.
3. One criteria used to assign part numbers.
5. One criteria used to assign part numbers.
6. A place where you can get a quick overall view of all the parts that comprise an assembly, how many of each are required and the material from which they are made.
7. The first sheet in a working drawing package is the .... drawing.
9. If we can purchase an item off the shelf, do we need to draw a detail of it?

<u>NOTES:</u>

ASSEMBLY PROBLEMS

P12-1) Consider the *Trolley* assembly shown. Sheets of an incomplete working drawing package are given in the following pages. Complete/draw the detailed drawings of the individual parts, create a standard parts sheet, and draw an assembly drawing. The *Trolley* dimensions are shown in the exploded assemblies shown on the following pages.

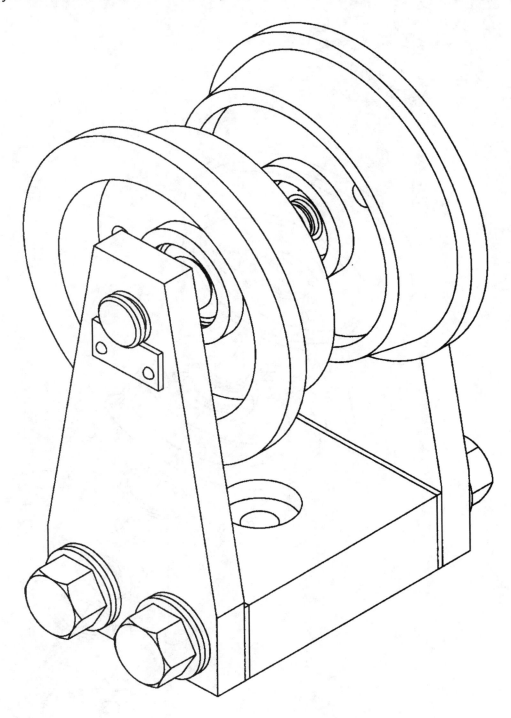

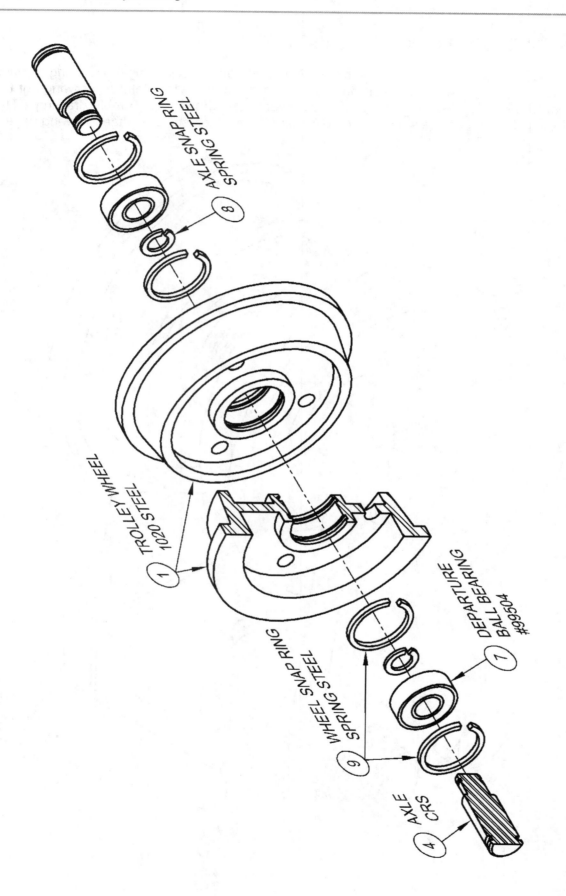

AXLE SNAP RING
SPRING STEEL
8

TROLLEY WHEEL
1020 STEEL
1

WHEEL SNAP RING
SPRING STEEL
9

DEPARTURE
BALL BEARING
#99504
7

AXLE
CRS
4

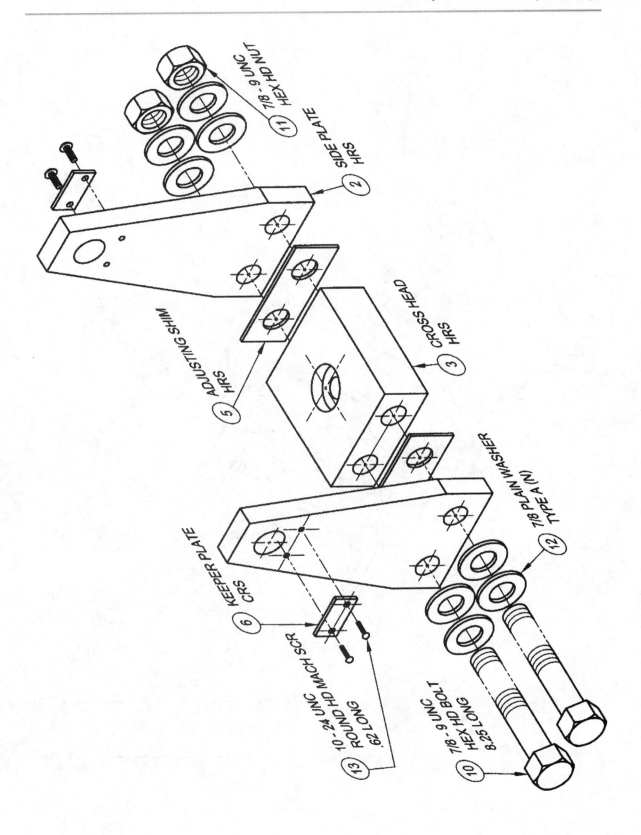

7/8 - 9 UNC
HEX HD NUT

11

SIDE PLATE
HRS

2

ADJUSTING SHIM
HRS

5

CROSS HEAD
HRS

3

7/8 PLAIN WASHER
TYPE A (N)

12

KEEPER PLATE
CRS

6

10 - 24 UNC
ROUND HD MACH SCR
.62 LONG

13

7/8 - 9 UNC
HEX HD BOLT
8.25 LONG

10

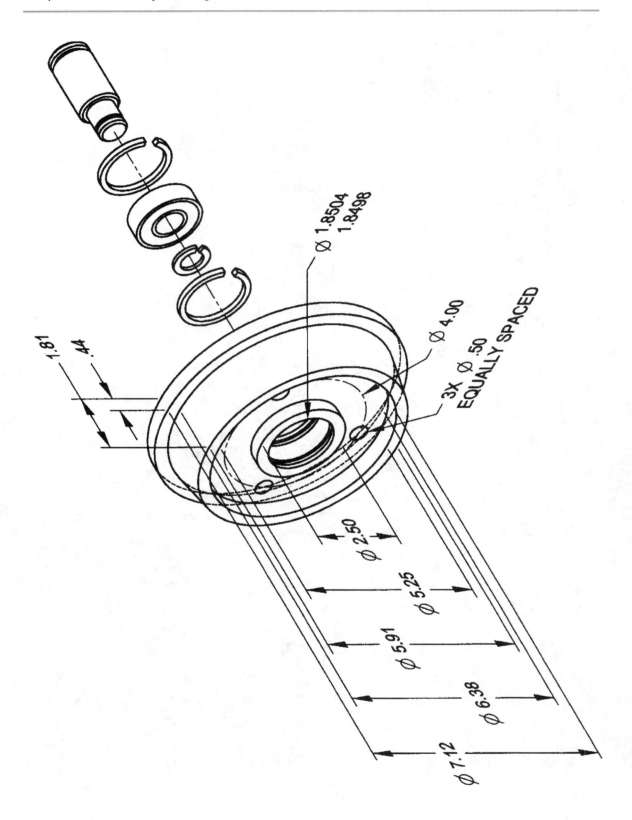

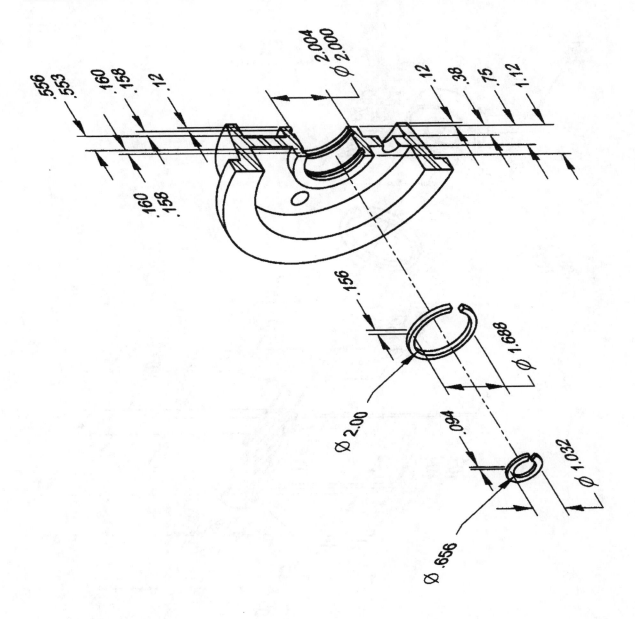

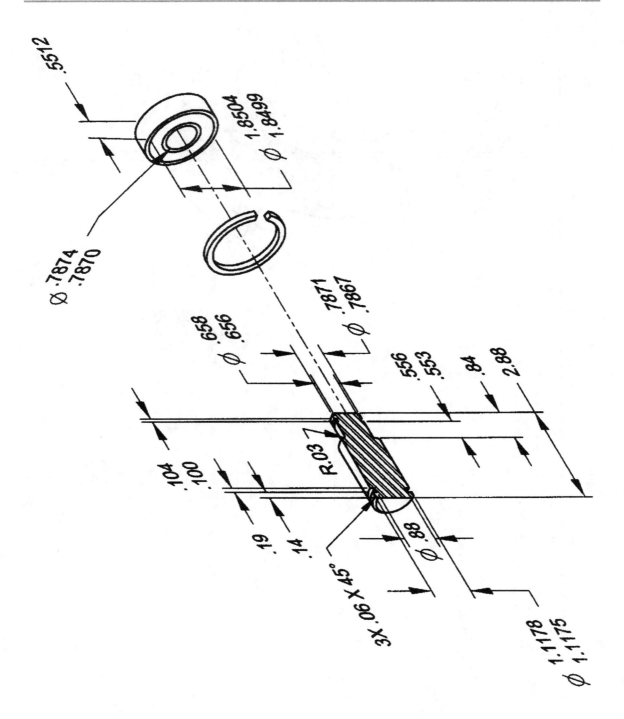

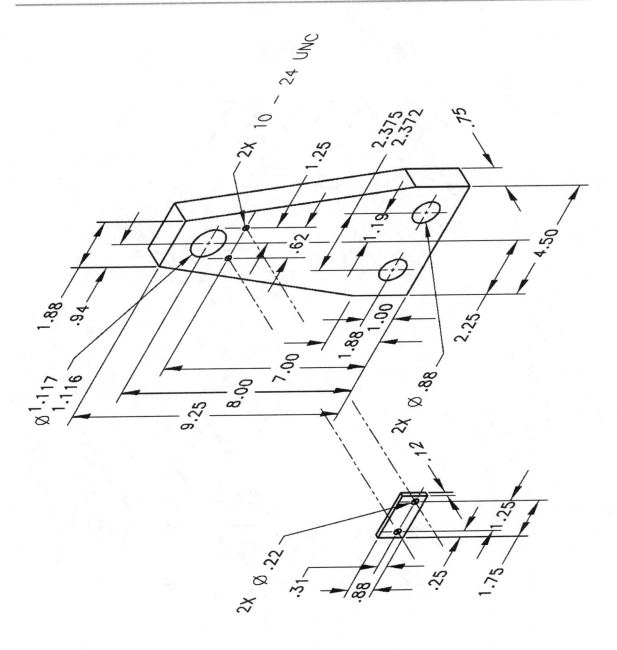

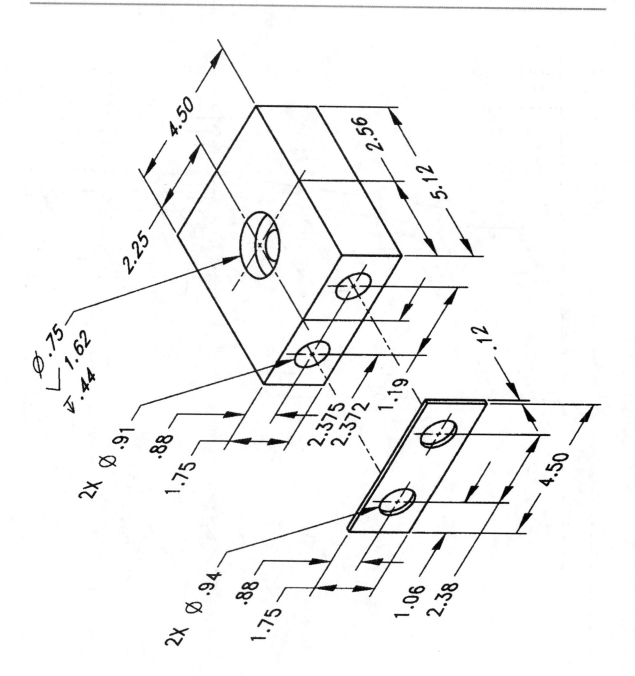

Name: _____ Date: _____

Fill in the part numbers in the appropriate balloons and complete the part list and title block information.

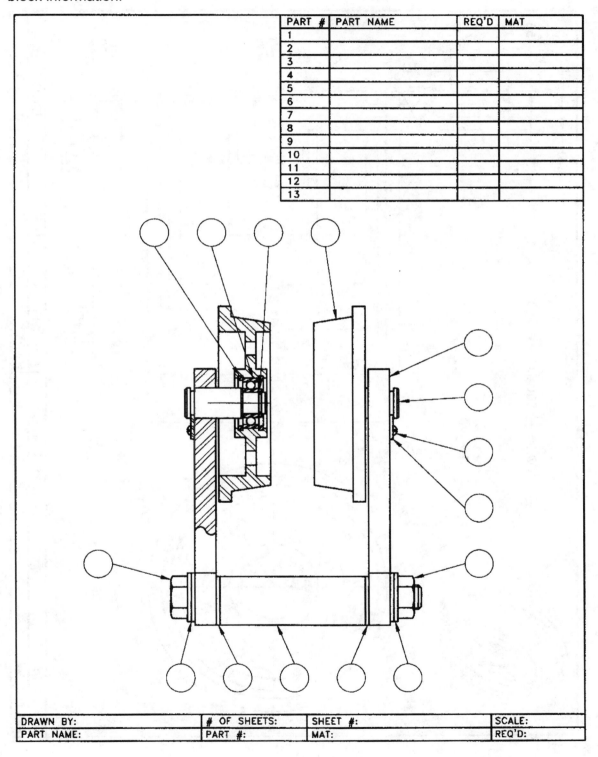

PART #	PART NAME	REQ'D	MAT
1			
2			
3			
4			
5			
6			
7			
8			
9			
10			
11			
12			
13			

DRAWN BY:		# OF SHEETS:	SHEET #:		SCALE:
PART NAME:		PART #:	MAT:		REQ'D:

Name: _____ Date: _____

Draw the missing section view and complete the title block information.

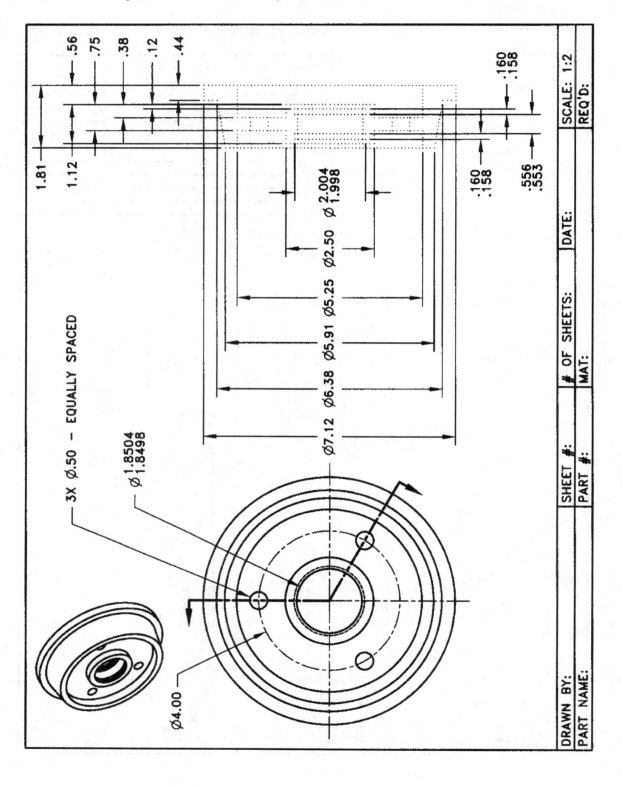

Name: _____ Date: _____

Place the remaining six dimensions and complete the title block information.

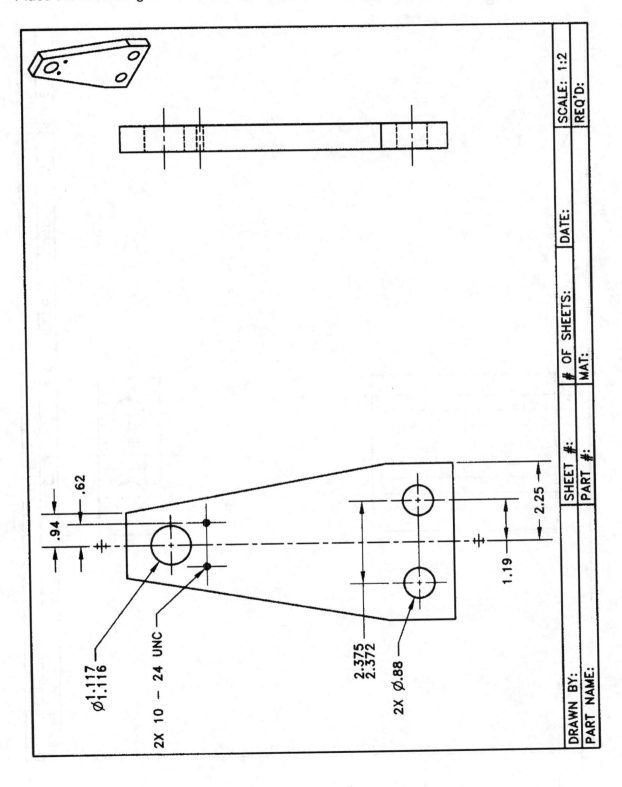

Name: _____ Date: _____

Place the remaining nine dimensions and complete the title block information.

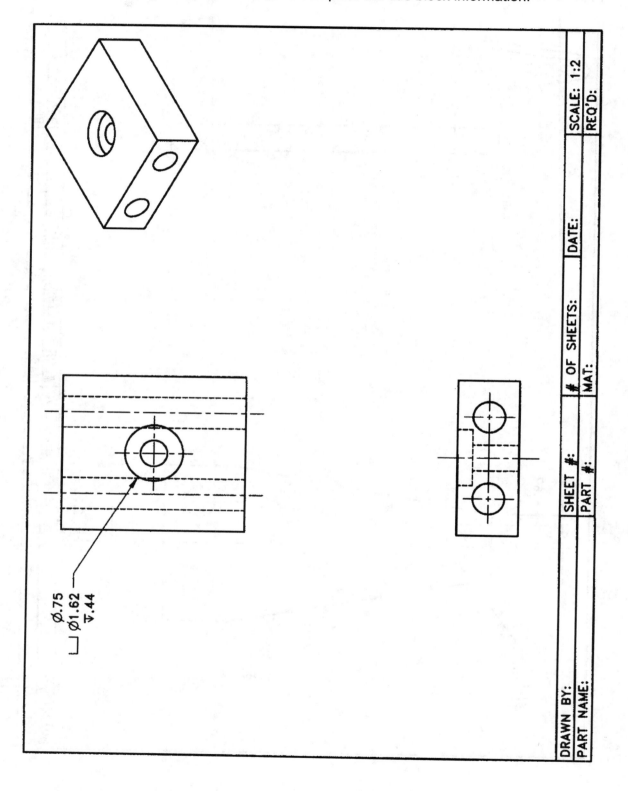

Name: _____ Date: _____

Draw in the missing dimensions and complete the title block information.

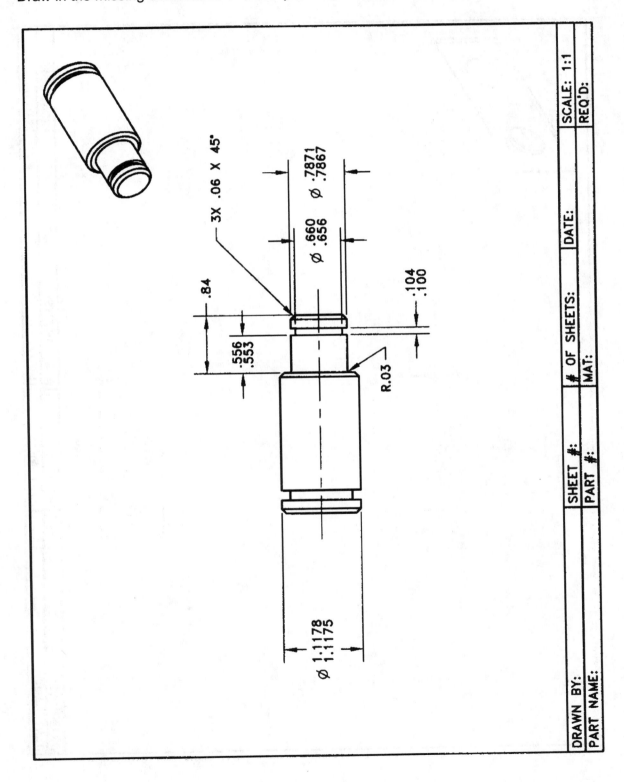

SCALE: 1:1
REQ'D:
DATE:
OF SHEETS:
MAT:
SHEET #:
PART #:
DRAWN BY:
PART NAME:

3X .06 X 45°

Ø .7871
.7867

Ø .660
.656

.84

.104
.100

.556
.553

R.03

Ø 1.1178
1.1175

Name: _____ Date: _____

Draw and dimension part #5, and fill in the title block.

SCALE: 1:1

REQ'D:

DATE:

OF SHEETS:

MAT:

SHEET #:

PART #:

DRAWN BY:

PART NAME:

Name: _____ Date: _____

Draw and dimension part #6, and fill in the title block.

SCALE: 1:1
REQ'D:

DATE:

OF SHEETS:
MAT:

SHEET #:
PART #:

DRAWN BY:
PART NAME:

Name: _____ Date: _____

Complete the information on the standard (stock) parts and fill in the title block.

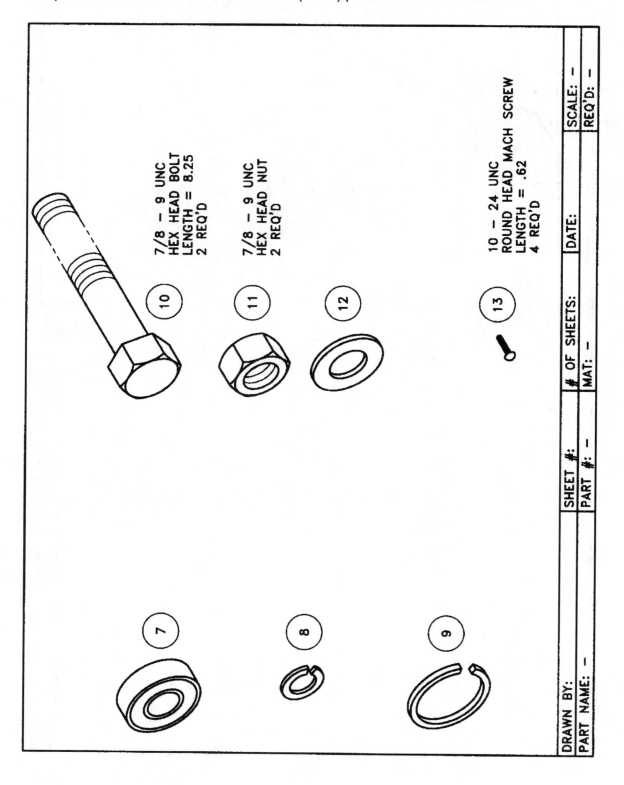

P12-2) Consider the *Drill Jig* assembly shown. Sheets of an incomplete working drawing package are given in the following pages. Complete/draw the detailed drawings of the individual parts, create a standard parts sheet, and draw an assembly drawing. The *Drill Jig* dimensions are shown in the exploded assembly shown on the next page.

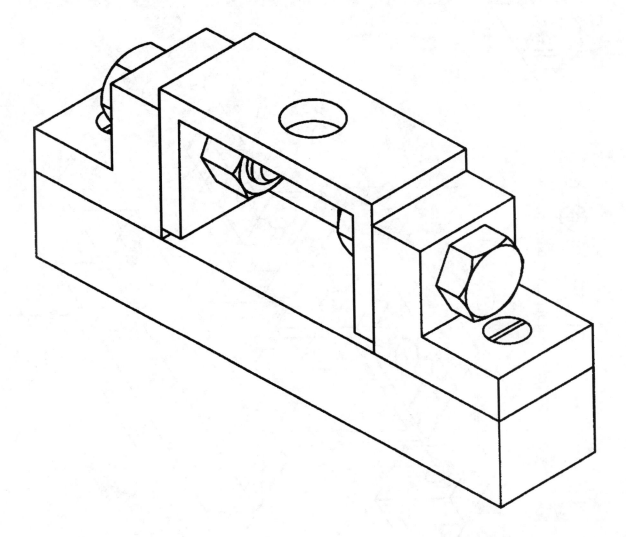

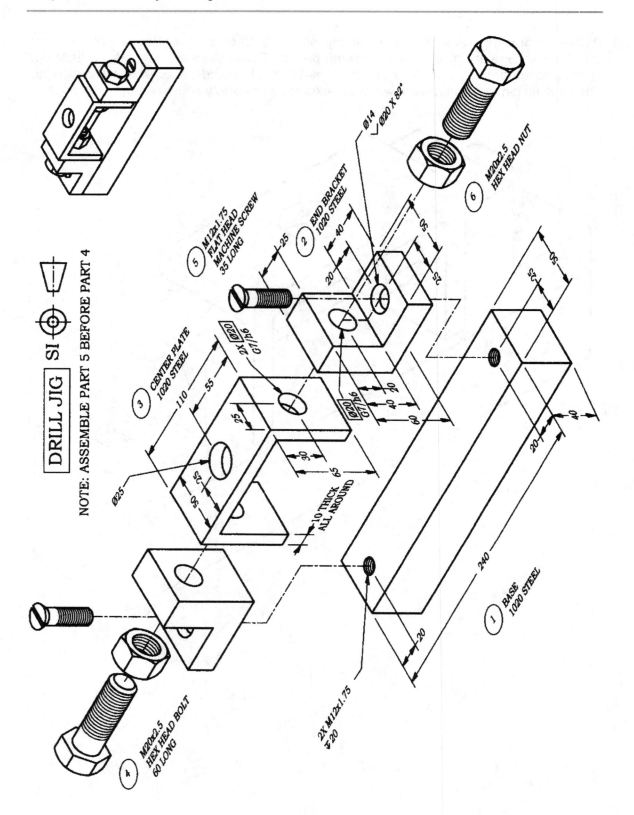

DRILL JIG SI

NOTE: ASSEMBLE PART 5 BEFORE PART 4

① BASE
1020 STEEL

② END BRACKET
1020 STEEL

③ CENTER PLATE
1020 STEEL

④ M20x2.5
HEX HEAD BOLT
60 LONG

⑤ M12x1.75
FLAT HEAD
MACHINE SCREW
35 LONG

⑥ M20x2.5
HEX HEAD NUT

Name: _____ Date: _____

Complete the section view by adding the appropriate section lines. Then, fill in the part numbers in the correct balloon, fill in the parts list, and fill in the title block.

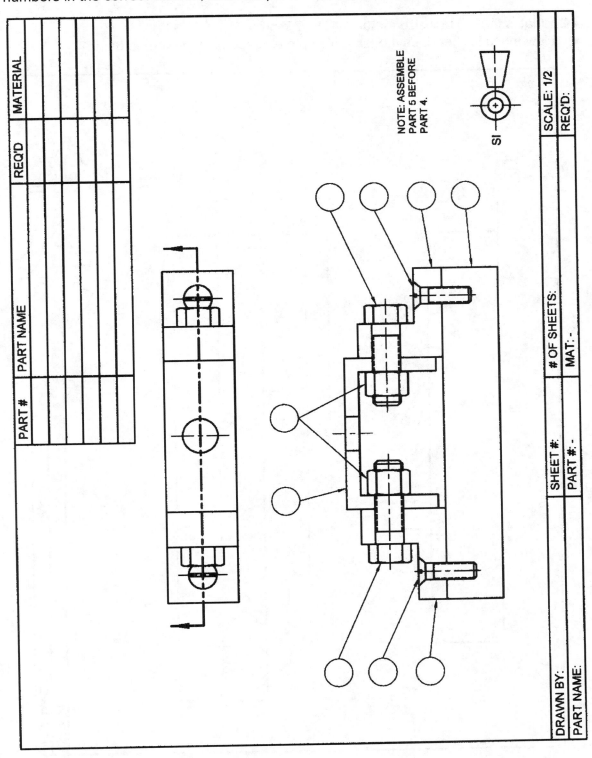

Name: _____ Date: _____

Draw and dimension the threaded features of part #1, fill in the title block, and answer the following questions.

- What is the tap drill size for the M12x1.75 thread?
- How much further does the tap drill depth proceed past the thread depth?

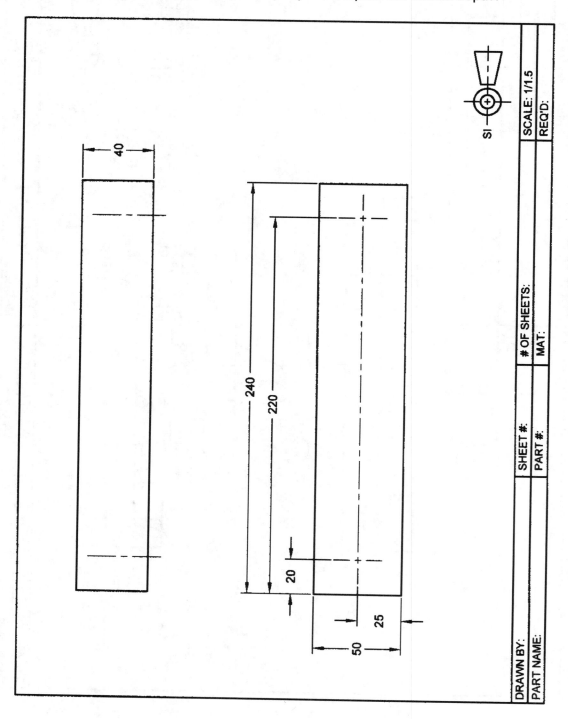

Name: _____ Date: _____

Dimension part #2 and fill in the title block.

SI

SCALE: 1/1.5

REQ'D:

OF SHEETS:

MAT:

SHEET #:

PART #:

DRAWN BY:

PART NAME:

Name: _____ Date: _____

Draw and dimension part #3, and fill in the title block.

SI

| DRAWN BY: | SHEET #: | # OF SHEETS: | SCALE: 1/1.5 |
| PART NAME: | PART #: | MAT: | REQ'D: |

Name: _____ Date: _____

Create a standard parts sheet and fill in the title block.

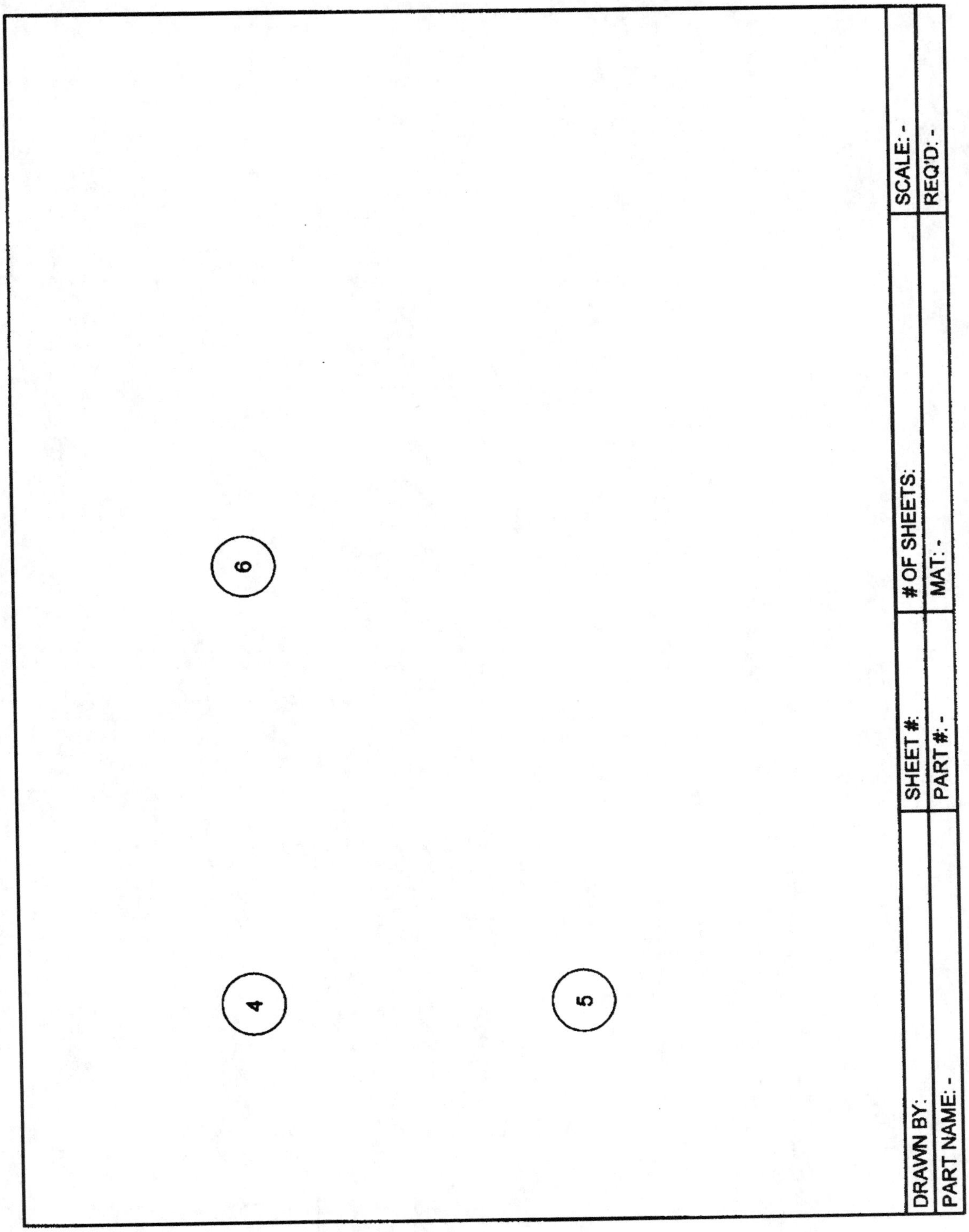

SCALE: -
REQ'D: -

# OF SHEETS:	SHEET #:
MAT: -	PART #: -

6

4   5

DRAWN BY:
PART NAME: -

NOTES:

CREATING ASSEMBLY DRAWINGS IN AUTOCAD

In Chapter 13 you will learn how to use individual part views to construct an assembly drawing. You will also learn how to balloon an assembly and make a parts list. By the end of this chapter, you will be able to construct a complete and fully annotated assembly drawing.

13.1) INTRODUCTION

The assembly drawing, included as part of a working drawing package, is usually created after all the detailed part drawings are completed. Conceptual or design idea assembly drawings are drawn at the beginning stages of the design process to test out an idea. However, these types of assembly drawings are not usually included as part of a working drawing package.

An assembly drawing is relatively easy to create if all the detailed part drawings are complete. Selected views of each part are copied and pasted into an assembly drawing file. Once all parts are combined into one file, an assembly may be created using various MODIFY commands. Some lines may have to be changed from visible to hidden or visa versa and some may need to be deleted. The only new parts that may need to be drawn are standard parts that were not detailed. And, the ballooning process has been greatly simplified with the advent of multileaders.

13.2) ASSEMBLY TUTORIAL

In this tutorial we will use previously drawn details to create a complete assembly drawing of the following *Drill Jig*. Assembly of the details will be accomplished using functionally related features and modify commands such as MOVE, MIRROR, COPY, etc...

> **IMPORTANT!** Throughout the tutorial you will be instructed to choose points that relate to geometric locations on an object. Select them with an *OSNAP*.

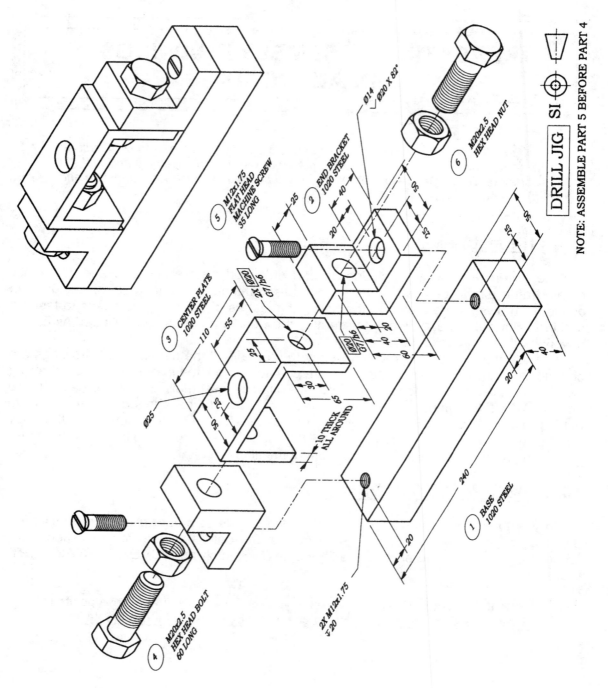

13.2.1) Creating the assembly drawing

1) View the *Assembly* video and read section 13.1).

2) *assembly_tut_student_2010.dwg* and **Assembly Tut.dwg.** The drawing should look like the figure below.

Refer to this figure when completing steps 3) – 5)

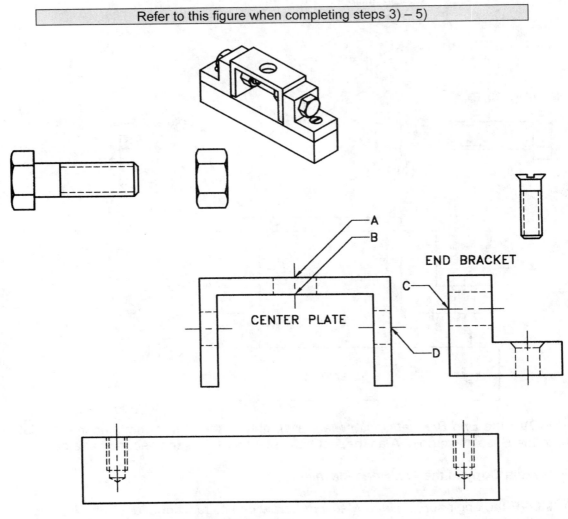

CENTER PLATE

END BRACKET

3) **MIRROR** the *End Bracket* to create the one for the left side. Use point A and B to create the mirror line. Select these points using an *OSNAP*.

4) **MOVE** the original *End Bracket* into its functional position with respect to the *Center Plate*. Use point C as the first base point and point D as the second base point.

5) Use a similar procedure to **MOVE** the *End Bracket* copy into its functional position.

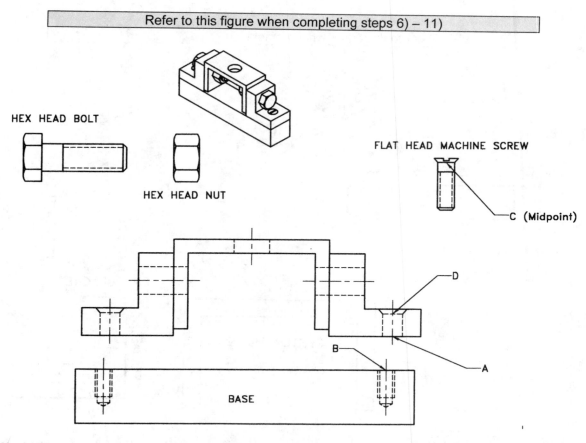

Refer to this figure when completing steps 6) – 11)

HEX HEAD BOLT

HEX HEAD NUT

FLAT HEAD MACHINE SCREW

C (Midpoint)

D

B

A

BASE

6) **MOVE** the *End Bracket/Center Plate* assembly to their functional placement relative to the *Base*. Use point A as the first base point and B as the second base point.

7) Make a **Copy** of the *Flat Head Machine Screw.*

8) **MOVE** the original *Flat Head Machine Screw* into its functional position. Use point C as the first base point. You will have to **ZOOM** in to locate point C. Use point D as the second base point.

9) Use a similar procedure to **MOVE** the *Flat Head Machine Screw* copy.

10) On your own, **MIRROR** the *Hex Head Bolt* and *Nut.*

11) Using similar procedures, as described above, to **MOVE** the *Hex Head Bolts* and *Hex Head Nuts* into their functional positions.

12)

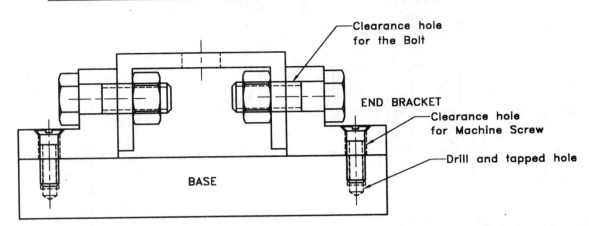

Refer to this figure when completing step 12)

Clearance hole
for the Bolt

END BRACKET

Clearance hole
for Machine Screw

Drill and tapped hole

BASE

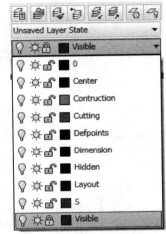

13) Clean up unwanted hidden lines in the assembly drawing.

a. **LOCK** the *Visible* layer by selecting the *Lock/Unlock* icon in the layer pull down window. (Note: When a layer is locked, you are not able to select any object on that layer. In this case, this will prevent you from accidentally selecting a visible line.)

b. **ERASE** all of the hidden lines associated with the *Machine Screw* clearance holes in the *End Bracket* and the drill and tapped holes in the *Base*.

c. **ERASE** all hidden lines associated with the *Hex Head Bolt* clearance holes in the *End Bracket* and *Center Plate*. (Note: If you are having difficulty selecting the hidden lines, you can turn the *Visible* layer off by selecting the On/Off icon (light bulb) in the layer pull down window.)

d. **UNLOCK** the *Visible* layer.

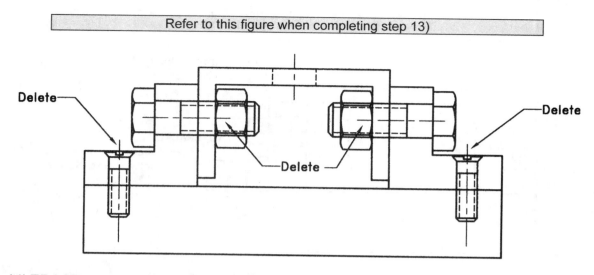

Refer to this figure when completing step 13)

14) **ERASE** duplicate centerlines and adjust their length.
  a. **ERASE** the four centerlines labeled in the above figure.
  b. Adjust the length of the remaining centerlines using grip boxes and *Polar Tracking*.

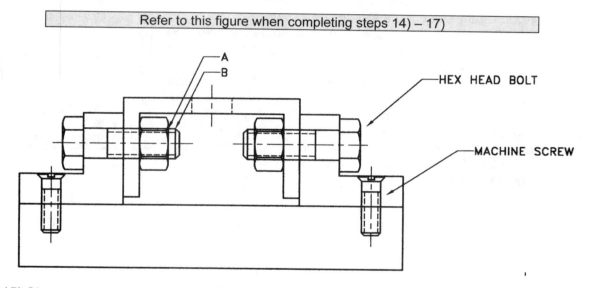

Refer to this figure when completing steps 14) – 17)

15) Change all visible lines in the *Machine Screws* to hidden lines. Select all visible lines in both *Machine Screws*. Don't worry if hidden lines also get selected. In the Layer pull down window select the *Hidden* layer. Hit **Esc** to get rid of the grip boxes.

16) On your own, change the visible lines of the *Hex Head Bolts* that run inside the *End Brackets* and *Center Plate* to hidden lines. (Note: You will end up changing a portion of some visible lines to hidden that should remain visible. We will fix that later.)

17) **Deselect all** and change your current layer to **Visible**.

18) Draw a visible line from point A to point B. Draw a similar visible line on the bottom portion of the bolt and on the other bolt.

13.2.2) Balloon the assembly

1) Create a multileader style that may be used to balloon the assembly.

a) <u>Command: **mleaderstyle**</u>   or   <u>Leaders panel:</u>

b) <u>*Multileader Style Manager* window:</u> Select ***New...***

c) <u>Create New Multileader Style window:</u> Name the style **Balloon**, start with the ***Standard*** style and select the ***Annotative*** check box.

d) <u>*Modify Multileader Style: Balloon* window – *Content* tab:</u>
   i. <u>*Multileader type* field:</u> ***Block***
   ii. <u>*Source block* field:</u> ***Circle***

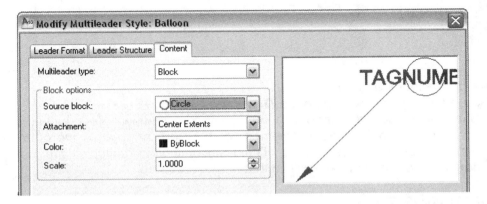

e) <u>*Modify Multileader Style: Balloon* window – *Leader Structure* tab:</u> Set the landing distance to **1.5**. This is set according to personal preference.

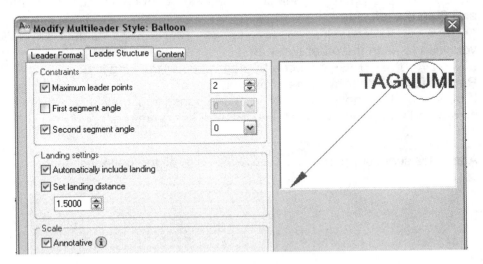

f) <u>*Multileader Style Manager* window:</u> Select the ***Balloon*** multileader style and then ***Set Current*** and then select ***Close***.

Refer to this figure when completing step 2) & 3)

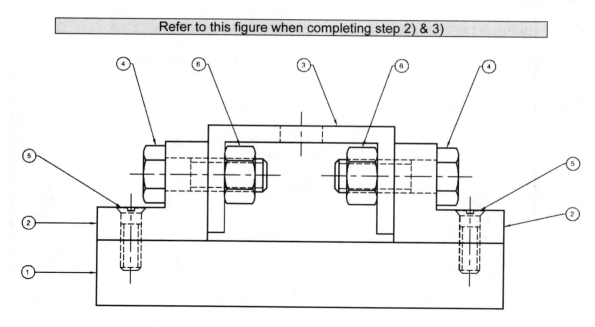

2) Draw the balloons and part numbers.
   a) Set your current layer to be the **Dimension** layer.
   b) Use the *Balloon* multileader to balloon the assembly. Your balloons and part numbers will look small, but remember they are annotative therefore; they will print out at the correct size. Don't worry if your balloons are not perfectly horizontal or vertical. We will fix that in the next step.

3) Align the balloons.

   a) <u>Command:</u> **mleaderalign**   or   *Leaders* <u>panel</u>:
   b) Select multileaders: Select the balloons containing the part numbers 1, 2, and 5 on the left side.
   c) Select multileader to align to or [Options]: Select the balloon that you wish to align the other two with.
   d) Specify direction: Select a 90 degree polar tracking line.
   e) Repeat for the other two sets of balloons.
   f) If you don't like the position of your balloons, you may move them using grip boxes and then reapply the MLEADERALIGN command.

4) Add a 1:2 scale support ⎡ Add/Delete Scales ⎤ to all the balloons.

Refer to this figure when completing steps 5) – 8)

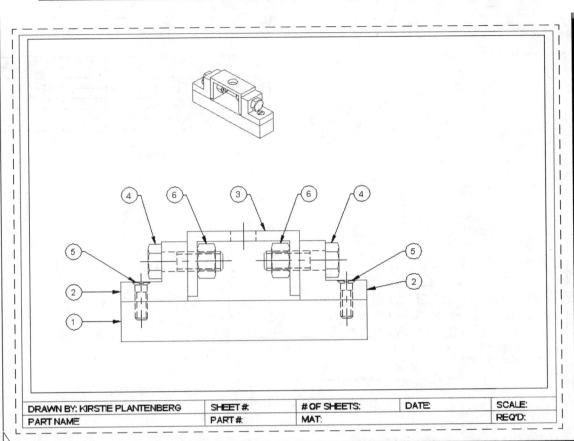

DRAWN BY: KIRSTIE PLANTENBERG	SHEET #:	# OF SHEETS:	DATE:	SCALE:
PART NAME	PART #:	MAT:		REQ'D:

5) Enter paper space on *Layout1*.

6) Enter the *Page Setup* and prepare your metric drawing to be printed on an *8.5 x 11* sheet of paper. Remember to set your plot scale to *1 inch = 25.4 units*.

7) Insert your title block at a scale of *25.4*.

8) Click on the viewport border, change it to the *Layout* layer, expand it to almost the size of the title block, and set the viewport scale to *1:2*. Notice that the multileaders adjust their size to match the viewport scale.

13.2.3) Create a parts list

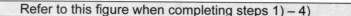
Refer to this figure when completing steps 1) – 4)

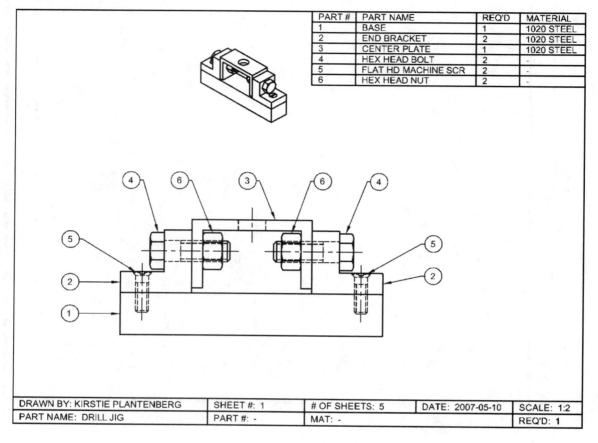

PART #	PART NAME	REQ'D	MATERIAL
1	BASE	1	1020 STEEL
2	END BRACKET	2	1020 STEEL
3	CENTER PLATE	1	1020 STEEL
4	HEX HEAD BOLT	2	-
5	FLAT HD MACHINE SCR	2	-
6	HEX HEAD NUT	2	-

DRAWN BY: KIRSTIE PLANTENBERG	SHEET #: 1	# OF SHEETS: 5	DATE: 2007-05-10	SCALE: 1:2
PART NAME: DRILL JIG	PART #: -	MAT: -		REQ'D: 1

1) In paper space, create the horizontal lines of the parts list.
   a) **EXPLODE** your title block.
   b) **OFFSET** the top horizontal line of the title block 7 times by **5** mm using the **MULTIPLE** option.

2) Create the vertical lines of the parts list. **OFFSET** the right vertical line of the title block border by **30, 50, 105** and **125** mm.

3) **TRIM** the unwanted lines.

4) In your **Dimension** layer, use **MTEXT** to fill in the parts list. Draw an inclosing box that covers the entire extents of the parts list compartment that you are entering text into. Use the **Middle Left** alignment and set the text indentation to 3.

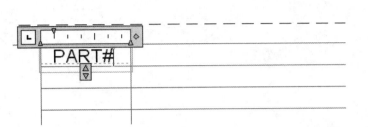
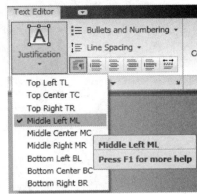

13.2.4) Title block information

1) Use the **DDEDIT** command to fill in the required title block information.

2) Turn the *Layout* layer off and print your drawing at a 1:2 scale.

<u>NOTES:</u>

CREATING ASSEMBLY DRAWINGS IN AUTOCAD PROBLEMS

P13-1) Create a working drawing package for the following *Pulley Assembly*. The working drawing package should contain an assembly drawing, details of all the parts, and a standard parts sheet. Notice that some of the dimensioned isometric drawings are not dimensioned using proper dimensioning techniques. When drawing the detailed drawings use proper symbols and dimensioning techniques.

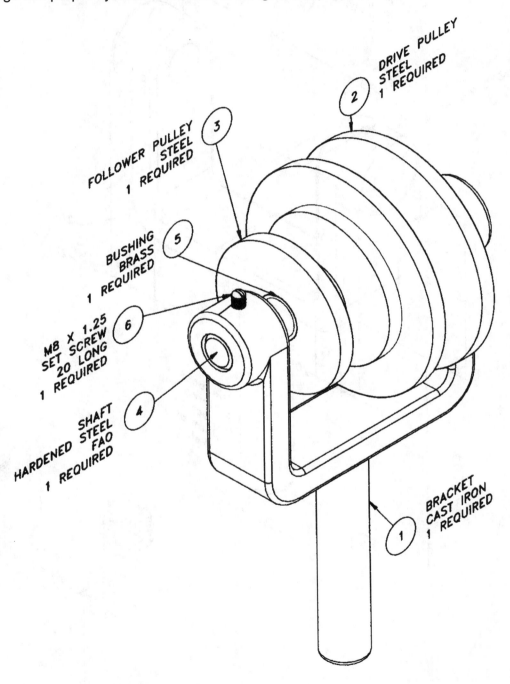

Bracket

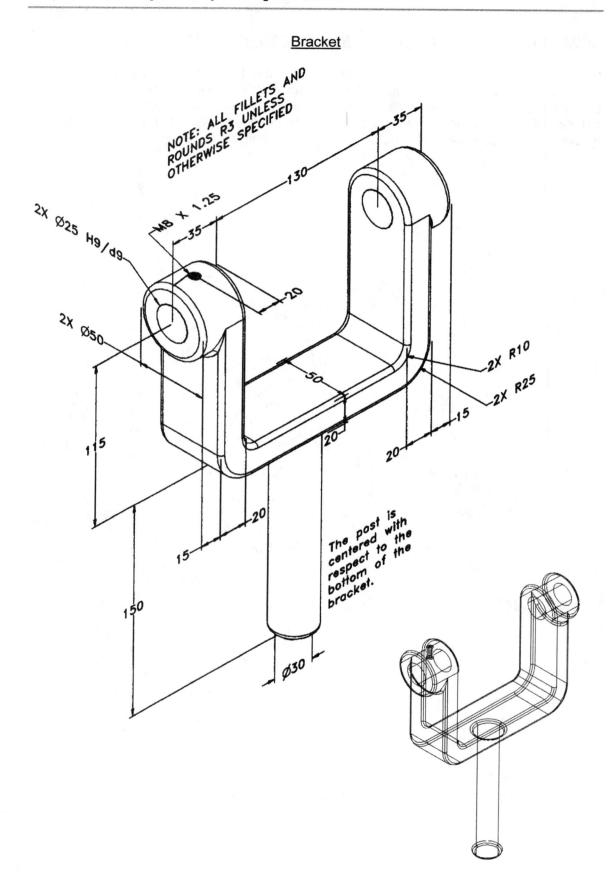

NOTE: ALL FILLETS AND ROUNDS R3 UNLESS OTHERWISE SPECIFIED

2X Ø25 H9/d9

2X Ø50

M8 X 1.25

130

35

35

20

50

2X R10

2X R25

15

20

115

20

15

150

The post is centered with respect to the bottom of the bracket.

Ø30

Drive Pulley

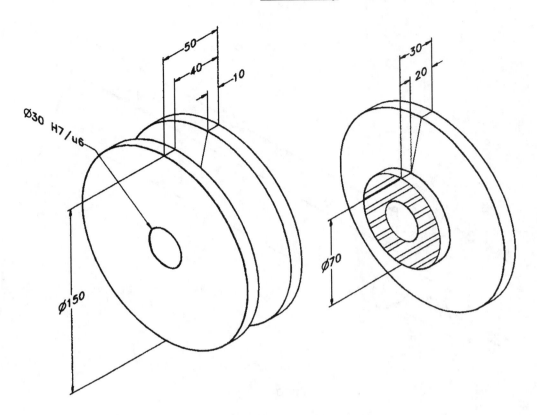

Follower Pulley

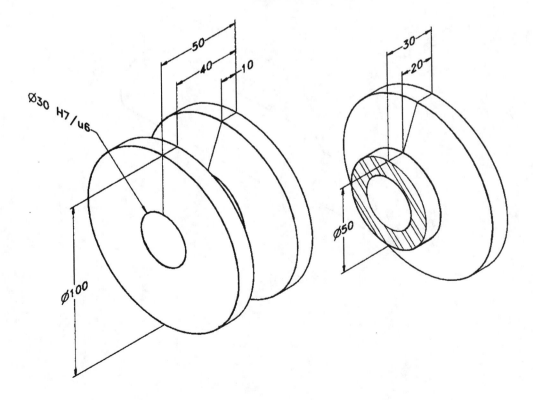

Shaft

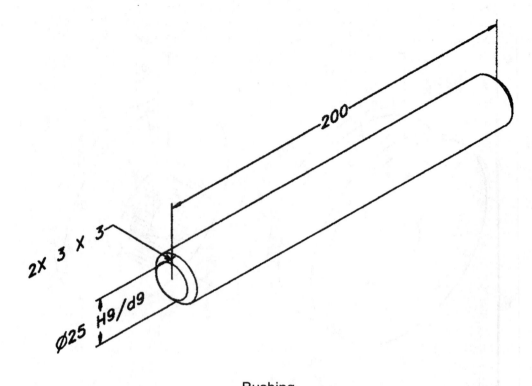

Bushing

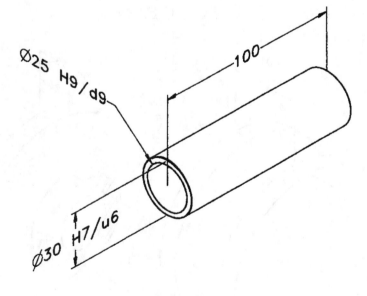

P13-2) Create a working drawing package for the following *Milling Jack*. The working drawing package should contain an assembly drawing, details of all the parts, and a standard parts sheet. Notice that some of the dimensioned isometric drawings are not dimensioned using proper dimensioning techniques. When drawing the detailed drawings use proper symbols and dimensioning techniques.

Milling Jack

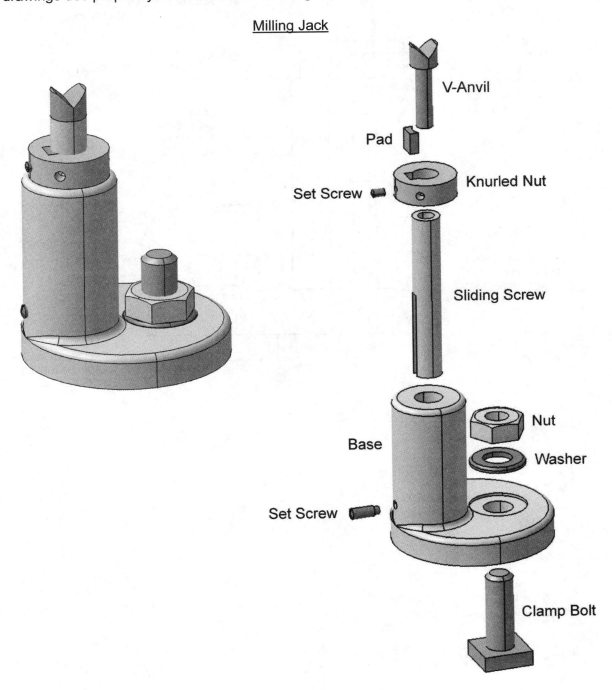

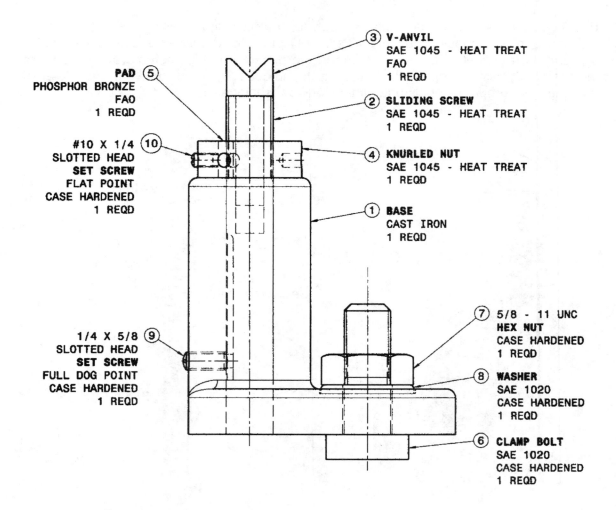

③ **V-ANVIL**
SAE 1045 - HEAT TREAT
FAO
1 REQD

PAD ⑤
PHOSPHOR BRONZE
FAO
1 REQD

② **SLIDING SCREW**
SAE 1045 - HEAT TREAT
1 REQD

#10 X 1/4 ⑩
SLOTTED HEAD
SET SCREW
FLAT POINT
CASE HARDENED
1 REQD

④ **KNURLED NUT**
SAE 1045 - HEAT TREAT
1 REQD

① **BASE**
CAST IRON
1 REQD

⑦ 5/8 - 11 UNC
HEX NUT
CASE HARDENED
1 REQD

1/4 X 5/8 ⑨
SLOTTED HEAD
SET SCREW
FULL DOG POINT
CASE HARDENED
1 REQD

⑧ **WASHER**
SAE 1020
CASE HARDENED
1 REQD

⑥ **CLAMP BOLT**
SAE 1020
CASE HARDENED
1 REQD

Base

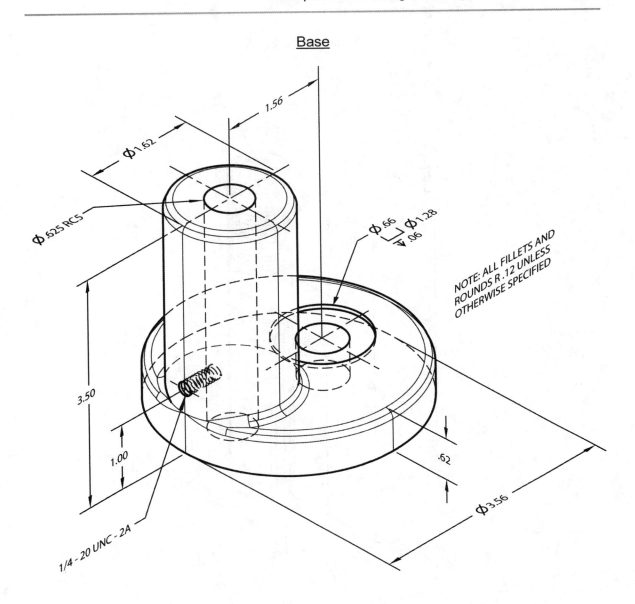

Sliding Screw

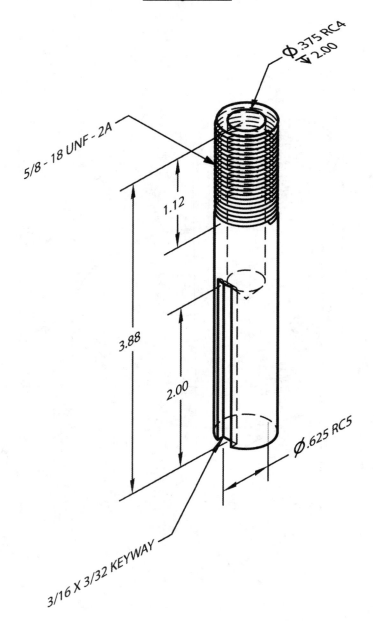

V-Anvil

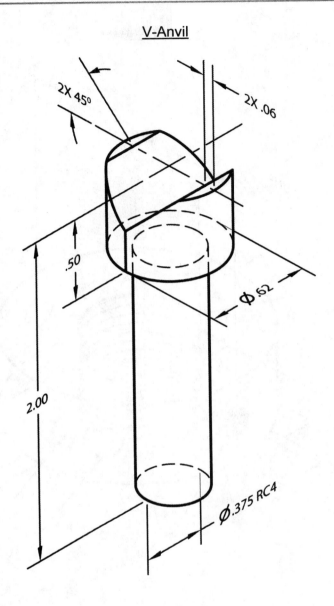

Knurled Nut

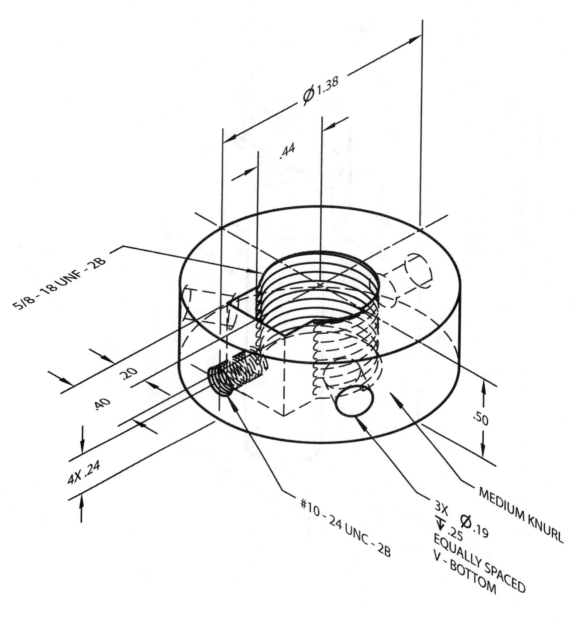

Ø1.38

.44

5/8 - 18 UNF - 2B

.20

.40

4X .24

#10 - 24 UNC - 2B

3X   Ø.19
.25
EQUALLY SPACED
V - BOTTOM

MEDIUM KNURL

.50

Pad

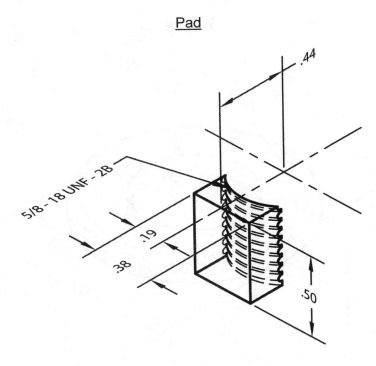

Clamp Bolt

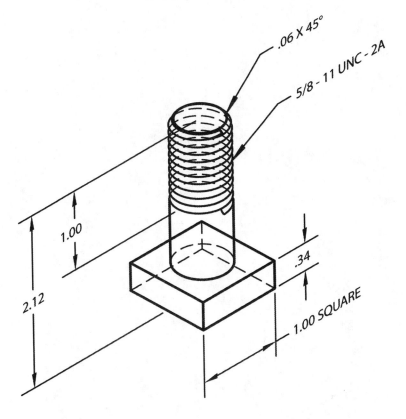

Washer

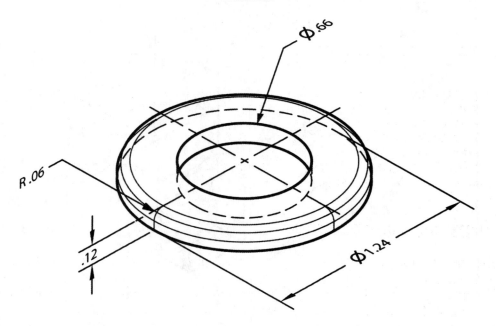

PICTORIALS

In Chapter 14 you will learn how to create isometric pictorial drawings. A pictorial drawing is a representation of an object created in two dimensions, which appears three dimensional. The two commonly used pictorials are Obliques and Isometrics. Pictorial use is important when trying to communicate a design idea to an audience that is unfamiliar with orthographic projections. By the end of this chapter you will be able to sketch an isometric pictorial based on an orthographic projection of the part.

14.1) PICTORIALS INTRODUCTION

Pictorials are pseudo 3-D drawings. That is, they are drawings of an object created in two dimensions that look three dimensional. A pictorial representation of a part is often included on a detailed drawing to help with the visualization of the part (see figure 14-1). Pictorials are also used to illustrate how parts fit together in an exploded assembly drawing (see figure 14-2).

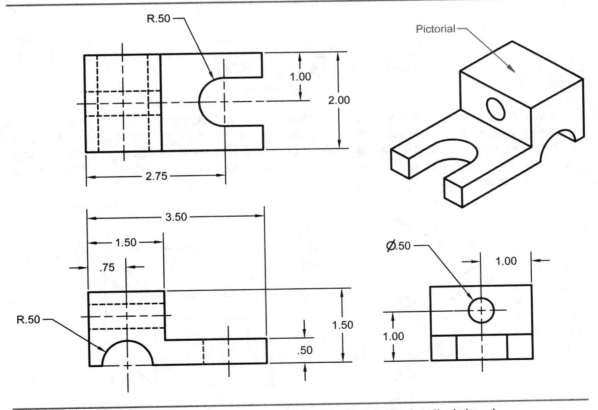

Figure 14-1: Pictorial representation added to a detailed drawing

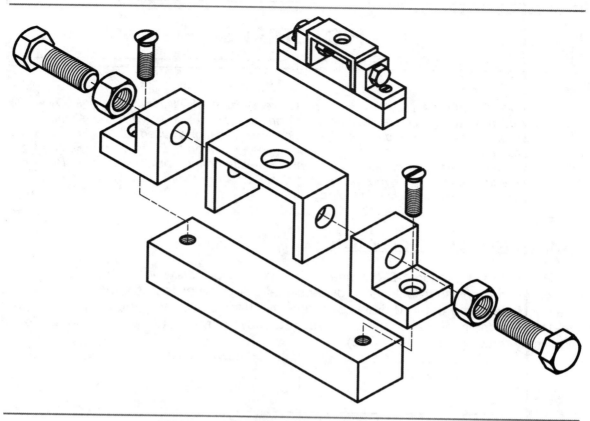

Figure 14-2: Exploded assembly drawing

Before computer assisted drawing, the two most commonly used pictorials were *isometric* and *oblique*. Most computer drawing and modeling packages are set up to create isometric pictorials. It is very difficult and sometimes impossible to create oblique pictorials in these packages. Therefore, only a procedure for creating isometric pictorials will be discussed in detail.

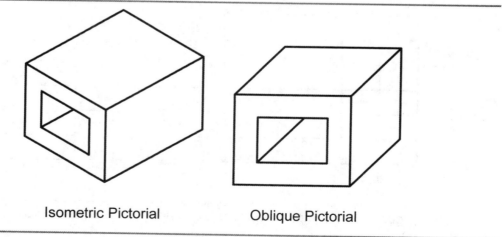

Isometric Pictorial   Oblique Pictorial

Figure 14-3: Types of pictorials

14.2) ISOMETRIC PICTORIAL AXES

Isometric pictorials are drawn in a coordinate system where the axes are 60 degrees apart as shown in Figure 14-4. The height of the object is drawn along the vertical axis and the width and depth are drawn along the axes that are at a 30 degree angle from the horizontal. The linear features on or parallel to these three axes are drawn at 80% of full scale to represent true size. However, isometric pictorials may be drawn at any scale as long as the scale is uniform on all axes.

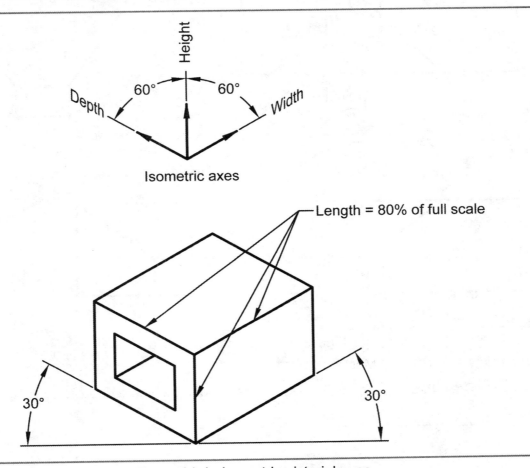

Figure 14-4: Isometric pictorial axes

14.3) DRAWING LINEAR FEATURES

The steps used to draw an isometric pictorial depend on the method of its creation. For example, you may use pencil and paper to sketch an isometric pictorial, or a computer drawing and/or modeling package such as AutoCAD or CATIA. If you are sketching an isometric pictorial, it is best to start with a box that contains or frames in your part. When using a 2-D drawing package, it is best to start with an isometric grid that will guide you along the appropriate axes. If you are using a 3-D modeling package, you don't have to draw an isometric pictorial at all because it will automatically generate one for you. The following steps describe a method that may be used to draw an isometric drawing by hand or with a 2-D drawing package. The object shown in Figure

14-5 will be used to illustrate the steps. Note that, for ease of illustration, the following steps produce a full scale isometric. A more realistic isometric is one that is drawn at 80% of full scale.

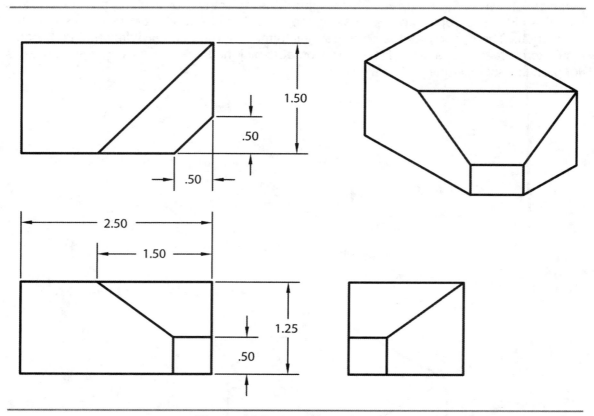

Figure 14-5: Isometric pictorial

Step 1) Draw three construction lines that represent the isometric axes (see Figure 14-6).

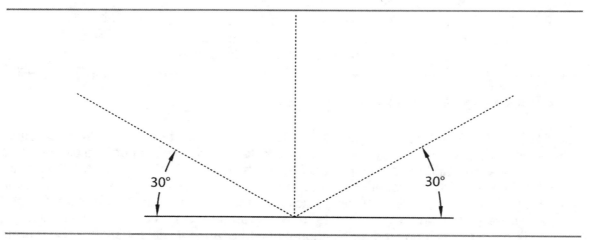

Figure 14-6: Creating an isometric pictorial step 1

Step 2) Draw a box whose sides are parallel to the three axes and whose dimensions are equal to the maximum height, width and depth dimension of the object (see Figure 14-7).

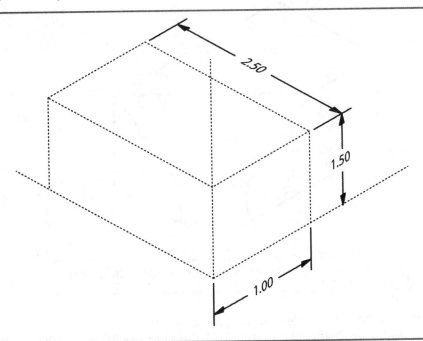

Figure 14-7: Creating an isometric pictorial step 2

Step 3) Draw the lines of the object that are parallel to the axes. These lines will be drawn full scale (see Figure 14-8).

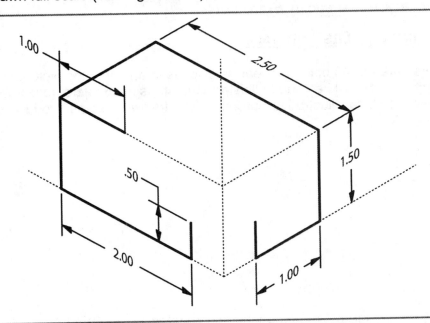

Figure 14-8: Creating an isometric pictorial step 3

Step 4)   The lines of the object that are not parallel to one of the axes are added by connecting the ends of existing lines (see Figure 14-9).

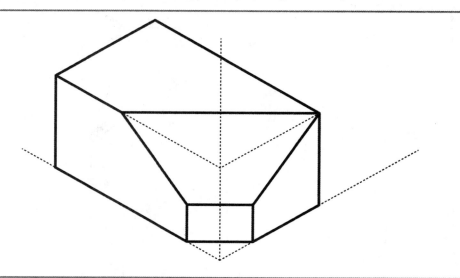

Figure 14-9: Creating an isometric pictorial step 4

Step 5)   Erase or remove the construction lines.
Step 6)   If the drawing is produced in a 2-D drawing package, it should be scaled by 80%.

If you plan to sketch an isometric pictorial by hand, a 30/60 triangle, an isometric (80%) ruler and an isometric ellipse template should be used.

View Video Exercise 14-1 and try Exercise 14-2

14.4) DRAWING CIRCLES AND RADII

Circular features of an object appear as ellipses in an isometric pictorial. The object shown in Figure 14-10 will be used to illustrate the steps used to create isometric circular features. Note that, for illustrative purposes, the following steps produce a full scale isometric.

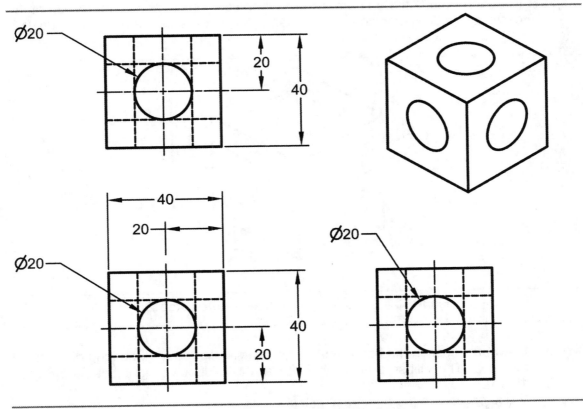

Figure 14-10: Creating circular features

Step 1)   Draw the linear features of the object using the procedure previously described (see Figure 14-11).

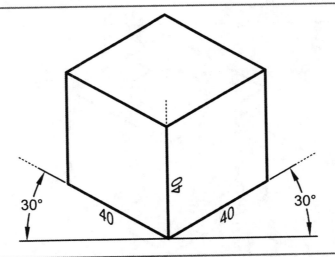

Figure 14-11: Creating circular features step 1

Step 2) For each circular feature, draw a box whose diagonals meet at the center of the circle and side dimensions are equal to the circle's diameter (see Figure 14-12).

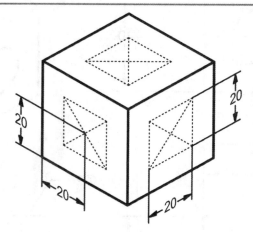

Figure 14-12: Creating circular features step 2

Step 3) Draw an ellipse in the box whose major axis is aligned with the long diagonal of the box. The ellipse touches the box at the midpoint of its sides (see Figure 14-13).
Step 4) Erase or remove the construction lines.
Step 5) If the drawing is produced in a 2-D drawing package, it should be scaled by 80%.

The same procedure is used to create radii except that the unwanted part of the ellipse is erased or trimmed. To sketch a more accurate isometric pictorial, an isometric ellipse template should be used.

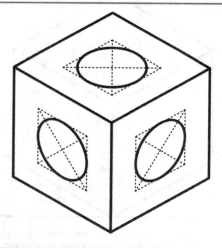

Figure 14-13: Creating circular features step 3

14.5) DRAWING CYLINDERS

Drawing cylinders in an isometric pictorial is just a matter of drawing two isometric circles and adding some connecting lines (see Figure 14-14).

Step 1) Draw a defining box whose height is equal to the height of the cylinder and whose width and depth dimensions are equal to the diameter of the cylinder.

Step 2) Draw the diagonals and ellipses in the boxes that define the beginning and end of the cylinder.

Step 3) Draw two lines that connect the two ellipses. The lines will start and end at the intersection between the ellipse and the major axis diagonal.

Step 4) Erase all construction lines and any lines that fall behind the cylinder.

Step 5) If the drawing is produced in a 2-D drawing package, it should be scaled by 80%.

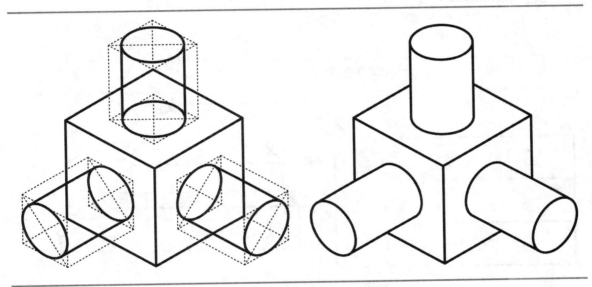

Figure 14-14: Drawing cylinders

View Video Exercise 14-3 and try Exercise 14-4

14.6) OBLIQUE PICTORIAL OVERVIEW

Oblique pictorials are drawn in a coordinate system where only one axes is at an angle from the horizontal. The angle of this axis may range between 0 and 90 degrees; however, the most commonly used angle is 45 degrees as shown in Figure 14-15. They are created by drawing the height in a vertical axis, the width along the horizontal axis and the depth along the axes that is at an angle from the horizontal. The features drawn on the plane defined by the vertical and horizontal axes are drawn at full scale and true shape. The linear features drawn on the angled axis may be full scale (cavalier projection) or may be drawn foreshortened. The most common, is a half scale cabinet projection (see Figure 14-16). The cabinet projection approach looks more realistic.

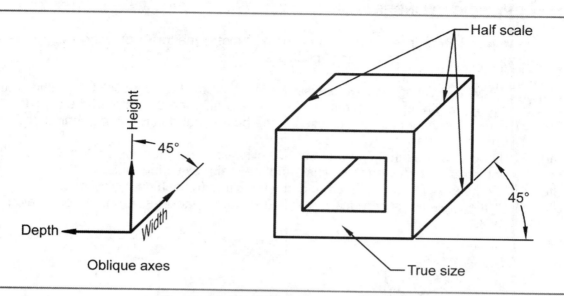

Figure 14-15: Oblique pictorial axes

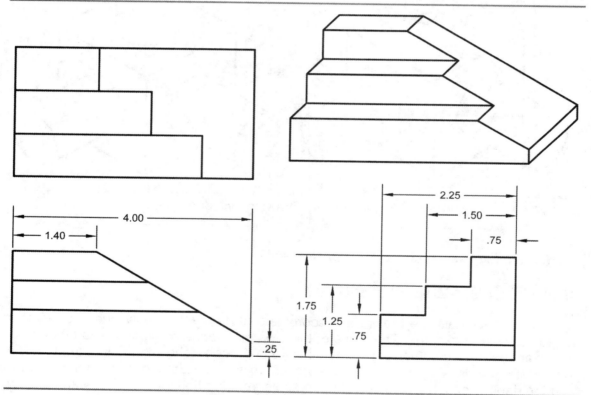

Figure 14-16: Oblique "cabinet" pictorial

Video Exercise 14-1: Beginning Isometric Pictorial 1

This video exercise will take you through creating an isometric pictorial based on the orthographic projection shown.

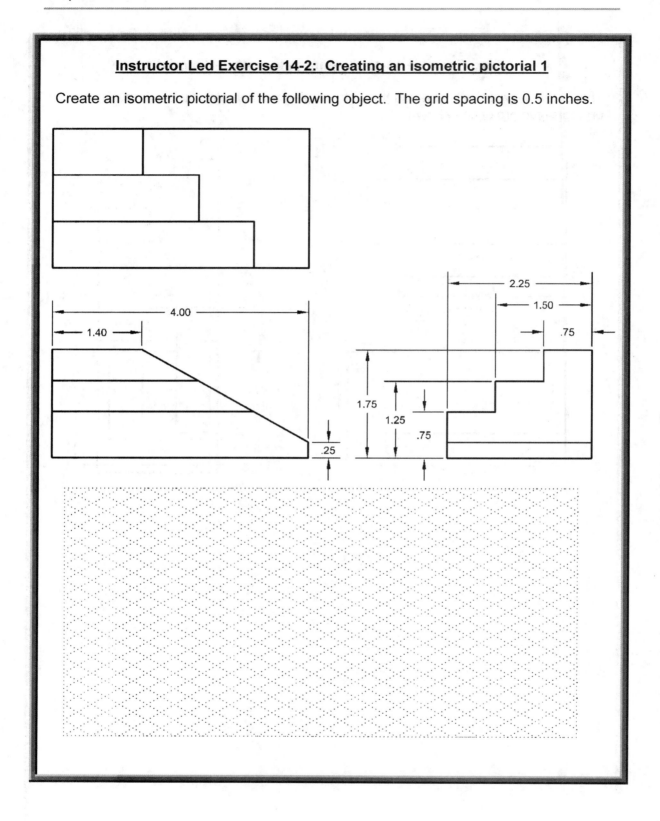

Instructor Led Exercise 14-2: Creating an isometric pictorial 1

Create an isometric pictorial of the following object. The grid spacing is 0.5 inches.

<u>Video Exercise 14-3: Beginning Isometric Pictorial 2</u>

This video exercise will take you through creating an isometric pictorial based on the orthographic projection shown.

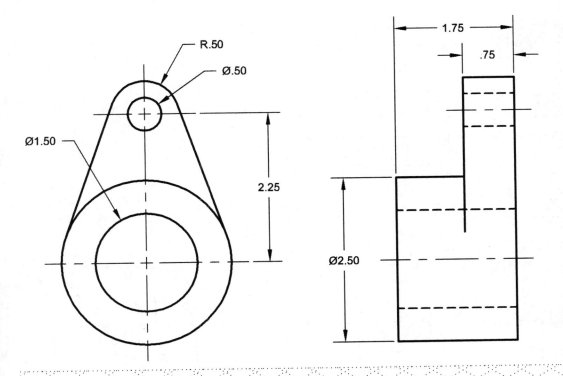

Instructor Led Exercise 14-4: Creating an isometric pictorial 2

Create a full scale isometric pictorial of the following object. The grid spacing is 10 mm.

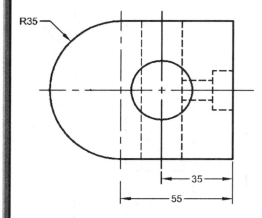

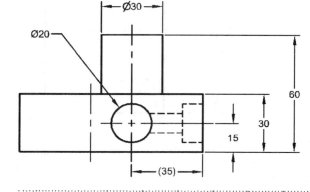

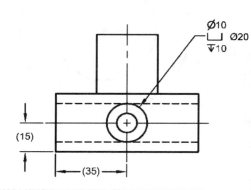

Video Exercise 14-5: Intermediate Isometric Pictorial

This video exercise will take you through creating an isometric pictorial based on the orthographic projection shown.

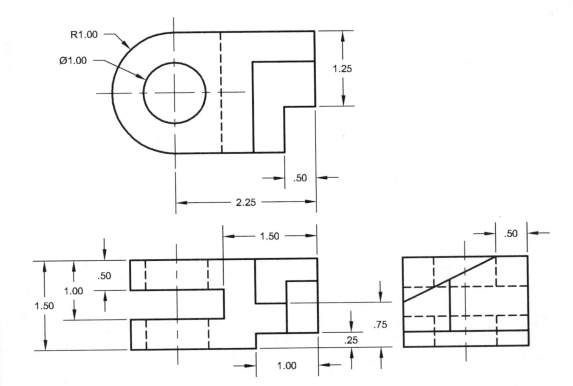

NOTES:

PICTORIAL CROSSWORD PUZZLE

Name: _____   Date: _____

CP14-1)

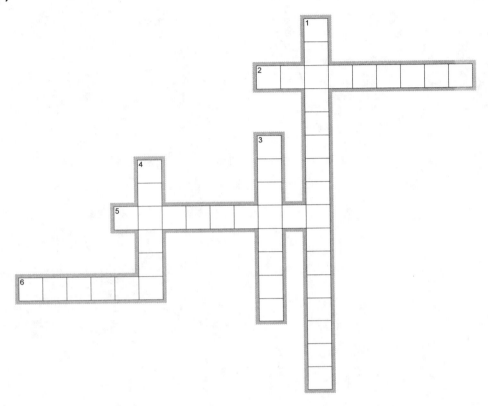

Across

2. Two of the oblique pictorial axes are drawn horizontally and vertically. The other axis is most commonly drawn .... degrees above the horizontal.
5. Pictorials help us .... the part.
6. An isometric pictorial looks more realistic if it is drawn at an .... percent scale.

Down

1. A pictorial drawing is a two dimensional rendering of a part that looks ....
3. Circular features in an isometric pictorial are drawn as ....
4. Two of the isometric axes are drawn .... above the horizontal.

NOTES:

PICTORIAL PROBLEMS

Name: _____ Date: _____

P14-1) Draw a full scale isometric pictorial by hand or in a drawing package per instructions. The grid spacing is 0.25 inch.

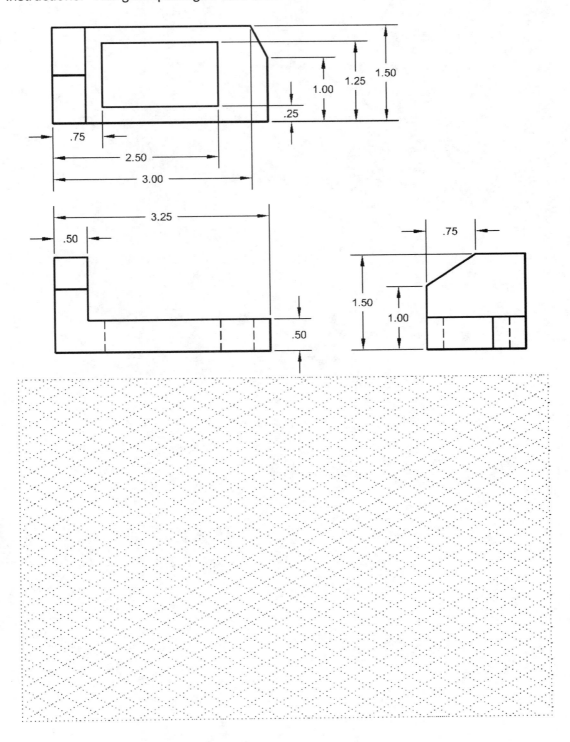

NOTES:

Name: _____ Date: _____

P14-2) Draw a full scale isometric pictorial by hand or in a drawing package per instructions. The grid spacing is 10 mm.

<u>NOTES:</u>

Name: _____ Date: _____

P14-3) Draw a full scale isometric pictorial by hand or in a drawing package per instructions. The grid spacing is 0.25 inch.

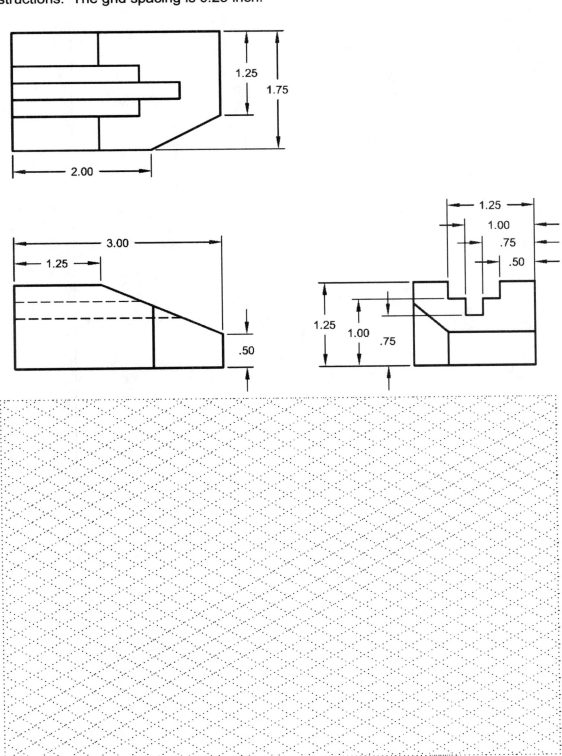

NOTES:

Name: _____   Date: _____

P14-4) Draw a full scale isometric pictorial by hand or in a drawing package per instructions. The grid spacing is 10 mm.

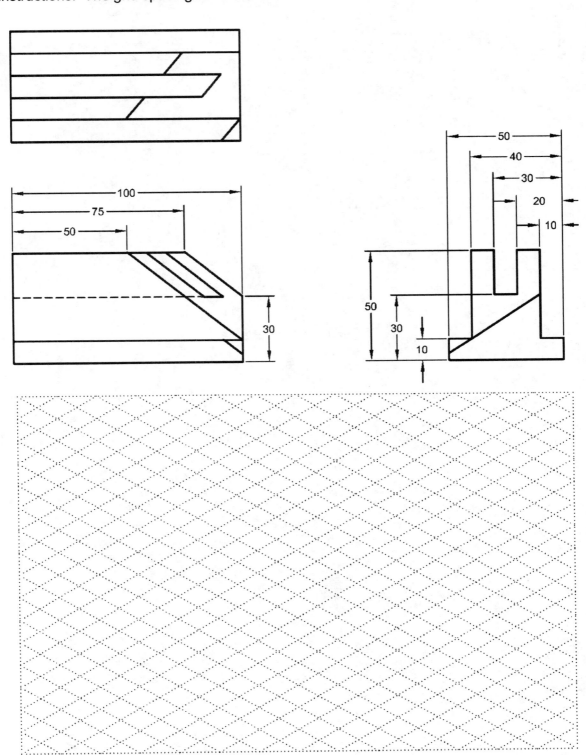

NOTES:

Name: _____   Date: _____

P14-5) Draw a full scale isometric pictorial by hand or in a drawing package per instructions. The grid spacing is 0.25 inch.

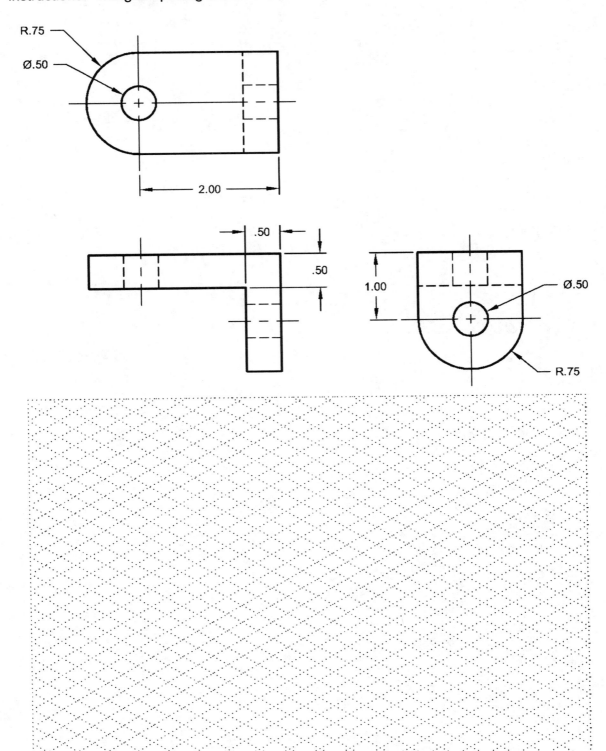

NOTES:

Name: _____ Date: _____

P14-6) Draw a full scale isometric pictorial by hand or in a drawing package per instructions. The grid spacing is 10 mm.

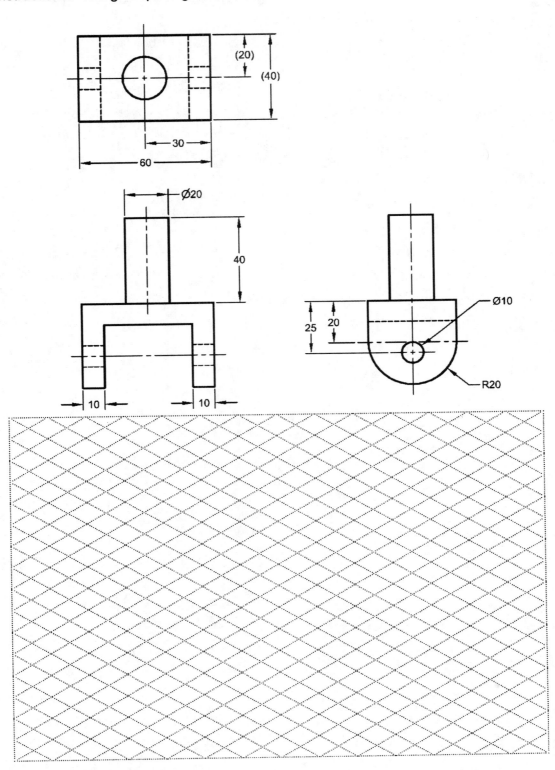

NOTES:

CREATING ISOMETRIC PICTORIALS IN AUTOCAD

In Chapter 15 you will learn how to use the isometric grid/snap and isocircles to create an isometric pictorial. The isometric snap option allows you to create a grid that aligns itself with the isometric pictorial axes. By the end of this chapter, you will be able to create an isometric pictorial that consists of lines, circles and radii.

15.1) ISOMETRIC SNAP

To facilitate the creation of an isometric pictorial, you may activate AutoCAD's isometric snap. Once the isometric snap is activated, the grid and snap will act along the isometric axes. Remember, these axes are oriented at 30 degrees above the horizontal. Figure 15-1 shows AutoCAD's isometric grid with an illustration of the isometric axes. An isometric pictorial may be created by following the isometric grid and snap directions. *Polar Tracking* set at increments of 30 degrees may also be helpful in the construction of an isometric pictorial.

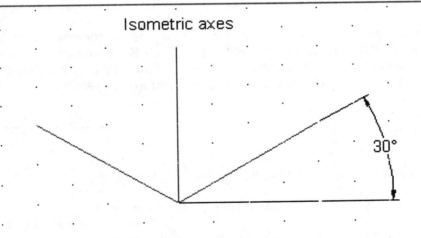

Figure 15-1: Isometric grid

Activating the isometric snap

1) <u>Command:</u> **snap**
2) Specify snap spacing or [ON/OFF/Aspect/Style/Type] <10>: **s**
3) Enter snap grid style [Standard/Isometric] <S>: **i**
4) Specify vertical spacing <10>: **Specify the isometric snap spacing.**

15.2) ISOCIRCLES

In an isometric pictorial, circular features are represented by an ellipse. The axes of the ellipse are not always horizontal and vertical. The angle of the ellipse axes depends on the isoplane in which the ellipse resides. Figure 15-2 shows a cube with a hole in each side. The representative ellipses and their defining boxes are shown. Notice the orientation of the ellipses and their associated isoplanes.

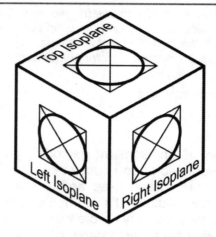

Figure 15-2: Isoplanes and ellipse orientation

AutoCAD makes creating the ellipses or isocircles used to represent circular features very easy. ISOCIRCLE is an option within the ELLIPSE command. When creating isocircles, you need to specify the desired isoplane. You may toggle between isoplanes by pressing **Ctrl+E**. You will know what isoplane you are currently in by looking at the crosshairs of your cursor.

Creating isocircles

1) <u>Command:</u> **ellipse**   or   *Draw* panel: ⊕ ▼
2) Specify axis endpoint of ellipse or [Arc/Center/Isocircle]: **i**
3) Specify center of isocircle: Specify the center of the isocircle.
4) Specify radius of isocircle or [Diameter]: Press **Ctrl+E** to toggle to the correct isoplane. Enter the radius of the circle that the isocircle is representing.

15.3) ISOMETRIC PICTORIAL TUTORIAL

The objective of this tutorial is to familiarize the user with the isometric snap and grid. You will draw the isometric pictorial shown.

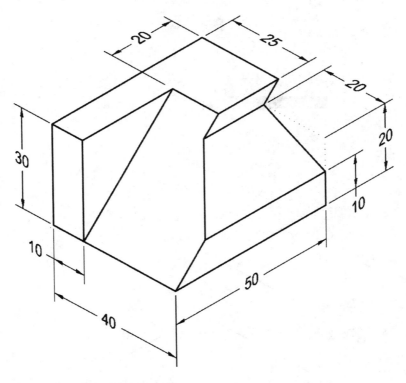

15.3.1) Setting up to draw an isometric pictorial

1) View the *Creating Isometric Pictorials* video and read sections 15.1) and 15.2).

2)   *set-mm.dwt* and   **Iso pictorial Tut.dwg**.

3) Turn your **GRID** on and set the spacing to be **10** mm.

4) Set your isometric snap.
   a) <u>Command:</u> **snap**
   b) `Specify snap spacing or [ON/OFF/Aspect/Style/Type] <10>:` **s**
   c) `Enter snap grid style [Standard/Isometric] <S>:` **i**
   d) `Specify vertical spacing <10>:` **5**

5) Notice that the grid is now at a 30 degree angle, in line with the isometric axes.

6) Set your polar tracking angle (**POLARANG**) to 30 degree increments.

15.3.2) Drawing the isometric pictorial

1) In your *Construction* layer, draw the object's defining box. Use the isometric grid/snap to guide you.

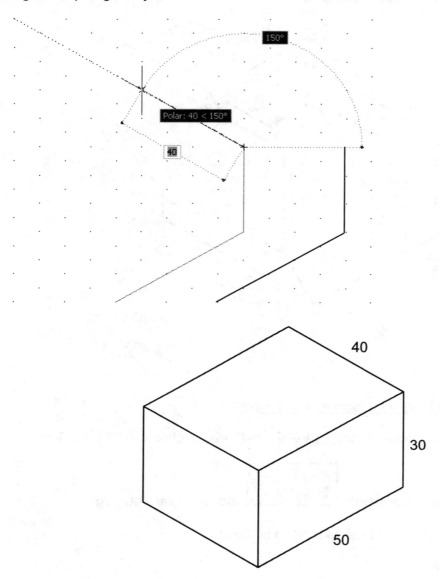

2) In your **Visible** layer, draw the features that are parallel to the sides of the defining box.

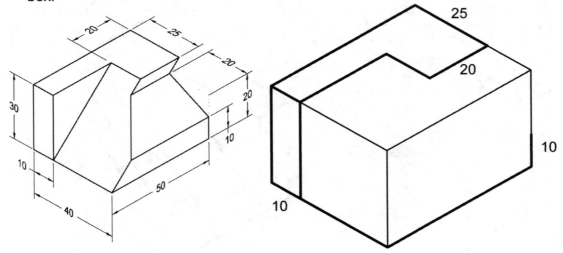

3) Draw the angled line shown in the left side figure.

4) Copy the angled line as shown in the right side figure.

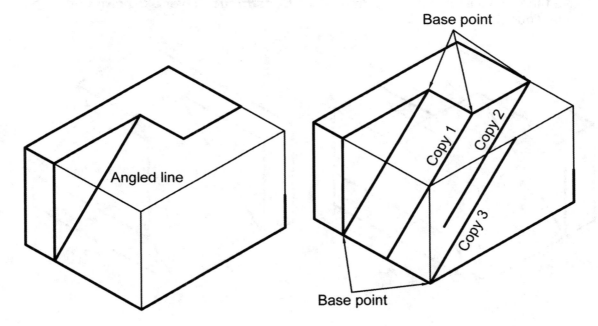

5) Add the lines shown.

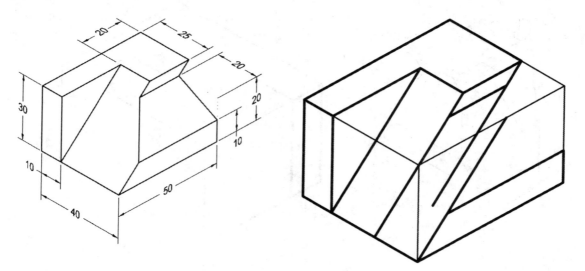

6) **TRIM** the unwanted lines as shown in the left side figure. It is easiest to trim lines if you temporarily turn your SNAP off.

7) Add the remaining lines and turn off your **Construction** layer as shown in the right side figure.

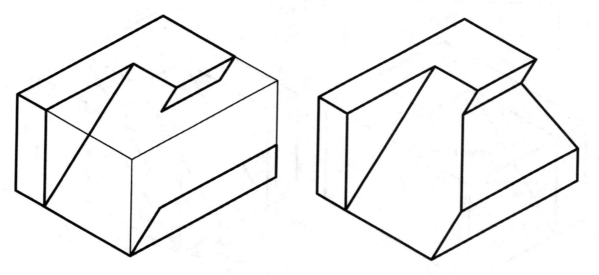

15.4) ISOCIRCLE TUTORIAL

The objective of this tutorial is to familiarize the user with creating isocircles. You will draw an isometric pictorial of the object shown.

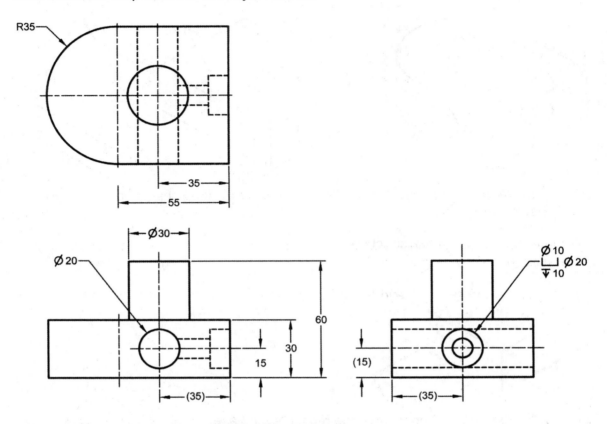

15.4.1) Setting up to draw an isometric pictorial

1) ___ **set-mm.dwt** and ___ **Isocircle Tut.dwg**.

2) Turn your **GRID** on and set the spacing to be **10** mm.

3) Set your **SNAP** style to **Isometric** and set the snap spacing to **5** mm.

15.4.2) Drawing the isometric pictorial

1) In your **Construction** layer, draw the object's defining box. Use the isometric grid/snap to guide you.

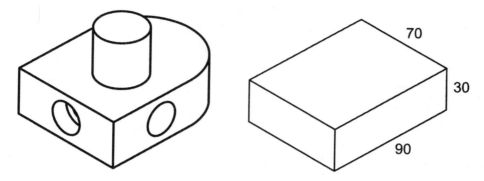

70

30

90

2) In your **Visible** layer, draw the **LINE**s indicated. Draw the construction line in your **Construction** layer.

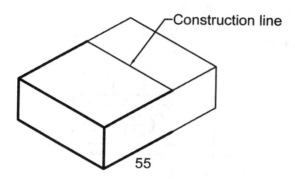

─Construction line

55

3) In your **Visible** layer, draw the large radius of the base.

 a) <u>Command:</u> **ellipse** or *Draw* panel:

 b) Specify axis endpoint of ellipse or [Arc/Center/Isocircle]: **i**

 c) Specify center of isocircle: **mid** or **midpoint**
    of Select the midpoint of the construction line.

 d) Specify radius of isocircle or [Diameter]: Move your mouse and notice the direction of the isocircle. Press **Ctrl+E** to change its direction to the top isoplane and then enter a radius of **35**.

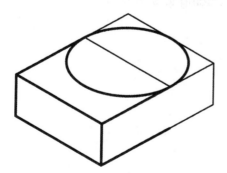

4) **COPY** the isocircle as shown.

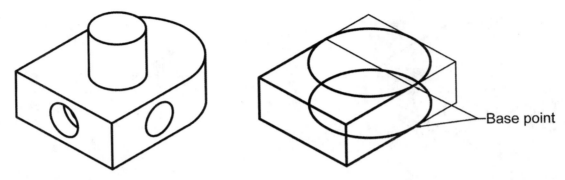

Base point

5) Draw a vertical **LINE** from the **QUADRANTS** of the isocircles and then **TRIM** off any unwanted lines as shown in the figure on the left side.

6) With the help of a construction line, draw an **ISOCIRCLE** of radius **10** mm as shown in the figure on the right side. The isocircle center is at the midpoint of the construction line. Use `Ctrl+E` to toggle to the appropriate isoplane.

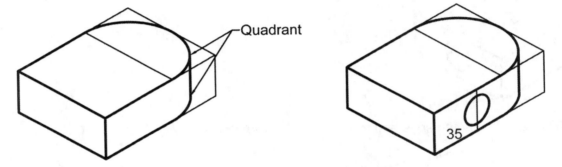

Quadrant

35

7) Add an **ISOCIRCLE** of radius **10** mm to represent the counterbored hole. (see left side figure)

8) **COPY** the counterbore isocircle using a first base point of anywhere and a second base point of **@10<30**. (see right side figure)

9) Use the **CENTER** of the copied isocircle to create the **ISOCIRCLE** of the drill (radius = **5** mm). (see right side figure)

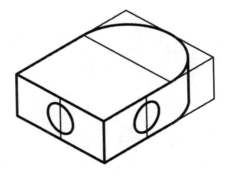

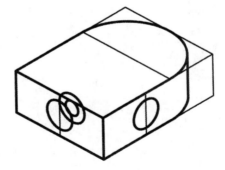

10) **TRIM** off any unwanted lines.

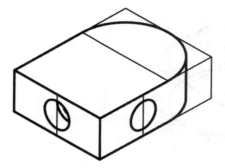

11) Draw an **ISOCIRCLE** that represents the base of the cylinder. **COPY** this isocircle using a second base point of **@30<90**. Draw vertical **LINE**s between the **QUADRANTS** of the isocircles.

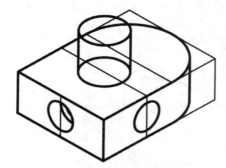

12) **TRIM** any unwanted lines and turn off your **Construction** layer.

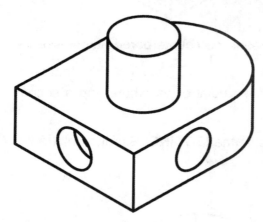

CREATING ISOMETRIC PICTORIALS IN AUTOCAD CROSSWORD PUZZLE

Name: _____   Date: _____

CP15-1)

Across

1. What command and options are used to access the isometric grid? The answer is the (command) followed by the first (option) and then the second (option).
3. What typed command is used to change the polar tracking angle increment?
4. How do you toggle between isoplanes?
5. A circular feature in an isometric pictorial is represented by an ...

Down

2. Within the ELLIPSE command, what option allows you to create a circular feature in an isometric pictorial?

NOTES:

CREATING ISOMETRIC PICTORIALS IN AUTOCAD PROBLEMS

P15-1) Draw an 80% scale isometric drawing of the following object.

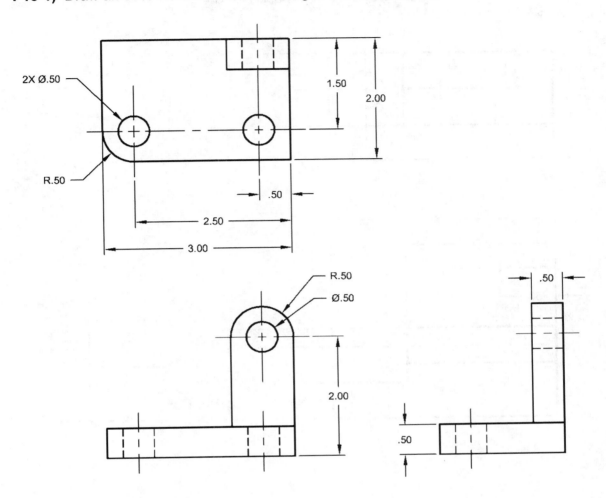

P15-2) Draw an 80% scale isometric drawing of the following object.

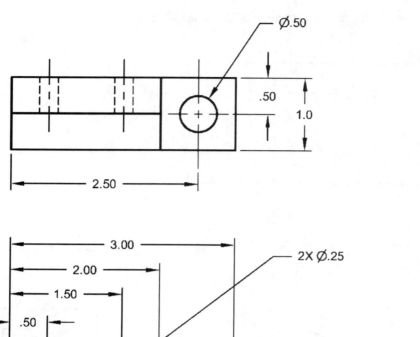

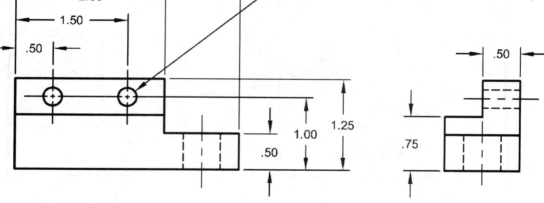

P15-3) Draw an 80% scale isometric drawing of the following object.

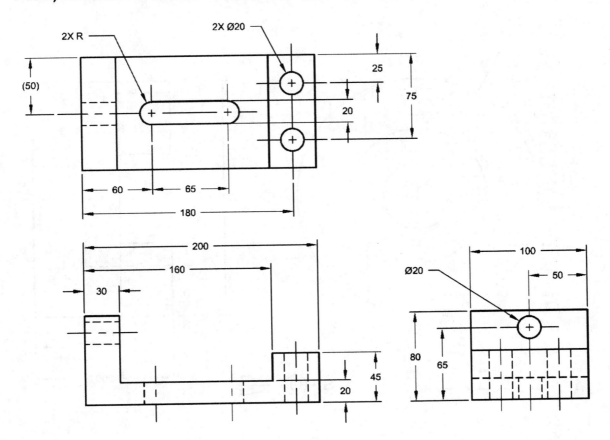

P15-4) Draw an 80% scale isometric drawing of the following object.

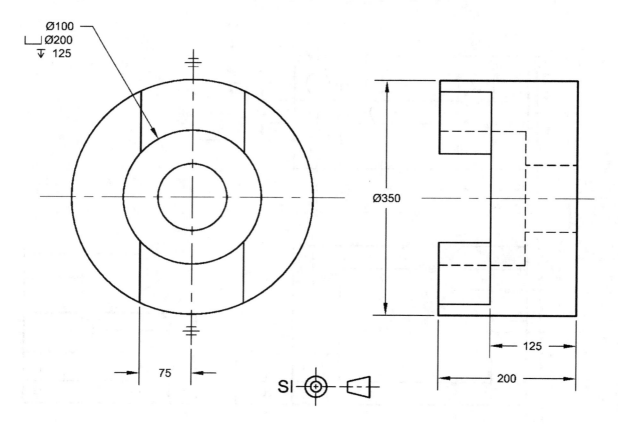

P15-5) Draw an 80% scale isometric drawing of the following object.

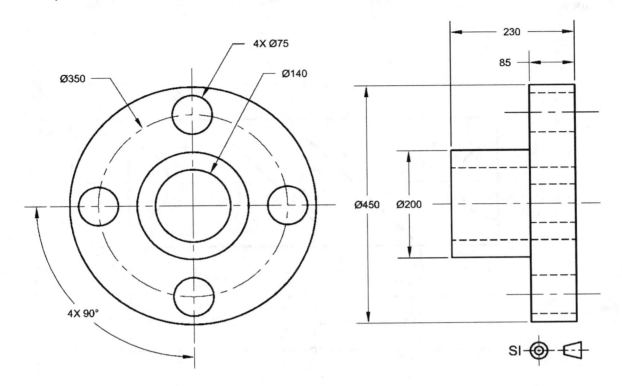

P15-6) Draw an 80% scale isometric drawing of the following object. Include all hidden lines.

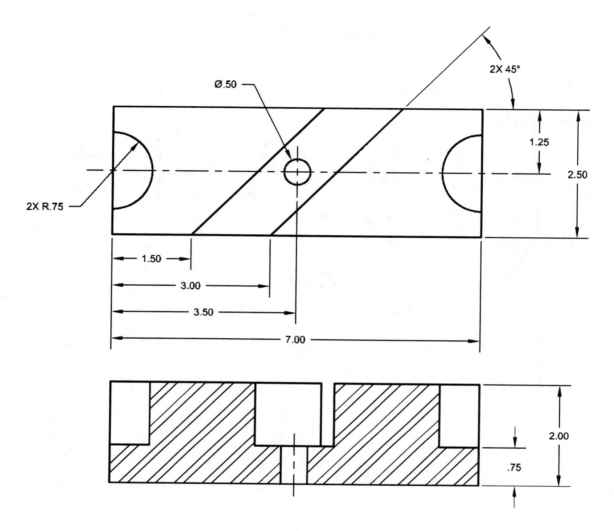

APPENDIX A: LIMITS AND FITS

A.1) LIMITS AND FITS (INCH)

A.1.1) Running or Sliding Clearance Fits

Basic hole system. Limits are in thousandths of an inch.
Limits for hole and shaft are applied algebraically to the basic size to obtain the limits of size for the parts.

Nominal Size Range Inches		Class RC1 Standard Limits		Class RC2 Standard Limits		Class RC3 Standard Limits		Class RC4 Standard Limits	
Over	To	Hole	Shaft	Hole	Shaft	Hole	Shaft	Hole	Shaft
0	− 0.12	+0.2 0	-0.1 -0.25	+0.25 0	-0.1 -0.3	+0.4 0	-0.3 -0.55	+0.6 0	-0.3 -0.7
0.12	− 0.24	+0.2 0	-0.15 -0.3	+0.3 0	-0.15 -0.35	+0.5 0	-0.4 -0.7	+0.7 0	-0.4 -0.9
0.24	− 0.40	+0.25 0	-0.2 -0.35	+0.4 0	-0.2 -0.45	+0.6 0	-0.5 -0.9	+0.9 0	-0.5 -1.1
0.40	− 0.71	+0.3 0	-0.25 -0.45	+0.4 0	-0.25 -0.55	+0.7 0	-0.6 -1.0	+1.0 0	-0.6 -1.3
0.71	− 1.19	+0.4 0	-0.3 -0.55	+0.5 0	-0.3 -0.7	+0.8 0	-0.8 -1.3	+1.2 0	-0.8 -1.6
1.19	− 1.97	+0.4 0	-0.4 -0.7	+0.6 0	-0.4 -0.8	+1.0 0	-1.0 -1.6	+1.6 0	-1.0 -2.0
1.97	− 3.15	+0.5 0	-0.4 -0.7	+0.7 0	-0.4 -0.9	+1.2 0	-1.2 -1.9	+1.8 0	-1.2 -2.4
3.15	− 4.73	+0.6 0	-0.5 -0.9	+0.9 0	-0.5 -1.1	+1.4 0	-1.4 -2.3	+2.2 0	-1.4 -2.8
4.73	− 7.09	+0.7 0	-0.6 -1.1	+1.0 0	-0.6 -1.3	+1.6 0	-1.6 -2.6	+2.5 0	-1.6 -3.2
7.09	− 9.85	+0.8 0	-0.6 -1.2	+1.2 0	-0.6 -1.4	+1.8 0	-2.0 -3.2	+2.8 0	-2.0 -3.8
9.85	− 12.41	+0.9 0	-0.8 -1.4	+1.2 0	-0.7 -1.6	+2.0 0	-2.5 -3.7	+3.0 0	-2.2 -4.2
12.41	− 15.75	+1.0 0	-1.0 -1.7	+1.4 0	-0.7 -1.7	+2.2 0	-3.0 -4.4	+3.5 0	-2.5 -4.7
15.75	− 19.69	+1.0 0	-1.2 -2.0	+1.6 0	-0.8 -1.8	+2.5 0	-4.0 -5.6	+4.0 0	-2.8 -5.3

Nominal Size Range Inches		Class RC5		Class RC6		Class RC7		Class RC8		Class RC9	
		Standard Limits		Standard Limits		Standard Limits		Standard Limits		Standard Limits	
Over	To	Hole	Shaft	Hole	Shaft	Hole	Shaft	Hole	Shaft	Hole	Shaft
0	− 0.12	+0.6 0	-0.6 -1.0	+1.0 0	-0.6 -1.2	+1.0 0	-1.0 -1.6	+1.6 0	-2.5 -3.5	+2.5 0	-4.0 -5.6
0.12	− 0.24	+0.7 0	-0.8 -1.3	+1.2 0	-0.8 -1.5	+1.2 0	-1.2 -1.9	+1.8 0	-2.8 -4.0	+3.0 0	-4.5 -6.0
0.24	− 0.40	+0.9 0	-1.0 -1.6	+1.4 0	-1.0 -1.9	+1.4 0	-1.6 -2.5	+2.2 0	-3.0 -4.4	+3.5 0	-5.0 -7.2
0.40	− 0.71	+1.0 0	-1.2 -1.9	+1.6 0	-1.2 -2.2	+1.6 0	-2.0 -3.0	+2.8 0	-3.5 -5.1	+4.0 0	-6.0 -8.8
0.71	− 1.19	+1.2 0	-1.6 -2.4	+2.0 0	-1.6 -2.8	+2.0 0	-2.5 -3.7	+3.5 0	-4.5 -6.5	+5.0 0	-7.0 -10.5
1.19	− 1.97	+1.6 0	-2.0 -3.0	+2.5 0	-2.0 -3.6	+2.5 0	-3.0 -4.6	+4.0 0	-5.0 -7.5	+6.0 0	-8.0 12.0
1.97	− 3.15	+1.8 0	-2.5 -3.7	+3.0 0	-2.5 -4.3	+3.0 0	-4.0 -5.8	+4.5 0	-6.0 -9.0	+7.0 0	-9.0 -13.5
3.15	− 4.73	+2.2 0	-3.0 -4.4	+3.5 0	-3.0 -5.2	+3.5 0	-5.0 -7.2	+5.0 0	-7.0 -10.5	+9.0 0	-10.0 -15.0
4.73	− 7.09	+2.5 0	-3.5 -5.1	+4.0 0	-3.5 -6.0	+4.0 0	-6.0 -8.5	+6.0 0	-8.0 -12.0	+10.0 0	-12.0 -18.0
7.09	− 9.85	+2.8 0	-4.0 -5.8	+4.5 0	-4.0 -6.8	+4.5 0	-7.0 -9.8	+7.0 0	-10.0 -14.5	+12.0 0	-15.0 -22.0
9.85	− 12.41	+3.0 0	-5.0 -7.0	+5.0 0	-5.0 -8.0	+5.0 0	-8.0 -11.0	+8.0 0	-12.0 -17.0	+12.0 0	-18.0 -26.0
12.41	− 15.75	+3.5 0	-6.0 -8.2	+6.0 0	-6.0 -9.5	+6.0 0	-10.0 -13.5	+9.0 0	-14.0 -20.0	+14.0 0	-22.0 -31.0
15.75	− 19.69	+4.0 0	-8.0 -10.5	+6.0 0	-8.0 -12.0	+6.0 0	-12.0 -16.0	+10.0 0	-16.0 -22.0	+16.0 0	-25.0 -35.0

USAS/ASME B4.1 – 1967 (R2004) Standard. For larger diameters, see the standard. ASME/ANSI B18.3.5M – 1986 (R2002) Standard. Reprinted from the standard listed by permission of the American Society of Mechanical Engineers. All rights reserved.

A.1.2) Locational Clearance Fits

Basic hole system. Limits are in thousandths of an inch.
Limits for hole and shaft are applied algebraically to the basic size to obtain the limits of size for the parts.

Nominal Size Range Inches		Class LC1 Standard Limits		Class LC2 Standard Limits		Class LC3 Standard Limits		Class LC4 Standard Limits	
Over	To	Hole	Shaft	Hole	Shaft	Hole	Shaft	Hole	Shaft
0	− 0.12	+0.25 0	0 -0.2	+0.4 0	0 -0.25	+0.6 0	0 -0.4	+1.6 0	0 -1.0
0.12	− 0.24	+0.3 0	0 -0.2	+0.5 0	0 -0.3	+0.7 0	0 -0.5	+1.8 0	0 -1.2
0.24	− 0.40	+0.4 0	0 -0.25	+0.6 0	0 -0.4	+0.9 0	0 -0.6	+2.2 0	0 -1.4
0.40	− 0.71	+0.4 0	0 -0.3	+0.7 0	0 -0.4	+1.0 0	0 -0.7	+2.8 0	0 -1.6
0.71	− 1.19	+0.5 0	0 -0.4	+0.8 0	0 -0.5	+1.2 0	0 -0.8	+3.5 0	0 -2.0
1.19	− 1.97	+0.6 0	0 -0.4	+1.0 0	0 -0.6	+1.6 0	0 -1.0	+4.0 0	0 -2.5
1.97	− 3.15	+0.7 0	0 -0.5	+1.2 0	0 -0.7	+1.8 0	0 -1.2	+4.5 0	0 -3.0
3.15	− 4.73	+0.9 0	0 -0.6	+1.4 0	0 -0.9	+2.2 0	0 -1.4	+5.0 0	0 -3.5
4.73	− 7.09	+1.0 0	0 -0.7	+1.6 0	0 -1.0	+2.5 0	0 -1.6	+6.0 0	0 -4.0
7.09	− 9.85	+1.2 0	0 -0.8	+1.8 0	0 -1.2	+2.8 0	0 -1.8	+7.0 0	0 -4.5
9.85	− 12.41	+1.2 0	0 -0.9	+2.0 0	0 -1.2	+3.0 0	0 -2.0	+8.0 0	0 -5.0
12.41	− 15.75	+1.4 0	0 -1.0	+2.2 0	0 -1.4	+3.5 0	0 -2.2	+9.0 0	0 -6.0
15.75	− 19.69	+1.6 0	0 -1.0	+2.5 0	0 -1.6	+4.0 0	0 -2.5	+10.0 0	0 -6.0

Nominal Size Range Inches		Class LC5 Standard Limits		Class LC6 Standard Limits		Class LC7 Standard Limits		Class LC8 Standard Limits	
Over	To	Hole	Shaft	Hole	Shaft	Hole	Shaft	Hole	Shaft
0	− 0.12	+0.4 0	-0.1 -0.35	+1.0 0	-0.3 -0.9	+1.6 0	-0.6 -1.6	+1.6 0	-1.0 -2.0
0.12	− 0.24	+0.5 0	-0.15 -0.45	+1.2 0	-0.4 -1.1	+1.8 0	-0.8 -2.0	+1.8 0	-1.2 -2.4
0.24	− 0.40	+0.6 0	-0.2 -0.6	+1.4 0	-0.5 -1.4	+2.2 0	-1.0 -2.4	+2.2 0	-1.6 -3.0
0.40	− 0.71	+0.7 0	-0.25 -0.65	+1.6 0	-0.6 -1.6	+2.8 0	-1.2 -2.8	+2.8 0	-2.0 -3.6
0.71	− 1.19	+0.8 0	-0.3 -0.8	+2.0 0	-0.8 -2.0	+3.5 0	-1.6 -3.6	+3.5 0	-2.5 -4.5
1.19	− 1.97	+1.0 0	-0.4 -1.0	+2.5 0	-1.0 -2.6	+4.0 0	-2.0 -4.5	+4.0 0	-3.0 -5.5
1.97	− 3.15	+1.2 0	-0.4 -1.1	+3.0 0	-1.2 -3.0	+4.5 0	-2.5 -5.5	+4.5 0	-4.0 -7.0
3.15	− 4.73	+1.4 0	-0.5 -1.4	+3.5 0	-1.4 -3.6	+5.0 0	-3.0 -6.5	+5.0 0	-5.0 -8.5
4.73	− 7.09	+1.6 0	-0.6 -1.6	+4.0 0	-1.6 -4.1	+6.0 0	-3.5 -7.5	+6.0 0	-6.0 -10.0
7.09	− 9.85	+1.8 0	-0.6 -1.8	+4.5 0	-2.0 -4.8	+7.0 0	-4.0 -8.5	+7.0 0	-7.0 -11.5
9.85	− 12.41	+2.0 0	-0.7 -1.9	+5.0 0	-2.2 -5.2	+8.0 0	-4.5 -9.5	+8.0 0	-7.0 -12.0
12.41	− 15.75	+2.2 0	-0.7 -2.1	+6.0 0	-2.5 -6.0	+9.0 0	-5.0 -11.0	+9.0 0	-8.0 -14.0
15.75	− 19.69	+2.5 0	-0.8 -2.4	+6.0 0	-2.8 -6.8	+10.0 0	-5.0 -11.0	+10.0 0	-9.0 -15.0

A - 3

Nominal Size Range Inches		Class LC9 Standard Limits		Class LC10 Standard Limits		Class LC11 Standard Limits	
Over	To	Hole	Shaft	Hole	Shaft	Hole	Shaft
0	– 0.12	+2.5 0	-2.5 -4.1	+4.0 0	-4.0 -8.0	+6.0 0	-5.0 -11.0
0.12	– 0.24	+3.0 0	-2.8 -4.6	+5.0 0	-4.5 -9.5	+7.0 0	-6.0 -13.0
0.24	– 0.40	+3.5 0	-3.0 -5.2	+6.0 0	-5.0 -11.0	+9.0 0	-7.0 -16.0
0.40	– 0.71	+4.0 0	-3.5 -6.3	+7.0 0	-6.0 -13.0	+10.0 0	-8.0 -18.0
0.71	– 1.19	+5.0 0	-4.5 -8.0	+8.0 0	-7.0 -15.0	+12.0 0	-10.0 -22.0
1.19	– 1.97	+6.0 0	-5.0 -9.0	+10.0 0	-8.0 -18.0	+16.0 0	-12.0 -28.0
1.97	– 3.15	+7.0 0	-6.0 -10.5	+12.0 0	-10.0 -22.0	+18.0 0	-14.0 -32.0
3.15	– 4.73	+9.0 0	-7.0 -12.0	+14.0 0	-11.0 -25.0	+22.0 0	-16.0 -38.0
4.73	– 7.09	+10.0 0	-8.0 -14.0	+16.0 0	-12.0 -28.0	+25.0 0	-18.0 -43.0
7.09	– 9.85	+12.0 0	-10.0 -17.0	+18.0 0	-16.0 -34.0	+28.0 0	-22.0 -50.0
9.85	– 12.41	+12.0 0	-12.0 -20.0	+20.0 0	-20.0 -40.0	+30.0 0	-28.0 -58.0
12.41	– 15.75	+14.0 0	-14.0 -23.0	+22.0 0	-22.0 -44.0	+35.0 0	-30.0 -65.0
15.75	– 19.69	+16.0 0	-16.0 -26.0	+25.0 0	-25.0 -50.0	+40.0 0	-35.0 -75.0

USAS/ASME B4.1 – 1967 (R2004) Standard. For larger diameters, see the standard. ASME/ANSI B18.3.5M – 1986 (R2002) Standard. Reprinted from the standard listed by permission of the American Society of Mechanical Engineers. All rights reserved.

A.1.3) Locational Transition Fits

Basic hole system. Limits are in thousandths of an inch.
Limits for hole and shaft are applied algebraically to the basic size to obtain the limits of size for the parts.

Nominal Size Range Inches		Class LT1 Standard Limits		Class LT2 Standard Limits		Class LT3 Standard Limits	
Over	To	Hole	Shaft	Hole	Shaft	Hole	Shaft
0	− 0.12	+0.4 0	+0.10 −0.10	+0.6 0	+0.2 −0.2		
0.12	− 0.24	+0.5 0	+0.15 −0.15	+0.7 0	+0.25 −0.25		
0.24	− 0.40	+0.6 0	+0.2 −0.2	+0.9 0	+0.3 −0.3	+0.6 0	+0.5 +0.1
0.40	− 0.71	+0.7 0	+0.2 −0.2	+1.0 0	+0.35 −0.35	+0.7 0	+0.5 +0.1
0.71	− 1.19	+0.8 0	+0.25 −0.25	+1.2 0	+0.4 −0.4	+0.8 0	+0.6 +0.1
1.19	− 1.97	+1.0 0	+0.3 −0.3	+1.6 0	+0.5 −0.5	+1.0 0	+0.7 +0.1
1.97	− 3.15	+1.2 0	+0.3 −0.3	+1.8 0	+0.6 −0.6	+1.2 0	+0.8 +0.1
3.15	− 4.73	+1.4 0	+0.4 −0.4	+2.2 0	+0.7 −0.7	+1.4 0	+1.0 +0.1
4.73	− 7.09	+1.6 0	+0.5 −0.5	+2.5 0	+0.8 −0.8	+1.6 0	+1.1 +0.1
7.09	− 9.85	+1.8 0	+0.6 −0.6	+2.8 0	+0.9 −0.9	+1.8 0	+1.4 +0.2
9.85	− 12.41	+2.0 0	+0.6 −0.6	+3.0 0	+1.0 −1.0	+2.0 0	+1.4 +0.2
12.41	− 15.75	+2.2 0	+0.7 −0.7	+3.5 0	+1.0 −1.0	+2.2 0	+1.6 +0.2

Nominal Size Range Inches		Class LT4 Standard Limits		Class LT5 Standard Limits		Class LT6 Standard Limits	
Over	To	Hole	Shaft	Hole	Shaft	Hole	Shaft
0	− 0.12			+0.4 0	+0.5 +0.25	+0.4 0	−0.65 +0.25
0.12	− 0.24			+0.5 0	+0.6 +0.3	+0.5 0	+0.8 +0.3
0.24	− 0.40	+0.9 0	+0.7 +0.1	+0.6 0	+0.8 +0.4	+0.6 0	+1.0 +0.4
0.40	− 0.71	+1.0 0	+0.8 +0.1	+0.7 0	+0.9 +0.5	+0.7 0	+1.2 +0.5
0.71	− 1.19	+1.2 0	+0.9 +0.1	+0.8 0	+1.1 +0.6	+0.8 0	+1.4 +0.6
1.19	− 1.97	+1.6 0	+1.1 +0.1	+1.0 0	+1.3 +0.7	+1.0 0	+1.7 +0.7
1.97	− 3.15	+1.8 0	+1.3 +0.1	+1.2 0	+1.5 +0.8	+1.2 0	+2.0 +0.8
3.15	− 4.73	+2.2 0	+1.5 +0.1	+1.4 0	+1.9 +1.0	+1.4 0	+2.4 +1.0
4.73	− 7.09	+2.5 0	+1.7 +0.1	+1.6 0	+2.2 +1.2	+1.6 0	+2.8 +1.2
7.09	− 9.85	+2.8 0	+2.0 +0.2	+1.8 0	+2.6 +1.4	+1.8 0	+3.2 +1.4
9.85	− 12.41	+3.0 0	+2.2 +0.2	+2.0 0	+2.6 +1.4	+2.0 0	+3.4 +1.4
12.41	− 15.75	+3.5 0	+2.4 +0.2	+2.2 0	+3.0 +1.6	+2.2 0	+3.8 +1.6

USAS/ASME B4.1 − 1967 (R2004) Standard. For larger diameters, see the standard. ASME/ANSI B18.3.5M − 1986 (R2002) Standard. Reprinted from the standard listed by permission of the American Society of Mechanical Engineers. All rights reserved.

A.1.4) Locational Interference Fits

Basic hole system. Limits are in thousandths of an inch.
Limits for hole and shaft are applied algebraically to the basic size to obtain the limits of size for the parts.

Nominal Size Range Inches		Class LN1 Standard Limits		Class LN2 Standard Limits		Class LN3 Standard Limits	
Over	To	Hole	Shaft	Hole	Shaft	Hole	Shaft
0	− 0.12	+0.25 0	+0.45 +0.25	+0.4 0	+0.65 +0.4	+0.4 0	+0.75 +0.5
0.12	− 0.24	+0.3 0	+0.5 +0.3	+0.5 0	+0.8 +0.5	+0.5 0	+0.9 +0.6
0.24	− 0.40	+0.4 0	+0.65 +0.4	+0.6 0	+1.0 +0.6	+0.6 0	+1.2 +0.8
0.40	− 0.71	+0.4 0	+0.8 +0.4	+0.7 0	+1.1 +0.7	+0.7 0	+1.4 +1.0
0.71	− 1.19	+0.5 0	+1.0 +0.5	+0.8 0	+1.3 +0.8	+0.8 0	+1.7 +1.2
1.19	− 1.97	+0.6 0	+1.1 +0.6	+1.0 0	+1.6 +1.0	+1.0 0	+2.0 +1.4
1.97	− 3.15	+0.7 0	+1.3 +0.8	+1.2 0	+2.1 +1.4	+1.2 0	+2.3 +1.6
3.15	− 4.73	+0.9 0	+1.6 +1.0	+1.4 0	+2.5 +1.6	+1.4 0	+2.9 +2.0
4.73	− 7.09	+1.0 0	+1.9 +1.2	+1.6 0	+2.8 +1.8	+1.6 0	+3.5 +2.5
7.09	− 9.85	+1.2 0	+2.2 +1.4	+1.8 0	+3.2 +2.0	+1.8 0	+4.2 +3.0
9.85	− 12.41	+1.2 0	+2.3 +1.4	+2.0 0	+3.4 +2.2	+2.0 0	+4.7 +3.5
12.41	− 15.75	+1.4 0	+2.6 +1.6	+2.2 0	+3.9 +2.5	+2.2 0	+5.9 +4.5
15.75	− 19.69	+1.6 0	+2.8 +1.8	+2.5 0	+4.4 +2.8	+2.5 0	+6.6 +5.0

A.1.5) Force and Shrink Fits

Basic hole system. Limits are in thousandths of an inch.
Limits for hole and shaft are applied algebraically to the basic size to obtain the limits of size for the parts.

Nominal Size Range Inches		Class FN1		Class FN2		Class FN3		Class FN4		Class FN5	
		Standard Limits		Standard Limits		Standard Limits		Standard Limits		Standard Limits	
Over	To	Hole	Shaft	Hole	Shaft	Hole	Shaft	Hole	Shaft	Hole	Shaft
0	− 0.12	+0.25 0	+0.5 +0.3	+0.4 0	+0.85 +0.6			+0.4 0	+0.95 +0.7	+0.6 0	+1.3 +0.9
0.12	− 0.24	+0.3 0	+0.6 +0.4	+0.5 0	+1.0 +0.7			+0.5 0	+1.2 +0.9	+0.7 0	+1.7 +1.2
0.24	− 0.40	+0.4 0	+0.75 +0.5	+0.6 0	+1.4 +1.0			+0.6 0	+1.6 +1.2	+0.9 0	+2.0 +1.4
0.40	− 0.56	+0.4 0	+0.8 +0.5	+0.7 0	+1.6 +1.2			+0.7 0	+1.8 +1.4	+1.0 0	+2.3 +1.6
0.56	− 0.71	+0.4 0	+0.9 +0.6	+0.7 0	+1.6 +1.2			+0.7 0	+1.8 +1.4	+1.0 0	+2.5 +1.8
0.71	− 0.95	+0.5 0	+1.1 +0.7	+0.8 0	+1.9 +1.4			+0.8 0	+2.1 +1.6	+1.2 0	+3.0 +2.2
0.95	− 1.19	+0.5 0	+1.2 +0.8	+0.8 0	+1.9 +1.4	+0.8 0	+2.1 +1.6	+0.8 0	+2.3 +1.8	+1.2 0	+3.3 +2.5
1.19	− 1.58	+0.6 0	+1.3 +0.9	+1.0 0	+2.4 +1.8	+1.0 0	+2.6 +2.0	+1.0 0	+3.1 +2.5	+1.6 0	+4.0 +3.0
1.58	− 1.97	+0.6 0	+1.4 +1.0	+1.0 0	+2.4 +1.8	+1.0 0	+2.8 +2.2	+1.0 0	+3.4 +2.8	+1.6 0	+5.0 +4.0
1.97	− 2.56	+0.7 0	+1.8 +1.3	+1.2 0	+2.7 +2.0	+1.2 0	+3.2 +2.5	+1.2 0	+4.2 +3.5	+1.8 0	+6.2 +5.0
2.56	− 3.15	+0.7 0	+1.9 +1.4	+1.2 0	+2.9 +2.2	+1.2 0	+3.7 +3.0	+1.2 0	+4.7 +4.0	+1.8 0	+7.2 +6.0
3.15	− 3.94	+0.9 0	+2.4 +1.8	+1.4 0	+3.7 +2.8	+1.4 0	+4.4 +3.5	+1.4 0	+5.9 +5.0	+2.2 0	+8.4 +7.0
3.94	− 4.73	+0.9 0	+2.6 +2.0	+1.4 0	+3.9 +3.0	+1.4 0	+4.9 +4.0	+1.4 0	+6.9 +6.0	+2.2 0	+9.4 +8.0
4.73	−5.52	+1.0 0	+2.9 +2.2	+1.6 0	+4.5 +3.5	+1.6 0	+6.0 +5.0	+1.6 0	+8.0 +7.0	+2.5 0	+11.6 +10.0
5.52	−6.30	+1.0 0	+3.2 +2.5	+1.6 0	+5.0 +4.0	+1.6 0	+6.0 +5.0	+1.6 0	+8.0 +7.0	+2.5 0	+13.6 +12.0
6.30	−7.09	+1.0 0	+3.5 +2.8	+1.6 0	+5.5 +4.5	+1.6 0	+7.0 +6.0	+1.6 0	+9.0 +8.0	+2.5 0	+13.6 +12.0
7.09	−7.88	+1.2 0	+3.8 +3.0	+1.8 0	+6.2 +5.0	+1.8 0	+8.2 +7.0	+1.8 0	+10.2 +9.0	+2.8 0	+15.8 +14.0
7.88	−8.86	+1.2 0	+4.3 +3.5	+1.8 0	+6.2 +5.0	+1.8 0	+8.2 +7.0	+1.8 0	+11.2 +10.0	+2.8 0	+17.8 +16.0
8.86	−9.86	+1.2 0	+4.3 +3.5	+1.8 0	+7.2 +6.0	+1.8 0	+9.2 +8.0	+1.8 0	+13.2 +12.0	+2.8 0	+17.8 +16.0
9.85	−11.03	+1.2 0	+4.9 +4.0	+2.0 0	+7.2 +6.0	+2.0 0	+10.2 +9.0	+2.0 0	+13.2 +12.0	+3.0 0	+20.0 +18.0

USAS/ASME B4.1 – 1967 (R2004) Standard. For larger diameters, see the standard. ASME/ANSI B18.3.5M – 1986 (R2002) Standard. Reprinted from the standard listed by permission of the American Society of Mechanical Engineers. All rights reserved.

A.2) __METRIC LIMITS AND FITS__

A.2.1) __Hole Basis Clearance Fits__

Preferred Hole Basis Clearance Fits. Dimensions in mm.

Basic Size	Loose Running		Free Running		Close Running		Sliding		Locational Clearance	
	Hole H11	Shaft c11	Hole H9	Shaft d9	Hole H8	Shaft f7	Hole H7	Shaft g6	Hole H7	Shaft h6
1 max	1.060	0.940	1.025	0.980	1.014	0.994	1.010	0.998	1.010	1.000
min	1.000	0.880	1.000	0.955	1.000	0.984	1.000	0.992	1.000	0.994
1.2 max	1.260	1.140	1.225	1.180	1.214	1.194	1.210	1.198	1.210	1.200
min	1.200	1.080	1.200	1.155	1.200	1.184	1.200	1.192	1.200	1.194
1.6 max	1.660	1.540	1.625	1.580	1.614	1.594	1.610	1.598	1.610	1.600
min	1.600	1.480	1.600	1.555	1.600	1.584	1.600	1.592	1.600	1.594
2 max	2.060	1.940	2.025	1.980	2.014	1.994	2.010	1.998	2.010	2.000
min	2.000	1.880	2.000	1.955	2.000	1.984	2.000	1.992	2.000	1.994
2.5 max	2.560	2.440	2.525	2.480	2.514	2.494	2.510	2.498	2.510	2.500
min	2.500	2.380	2.500	2.455	2.500	2.484	2.500	2.492	2.500	2.494
3 max	3.060	2.940	3.025	2.980	3.014	2.994	3.010	2.998	3.010	3.000
min	3.000	2.880	3.000	2.955	3.000	2.984	3.000	2.992	3.000	2.994
4 max	4.075	3.930	4.030	3.970	4.018	3.990	4.012	3.996	4.012	4.000
min	4.000	3.855	4.000	3.940	4.000	3.978	4.000	3.988	4.000	3.992
5 max	5.075	4.930	5.030	4.970	5.018	4.990	5.012	4.996	5.012	5.000
min	5.000	4.855	5.000	4.940	5.000	4.978	5.000	4.988	5.000	4.992
6 max	6.075	5.930	6.030	5.970	6.018	5.990	6.012	5.996	6.012	6.000
min	6.000	5.855	6.000	5.940	6.000	5.978	6.000	5.988	6.000	5.992
8 max	8.090	7.920	8.036	7.960	8.022	7.987	8.015	7.995	8.015	8.000
min	8.000	7.830	8.000	7.924	8.000	7.972	8.000	7.986	8.000	7.991
10 max	10.090	9.920	10.036	9.960	10.022	9.987	10.015	9.995	10.015	10.000
min	10.000	9.830	10.000	9.924	10.000	9.972	10.000	9.986	10.000	9.991
12 max	12.110	11.905	12.043	11.950	12.027	11.984	12.018	11.994	12.018	12.000
min	12.000	11.795	12.000	11.907	12.000	11.966	12.000	11.983	12.000	11.989
16 max	16.110	15.905	16.043	15.950	16.027	15.984	16.018	15.994	16.018	16.000
min	16.000	15.795	16.000	15.907	16.000	15.966	16.000	15.983	16.000	15.989
20 max	20.130	19.890	20.052	19.935	20.033	19.980	20.021	19.993	20.021	20.000
min	20.000	19.760	20.000	19.883	20.000	19.959	20.000	19.980	20.000	19.987
25 max	25.130	24.890	25.052	24.935	25.033	24.980	25.021	24.993	25.021	25.000
min	25.000	24.760	25.000	24.883	25.000	24.959	25.000	24.980	25.000	24.987
30 max	30.130	29.890	30.052	29.935	30.033	29.980	30.021	29.993	30.021	30.000
min	30.000	29.760	30.000	29.883	30.000	29.959	30.000	29.980	30.000	29.987

ANSI B4.2 – 1978 (R2004) Standard. ASME/ANSI B18.3.5M – 1986 (R2002) Standard. Reprinted from the standard listed by permission of the American Society of Mechanical Engineers. All rights reserved.

A.2.2) Hole Basis Transition and Interference Fits

Preferred Hole Basis Clearance Fits. Dimensions in mm.

Basic Size	Locational Transition		Locational Transition		Locational Interference		Medium Drive		Force	
	Hole H7	Shaft k6	Hole H7	Shaft n6	Hole H7	Shaft p6	Hole H7	Shaft s6	Hole H7	Shaft u6
1 max	1.010	1.006	1.010	1.010	1.010	1.012	1.010	1.020	1.010	1.024
min	1.000	1.000	1.000	1.004	1.000	1.006	1.000	1.014	1.000	1.018
1.2 max	1.210	1.206	1.210	1.210	1.210	1.212	1.210	1.220	1.210	1.224
min	1.200	1.200	1.200	1.204	1.200	1.206	1.200	1.214	1.200	1.218
1.6 max	1.610	1.606	1.610	1.610	1.610	1.612	1.610	1.620	1.610	1.624
min	1.600	1.600	1.600	1.604	1.600	1.606	1.600	1.614	1.600	1.618
2 max	2.010	2.006	2.010	2.020	2.010	2.012	2.010	2.020	2.010	2.024
min	2.000	2.000	2.000	2.004	2.000	2.006	2.000	1.014	2.000	2.018
2.5 max	2.510	2.506	2.510	2.510	2.510	2.512	2.510	2.520	2.510	2.524
min	2.500	2.500	2.500	2.504	2.500	2.506	2.500	2.514	2.500	2.518
3 max	3.010	3.006	3.010	3.010	3.010	3.012	3.010	3.020	3.010	3.024
min	3.000	3.000	3.000	3.004	3.000	3.006	3.000	3.014	3.000	3.018
4 max	4.012	4.009	4.012	4.016	4.012	4.020	4.012	4.027	4.012	4.031
min	4.000	4.001	4.000	4.008	4.000	4.012	4.000	4.019	4.000	4.023
5 max	5.012	5.009	5.012	5.016	5.012	5.020	5.012	5.027	5.012	5.031
min	5.000	5.001	5.000	5.008	5.000	5.012	5.000	5.019	5.000	5.023
6 max	6.012	6.009	6.012	6.016	6.012	6.020	6.012	6.027	6.012	6.031
min	6.000	6.001	6.000	6.008	6.000	6.012	6.000	6.019	6.000	6.023
8 max	8.015	8.010	8.015	8.019	8.015	8.024	8.015	8.032	8.015	8.037
min	8.000	8.001	8.000	8.010	8.000	8.015	8.000	8.023	8.000	8.028
10 max	10.015	10.010	10.015	10.019	10.015	10.024	10.015	10.032	10.015	10.037
min	10.000	10.001	10.000	10.010	10.000	10.015	10.000	10.023	10.000	10.028
12 max	12.018	12.012	12.018	12.023	12.018	12.029	12.018	12.039	12.018	12.044
min	12.000	12.001	12.000	12.012	12.000	12.018	12.000	12.028	12.000	12.033
16 max	16.018	16.012	16.018	16.023	16.018	16.029	16.018	16.039	16.018	16.044
min	16.000	16.001	16.000	16.012	16.000	16.018	16.000	16.028	16.000	16.033
20 max	20.021	20.015	20.021	20.028	20.021	20.035	20.021	20.048	20.021	20.054
min	20.000	20.002	20.000	20.015	20.000	20.022	20.000	20.035	20.000	20.041
25 max	25.021	25.015	25.021	25.028	25.021	25.035	25.021	25.048	25.021	25.061
min	25.000	25.002	25.000	25.015	25.000	25.022	25.000	25.035	25.000	25.048
30 max	30.021	30.015	30.021	30.028	30.021	30.035	30.021	30.048	30.021	30.061
min	30.000	30.002	30.000	30.015	30.000	30.022	30.000	30.035	30.000	30.048

A.2.3) <u>Shaft Basis Clearance Fits</u>

Preferred Shaft Basis Clearance Fits. Dimensions in mm.

Basic Size	Loose Running		Free Running		Close Running		Sliding		Locational Clearance	
	Hole C11	Shaft h11	Hole D9	Shaft h9	Hole F8	Shaft h7	Hole G7	Shaft h6	Hole H7	Shaft h6
1 max	1.120	1.000	1.045	1.000	1.020	1.000	1.012	1.000	1.010	1.000
min	1.060	0.940	1.020	0.975	1.006	0.990	1.002	0.994	1.000	0.994
1.2 max	1.320	1.200	1.245	1.200	1.220	1.200	1.212	1.200	1.210	1.200
min	1.260	1.140	1.220	1.175	1.206	1.190	1.202	1.194	1.200	1.194
1.6 max	1.720	1.600	1.645	1.600	1.620	1.600	1.612	1.600	1.610	1.600
min	1.660	1.540	1.620	1.575	1.606	1.590	1.602	1.594	1.600	1.594
2 max	2.120	2.000	2.045	2.000	2.020	2.000	2.012	2.000	2.010	2.000
min	2.060	1.940	2.020	1.975	2.006	1.990	2.002	1.994	2.000	1.994
2.5 max	2.620	2.500	2.545	2.500	2.520	2.500	2.512	2.500	2.510	2.500
min	2.560	2.440	2.520	2.475	2.506	2.490	2.502	2.494	2.500	2.494
3 max	3.120	3.000	3.045	3.000	3.020	3.000	3.012	3.000	3.010	3.000
min	3.060	2.940	3.020	2.975	3.006	2.990	3.002	2.994	3.000	2.994
4 max	4.145	4.000	4.060	4.000	4.028	4.000	4.016	4.000	4.012	4.000
min	4.070	3.925	4.030	3.970	4.010	3.988	4.004	3.992	4.000	3.992
5 max	5.145	5.000	5.060	5.000	5.028	5.000	5.016	5.000	5.012	5.000
min	5.070	4.925	5.030	4.970	5.010	4.988	5.004	4.992	5.000	4.992
6 max	6.145	6.000	6.060	6.000	6.028	6.000	6.016	6.000	6.012	6.000
min	6.070	5.925	6.030	5.970	6.010	5.988	6.004	5.992	6.000	5.992
8 max	8.170	8.000	8.076	8.000	8.035	8.000	8.020	8.000	8.015	8.000
min	8.080	7.910	8.040	7.964	8.013	7.985	8.005	7.991	8.000	7.991
10 max	10.170	10.000	10.076	10.000	10.035	10.000	10.020	10.000	10.015	10.000
min	10.080	9.910	10.040	9.964	10.013	9.985	10.005	9.991	10.000	9.991
12 max	12.205	12.000	12.093	12.000	12.043	12.000	12.024	12.000	12.018	12.000
min	12.095	11.890	12.050	11.957	12.016	11.982	12.006	11.989	12.000	11.989
16 max	16.205	16.000	16.093	16.000	16.043	16.000	16.024	16.000	16.018	16.000
min	16.095	15.890	16.050	15.957	16.016	15.982	16.006	15.989	16.000	15.989
20 max	20.240	20.000	20.117	20.000	20.053	20.000	20.028	20.000	20.021	20.000
min	20.110	19.870	20.065	19.948	20.020	19.979	20.007	19.987	20.000	19.987
25 max	25.240	25.000	25.117	25.000	25.053	25.000	25.028	25.000	25.021	25.000
min	25.110	24.870	25.065	24.948	25.020	24.979	25.007	24.987	25.000	24.987
30 max	30.240	30.000	30.117	30.000	30.053	30.000	30.028	30.000	30.021	30.000
min	30.110	29.870	30.065	29.948	30.020	29.979	30.007	29.987	30.000	29.987

ANSI B4.2 – 1978 (R2004) Standard. ASME/ANSI B18.3.5M – 1986 (R2002) Standard. Reprinted from the standard listed by permission of the American Society of Mechanical Engineers. All rights reserved.

A.2.4) <u>Shaft Basis Transition and Interference Fits</u>

Preferred Shaft Basis Transition and Interference Fits. Dimensions in mm.

Basic Size	Locational Transition		Locational Transition		Locational Interference		Medium Drive		Force	
	Hole K7	Shaft h6	Hole N7	Shaft h6	Hole P7	Shaft h6	Hole S7	Shaft h6	Hole U7	Shaft h6
1 max	1.000	1.000	0.996	1.000	0.994	1.000	0.986	1.000	0.982	1.000
min	0.990	0.994	0.986	0.994	0.984	0.994	0.976	0.994	0.972	0.994
1.2 max	1.200	1.200	1.196	1.200	1.194	1.200	1.186	1.200	1.182	1.200
min	1.190	1.194	1.186	1.194	1.184	1.194	1.176	1.194	1.172	1.194
1.6 max	1.600	1.600	1.596	1.600	1.594	1.600	1.586	1.600	1.582	1.600
min	1.590	1.594	1.586	1.594	1.584	1.594	1.576	1.594	1.572	1.594
2 max	2.000	2.000	1.996	2.000	1.994	2.000	1.986	2.000	1.982	2.000
min	1.990	1.994	1.986	1.994	1.984	1.994	1.976	1.994	1.972	1.994
2.5 max	2.500	2.500	2.496	2.500	2.494	2.500	2.486	2.500	2.482	2.500
min	2.490	2.494	2.486	2.494	2.484	2.494	2.476	2.494	2.472	2.494
3 max	3.000	3.000	2.996	3.000	2.994	3.000	2.986	3.000	2.982	3.000
min	2.990	2.994	2.986	2.994	2.984	2.994	2.976	2.994	2.972	2.994
4 max	4.003	4.000	3.996	4.000	3.992	4.000	3.985	4.000	3.981	4.000
min	3.991	5.992	3.984	5.992	3.980	5.992	3.973	5.992	3.969	5.992
5 max	5.003	5.000	4.996	5.000	4.992	5.000	4.985	5.000	4.981	5.000
min	4.991	4.992	4.984	4.992	4.980	4.992	4.973	4.992	4.969	4.992
6 max	6.003	6.000	5.996	6.000	5.992	6.000	5.985	6.000	5.981	6.000
min	5.991	5.992	5.984	5.992	5.980	5.992	5.973	5.992	5.969	5.992
8 max	8.005	8.000	7.996	8.000	7.991	8.000	7.983	8.000	7.978	8.000
min	7.990	7.991	7.981	7.991	7.976	7.991	7.968	7.991	7.963	7.991
10 max	10.005	10.000	9.996	10.000	9.991	10.000	9.983	10.000	9.978	10.000
min	9.990	9.991	9.981	9.991	9.976	9.991	9.968	9.991	9.963	9.991
12 max	12.006	12.000	11.995	12.000	11.989	12.000	11.979	12.000	11.974	12.000
min	11.988	11.989	11.977	11.989	11.971	11.989	11.961	11.989	11.956	11.989
16 max	16.006	16.000	15.995	16.000	15.989	16.000	15.979	16.000	15.974	16.000
min	15.988	15.989	15.977	15.989	15.971	15.989	15.961	15.989	15.956	15.989
20 max	20.006	20.000	19.993	20.000	19.986	20.000	19.973	20.000	19.967	20.000
min	19.985	19.987	19.972	19.987	19.965	19.987	19.952	19.987	19.946	19.987
25 max	25.006	25.000	24.993	25.000	24.986	25.000	24.973	25.000	24.960	25.000
min	24.985	24.987	24.972	24.987	24.965	24.987	24.952	24.987	24.939	24.987
30 max	30.006	30.000	29.993	30.000	29.986	30.000	29.973	30.000	29.960	30.000
min	29.985	29.987	29.972	29.987	29.965	29.987	29.952	29.987	29.939	29.987

ANSI B4.2 – 1978 (R2004) Standard. ASME/ANSI B18.3.5M – 1986 (R2002) Standard. Reprinted from the standard listed by permission of the American Society of Mechanical Engineers. All rights reserved.

NOTES:

APPENDIX B: THREADS AND FASTENERS

B.1) UNIFIED NATIONAL THREAD FORM

(External Threads) Approximate Minor diameter = $D - 1.0825P$ P = Pitch

Nominal Size, in.	Basic Major Diameter (D)	Coarse UNC		Fine UNF		Extra Fine UNEF	
		Thds. Per in.	Tap Drill Dia.	Thds. Per in.	Tap Drill Dia.	Thds. Per in.	Tap Drill Dia.
#0	0.060	…	…	80	3/64	…	…
#1	0.0730	64	0.0595	72	0.0595	…	…
#2	0.0860	56	0.0700	64	0.0700	…	…
#3	0.0990	48	0.0785	56	0.0820	…	…
#4	0.1120	40	0.0890	48	0.0935	…	…
#5	0.1250	40	0.1015	44	0.1040	…	…
#6	0.1380	32	0.1065	40	0.1130	…	…
#8	0.1640	32	0.1360	36	0.1360	…	…
#10	0.1900	24	0.1495	32	0.1590	…	…
#12	0.2160	24	0.1770	28	0.1820	32	0.1850
1/4	0.2500	20	0.2010	28	0.2130	32	7/32
5/16	0.3125	18	0.257	24	0.272	32	9/32
3/8	0.3750	16	5/16	24	0.332	32	11/32
7/16	0.4375	14	0.368	20	25/64	28	13/32
1/2	0.5000	13	27/64	20	29/64	28	15/32
9/16	0.5625	12	31/64	18	33/64	24	33/64
5/8	0.6250	11	17/32	18	37/64	24	37/64
11/16	0.675	…	…	…	…	24	41/64
3/4	0.7500	10	21/32	16	11/16	20	45/64
13/16	0.8125	…	…	…	…	20	49/64
7/8	0.8750	9	49/64	14	13/16	20	53/64
15/16	0.9375	…	…	…	…	20	57/64
1	1.0000	8	7/8	12	59/64	20	61/64
1 1/8	1.1250	7	63/64	12	1 3/64	18	1 5/64
1 1/4	1.2500	7	1 7/64	12	1 11/64	18	1 3/16
1 3/8	1.3750	6	1 7/32	12	1 19/64	18	1 5/16
1 1/2	1.5000	6	1 11/32	12	1 27/64	18	1 7/16
1 5/8	1.6250	…	…	…	…	18	1 9/16
1 3/4	1.7500	5	1 9/16	…	…	…	…
1 7/8	1.8750	…	…	…	…	…	…
2	2.0000	4 1/2	1 25/32	…	…	…	…
2 1/4	2.2500	4 1/2	2 1/32	…	…	…	…
2 1/2	2.5000	4	2 1/4	…	…	…	…
2 3/4	2.7500	4	2 1/2	…	…	…	…

B.2) METRIC THREAD FORM

(External Threads) Approximate Minor diameter = $D - 1.2075P$ $\qquad$ P = Pitch

Preferred sizes for commercial threads and fasteners are shown in boldface type.

Coarse (general purpose)		Fine	
Nominal Size (D) & Thread Pitch	Tap Drill Diameter, mm	Nominal Size & Thread Pitch	Tap Drill Diameter, mm
M1.6 x 0.35	1.25	---	---
M1.8 x 0.35	1.45	---	
M2 x 0.4	1.6	---	---
M2.2 x 0.45	1.75	---	---
M2.5 x 0.45	2.05	---	---
M3 x 0.5	2.5	---	---
M3.5 x 0.6	2.9	---	---
M4 x 0.7	3.3	---	---
M4.5 x 0.75	3.75	---	---
M5 x 0.8	4.2	---	---
M6 x 1	5.0	---	---
M7 x 1	6.0	---	---
M8 x 1.25	6.8	**M8 x 1**	7.0
M9 x 1.25	7.75	---	---
M10 x 1.5	8.5	**M10 x 1.25**	8.75
M11 x 1.5	9.50	---	---
M12 x 1.75	10.30	**M12 x 1.25**	10.5
M14 x 2	12.00	**M14 x 1.5**	12.5
M16 x 2	14.00	**M16 x 1.5**	14.5
M18 x 2.5	15.50	**M18 x 1.5**	16.5
M20 x 2.5	17.5	**M20 x 1.5**	18.5
M22 x 2.5[b]	19.5	**M22 x 1.5**	20.5
M24 x 3	21.0	**M24 x 2**	22.0
M27 x 3[b]	24.0	**M27 x 2**	25.0
M30 x 3.5	26.5	**M30 x 2**	28.0
M33 x 3.5	29.5	M33 x 2	31.0
M36 x 4	32.0	**M36 x 2**	33.0
M39 x 4	35.0	M39 x 2	36.0
M42 x 4.5	37.5	**M42 x 2**	39.0
M45 x 4.5	40.5	M45 x 1.5	42.0
M48 x 5	43.0	**M48 x 2**	45.0
M52 x 5	47.0	M52 x 2	49.0
M56 x 5.5	50.5	**M56 x 2**	52.0
M60 x 5.5	54.5	M60 x 1.5	56.0
M64 x 6	58.0	**M64 x 2**	60.0
M68 x 6	62.0	M68 x 2	64.0
M72 x 6	66.0	**M72 x 2**	68.0
M80 x 6	74.0	**M80 x 2**	76.0
M90 x 6	84.0	**M90 x 2**	86.0
M100 x 6	94.0	**M100 x 2**	96.0

[b]Only for high strength structural steel fasteners

B.3) **FASTENERS (INCH SERIES)**

CAUTION! All fastener dimensions have a tolerance. Therefore, each dimension has a maximum and minimum value. Only one size for each dimension is given in this appendix. That is all that is necessary to complete the problems given in the "Threads and Fasteners" chapter. For both values, please refer to the standards noted.

B.3.1) Dimensions of Hex Bolts and Heavy Hex Bolts

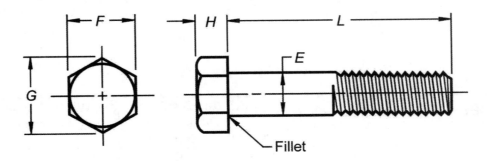

Regular Hex Head Bolts

Size (D)	Head Height Basic*	Width Across Flats Basic Adjust to sixteenths	Width Across Corners Max.
1/4	$H = 0.625\ D + 0.016$	$F = 1.500\ D + 0.062$	
5/16 – 7/16	$H = 0.625\ D + 0.016$		
1/2 – 7/8	$H = 0.625\ D + 0.031$		Max. $G = 1.1547\ F$
1 – 1 7/8	$H = 0.625\ D + 0.062$	$F = 1.500\ D$	
2 – 3 3/4	$H = 0.625\ D + 0.125$		
4	$H = 0.625\ D + 0.188$		

Heavy Hex Head Bolts

Size (D)	Head Height Basic*	Width Across Flats Basic Adjust to sixteenths	Width Across Corners Max.
1/2 - 3	Same as for regular hex head bolts.	$F = 1.500\ D + 0.125$	Max. $G = 1.1547\ F$

* Size to 1 in. adjusted to sixty-fourths. 1 1/8 through 2 1/2 in. sizes adjusted upward to thirty-seconds. 2 3/4 thru 4 in. sizes adjusted upward to sixteenths.

ASME B18.2.1 – 1996 Standard. Reprinted from the standard listed by permission of the American Society of Mechanical Engineers. All rights reserved.

B.3.2) Dimensions of Hex Nuts and Hex Jam Nuts

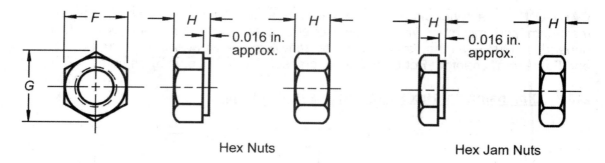

Hex Nuts   Hex Jam Nuts

Hex Nuts

Nut Size (D)	Nut Thickness Basic[*]	Width Across Flats Basic Adjust to sixteenths	Width Across Corners Max.
1/4	H = 0.875 D	F = 1.500 D + 0.062	
5/16 – 5/8	H = 0.875 D		Max. G = 1.1547 F
3/4 – 1 1/8	H = 0.875 D – 0.016	F = 1.500 D	
1 1/4 – 1 1/2	H = 0.875 D – 0.031		

Hex Thick Nuts

Nut Size (D)	Width Across Flats Basic Adjust to sixteenths	Width Across Corners Max.	Nut Thickness Basic
1/4	F = 1.500 D + 0.062		
5/16 – 5/8	F = 1.500 D	Max. G = 1.1547 F	See Table
3/4 – 1 1/2	F = 1.500 D		

Nut Size (D)	1/4	5/16	3/8	7/16	1/2	9/16	5/8
Nut Thickness Basic	9/32	21/64	13/32	29/64	9/16	39/64	23/32

Nut Size (D)	3/4	7/8	1	1 1/8	1 1/4	1 3/8	1 1/2
Nut Thickness Basic	13/16	29/32	1	1 5/32	1 1/4	1 3/8	1 1/2

Hex Jam Nut

Nut Size (D)	Nut Thickness Basic*	Width Across Flats Basic Adjust to sixteenths	Width Across Corners Max.
1/4	See Table	$F = 1.500\ D + 0.062$	Max. $G = 1.1547\ F$
5/16 – 5/8	See Table	$F = 1.500\ D$	
3/4 – 1 1/8	$H = 0.500\ D - 0.047$		
1 1/4 – 1 1/2	$H = 0.500\ D - 0.094$		

Nut Size (D)	1/4	5/16	3/8	7/16	1/2	9/16	5/8
Nut Thickness Basic	5/32	3/16	7/32	1/4	5/16	5/16	3/8

B.3.3) Dimensions of Hexagon and Spline Socket Head Cap Screws

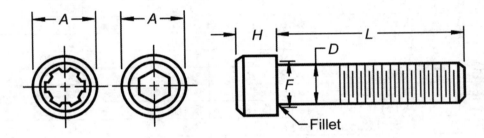

Screw Size (D)	Head Diameter	Head Height
#0 - #10	See Table	Max. $H = D$
1/4 - 4	Max. $A = 1.50\ D$	

Screw Size (D)	#0	#1	#2	#3	#4
Max. Head Diameter (A)	0.096	0.118	0.140	0.161	0.183

Screw Size (D)	#5	#6	#8	#10
Max. Head Diameter (A)	0.205	0.226	0.270	0.312

B.3.4) Drill and Counterbore Sizes for Socket Head Cap Screws

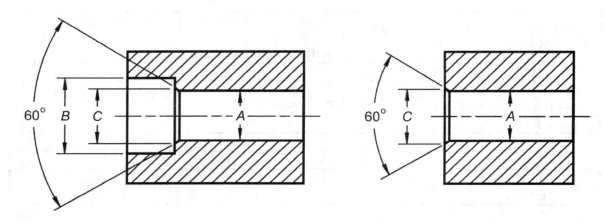

Nominal Size of Screw (*D*)	Nominal Drill Size (*A*)		Counterbore Diameter (*B*)	Countersink (*C*)
	Close Fit	**Normal Fit**		
#0 (0.0600)	(#51) 0.067	(#49) 0.073	1/8	0.074
#1 (0.0730)	(#46) 0.081	(#43) 0.089	5/32	0.087
#2 (0.0860)	3/32	(#36) 0.106	3/16	0.102
#3 (0.0990)	(#36) 0.106	(#31) 0.120	7/32	0.115
#4 (0.1120)	1/8	(#29) 0.136	7/32	0.130
#5 (0.1250)	9/64	(#23) 0.154	1/4	0.145
#6 (0.1380)	(#23) 0.154	(#18) 0.170	9/32	0.158
#8 (0.1640)	(#15) 0.180	(#10) 0.194	5/16	0.188
#10 (0.1900)	(#5) 0.206	(#2) 0.221	3/8	0.218
1/4	17/64	9/32	7/16	0.278
5/16	21/64	11/32	17/32	0.346
3/8	25/64	13/32	5/8	0.415
7/16	29/64	15/32	23/32	0.483
1/2	33/64	17/32	13/16	0.552
5/8	41/64	21/32	1	0.689
3/4	49/64	25/32	1 3/16	0.828
7/8	57/64	29/32	1 3/8	0.963
1	1 1/64	1 1/32	1 5/8	1.100
1 1/4	1 9/32	1 5/16	2	1.370
1 1/2	1 17/32	1 9/16	2 3/8	1.640
1 3/4	1 25/32	1 13/16	2 3/4	1.910
2	2 1/32	2 1/16	3 1/8	2.180

Notes on next page.

Notes:
(1) *Countersink.* It is considered good practice to countersink or break the edges of holes that are smaller than F (max.) in parts having a hardness which approaches, equals, or exceeds the screw hardness. If such holes are not countersunk, the heads of screws may not seat properly or the sharp edges on hols may deform the fillets on screws thereby making them susceptible to fatigue in applications involving dynamic loading. The countersink or corner relief, however, should not be larger than is necessary to insure that the fillet on the screw is cleared. Normally, the diameter of countersink does not heave to exceed F (max.). Countersinks or corner reliefs in excess of this diameter reduce the effective bearing area and introduce the possibility of imbedment where the parts to be fastened are softer than the screws or brinnelling or flaring of the heads of the screws where the parts to be fastened are harder than the screws.

(2) *Close Fit.* The close fit is normally limited to holes for those lengths of screws that are threaded to the head in assemblies where only one screw is to be used or where two or more screws are to be used and the mating holes are to be produced either at assembly or by matched and coordinated tooling.

(3) *Normal Fit.* The normal fit is intended for screws of relatively long length or for assemblies involving two or more screws where the mating holes are to be produced by conventional tolerancing methods. It provides for the maximum allowable eccentricity of the longest standard screws and for certain variations in the parts to be fastened, such as: deviations in hole straightness, angularity between the axis of the tapped hole and that of the hole for the shank, differences in center distances of the mating holes, etc.

B.3.5) <u>Dimensions of Hexagon and Spline Socket Flat Countersunk Head Cap Screws</u>

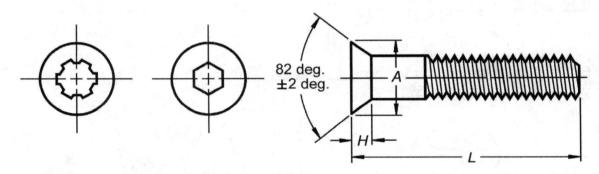

Screw Size (*D*)	Head Diameter (*A*) Theor. Sharp	Max. Head Height (*H*)
#0 - #3	See Table	
#4 – 3/8	Max. $A = 2D + 0.031$	Max. $H = 0.5$ (Max. $A - D$) * cot (41°)
7/16	Max. $A = 2D - 0.031$	
1/2 – 1 1/2	Max. $A = 2D - 0.062$	

Screw Size (*D*)	Head Diameter (*A*) Theor. Sharp
#0	0.138
#2	0.168
#3	0.197
#4	0.226

B.3.6) <u>Dimensions of Slotted Flat Countersunk Head Cap Screws</u>

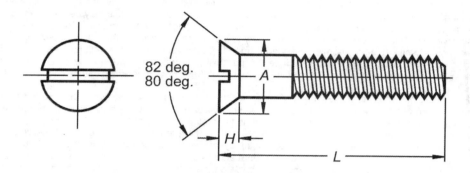

Screw Size (*D*)	Head Diameter (*A*) Thero. Sharp	Head Height (*H*)
1/4 through 3/8	Max. *A* = 2.000 *D*	Max. *H* = 0.596 *D*
7/16	Max. *A* = 2.000 *D* – 0.063	Max. *H* = 0.596 *D* – 0.0375
1/2 through 1	Max. *A* = 2.000 *D* – 0.125	Max. *H* = 0.596 *D* – 0.075
1 1/8 through 1 1/2	Max. *A* = 2.000 *D* – 0.188	Max. *H* = 0.596 *D* – 0.112

ASME B18.6.2 – 1998 Standard. Reprinted from the standard listed by permission of the American Society of Mechanical Engineers. All rights reserved.

B.3.7) <u>Dimensions of Slotted Round Head Cap Screws</u>

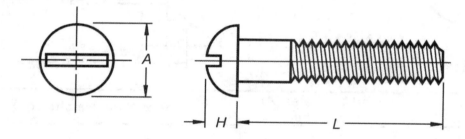

Screw Size (*D*)	Head Diameter (*A*) Thero. Sharp	Head Height (*H*)
1/4 and 5/16	Max. *A* = 2.000 *D* – 0.063	Max. *H* = 0.875 *D* – 0.028
3/8 and 7/16	Max. *A* = 2.000 *D* – 0.125	Max. *H* = 0.875 *D* – 0.055
1/2 and 9/16	Max. *A* = 2.000 *D* – 0.1875	Max. *H* = 0.875 *D* – 0.083
5/8 and 3/4	Max. *A* = 2.000 *D* – 0.250	Max. *H* = 0.875 *D* – 0.110

ASME B18.6.2 – 1998 Standard. Reprinted from the standard listed by permission of the American Society of Mechanical Engineers. All rights reserved.

B.3.8) Dimensions of Preferred Sizes of Type A Plain Washers

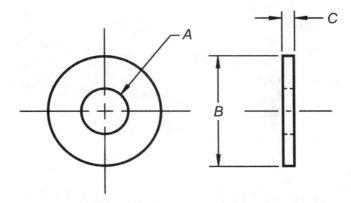

Nominal Washer Size*	Inside Diameter (A) Basic	Outside Diameter (B) Basic	Thickness (C)	Nominal Washer Size*	Inside Diameter (A) Basic	Outside Diameter (B) Basic	Thickness (C)
	0.078	0.188	0.020	1 N	1.062	2.000	0.134
	0.094	0.250	0.020	1 W	1.062	2.500	0.165
	0.125	0.312	0.032	1 1/8 N	1.250	2.250	0.134
#6 (0.138)	0.156	0.375	0.049	1 1/8 W	1.250	2.750	0.165
#8 (0.164)	0.188	0.438	0.049	1 1/4 N	1.375	2.500	0.165
#10 (0.190)	0.219	0.500	0.049	1 1/4 W	1.375	3.000	0.165
3/16	0.250	0.562	0.049	1 3/8 N	1.500	2.750	0.165
#12 (0.216)	0.250	0.562	0.065	1 3/8 W	1.500	3.250	0.180
1/4 N	0.281	0.625	0.065	1 1/2 N	1.625	3.000	0.165
1/4 W	0.312	0.734	0.065	1 1/2 W	1.625	3.500	0.180
5/16 N	0.344	0.688	0.065	1 5/8	1.750	3.750	0.180
5/16 W	0.375	0.875	0.083	1 3/4	1.875	4.000	0.180
3/8 N	0.406	0.812	0.065	1 7/8	2.000	4.250	0.180
3/8 W	0.438	1.000	0.083	2	2.125	4.500	0.180
7/16 N	0.469	0.922	0.065	2 1/4	2.375	4.750	0.220
7/16 W	0.500	1.250	0.083	2 1/2	2.625	5.000	0.238
1/2 N	0.531	1.062	0.095	2 3/4	2.875	5.250	0.259
1/2 W	0.562	1.375	0.109	3	3.125	5.500	0.284
9/16 N	0.594	1.156	0.095				
9/16 W	0.625	1.469	0.109				
5/8 N	0.656	1.312	0.095				
5/8 W	0.688	1.750	0.134				
3/4 N	0.812	1.469	0.134				
3/4 W	0.812	2.000	0.148				
7/8 N	0.938	1.750	0.134				
7/8 W	0.938	2.250	0.165				

* Nominal washer sizes are intended for use with comparable nominal screw or bolt sizes.

B.3.9) Dimensions of Regular Helical Spring-Lock Washers

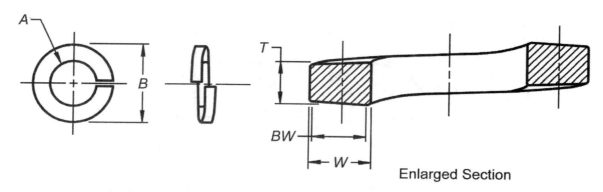

Enlarged Section

Nominal Washer Size	Min. Inside Diameter (A)	Max. Outside Diameter (B)	Mean Section Thickness (T)	Min. Section Width (W)	Min. Bearing Width (BW)
#2 (0.086)	0.088	0.172	0.020	0.035	0.024
#3 (0.099)	0.101	0.195	0.025	0.040	0.028
#4 (0.112)	0.114	0.209	0.025	0.040	0.028
#5 (0.125)	0.127	0.236	0.031	0.047	0.033
#6 (.0138)	0.141	0.250	0.031	0.047	0.033
#8 (0.164)	0.167	0.293	0.040	0.055	0.038
#10 (0.190)	0.193	0.334	0.047	0.062	0.043
#12 (0.216)	0.220	0.377	0.056	0.070	0.049
1/4	0.252	0.487	0.062	0.109	0.076
5/16	0.314	0.583	0.078	0.125	0.087
3/8	0.377	0.680	0.094	0.141	0.099
7/16	0.440	0.776	0.109	0.156	0.109
1/2	0.502	0.869	0.125	0.171	0.120
9/16	0.564	0.965	0.141	0.188	0.132
5/8	0.628	1.073	0.156	0.203	0.142
11/16	0.691	1.170	0.172	0.219	0.153
3/4	0.753	1.265	0.188	0.234	0.164
13/16	0.816	1.363	0.203	0.250	0.175
7/8	0.787	1.459	0.219	0.266	0.186
15/16	0.941	1.556	0.234	0.281	0.197
1	1.003	1.656	0.250	0.297	0.208
1 1/16	1.066	1.751	0.266	0.312	0.218
1 1/8	1.129	1.847	0.281	0.328	0.230
1 3/16	1.192	1.943	0.297	0.344	0.241
1 1/4	1.254	2.036	0.312	0.359	0.251
1 5/16	1.317	2.133	0.328	0.375	0.262
1 3/8	1.379	2.219	0.344	0.391	0.274
1 7/16	1.442	2.324	0.359	0.406	0.284
1 1/2	1.504	2.419	0.375	0.422	0.295
1 5/8	1.633	2.553	0.389	0.424	0.297
1 3/4	1.758	2.679	0.389	0.424	0.297
1 7/8	1.883	2.811	0.422	0.427	0.299
2	2.008	2.936	0.422	0.427	0.299
2 1/4	2.262	3.221	0.440	0.442	0.309
2 1/2	2.512	3.471	0.440	0.422	0.309
2 3/4	2.762	3.824	0.458	0.491	0.344
3	3.012	4.074	0.458	0.491	0.344

B.4) METRIC FASTENERS

B.4.1) Dimensions of Hex Bolts

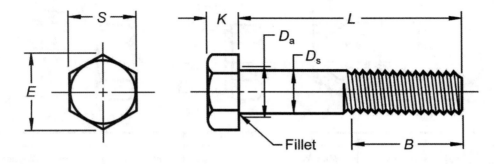

D	D_s	S	E	K	D_a	Thread Length (B)		
Nominal Bolt Diameter and Thread Pitch	Max. Body Diameter	Max. Width Across Flats	Max. Width Across Corners	Max. Head Height	Fillet Transition Diameter	Bolt Lengths ≤ 125	Bolt Lengths > 125 and ≤ 200	Bolt Lengths > 200
M5 x 0.8	5.48	8.00	9.24	3.88	5.7	16	22	35
M6 x 1	6.19	10.00	11.55	4.38	6.8	18	24	37
M8 x 1.25	8.58	13.00	15.01	5.68	9.2	22	28	41
M10 x 1.5	10.58	16.00	18.48	6.85	11.2	26	32	45
M12 x 1.75	12.70	18.00	20.78	7.95	13.7	30	36	49
M14 x 2	14.70	21.00	24.25	9.25	15.7	34	40	53
M16 x 2	16.70	24.00	27.71	10.75	17.7	38	44	57
M20 x 2.5	20.84	30.00	34.64	13.40	22.4	46	52	65
M24 x 3	24.84	36.00	41.57	15.90	26.4	54	60	73
M30 x 3.5	30.84	46.00	53.12	19.75	33.4	66	72	85
M36 x 4	37.00	55.00	63.51	23.55	39.4	78	84	97
M42 x 4.5	43.00	65.00	75.06	27.05	45.4	90	96	109
M48 x 5	49.00	75.00	86.60	31.07	52.0	102	108	121
M56 x 5.5	57.00	85.00	98.15	36.20	62.0		124	137
M64 x 6	65.52	95.00	109.70	41.32	70.0		140	153
M72 x 6	73.84	105.00	121.24	46.45	78.0		156	169
M80 x 6	82.16	115.00	132.79	51.58	86.0		172	185
M90 x 6	92.48	130.00	150.11	57.74	96.0		192	205
M100 x 6	102.80	145.00	167.43	63.90	107.0		212	225

B.4.2) Dimensions of Hex Nuts, Style 1

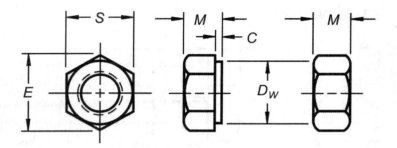

D	S	E	M	D_W	C
Nominal Bolt Diameter and Thread Pitch	**Max. Width Across Flats**	**Max. Width Across Corners**	**Max. Thickness**	**Min. Bearing Face Diameter**	**Max. Washer Face Thickness**
M1.6 x 0.35	3.20	3.70	1.30	2.3	
M2 x 0.4	4.00	4.62	1.60	3.1	
M2.5 x 0.45	5.00	5.77	2.00	4.1	
M3 x 0.5	5.50	6.35	2.40	4.6	
M3.5 x 0.6	6.00	6.93	2.80	5.1	
M4 x 0.7	7.00	8.08	3.20	6.0	
M5 x 0.8	8.00	9.24	4.70	7.0	
M6 x 1	10.00	11.55	5.20	8.9	
M8 x 1.25	13.00	15.01	6.80	11.6	
M10 x 1.5	15.00	17.32	9.10	13.6	
M10 x 1.5	16.00	18.45	8.40	14.6	
M12 x 1.75	18.00	20.78	10.80	16.6	
M14 x 2	21.00	24.25	12.80	19.4	
M16 x 2	24.00	27.71	14.80	22.4	
M20 x 2.5	30.00	34.64	18.00	27.9	0.8
M24 x 3	36.00	41.57	21.50	32.5	0.8
M30 x 3.5	46.00	53.12	25.60	42.5	0.8
M36 x 4	55.00	63.51	31.00	50.8	0.8

ASME B18.2.4.1M – 2002 Standard. Reprinted from the standard listed by permission of the American Society of Mechanical Engineers. All rights reserved.

B.4.3) Dimensions of Metric Socket Head Cap Screws

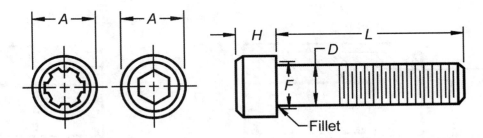

Dimensions in mm

Screw Size (*D*)	Head Diameter (*A*)	Head Height (*H*)
1.6 through 2.5	See Table	
3 through 8	Max. *A* = 1.5 *D* + 1	Max. *H* = *D*
> 10	Max. *A* = 1.5 *D*	

Screw Size (*D*)	1.6	2	2.5
Max. Head Diameter (*A*)	3.00	3.80	4.50

B.4.4) Drill and Counterbore Sizes for Socket Head Cap Screws

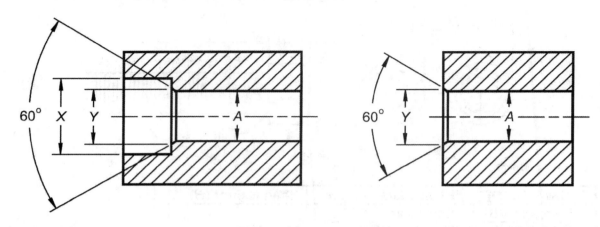

Nominal Size or Basic Screw Diameter	A		X	Y
	Nominal Drill Size		Counterbore Diameter	Countersink Diameter
	Close Fit	Normal Fit		
M1.6	1.80	1.95	3.50	2.0
M2	2.20	2.40	4.40	2.6
M2.5	2.70	3.00	5.40	3.1
M3	3.40	3.70	6.50	3.6
M4	4.40	4.80	8.25	4.7
M5	5.40	5.80	9.75	5.7
M6	6.40	6.80	11.25	6.8
M8	8.40	8.80	14.25	9.2
M10	10.50	10.80	17.25	11.2
M12	12.50	12.80	19.25	14.2
M14	14.50	14.75	22.25	16.2
M16	16.50	16.75	25.50	18.2
M20	20.50	20.75	31.50	22.4
M24	24.50	24.75	37.50	26.4
M30	30.75	31.75	47.50	33.4
M36	37.00	37.50	56.50	39.4
M42	43.00	44.00	66.00	45.6
M48	49.00	50.00	75.00	52.6

B.4.5) Dimensions of Metric Countersunk Socket Head Cap Screws

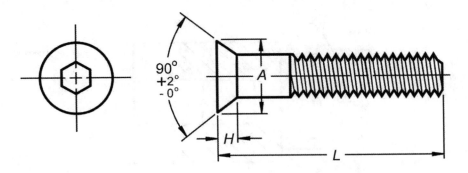

Basic Screw Diameter and Thread Pitch	Head Diameter (A) Theor. Sharp	Head Height (H)
M3 x 0.5	6.72	1.86
M4 x 0.7	8.96	2.48
M5 x 0.8	11.20	3.10
M6 x 1	13.44	3.72
M8 x 1.25	17.92	4.96
M10 x 1.5	22.40	6.20
M12 x 1.75	26.88	7.44
M14 x 2	30.24	8.12
M16 x 2	33.60	8.80
M20 x 2.5	40.32	10.16

ASME/ANSI B18.3.5M – 1986 (R2002) Standard. Reprinted from the standard listed by permission of the American Society of Mechanical Engineers. All rights reserved.

B.4.5) Drill and Countersink Sizes for Flat Countersunk Head Cap Screws

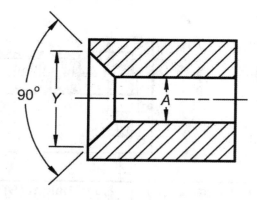

D	A	Y
Nominal Screw Size	**Nominal Hole Diameter**	**Min. Countersink Diameter**
M3	3.5	6.72
M4	4.6	8.96
M5	6.0	11.20
M6	7.0	13.44
M8	9.0	17.92
M10	11.5	22.40
M12	13.5	26.88
M14	16.0	30.24
M16	18.0	33.60
M20	22.4	40.32

B.5) BOLT AND SCREW CLEARANCE HOLES

B.5.1) Inch Clearance Holes

Nominal Screw Size	Fit Classes		
	Normal	Close	Loose
	Nominal Drill Size		
#0 (0.06)	#48 (0.0760)	#51 (0.0670)	3/32
#1 (0.073)	#43 (0.0890)	#46 (0.0810)	#37 (0.1040)
#2 (0.086)	#38 (0.1015)	3/32	#32 (0.1160)
#3 (0.099)	#32 (0.1160)	#36 (0.1065)	#30 (0.1285)
#4 (0.112)	#30 (0.1285)	#31 (0.1200)	#27 (0.1440)
#5 (0.125)	5/32	9/64	11/64
#6 (0.138)	#18 (0.1695)	#23 (0.1540)	#13 (0.1850)
#8 (0.164)	#9 (0.1960)	#15 (0.1800)	#3 (0.2130)
#10 (0.190)	#2 (0.2210)	#5 (0.2055)	B (0.238)
1/4	9/32	17/64	19/64
5/16	11/32	21/64	23/64
3/8	13/32	25/64	27/64
7/16	15/32	29/64	31/64
1/2	9/16	17/32	39/64
5/8	11/16	21/32	47/64
3/4	13/16	25/32	29/32
7/8	15/16	29/32	1 1/32
1	1 3/32	1 1/32	1 5/32
1 1/8	1 7/32	1 5/32	1 5/16
1 1/4	1 11/32	1 9/32	1 7/16
1 3/8	1 1/2	1 7/16	1 39/64
1 1/2	1 5/8	1 9/16	1 47/64

ASME B18.2.8 – 1999 Standard. Reprinted from the standard listed by permission of the American Society of Mechanical Engineers. All rights reserved.

B.5.2) Metric Clearance Holes

Nominal Screw Size	Fit Classes		
	Normal	Close	Loose
	Nominal Drill Size		
M1.6	1.8	1.7	2
M2	2.4	2.2	2.6
M2.5	2.9	2.7	3.1
M3	3.4	3.2	3.6
M4	4.5	4.3	4.8
M5	5.5	5.3	5.8
M6	6.6	6.4	7
M8	9	8.4	10
M10	11	10.5	12
M12	13.5	13	14.5
M14	15.5	15	16.5
M16	17.5	17	18.5
M20	22	21	24
M24	26	25	28
M30	33	31	35
M36	39	37	42
M42	45	43	48
M48	52	50	56
M56	62	58	66
M64	70	66	74
M72	78	74	82
M80	86	82	91
M90	96	93	101
M100	107	104	112

APPENDIX C: REFERENCES

- ASME B1.1 – 2003: Unified Inch Screw Threads (UN and UNR Thread Form)
- ASME B1.13M – 2001: Metric Screw Threads: M Profile
- USAS/ASME B4.1 – 1967 (R2004): Preferred Limits and Fits for Cylindrical Parts
- ANSI B4.2 – 1978 (R2004): Preferred Metric Limits and Fits
- ASME B18.2.1 – 1996: Square and Hex Bolts and Screws (Inch Series)
- ASME/ANSI B18.2.2 – 1987 (R1999): Square and Hex Nuts (Inch Series)
- ANSI B18.2.3.5M – 1979 (R2001): Metric Hex Bolts
- ASME B18.2.4.1M – 2002: Metric Hex Nuts, Style 1
- ASME B18.2.8 – 1999: Clearance Holes for Bolts, Screws, and Studs
- ASME B18.3 – 2003: Socket Cap, Shoulder, and Set Screws, Hex and Spline Keys (Inch Series)
- ASME/ANSI B18.3.1M – 1986 (R2002): Socket Head Cap Screws (Metric Series)
- ASME/ANSI B18.3.5M – 1986 (R2002): Hexagon Socket Flat Countersunk Head Cap Screws (Metric Series)
- ASME 18.6.2 – 1998: Slotted Head Cap Screws, Square Head Set Screws, and Slotted Headless Set Screws (Inch Series)
- ASME B18.21.1 – 1999: Lock Washers (Inch Series)
- ANSI B18.22.1 – 1965 (R2003): Plain Washers
- ASME Y14.2M – 1992 (R2003): Line Conventions and Lettering
- ASME Y14.3 – 2003: Multiview and Sectional view Drawings
- ASME Y14.4M – 1989 (R1999): Pictorial Drawings
- ASME Y14.5M – 1994: Dimensioning and Tolerancing
- ASME Y14.6 – 2001: Screw Thread Representation
- ASME Y14.100 – 2000: Engineering Drawing Practices
- 26th Edition of the Machinery's Handbook

NOTES:

NOTES:

NOTES: